Dissemination

Jacques Derrida

Dissemination

Translated, with an Introduction and Additional Notes, by
Barbara Johnson

The University of Chicago Press

The University of Chicago Press, Chicago 60637
The Athlone Press, London

© 1981 by The University of Chicago
All rights reserved. Published 1981
Printed in the United States of America
13 12 11 10 09 08 07 06 05 04   9 10 11 12 13

This work was published in Paris under the title *La Dissémination*,
© Editions du Seuil, 1972

Library of Congress Cataloging-in-Publication Data

Derrida, Jacques.
 Dissemination.
 Translation of: La dissémination.
 I. Title.
AC25.D45513   808'.00141   81-3359
ISBN 0-226-14334-1 (paper)   AACR2

Contents

Dissemination

Translator's Introduction

All translation is only a somewhat provisional way of coming to terms with the foreignness of languages.

—Walter Benjamin, "The Task of the Translator"

What is translation? On a platter
A poet's pale and glaring head,
A parrot's screech, a monkey's chatter,
And profanation of the dead.

—Vladimir Nabokov, "On Translating 'Eugene Onegin' "

Jacques Derrida, born in Algiers in 1930, teaches philosophy at the Ecole Normale Supérieure in Paris. His tremendous impact on contemporary theoretical thought began in 1967 with the simultaneous publication of three major philosophical works: *La Voix et le phénomène* (an introduction to the problem of the *sign* in Husserl's phenomenology; translated by David Allison as *Speech and Phenomena* [Evanston: Northwestern University Press, 1973]), *L'écriture et la différence* (a collection of essays on the problematics of writing in literature, philosophy, psychoanalysis, and anthropology; translated by Alan Bass as *Writing and Difference* [Chicago: University of Chicago Press, 1978]), and *De la grammatologie* (a sustained analysis of the repression of writing in Western theories of language and culture and a methodological and theoretical outline of a new "science" of writing; translated by Gayatri Chakravorty Spivak as *Of Grammatology* [Baltimore: Johns Hopkins University Press, 1974]).

Five years later, in 1972, came another tripartite Derridean biblioblitz: *Positions* (a collection of interviews; translated by Alan Bass as *Positions* [Chicago: University of Chicago Press, 1981]), *Marges: de la philosophie* (a collection of essays in/on the "margins" of philosophy, linguistics, and literature [translation in preparation, University of Chicago Press]), and *La Dissémination*.

Since 1972, Derrida's work has continued to proliferate and diversify. *Glas* (a giant montage of textual grafts and hardworking wordplays in which Hegel and Genet are shuffled into each other from juxtaposed columns of print) appeared in 1974, followed, among numerous articles and short works, by a collection of critical essays on painting, *La Vérité en peinture* (1978), and, in 1980, by *La Carte Postale: de Socrate à Freud et au-delà*, an intriguing collection of essays that treat the psychoanalytical writings of Freud and Jacques Lacan, preceded by a pseudo-fictional, pseudo-autobiographical epistolary preface that hinges on a postcard depicting Plato dictating behind the back of a writing Socrates.

I. A Critique of Western Metaphysics

Best known in this country for having forged the term "deconstruction," Jacques Derrida follows Nietzsche and Heidegger in elaborating a critique of "Western metaphysics," by which he means not only the Western philosophical tradition but "everyday" thought and language as well. Western thought, says Derrida, has always been structured in terms of dichotomies or polarities: good vs. evil, being vs. nothingness, presence vs. absence, truth vs. error, identity vs. difference, mind vs. matter, man vs. woman, soul vs. body, life vs. death, nature vs. culture, speech vs. writing. These polar opposites do not, however, stand as independent and equal entities. The second term in each pair is considered the negative, corrupt, undesirable version of the first, a fall away from it. Hence, absence is the lack of presence, evil is the fall from good, error is a distortion of truth, etc. In other words, the two terms are not simply opposed in their meanings, but are arranged in a hierarchical order which gives the first term *priority*, in both the temporal and the qualitative sense of the word. In general, what these hierarchical oppositions do is to privilege unity, identity, immediacy, and temporal and spatial *presentness* over distance, difference, dissimulation, and deferment. In its search for the answer to the question of Being, Western philosophy has indeed always determined Being as *presence*.

Derrida's critique of Western metaphysics focuses on its privileging of the spoken word over the written word. The spoken word is given a higher value because the speaker and listener are both present to the utterance simultaneously. There is no temporal or spatial distance between speaker, speech, and listener, since the speaker hears himself speak at the same moment the listener does. This immediacy seems to guarantee the notion that in the spoken word we know what we mean, mean what we say, say what we mean, and know what we have said. Whether or not perfect understanding always occurs *in fact*, this image of perfectly self-present meaning is, according to Derrida, the underlying ideal of Western culture. Derrida has termed this belief in the self-presentation of meaning "Logocentrism," from the Greek word *Logos* (meaning speech, logic, reason, the Word of God). Writing, on the other hand, is considered by the logocentric system to be only a *representation* of speech, a secondary substitute designed for use only when speaking is impossible. Writing is thus a second-rate activity that tries to overcome distance by making use of it: the writer puts his thought on paper, distancing it from himself, transforming it into something that can be read by someone far away, even after the writer's death. This inclusion of death, distance, and difference is thought to be a corruption of the self-presence of meaning, to open meaning up to all forms of adulteration which immediacy would have prevented.

In the course of his critique, Derrida does not simply reverse this value system and say that writing is better than speech. Rather, he attempts to show that the very possibility of opposing the two terms on the basis of presence vs. absence or immediacy vs. representation is an illusion, since speech is *already* structured by difference and distance as much as writing is. The very fact that a word is divided into a phonic *signifier* and a mental *signified*, and that, as Saussure pointed out, language is a system of differences rather than a collection of independently meaningful units, indicates that language as such is already constituted by the very distances and differences it seeks to overcome. To mean, in other words, is automatically *not* to be. As soon as there is meaning, there is difference. Derrida's word for this lag inherent in any signifying act is *différance*, from the French verb *différer*, which means both "to differ" and "to defer." What Derrida attempts to demonstrate is that this *différance* inhabits the very core of what appears to be immediate and present. Even in the seemingly nonlinguistic areas of the structures of consciousness and the unconscious, Derrida analyzes the underlying necessity that induces Freud to compare the psychic apparatus to a structure of scriptural *différance*, a "mystic writing-pad."[1] The illusion of the self-presence of meaning or of consciousness is thus produced by the repression of the differential structures from which they spring.

Derrida's project in his early writings is to elaborate a science of writing called *grammatology*: a science that would study the effects of this *différance* which Western metaphysics has systematically repressed in its search for

---

1. See "Freud and the Scene of Writing," in *Writing and Difference*, trans. Alan Bass (Chicago: University of Chicago Press, 1978), pp. 196–231.

self-present Truth. But, as Derrida himself admits, the very notion of a perfectly adequate *science* or *-logy* belongs to the logocentric discourse which the science of writing would try, precisely, to put in question. Derrida thus finds himself in the uncomfortable position of attempting to account for an error by means of tools derived from that very error. For it is not possible to show that the belief in truth is an error without implicitly believing in the notion of Truth. By the same token, to show that the binary oppositions of metaphysics are illusions is *also*, and perhaps most importantly, to show that such illusions cannot simply in turn *be opposed* without repeating the very same illusion. The task of undoing the history of logocentrism in order to disinter *différance* would thus appear to be a doubly impossible one: on the one hand, it can only be conducted by means of notions of revelation, representation, and rectification, which are *the* logocentric notions par excellence, and, on the other hand, it can only dig up something that is really nothing—a difference, a gap, an interval, a trace. How, then, can such a task be undertaken?

II. Supplementary Reading

Any attempt to disentangle the weave of *différance* from the logocentric blanket can obviously not long remain on the level of abstraction and generality of the preceding remarks. Derrida's writing, indeed, is always explicitly inscribed in the margins of some preexisting text. Derrida is, first and foremost, a *reader*, a reader who constantly reflects on and transforms the very nature of the act of reading. It would therefore perhaps be helpful to examine some of the specific reading strategies he has worked out. I begin with a chapter from *Of Grammatology* entitled "That Dangerous Supplement," in which Derrida elaborates not only a particularly striking reading of Rousseau's *Confessions* but also a concise reflection on his own methodology.

Derrida's starting point is the rhetoric of Rousseau's discussions of writing, on the one hand, and masturbation, on the other. Both activities are called *supplements* to natural intercourse, in the sense both of conversation and of copulation. What Derrida finds in Rousseau's account is a curious bifurcation within the values of writing and masturbation with respect to the desire for presence.

Let us take writing first. On the one hand, Rousseau condemns writing for being only a representation of direct speech and therefore less desirable because less immediate. Rousseau, in this context, privileges speech as the more direct expression of the self. But on the other hand, in the actual experience of living speech, Rousseau finds that he expresses himself much less successfully in person than he does in his writing. Because of his shyness, he tends to blurt out things that represent him as the opposite of what he thinks he is:

> I would love society like others, if I were not sure of showing myself not only at a disadvantage, but as completely different from what I am. The part that I have taken of *writing and hiding myself* is precisely the one that suits me. If I were present, one would never know what I was worth.[2]

It is thus absence that assures the presentation of truth, and presence that entails its distortion. Derrida's summation of this contradictory stance is as follows:

> Straining toward the reconstruction of presence, [Rousseau] valorizes and disqualifies writing at the same time. . . . Rousseau condemns writing as destruction of presence and as disease of speech. He rehabilitates it to the extent that it promises the reappropriation of that of which speech allowed itself to be dispossessed. But by what, if not already a writing older than speech and already installed in that place? (Pp. 141–42)

In other words, the loss of presence has always already begun. Speech itself springs out of an alienation or differance that has the very structure of writing.

It would seem, though, that it is precisely through this assumption of the necessity of absence that Rousseau ultimately succeeds in reappropriating the lost presence. In sacrificing himself, he recuperates himself. This notion that self-sacrifice is the road to self-redemption is a classical structure in Western metaphysics. Yet it can be shown that this project of reappropriation is inherently self-subverting because its very starting point is not presence itself but the *desire* for presence, that is, the *lack* of presence. It is not possible to desire that with which one coincides. The starting point is thus not a *point* but a differance:

> Without the possibility of differance, the desire of presence as such would not find its breathing-space. That means by the same token that

2. Quoted in *Of Grammatology* (trans. Gayatri Chakravorty Spivak [Baltimore: Johns Hopkins University Press, 1974]), p. 142. Page numbers in brackets following references to *Of Grammatology* refer to J. M. Cohen's translation of Rousseau's *Confessions* (Penguin, 1954), which I have sometimes substituted for the translation used by Spivak.

this desire carries in itself the destiny of its nonsatisfaction. Differance produces what it forbids, making possible the very thing that it makes impossible. (P. 143)

The same paradoxical account of the desire for presence occurs in Rousseau's discussions of sexuality. On the one hand, masturbation is condemned as a means of "cheating Nature" and substituting a mere image (absence) for the presence of a sexual partner. On the other hand:

> This vice, which shame and timidity find so convenient, has a particular attraction for lively imaginations. It allows them to dispose, so to speak, of the whole female sex at their will, and to make any beauty who tempts them serve their pleasure without the need of first obtaining her consent. (P. 151 [109])

It is thus the woman's absence that gives immediacy to her imaginary possession, while to deal with the woman's presence would inevitably be to confront differance. Masturbation is both a symbolic form of ideal union, since in it the subject and object are truly one, and a radical alienation of the self from any contact with an other. The union that would perfectly fulfill desire would also perfectly exclude the space of its very possibility.

Just as speech was shown to be structured by the same differance as writing, so, too, the desire to possess a "real" woman is grounded in distance, both because the prohibition of incest requires that one's love-object always be a substitute for the original object, and because of the fundamental structure of desire itself. Rousseau's autobiography offers us a particularly striking example of the essential role of differance in desire. Faced with the possibility of a quasi-incestuous relation with the woman he called "Mama"—incest being the very model of the elimination of differance—Rousseau finds that his desire manifests itself in inverse proportion to Mama's physical proximity: "I only felt the full strength of my attachment to her when she was out of my sight" (p. 152 [107]). Not only does the enjoyment of presence appear to Rousseau to be impossible; it also could be fatal: "If I had ever in my life tasted the delights of love even once in their plenitude," he writes, "I do not imagine that my frail existence would have been sufficient for them. I would have been dead in the act" (p. 155).

Presence, then, is an ambiguous, even dangerous, ideal. Direct speech is self-violation; perfect heteroeroticism is death. Recourse to writing and autoeroticism is necessary to recapture a presence whose lack has not been preceded by any fullness. Yet these two compensatory activities are themselves condemned as unnecessary, even dangerous, supplements.

In French, the word *supplément* has two meanings: it means both "an addition" and "a substitute." Rousseau uses this word to describe both writing and masturbation. Thus, writing and masturbation may *add to* something that is already present, in which case they are *superfluous*, AND/OR they may *replace* something that is *not* present, in which case they are *necessary*. Superfluous and necessary, dangerous and redemptive, the supplement moves through Rousseau's text according to a very strange logic.

What Derrida's reading of Rousseau sketches out is indeed nothing less than a revolution in the very logic of meaning. The logic of the supplement wrenches apart the neatness of the metaphysical binary oppositions. Instead of "A is opposed to B" we have "B is both added to A and replaces A." A and B are no longer opposed, nor are they equivalent. Indeed, they are no longer even equivalent to themselves. They are their own differance from themselves. "Writing," for example, no longer means simply "words on a page," but rather any differential trace structure, a structure that *also* inhabits speech. "Writing" and "speech" can therefore no longer be simply opposed, but neither have they become identical. Rather, the very notion of their "identities" is put in question.

In addition to this supplementary logic in the text's *signified*, the inseparability of the two senses of the *word* "supplément" renders any affirmation that contains it problematic. While Rousseau's explicit intentions are to keep the two senses rigorously distinct—to know when he means "substitute" and when he means "addition"—the shadow presence of the other meaning is always there to undermine the distinction. On the level both of the signified and of the signifier, therefore, it is not possible to pin down the dividing lines between excess and lack, compensation and corruption. The doubleness of the word *supplément* carries the text's signifying possibilities beyond what could reasonably be attributed to Rousseau's conscious intentions. Derrida's reading shows how Rousseau's text functions *against* its own explicit (metaphysical) assertions, not just by creating ambiguity, but by inscribing a *systematic* "other message" behind or through what is being said.

III. Deconstruction

Let us now examine more closely the strategies and assumptions involved in this type of critical reading. It is clear that Derrida is not seeking the "meaning" of Rousseau's text in any traditional sense. He neither adds the text up into a final set of themes or affirmations nor looks for the reality of Rousseau's life outside the text. Indeed, says Derrida, there *is* no outside of the text:

> *There is nothing outside of the text* [*il n'y a pas de hors-texte*]. And that is
> neither because Jean-Jacques' life, or the existence of Mama or Thérèse
> *themselves*, is not of prime interest to us, nor because we have access to
> their so-called "real" existence only in the text and we have neither any
> means of altering this, nor any right to neglect this limitation. All
> reasons of this type would already be sufficient, to be sure, but there are
> more radical reasons. What we have tried to show by following the
> guiding line of the "dangerous supplement," is that in what one calls
> the real life of these existences "of flesh and bone," beyond and behind
> what one believes can be circumscribed as Rousseau's text, there has
> never been anything but writing; there have never been anything but
> supplements, substitutive significations which could only come forth
> in a chain of differential references, the "real" supervening, and being
> added only while taking on meaning from a trace and from an invoca-
> tion of the supplement, etc. And thus to infinity, for we have read, *in
> the text*, that the absolute present, Nature, that which words like "real
> mother" name, have always already escaped, have never existed; that
> what opens meaning and language is writing as the disappearance of
> natural presence. (Pp. 158–59; emphasis in original)

Far from being a simple warning against the biographical or referential
fallacy, *il n'y a pas de hors-texte* is a statement derived from Rousseau's
autobiography itself. For what Rousseau's text tells us is that our very
relation to "reality" already functions like a text. Rousseau's account of his
life is not only itself a text, but it is a text that speaks only about the
textuality of life. Rousseau's life does not *become* a text through his writing:
it always already *was* one. Nothing, indeed, can be said to be *not* a text.

Derrida's reading of Rousseau's autobiography thus proposes a "deconstruction" of its logocentric claims and metaphysical assumptions. Deconstruction is not a form of textual vandalism designed to prove that meaning
is impossible. In fact, the word "de-construction" is closely related not to
the word "destruction" but to the word "analysis," which etymologically
means "to undo"—a virtual synonym for "to de-construct." The deconstruction of a text does not proceed by random doubt or generalized
skepticism, but by the careful teasing out of warring forces of signification
within the text itself. If anything is destroyed in a deconstructive reading, it is
not meaning but the claim to unequivocal domination of one mode of
signifying over another. This, of course, implies that a text signifies in more
than one way, and to varying degrees of explicitness. Sometimes the
discrepancy is produced, as here, by a double-edged word, which serves as a
hinge that both articulates and breaks open the explicit statement being

made. Sometimes it is engendered when the figurative level of a statement is at odds with the literal level. And sometimes it occurs when the so-called starting point of an argument is based on presuppositions that render its conclusions problematic or circular.

Derrida defines his reading strategy as follows:

> The reading must always aim at a certain relationship, unperceived by the writer, between what he commands and what he does not command of the patterns of the language that he uses. This relationship is not a certain quantitative distribution of shadow and light, of weakness or of force, but a signifying structure that the critical reading should *produce*. (p. 158; emphasis in original)

In other words, the deconstructive reading does not point out the flaws or weaknesses or stupidities of an author, but the *necessity* with which what he *does* see is systematically related to what he does *not* see.

It can thus be seen that deconstruction is a form of what has long been called a *critique*. A critique of any theoretical system is not an examination of its flaws or imperfections. It is not a set of criticisms designed to make the system better. It is an analysis that focuses on the grounds of that system's possibility. The critique reads backwards from what seems natural, obvious, self-evident, or universal, in order to show that these things have their history, their reasons for being the way they are, their effects on what follows from them, and that the starting point is not a (natural) given but a (cultural) construct, usually blind to itself. For example, Copernicus can be said to have written a critique of the Ptolemeic conception of the universe. But the idea that the earth goes around the sun is not an *improvement* of the idea that the sun goes around the earth. It is a shift in perspective which literally makes the ground move. It is a deconstruction of the validity of the commonsense perception of the obvious. In the same way, Marx's critique of political economy is not an improvement in it but a demonstration that the theory which starts with the commodity as the basic unit of economy is blind to what *produces* the commodity—namely, labor. Every theory starts somewhere; every critique exposes what that starting point conceals, and thereby displaces all the ideas that follow from it. The critique does not ask "what does this statement *mean*?" but "where is it being made from? What does it presuppose? Are its presuppositions compatible with, independent of, and anterior to the statement that seems to follow from them, or do they already follow from it, contradict it, or stand in a relation of mutual dependence such that neither can exist without positing that the other is prior to it?"

In its elaboration of a critique of the metaphysical forces that structure and smother differance in every text, a deconstructive reading thus assumes:

1. That the rhetoric of an assertion is not necessarily compatible with its explicit meaning.

2. That this incompatibility can be read as systematic and significant *as such*.

3. That an inquiry that attempts to study an object by means of that very object is open to certain analyzable aberrations (this pertains to virtually all important investigations: the self analyzing itself, man studying man, thought thinking about thought, language speaking about language, etc.).

4. That certain levels of any rigorous text will engender a systematic double mark of the insistent but invisible contradiction or differance (the repression of) which is necessary for and in the text's very elaboration.

But if the traditional logic of meaning as an unequivocal structure of mastery *is* Western metaphysics, the deconstruction of metaphysics cannot simply combat logocentric meaning by opposing some other meaning to it. Differance is not a "concept" or "idea" that is "truer" than presence. It can only be a process of textual *work*, a strategy of *writing*.

IV. Derrida's Styles

Early in "The Double Session," in the course of a discussion of the possible Hegelian or Platonic overtones of the word "Idea" in Mallarmé's writing, we read the following warning:

> But a reading here should no longer be carried out as a simple table of concepts or words, as a static or statistical sort of punctuation. One must reconstitute a chain in motion, the effects of a network and the play of a syntax. (P. 194)

This warning applies equally well to Derrida's own writing, in which it is all too tempting to focus on certain "key" terms and to compile them into a static lexicon: *supplément*, *différance*, *pharmakon*, *hymen*, etc. Because Derrida's text is constructed as a moving chain or network, it constantly frustrates the desire to "get to the point" (see the remarks on the dancer's "points" in "The Double Session"). In accordance with its deconstruction of summary meaning, Derrida's writing mimes the *movement* of desire rather than its fulfillment, refusing to stop and totalize itself, or doing so only by feint. Some of the mechanisms of this signifying frustration include:

1. *Syntax*. Derrida's grammar is often "unspeakable"—i.e., it conforms to the laws of writing but not necessarily to the cadences of speech. Ambiguity is rampant. Parentheses go on for pages. A sentence beginning

on p. 319 does not end until p. 323, having embraced two pages of *Un Coup de dés* and a long quotation from Robert Greer Cohn. Punctuation arrests without necessarily clarifying.

2. *Allusions*. The pluralization of writing's references and voices often entails the mobilization of unnamed sources and addressees. All references to castration, lack, talking truth, and letters not reaching their destination, for example, are part of Derrida's ongoing critique of the writings of Jacques Lacan.

3. *Fading in and out*. The beginnings and endings of these essays are often the most mystifying parts. Sometimes, as in the description of Plato working after hours in his pharmacy, they are also cryptically literary, almost lyrical. It is as though the borderlines of the text had to be made to bear the mark of the silence—and the pathos—that lie beyond its fringes, as if the text had first and last to more actively disconnect itself from the logos toward which it still aspires.

4. *Multiple coherences*. The unit of coherence here is not necessarily the sentence, the word, the paragraph, or even the essay. Different threads of *Dissemination* are woven together through the bindings of grammar (the future perfect), "theme" (stones, columns, folds, caves, beds, textiles, seeds, etc.), letters (*or*, *d*, *i*), anagrammatical plays (graft/graph, semen/semantics, *lit/lire*), etc.

5. *Nonbinary logic*. In its deconstruction of the either/or logic of noncontradiction that underlies Western metaphysics, Derrida's writing attempts to elaborate an "other" logic. As he puts it in *Positions*:

> It has been necessary to analyze, to set to work, *within* the text of the history of philosophy, as well as *within* the so-called literary text . . . certain marks . . . that *by analogy* . . . I have called undecidables, that is, unities of simulacrum, "false" verbal properties (nominal or semantic) that can no longer be included within philosophical (binary) opposition, resisting and disorganizing it, *without ever* constituting a third term, without ever leaving room for a solution in the form of speculative dialectics (the *pharmakon* is neither remedy nor poison, neither good nor evil, neither the inside nor the outside, neither speech nor writing; the *supplement* is neither a plus nor a minus, neither an outside nor the complement of an inside, neither accident nor essence, etc.; the *hymen* is neither confusion nor distinction, neither identity nor difference, neither consummation nor virginity, neither the veil nor the unveiling, neither the inside nor the outside, etc. . . . Neither/nor, that is, *simultaneously* either/or. . . .)[3]

3. *Positions*, trans. Alan Bass (Chicago: University of Chicago Press, 1981), pp. 42–43.

Because Derrida's writing functions according to this type of "other" logic, it is not surprising that it does not entirely conform to traditional binary notions of "clarity."

V. Translation

To translate an author so excruciatingly aware of the minutest linguistic differance is an exercise in violent approximation. On the one hand, one must try to find an English equivalent not only for what Derrida *says* but also for the way in which his text *differs* from its own statements and from standard French usage. But on the other hand, these microstructural differances cannot be privileged at the expense of the text's power to *intervene* in the history of philosophy and criticism. Nonetheless, since Derrida's most striking intervention is precisely his way of reworking writing, I have generally tried to align my English with Derrida's disseminative infidelity to French rather than reduce his French to the statement of a thought *about* dissemination. Hence, every weapon available—from Latin to neologisms to American slang—has been mobilized to keep the juggling-puns in the air. The normal English equivalent of *n'avoir rien à voir avec*, for instance, is "to have nothing to do with." But since the literal meaning of the expression is "to have nothing to *see* with," Derrida sometimes uses it in the context of a discussion of "seeing." It was therefore necessary to resort to the colloquial use of "a damn sight" (meaning "a bit") and to translate *L'écriture . . . n' a rien à y voir. Elle a plutôt à (s')y aveugler* as "Writing . . . hasn't a damn sight to do with it. It has rather a blindness to do with it" (p. 135). Or again *médusée par ses propres signes* literally means "mesmerized by its own signs," but the word *médusée*, referring as it does to the Medusa, also implies "being turned to stone." Hence, the (doubtless related) contemporary sense of "getting stoned" has been called upon in rendering *médusée par ses propres signes* as "letting itself get stoned by its own signs" (p. 105). Or yet again, the expression *frayer avec* means "to associate with," but *frayer* alone means "to blaze a trail." Hence *un texte . . . avec lequel il faut frayer* becomes "a text one must make tracks with" (p. 270).

Syntax has been the greatest stumbling block. The "in fact" included in "nothing was any more, in fact, real" (p. 43), for example, has as its sole function the creation of ambiguity in the "any more" (which becomes both quantitative and temporal). In Mallarmé's *Mimique*, the comma after *qui le lit* serves to problematize the antecedent of *qui*. Hence, *le rôle, qui le lit, tout de suite comprend* can mean either "the role, whoever reads it instantly understands" or "the role, which reads him, instantly includes." I have attempted to render the ambiguity by translating this as "the role, the one that reads, will instantly comprehend."

Some justification may be in order regarding my rendering of the title of the opening essay of the book ("Hors livre, préfaces") as "Outwork, Hors d'œuvre, Extratext, Foreplay, Bookend, Facing, Prefacing" (see p. 1). Since no perfect equivalent presented itself, and since that essay, in its complex way of questioning the relations between "prefaces" and "books," is particularly difficult to follow, it seemed to me useful to conjugate out some of the ramifications of this "title" and to open *Dissemination* with a kind of miniaturized version of its strange textual logic.

Many of the word plays, alas, have been lost. While *fils* (threads) is typographically identical to *fils* (sons), "threads" does not sound anything like "sons" (the closest I could get was "filial filaments" [p. 84]). Yet it has been interesting to discover that, while many of these word plays were disappearing, others, just as pervasive, through a strange sort of sympathetic ink, kept appearing. One might almost believe, for instance, that, with its recurring emphasis on weaving and seeding, *Dissemination* had been waiting all along for the English homonymy between "sow" and "sew" to surface.

There is one passage in the book that I have been sorely tempted not to tackle: it is a letter written by Philippe Sollers to Derrida between the two halves of the "Double Session." The letter plays on Mallarmé's *Mimique*, whose text it transforms by twisting its graphic and phonic signifiers in such a way as to reveal surprising associations and unexpected intersections with the text of "The Double Session" into which it is inserted. To translate Sollers' letter, one must find an equivalent not for its words but for its *relation* to Mallarmé's *Mimique*. Hence, the translation is a fourfold process of transformation: the English version of the letter must relate to the English version of *Mimique* as the French version of the letter relates to the French version of *Mimique*, but *at the same time* the transformations wrought by the English version of the letter must produce results *analogous* to those produced in the French. "Meaning" here thus functions not as a primary focus but as a *constraint* on the translation of textual differance.

This fourfold system of relations is, indeed, paradigmatic of the difficulties involved in translating the whole of *Dissemination*. Just as Sollers' letter reproduces and reworks Mallarmé's *Mimique*, so Derrida's writing both employs and subverts the standard usage of French. In both cases, it is the transformational work rather than the "ideas" that must be rendered in translation. In addition, the word "translate" figures prominently *within* Mallarmé's text, just as the problematics of translation pervade all of Derrida's writings. I therefore here offer the following parallel texts in lieu of a theory of translation (see pp. xx–xxiii).

Mimique

Le silence, seul luxe après les rimes, un orchestre ne faisant avec son or, ses frôlements de pensée et de soir, qu'en détailler la signification à l'égal d'une ode tue et que c'est au poète, suscité par un défi, de traduire! le silence aux après-midi de musique; je le trouve, avec contentement, aussi, devant la réapparition toujours inédite de Pierrot ou du poignant et élégant mime Paul Margueritte.

Ainsi ce PIERROT ASSASSIN DE SA FEMME composé et rédigé par lui-même, soliloque muet que, tout du long à son âme tient et du visage et des gestes le fantôme blanc comme une page pas encore écrite. Un tourbillon de raisons naïves ou neuves émane, qu'il plairait de saisir avec sûreté: l'esthétique du genre situé plus près de principes qu'aucun! rien en cette région du caprice ne contrariant l'instinct simplificateur direct... Voici—"La scène n'illustre que l'idée, pas une action effective, dans un hymen (d'où procède le Rêve), vicieux mais sacré, entre le désir et l'accomplissement, la perpétration et son souvenir: ici devançant, là remémorant, au futur, au passé, *sous une apparence fausse de présent*. Tel opère le Mime, dont le jeu se borne à une allusion perpétuelle sans briser la glace: il installe, ainsi, un milieu, pur, de fiction." Moins qu'un millier de lignes, le rôle, qui le lit, tout de suite comprend les règles comme placé devant un tréteau, leur dépositaire humble. Surprise, accompagnant l'artifice d'une notation de sentiments par phrases point proférées—que, dans le seul cas, peut-être, avec authenticité, entre les feuillets et le regard règne un silence encore, condition et délice de la lecture.

Lettre de Sollers

"le 12 (minuit).

MIMIQUE, ou plutôt mi + mi + que, c'est-à-dire deux fois les moitiés plus l'indication ou l'intimation subjonctive de la subordination mimée; mi-mais? mais-qui? mimi à que(ue)? queue de mémé?

Le *si* lance et défie le texte en excès comme ce qui succède—dans l'après mi-dit—à la répétition du rire en écho mimé (rimé) l'arrivée d'or étant tout d'abord musique (or-chestre) et cela fait (si + or) = *soir* au milieu des rôles et du lustre qui ment—silence meurtrier, silence tué—

(*synodique*: temps qui s'écoule entre deux nouvelles lunes consécutives)—pas tant qu'il ne soient freinés—LIT/DES (il y en a *des* qui sont dans le *lit*) (scène primitive) (coup de dés)— queue déliant l'idée—

la scène ne rend pas illustre, sous le lustre, que lit le dés (ir)—

le vice est plus près des cieux que le rêve, sacré—ça crée en cédant au rêve—en s'aidant au rêve—pas de cadeau non plus (présent) apparent—le fantasme blanc—procédant, pro-

créant—

plissement du con, pétration du père

(ô père)

per/pro

foutre futur passé glacé opéra—

mimère—

L'I mène—

Le MIME (neutre) est un demi-moi opéré, infini borné dans son unique stalle pur de toute fiction, un demi-lieu et un demi-dieu—

retour des règles—

mime/milieu = moins/millier

(qu'y le lit/qui le l'y) (lie)

très tôt en dépot : s'y taire

lignes : phrases-points, que/con, sur-prise liée—

au temps cité, luxe du silence ferré : *un si lance en qu'or*—condiction d'hélice au regard feuilleté : dés lisses—"

Mimique

Silence, sole luxury after rhymes, an orchestra only marking with its gold, its brushes with thought and dusk, the detail of its signification on a par with a stilled ode and which it is up to the poet, roused by a dare, to translate! the silence of an afternoon of music; I find it, with contentment, also, before the ever original reappearance of Pierrot or of the poignant and elegant mime Paul Marguerritte.

Such is this PIERROT MURDERER OF HIS WIFE composed and set down by himself, a mute soliloquy that the phantom, white as a yet unwritten page, holds in both face and gesture at full length to his soul. A whirlwind of naive or new reasons emanates, which it would be pleasing to seize upon with security; the aesthetics of the genre situated closer to principles than any!(no)thing in this region of caprice foiling the direct simplifying instinct . . . This—"The scene illustrates but the idea, not any actual action, in a hymen (out of which flows Dream), tainted with vice yet sacred, between desire and fulfillment, perpetration and remembrance: here anticipating, there recalling, in the future, in the past, *under the false appearance of a present*. That is how the Mime operates, whose act is confined to a perpetual allusion without breaking the ice or the mirror: he thus sets up a medium, a pure medium, of fiction." Less than a thousand lines, the role, the one that reads, will instantly comprehend the rules as if placed before the stage-boards, their humble depository. Surprise, accompanying the artifice of a notation of sentiments by unproffered sentences—that, in the sole case, perhaps, with authenticity, between the sheets and the eye there reigns a silence still, the condition and delight of reading.

Sollers' Letter

"the 12 (midnight)

MIMIQUE, or rather me + meek, that is, mimed self-effacement; mimicry—me, me cry? crime, me? my mere key? mama's queue?

The sigh lends and dares the text in excess as that which follows—in the after-no one—the repetition of l'after in a mimed (rhymed) echo, the coming of the golden ore being at first music (or-chestra), the son or us, and then, amid the roles, the soul luxury of the lying lustre, the sigh node, the sign ode, the synodical stillness, the killed ode—

(synodical: the interval between two successive conjunctions of a planet or the moon with the sun)—not successive in conjunction with the son—

There are eyes between the sheets, eye-dice, I.D.'s, i-deas, "I" dies, the eyes dive between the sheets (primal scene) (throw of (d)ice)

de-tail on a par(ent)

the poignant poll, the elegant pall

the scene makes illustrious, beneath the lustre, only the well red sheets of d's(ire)

(v)ice in the tain, out of the dream floe no gift (ap)parently (present) either—the phantasm

> why—
> flowing, foiling
> the fillment of the full
> father and father in
> remembranes
> the me(1)you of fuction

The high men

The I menses

the I's or/a thou's and

lesson a thousand lies, the one that reads

come, pretend the rules

be for the bored, their hymn bled Poe's story

sure prize? oh, then tent city

between the she and the I, the diction and the light of reading."

VI. Dissemination

In *Dissemination*, then, Jacques Derrida undertakes a finely (dis)articulated meditation on the problematics of presentation and representation in the history of Western philosophy and literature. The "pre-texts" for this inquiry are Plato's *Phaedrus* (in "Plato's Pharmacy"), Mallarmé's *Mimique* (in "The Double Session"), Philippe Sollers' *Nombres* (in "Dissemination"), and an encyclopedic array of prefaces and pseudonyms (in "Outwork"). These, of course, are only the most prominent figures in a text that combs the history of reading as well as that of writing for the threads with which to weave its signifying warp.

In the following remarks, I shall attempt to offer not a summary of the major themes and theses of *Dissemination* but rather a kind of roadmap that will detail some of its prominent routes and detours.

A. Plato's Pharmacy, or the Doctoring of Philosophy

"Plato's Pharmacy" takes off from the *Phaedrus*, a Platonic dialogue in which the function and value of writing are explicitly discussed. Socrates is taking a stroll with the handsome young Phaedrus, who holds, hidden under his cloak, the text of a speech by the sophist Lysias in which it is demonstrated that one should yield rather to a nonlover than to a lover. In the course of the dialogue, Socrates listens to Phaedrus read Lysias' speech and then utters two speeches of his own. This exchange of discourses on love is followed by a discussion of speech, rhetoric, writing, seed sowing, and play, in the course of which Socrates recounts the myth of Theuth, the inventor of writing.

Socrates' condemnation of writing and his panegyric to direct speech as the proper vehicle for dialectics and Truth have for centuries been taken almost exclusively at face value. "Platonism" can indeed be seen as another name for the history of strongly stressed metaphysical binarity. What Derrida does in his reading of Plato is to unfold those dimensions of Plato's *text* that work against the grain of (Plato's own) Platonism. Although Derrida does not make his procedures explicit, he can be seen to intervene along the following routes:

1. *Translation.* It can be said that everything in Derrida's discussion of the *Phaedrus* hinges on the translation of a single word: the word *pharmakon*, which in Greek can mean *both* "remedy" *and* "poison." In referring to writing as a *pharmakon*, Plato is thus not making a *simple* value judgment. Yet translators, by choosing to render the word sometimes by "remedy" and sometimes by "poison," have consistently *decided* what in Plato remains

undecidable, and thus influenced the course of the entire history of "Platonism." When one recalls the means of Socrates' death, one begins to see just how crucial the undecidability between poison and remedy might be. But the notion of translation at work here cannot be confined to the exactitude or inexactitude of the rendering of a single "word." By focusing on the translation of *pharmakon*, Derrida strikes at the heart of philosophy itself:

> We hope to display in the most striking manner the regular, ordered polysemy that has, through skewing, indetermination, or overdetermination, but without mistranslation, permitted the rendering of the same word by "remedy," "recipe," "poison," "drug," "philter," etc. It will also be seen to what extent the malleable unity of this concept, or rather its rules and the strange logic that links it with its signifier, has been dispersed, masked, obliterated, and rendered almost unreadable not only by the imprudence or empiricism of the translators, but first and foremost by the redoubtable, irreducible difficulty of translation. It is a difficulty inherent in its very principle, situated less in the passage from one language to another, from one philosophical language to another, than already, as we shall see, in the tradition between Greek and Greek; a violent difficulty in the transference of a non-philosopheme into a philosopheme. With this problem of translation we will thus be dealing with nothing less than the problem of the very passage into philosophy (Pp. 71–72).

Plato's "original" text is thus itself already the battlefield of an impossible process of translation.

2. *Anagrammatical texture.* Derived from Saussure's discovery of the anagrammatical dispersal of certain proper names in Latin poetry, this expression designates the systematic insistence of the word *pharmakon* and its relatives in Plato's text. Beginning with the passing mention of a mythical figure named "Pharmacia," and continuing through the word "pharmakeus" (sorcerer, magician), Derrida also notes the *absence* of the word "pharmakos," which means "scapegoat." In this way, a signifying chain belonging neither entirely to Plato's text nor entirely to the Greek language enables Derrida to reflect on the very relation between individual discourse and language itself.

3. *Lateral association.* By following all the senses of the word *pharmakon*, Derrida brings into play many other contexts in which the word is used by Plato, thus folding onto the problematics of writing such "other" domains as medicine, painting, politics, farming, law, sexuality, festivity, and family relations.

4. *Myth*. In amassing a detailed account of other Western myths of writing, Derrida shows the overdetermination of certain structures in the supposedly "original" Platonic myth of Theuth.

5. *Writing: literal and figurative*. Paradoxically enough, Plato resorts to the notion of "writing in the soul" in order to name the *other* of writing, the self-present Truth that speech—*not* writing—is designed to convey. This return of writing precisely as *what returns* throws the explicit opposition between speech and writing—and between literal and figurative—askew.

6. *Family scenes*. The insistence of a paternal and parricidal vocabulary leads Derrida to reflect both on the relations between paternity and language and on the ambiguities entailed by the fact that Plato, a son figure, is *writing*, from out of the death of Socrates, of Socrates' condemnation of writing as parricide.

B. *The Double Session, or Mallarmé's Miming of Mimesis*

Now shall we make use of this example to throw light on our question as to the true nature of this artist who represents things? We have here three sorts of bed: one which exists in the nature of things and which, I imagine, we could only describe as a product of divine workmanship; another made by the carpenter; and a third by the painter. . . .

We must not be surprised, then, if even an actual bed is a somewhat shadowy thing as compared with reality. . . .

Like ourselves, I replied; for in the first place prisoners so confined would have seen nothing of themselves or of one another, except the shadows thrown by the fire-light on the wall of the Cave facing them, would they? . . . And suppose their prison had an echo from the wall facing them? . . .

Suppose one of them set free and forced suddenly to stand up, turn his head, and walk with eyes lifted to the light. . . . They would laugh at him and say that he had gone up only to come back with his sight ruined; it was worth no-one's while even to attempt the ascent. If they could lay hands on the man who was trying to set them free and lead them up, they would kill him.

 —Plato, *The Republic*, XXXV, XXV

Yes, Literature exists and, if you will, alone, excepting everything.

We know, captives of an absolute formula that, of course, there is nothing but what is. However, incontinent(ly) to put aside, under a pretext, the lure, would point up our inconsequence, denying the pleasure that we wish to take: for that *beyond* is its agent, and its motor might I say were I not loath to operate, in public, the impious dismantling of (the) fiction and consequently of the literary mechan-

ism, so as to display the principal part or nothing. But, I venerate
how, by some flimflam, we project, toward a height both forbidden
and thunderous! the conscious lacks in us (of) what, above, bursts
out.
   What is that for—
   For play.
      —Mallarmé, *La Musique et les Lettres*

In "The Double Session," Derrida executes a kind of "pas de deux"—both a
dance of duplicity and an erasure of binarity—with the history of a certain
interpretation of *mimesis*. The classical understanding of mimesis, derived
in part from Plato's examples of the Bed and the Cave (which Derrida here
calls the Antre), is fundamentally ontological: it involves either the self-
presentation of a being-present or a relation of adequation between an
imitator and an imitated. Alongside the mimetic hierarchies of Plato,
Derrida has placed a short text by Stéphane Mallarmé, *Mimique*, in which,
according to Derrida's reading, what is imitated is not a referent or a reality
but rather the very scheme of mimesis itself.

Simultaneously revealed and concealed behind a vast panoply of erudition, allusion, and wordplay, the following operations can be discerned in
Derrida's text:

1. *Shortsheeting Plato's bed*. Into Plato's catalogue of variously made
beds, Derrida inserts Mallarmé's short account of a Pierrot miming the
murder of his wife. Writ(h)ing upon the conjugal sheets, the Mime plays
both man and woman, pleasure and death, "in a hymen (out of which flows
Dream), tainted with vice yet sacred, between desire and fulfillment,
perpetration and remembrance: here anticipating, there recalling, in the
future, in the past, *under the false appearance of a present*." Through the
syntactical ambiguities of *Mimique* and the double meaning of the word
"hymen" (both "membrane" and, archaically, "marriage") Derrida man-
ages to show that the mime's "operation" is a "perpetual allusion" to
himself on the point of alluding, in which the differance between the
imitator and the imitated is at once preserved and erased. The fact that the
French word for bed, *lit*, can also mean "reads" is pivotal to this analysis, in
which what Mallarmé calls the "desperate practice" of reading is so deeply
embedded. "Reading," indeed, is the last word of *Mimique*.

2. *Spelunking in the Antre*. Plato's second mimetic paradigm, the cave,
finds itself translated, through the homonymy between ANTRE ("cave") and
ENTRE ("between"), into various figures of penetration and articulation.
The most important of these is the "hymen," which, in signifying both
membrane and marriage, designates both the virginal intactness of the

distinction between the inside and the outside and the erasing of that distinction through the commingling of self and other. Yet that alluringly foregrounded hymen—like the rest of the Derridean "lexicon" of double-edged words—is not indispensable:

> What counts here is not the lexical richness, the semantic infiniteness of a word or concept, its depth or breadth, the sedimentation that has produced inside it two contradictory layers of signification (continuity and discontinuity, inside and outside, identity and difference, etc.). What counts here is the formal or syntactical *praxis* that composes and decomposes it. We have indeed been making believe that everything could be traced to the word *hymen*. But the irreplaceable character of this signifier, which everything seemed to grant it, was laid out like a trap. . . . It produces its effect first and foremost through the syntax, which disposes the *"entre"* in such a way that the suspense is due only to the placement and not to the content of the words. . . . It is the "between," whether it names fusion or separation, that thus carries all the force of the operation. The hymen must be determined through the *entre* and not the other way around. . . . What holds for "hymen" also holds, mutatis mutandis, for all other signs which, like pharmakon, supplement, differance, and others, have a double, contradictory, undecidable value that always derives from their syntax. . . .(pp. 220-21)

The passage from Plato's *antre* to Mallarmé's *entre* is thus a passage from ontological semantics to undecidable syntax, from the play of light and shadow to the play of articulation.

3. *A Practice of spacing.* One of the first things one notices about "The Double Session" is its provocative use of typographic spacing. From the insertion of *Mimique* into an L-shaped quotation from Plato to the quotations in boxes, the passages from *Un Coup de dés* and *Le Livre*, the reproduction of Mallarmé's handwriting, and the pages bottom-heavy with footnotes, it is clear that an effort is being made to call the reader's attention to the syntactical function of spacing in the act of reading. Through such supplementary syntactical effects, Derrida duplicates and analyzes the ways in which Mallarmé's texts mime their own articulation, include their own blank spaces among their referents, and deploy themselves consistently with one textual fold too many or too few to be accounted for by a reading that would seek only the text's "message" or "meaning." By thus making explicit the role of the materiality of space within the act of understanding, Mallarmé—and Derrida—demonstrate the untenability of the logocentric

distinction between the sensible and the intelligible, between ideality and materiality.

4. *A critique of the dialectics of reading.* The history of Mallarmé criticism prior to Derrida can be grouped into two general moments: the Hegelian/ Platonic and the thematic/formalist. Derrida's reading of *Mimique* enables him to work out a far-reaching critique of both moments. By skewing the form/content division, tracing the proliferation of plays of the signifier, problematizing *mimesis*, and putting the text's materiality to work as an excess of syntax over semantics, Derrida puts in question the classical mentalist, expressionist presuppositions and procedures of the act of reading itself.

C. Dissemination, or the Recounting of Numbers

The ostensible subject of the essay entitled "Dissemination" is a novel by Philippe Sollers entitled *Numbers*. The novel presents itself as a series of 100 passages numbered from 1. to 4.100, in which the number preceding the decimal point varies cyclically from 1 to 4 and the number following the decimal point goes numerically from 5 to 100 after the first group of 1–4. The text of the novel is explicitly heterogeneous and discontinuous: quotations, parentheses, dashes, cuts, figures, and Chinese characters are only the most visible manifestations of continual textual upheaval. On the jacket of *Numbers*, Sollers presents the book in the following terms:

> How can the contradiction between discourse and (hi)story be lifted? unless it be through an exit out of the representational scene that maintains their opposition? through a text whose orderly permutations open not upon some spoken expression, but upon the constantly active historical real?
>
> Between the imperfect (sequences 1/2/3) and the present (sequence 4), which make up the square matrix that engenders the narrative and its reflection, is inscribed the textual work that destroys any spectacular or imaginary "truth." That destruction affects not only the hypothetical "subject" of the story—his/her body, sentences, and dreams—but also the story itself, which is overturned and gradually immersed in texts of various cultures. Writing thus begins to function "outside," to burn in a self-constructing, self-effacing, self-extending space according to the infinity of its production. Such a theater, having neither stage nor house, where words have become the actors and spectators of a new community of play, should also enable us to capture, across its intersecting surfaces, our own "time": the advent of

a dialogue between West and East, the question of the passage from alienated writing to a writing of the trace, through war, sex, and the mute, hidden work of transformation.

The novel printed here *is not* a printed novel. It refers to the mythical milieu that is now washing over you, slipping into you, out of you, everywhere, forever, as of tomorrow. It attempts to winnow out the movement of the depths, the depths that follow upon books, the depths of the thought of masses, capable of shaking the very foundations of the old mentalist, expressionist world, whose end, if one takes the risk of reading, is at hand. (My translation)

Among other challenges is "Dissemination" 's generalized citationality, which is particularly difficult to render in a translation. In keeping with the pattern set by the essay in French, "Dissemination" appears without footnotes. Quotations from *Numbers* are printed both in quotation marks and in italics. Quotations from other works by Sollers—*The Park, Drama, Logics*—are generally identified as such in the body of the text. Other authors cited but not always identified include such diverse figures as Claudel, Lautréamont, Robert Greer Cohn, Montaigne, Freud, Heidegger, Sophocles, Artaud, Hegel, and Marx.[4] Mallarmé is a constant presence, but his texts—often modified before insertion—do not always appear in quotation marks. To take just one example: in the opening pages, a discussion of the word "therefore" is preceded by a modified quotation from Mallarmé's *Igitur* (= "therefore" in Latin), which reads: "The tale is thereby addressed to the reader's body, which is put by things on stage, itself." The original quotation reads: "Ce conte s'adresse à l'Intelligence du lecteur qui met les choses en scène, elle-même" ["This tale is addressed to the reader's *Intelligence*, which *puts things* on stage, itself."]. In changing "Intelligence" to "body," in making the reader into an *object* of the activity of things, and in leaving the word "elle-même" ["itself"] without a clear antecedent ("body" is masculine), Derrida gives us a clue to the type of transformation entailed by "Dissemination."

The multiplication of sources and the disappearance of proper names is a literal enactment of Mallarmé's insight into the "elocutionary disappear-

4. I have quoted from the following English translations of texts "cited": Philippe Sollers, *The Park* (trans. A. M. Sheridan Smith [New York: Red Dust, 1969]); Martin Heidegger, *The Question of Being* (trans. W. Kluback and J. T. Wilde [New York: Twayne Publishers, 1958]) and *Poetry, Language, Thought* (trans. Albert Hofstadter [New York: Harper & Row, 1971]); Lautrèamont, *Maldoror and Poems* (trans. Paul Knight [Penguin, 1978]); Karl Marx, *Capital* (trans. Samuel Moore and Edward Aveling [New York: International publishers, 1967]); Sophocles, *Oedipus the King* (trans. David Grene) and *Oedipus at Colonus* (trans. Robert Fitzgerald) in *Greek Tragedies*, vols 1 and 3 (Chicago: University of Chicago Press, 1960).

ance of the author, who leaves the initiative to words." Yet the proper name does not remain entirely effaced in "Dissemination." It returns through the mouth of the other, as a textual effect. "Dissemination" cleverly enacts the name's return in the following passage:

> *Numbers* thus has no proper, unified, present origin; no one, outside the mask or simulacrum of some very clever pseudonym, is entitled to the property rights or author's royalties . . . Authority and property still remain, though, as pretentions of the attending discourse and as dead surface effects. (Even though, if two specific emblems are taken into account, while the proper name of the author is disappearing in a constant equivocal motion of death and safe-keeping or salvation, the name is only in fact in hiding: it conceals itself behind the screen, behind *"the multiplication of screens as emblems of this new reign"* (1.25), or finds refuge, without ceasing to shine, a gem without air at the bottom of the book, the clasp, or the jewel-case, thanks to *"that writing that comprises a tangle of serpents, plumes, and the emblem of the eagle, which refers to the tensed force of the sun—a precious stone—a stone that must be reached if one wishes to go on behind the sun"* (2.34), behind death. A proper name, then, as it was once penciled at the theater, "always ready to regain control. An intact jewel [*joyau*] beneath the disaster." All you will have had to do, once this stone has been thrown out, is to go a bit further, behind the citing of the solar star [*l'astre solaire*] (sun = death = mirror) in order to glimpse a poisoned ring. Then an antidote and then the key. Which are all the same.) (pp.328–29)

The reader has probably divined behind the proliferation of solar imagery the pseudonym Sollers. But he has probably not seen in the "intact jewel" from Mallarmé a second name ready to regain control. Philippe Sollers' "real" name is Joyaux.

Both *Numbers* and "Dissemination" are attempts to *enact* rather than simply *state* the theoretical upheavals produced in the course of a radical reevaluation of the nature and function of writing undertaken by Derrida, Sollers, Roland Barthes, Julia Kristeva and other contributors to the journal *Tel Quel* in the late 1960s. Ideological and political as well as literary and critical, the *Tel Quel* program attempted to push to their utmost limits the theoretical revolutions wrought by Marx, Freud, Nietzsche, Mallarmé, Lévi-Strauss, Saussure, and Heidegger.

It is not surprising, therefore, to find that "Dissemination" operates at the very limits of intelligibility. Crucial metaphysical guideposts such as the notions of "first," "last," "here," "now," "I," "you," "unique," "repeated," "author," "reader," "matter," "mind," "beginning," "end," etc.

are fragmented, fictionalized, put in quotation marks. New linguistic and numerical logics are employed with baffling virtuosity. Through the pun linking *"Est"* ["East"] and *"est"* ["is"], for instance, "Dissemination" inscribes the West's orientation toward Being as a relation to the *Est* it both desires and shuns. And through its insistence upon squares, crossroads, and other four-sided figures, "Dissemination" attempts to work a violent but imperceptible displacement of the "triangular"—Dialectical, Trinitarian, Oedipal—foundations of Western thought. This passage from three to four may perhaps be seen as a warning to those who, having understood the necessity for a deconstruction of metaphysical binarity, might be tempted to view the number "three" as a guarantee of liberation from the blindness of logocentrism.

D. OUTWORK, or Disseminating Prefacing

This book begins with a denial both of the book and of the beginning. The opening sentence, "This (therefore) will not have been a book," written in the future perfect tense, marks itself as presentation ("this"), anticipation ("will"), negation ("not"), recapitulation ("have been"), and conclusion ("therefore"). The juxtaposition of the title (*Hors livre*, lit. "outside the book") and the opening sentence is thus designed to map out the play of anticipatory retrospection and internalized exteriority involved in that metalinguistic moment of self-reflection traditionally known as the *Preface*. Situated both inside and outside, both before and after the "book" whose "book-ness" it both promotes and transgresses, the preface has always inscribed itself in a strange warp of both time and space.

In writing a preface that deals with the simultaneous impossibility and necessity of prefacing, Derrida has raised the prefatory double bind to a higher degree. The fact that his preface at once prefaces *and* deconstructs the preface is perhaps an instance of the "systematic double mark" with which it deals. While the reader expects to read a preface to *Dissemination*, what he finds is the word "dissemination" disseminated here and there within a preface on prefaces.

The Book, the Preface, and the Encyclopedia are all structures of unification and totalization. Dissemination, on the other hand, is what subverts all such recuperative gestures of mastery. It is what foils the attempt to progress in an orderly way toward meaning or knowledge, what breaks the circuit of intentions or expectations through some ungovernable excess or loss.

The challenge here is to "present" dissemination in a disseminative way. In a sense, the very success of such an attempt would be a sign of failure. To perfectly disseminate the exposition of dissemination would require a kind of textual mastery that would belong among the recuperative gestures that dissemination undercuts. It could perhaps be said, however, that the most compelling achievement of *Dissemination*, in the final analysis, lies precisely in its *inscription* of the ways in which all theoretical discourse—including its own—forever remains both belated and precipitous with respect to the textual practice it attempts to comprehend.

* * *

I have attempted to refer to English editions of texts cited whenever possible. Where no reference to an English translation is given, however, the translation is my own. Brackets are generally my interpolations unless they occur within quotations, in which case they are Derrida's (e.g. p. 16). Footnotes preceded by the abbreviation TN are my translator's notes.

I would like to take this opportunity to thank the following for their support: Yale University, for granting me a Morse Fellowship, which provided me with the freedom necessary for the completion of this translation; Steven Rendall, for letting me look at his draft of a translation of "Plato's Pharmacy"; Sheila Brewer, for her superb typing and moral support; Chris Miller, for his help with last-minute bibliographical lacunae; and Roger Gilbert, for his help with the proofreading.

HORS LIVRE:

OUTWORK
HORS D'OEUVRE
EXTRATEXT
FOREPLAY

BOOKEND

FACING

PREFACING

This (therefore) will not have been a book.

Still less, despite appearances, will it have been a collection of *three* "essays" whose itinerary it would be time, after the fact, to recognize; whose continuity and underlying laws could now be pointed out; indeed, whose overall concept or meaning could at last, with all the insistence required on such occasions, be squarely set forth. I will not feign, according to the code, either premeditation or improvisation. These texts are assembled otherwise; it is not my intention here to *present* them.

The question astir here, precisely, is that of presentation.

While the form of the "book" is now going through a period of general upheaval, and while that form now appears less natural, and its history less transparent, than ever, and while one cannot tamper with it without disturbing everything else, the book form alone can no longer settle—here for example—the case of those writing processes which, in *practically* questioning that form, must also dismantle it.

Hence the necessity, today, of working out at every turn, with redoubled effort, the question of the preservation of names: of *paleonymy*. Why should an old name, for a determinate time, be retained? Why should the effects of a new meaning, concept, or object be damped by memory?

Posed in these terms, the question would already be caught up in a whole system of presuppositions that have now been elucidated: for example, here, that of the signifier's *simple* exteriority to "its" concept. One must therefore proceed otherwise.

Let us begin again. To take some examples: why should "literature" still designate that which already breaks away from literature—away from what has always been conceived and signified under that name—or that which, not merely escaping literature, implacably destroys it? (Posed in these terms, the question would already be caught in the assurance of a certain fore-knowledge: can "what has always been conceived and signified under

3

that name" be considered fundamentally homogeneous, univocal, or non-conflictual?) To take other examples: what historical and strategic function should henceforth be assigned to the quotation marks, whether visible or invisible, which transform this into a "book," or which still make the deconstruction of philosophy into a "philosophical discourse"?

This structure of the *double mark* (*caught*—both seized and entangled—in a binary opposition, one of the terms retains its old name so as to destroy the opposition to which it no longer quite belongs, to which in *any* event it has *never* quite yielded, the history of this opposition being one of incessant struggles generative of hierarchical configurations) works the entire field within which these texts move. This structure itself is worked in turn: the rule according to which every concept necessarily receives two similar marks—a repetition without identity—one mark inside and the other outside the deconstructed system, should give rise to a double reading and a double writing. And, as will appear in due course: a *double science*.

No concept, no name, no signifier can escape this structure. We will try to determine the law which compels us (by way of example and taking into account a general remodeling of theoretical discourse which has recently been rearticulating the fields of philosophy, science, literature, etc.) to apply the name "writing" to that which critiques, deconstructs, wrenches apart the traditional, hierarchical opposition between writing and speech, between writing and the (idealist, spiritualist, phonocentrist: first and foremost logocentric)[1] system of all of what is customarily opposed to writing; to apply the name "work" or "practice" to that which disorganizes the philosophical opposition *praxis/theoria* and can no longer be sublated[2] according to the process of Hegelian negativity; to apply the name "unconscious" to that which can never have been the symmetrical negative or the potential reservoir of "consciousness"; to apply the name "matter" to that which lies outside all classical oppositions and which, provided one takes into account certain theoretical achievements and a certain philosophical deconstruction belonging to a not so distant time, should no longer be able to assume any reassuring form: neither that of a referent (at least if conceived as a real thing or cause, anterior and exterior to the system of general

1. TN. "Logocentric"—that which is "centered" on the "Logos" (= speech, logic, reason, the Word of God)—is the term used by Derrida to characterize any signifying system governed by the notion of the self-presence of meaning; i.e. any system structured by a valorization of speech over writing, immediacy over distance, identity over difference, and (self-) presence over all forms of absence, ambiguity, simulation, substitution, or negativity.

2. TN. "Sublation" is the traditional English translation of the German *Aufhebung*, which is Hegel's term for the simultaneous negation and retention of what is being surpassed by the progress of dialectical thought.

textuality), nor that of presence in any of its modes (meaning, essence, existence—whether objective or subjective; form, i.e. appearance, content, substance, etc.; sensible presence or intelligible presence), nor that of a fundamental or totalizing principle, nor even of a last instance: in short, the classical system's "outside" can no longer take the form of the sort of extra-text which would arrest the concatenation of writing (i.e. that movement which situates every signified as a differential trace) and for which I had proposed the concept of "transcendental signified." "Differance"[3] also designated, within the same problematic field, that kind of economy—that war economy—which brings the radical otherness or the absolute exteriority of the outside into relation with the closed, agonistic, hierarchical field of philosophical oppositions, of "differends" or "difference":[4] an economic movement of the trace that implies both its mark and its erasure—the margin of its impossibility—according to a relation that no speculative dialectic of the same and the other can master, for the simple reason that such a dialectic always remains an operation of mastery.[5]

To put the old names to work, or even just to leave them in circulation, will always, of course, involve some risk: the risk of settling down or of regressing into the system that has been, or is in the process of being, deconstructed. To deny this risk would be to confirm it: it would be to see the signifier—in this case the name—as a merely circumstantial, conventional occurrence of the concept or as a concession without any specific effect. It would be an affirmation of the autonomy of meaning, of the ideal purity of an abstract, theoretical history of the concept. Inversely, to claim to do away immediately with previous marks and to cross over, by decree, by a simple leap, into the outside of the classical oppositions is, apart from the risk of engaging in an interminable "negative theology," to forget that these oppositions have never constituted a *given* system, a sort of ahistorical, thoroughly homogeneous table, but rather a dissymmetric, hierarchically ordered space whose closure is constantly being traversed by the forces, and worked by the exteriority, that it represses: that is, expels and, which amounts to the same, internalizes as one of *its* moments. This is why

3. TN. *Differance* is a Derridean neologism combining the two senses of the French verb *différer*—"to differ" and "to defer or postpone"—into a noun designating active non-self-presence both in space and time.
4. Cf. "La différance," in *Théorie d'ensemble*, coll. "Tel Quel" (Paris: Le Seuil, 1968), pp. 58 ff. [Reprinted in *Marges* (Paris: Editions de Minuit, 1972). Translated as "Differance" by David Allison in *Speech and Phenomena* (Evanston: Northwestern University Press, 1973).]
5. Cf. "De l'économie restreinte à l'économie générale," in *L'Ecriture et la différence*, coll. "Tel Quel," Paris: Le Seuil, 1967. [Translated as "From Restricted to General Economy," in *Writing and Difference*, trans. Alan Bass (Chicago: Chicago University Press, 1978).]

deconstruction involves an indispensable phase of *reversal*. To remain content with reversal is of course to operate within the immanence of the system to be destroyed. But to sit back, in order to go *further*, in order to be more radical or more daring, and take an attitude of neutralizing indifference with respect to the classical oppositions would be to give free rein to the existing forces that effectively and historically dominate the field. It would be, for not having seized the means to *intervene*,[6] to confirm the established equilibrium.

These two operations must be conducted in a kind of disconcerting *simul*, in a movement of the entire field that must be coherent, of course, but at the same time divided, differentiated, and stratified. The gap between the two operations must remain open, must let itself be ceaselessly marked and remarked. This is already a sufficient indication of the necessary heterogeneity of each text participating in this operation and of the impossibility of summing up the gap at a single point or under a single name. Responsibility and individuality are values that can no longer predominate here: that is the first effect of dissemination.

There is no such thing as a "metaphysical-concept." There is no such thing as a "metaphysical-name." The "metaphysical" is a certain determination or direction taken by a sequence or "chain." It cannot as such be opposed by a concept but rather by a process of textual labor and a different sort of articulation. This being the case, the development of this problematic will inevitably involve the movement of differance as it has been discussed elsewhere: a "productive," conflictual[7] movement which cannot be preceded by any identity, any unity, or any original simplicity; which cannot be "relieved" [*relevé*],[8] resolved, or appeased by any philosophical

---

6. On the concepts of *intervention* and *paleonymy*, and on the conceptual operation of reversal/displacement (the withdrawal of a predicate, the adherence of a name, the processes of grafting, extending, and reorganizing), cf. "Positions," in *Promesse* No. 30-31, p. 37. [Reprinted in *Positions* (Paris: Editions de Minuit, 1972). Translated as *Positions* by Alan Bass (Chicago: Chicago University Press, 1981).]

7. "La différance," pp. 46 ff.

8. *Aufgehoben* (concerning this translation of "aufheben" [to sublate] by "relever" [to relieve], cf. "Le puits et la pyramide," in *Hegel et la pensée moderne* [Paris: P.U.F., 1971]). The movement by which Hegel determines difference as contradiction ("Der Unterschied überhaupt ist schon der Widerspruch *an sich*," *The Science of Logic* II, I, chap. 2, C) is designed precisely to make possible the ultimate (onto-theo-teleo-logical) sublation [la relève] of difference. *Differance*—which is thus by no means dialectical contradiction in this Hegelian sense—marks the critical limit of the idealizing powers of relief [la relève] wherever they are able, directly or indirectly, to operate. Differance *inscribes* contradiction, or rather, since it remains irreducibly differentiating and disseminating, contradiction*s*. In marking the "productive" (in the sense of general economy and in accordance with the loss of presence) and differentiating movement, the *economic* "concept" of differance does not reduce all

dialectic; and which disorganizes "historically," "practically," textually, the opposition or the difference (the static distinction) between opposing terms.

A *preface* would retrace and presage here a *general* theory and practice of deconstruction, that strategy without which the possibility of a critique could exist only in fragmentary, empiricist surges that amount in effect to a non-equivocal confirmation of metaphysics. The preface would announce in the future tense ("this is what you are going to read") the conceptual content or significance (here, that strange strategy without finality, the debility or failure that organizes the *telos* or the *eschaton*, which reinscribes restricted economy within general economy) of what will *already* have been *written*. And thus sufficiently *read* to be gathered up in its semantic tenor and proposed in advance. From the viewpoint of the fore-word, which recreates an intention-to-say after the fact, the text exists as something written—a past—which, under the false appearance of a present, a hidden omnipotent author (in full mastery of his product) is presenting to the reader as his future. Here is what I wrote, then read, and what I am writing that you are going to read. After which you will again be able to take possession of this preface which in sum you have not yet begun to read, even though, once having read it, you will already have anticipated everything that follows and thus you might just as well dispense with reading the rest. The *pre* of the preface makes the future present, represents it, draws it closer, breathes it in, and in going ahead of it puts it ahead. The *pre* reduces the future to the form of manifest presence.

This is an essential and ludicrous operation: not only because writing as such does not consist in any of these tenses (present, past, or future insofar as they are all modified presents); not only because such an operation would confine itself to the discursive effects of an intention-to-mean, but because, in pointing out a single thematic nucleus or a single guiding thesis, it would cancel out the textual displacement that is at work "here." (Here? Where? The question of the here and now is explicitly enacted in dissemination.) Indeed, if such a thing were justifiable, we would have to assert right now that one of the theses—there is more than one—inscribed within dissemination is precisely the impossibility of reducing a text as such to its effects of meaning, content, thesis, or theme. Not the impossibility, perhaps, since *it is commonly done*, but the resistance—we shall call it the

---

contradictions to the homogeneity of a single model. It is the opposite that is likely to happen when Hegel makes difference into a moment within general contradiction. The latter is always ontotheological in its foundation. As is the reduction of the complex general economy of differ*a*nce to difference. (Belated residual note for a postface.)

restance[9]—of a sort of writing that can neither adapt nor adopt such a reduction.

Hence this is not a preface, at least not if by preface we mean a table, a code, an annotated summary of prominent signifieds, or an index of key words or of proper names.

But what do prefaces actually do? Isn't their logic more surprising than this? Oughtn't we some day to reconstitute their history and their typology? Do they form a genre? Can they be grouped according to the necessity of some common predicate, or are they otherwise and in themselves divided?

These questions will not be answered, at least not finally in the declarative mode. *Along the way*, however, a certain *protocol* will have—destroying this future perfect[10]—taken up the pre-occupying place of the *preface*.[11] If one insists on fixing this protocol in a representation, let us say in advance that, with a few supplementary complications, it has the structure of a *magic slate*.[12]

---

9. TN. The word *restance*, coined from the verb *rester* (to remain), means "the fact or act of remaining or of being left over."

10. TN. The French designation of the future perfect tense, *le futur antérieur*, literally means "the prior future." Derrida here both plays upon the simultaneous pastness and futureness of a book with respect to its preface and employs the future perfect tense in the very sentence in which he speaks about it. In French, the future perfect is often used to express hypothesis or opinion. Although this usage is not common in English, I have retained the future perfect in such cases whenever its temporal paradoxes are relevant to the context (cf. the first sentence of the book).

11. The preface does not expose the frontal, preambulary façade of a certain space. It does not exhibit the first face or the sur-face of a development that can thus be fore-seen and presented. It is what comes in advance of a speech (*praefatio, prae-fari*). In place of this discursive anticipation, the notion of "protocol" substitutes a textual monument: the *first* (*proto-*) page *glued* (*kollon*) over the opening—the first page—of a register or set of records. In all contexts in which it intervenes, the protocol comprises the meanings of priority, formula (form, pharmacopoeia), and writing: pre-scription. And through its "collage," the *protokol-lon* divides and undoes the inaugural pretention of the first page, as of any *incipit*. Everything, then, begins—this is a law of dissemination—doubled by a "facing." Of course, if the protocol itself amounted to the gluing in of a simple sheet (for example the recto/verso of the sign), it would become a preface again, in accordance with an order in which one can recognize the features of the Greater Logic. It avoids this only insofar as it forms a block, magically slated according to the "graphics" of a completely different structure: neither depth nor surface, neither substance nor phenomenon, neither in itself nor for itself.

(This outwork would then constitute—for example—the sketch, according to protocol, of an oblique introduction to two treatises (treatments, rather, and so strangely contemporaneous: to their own practice), the two most remarkable treatises, indefinitely re-markable, on the *pre written* [*le pré écrit*: can also mean "the written meadow"]: these two musical machines, as different as they can be—Francis Ponge's *le Pré* [*The Meadow*] or *la Fabrique du pré* [*Meadow Making*] and Roger Laporte's *Fugue*.)

12. TN. *Un bloc magique*. This is a reference to Freud's comparison of the psychic apparatus to a "mystic writing-pad," [*Wunderblock*] ("Note on the Mystic Writing-Pad,"

Prefaces, along with forewords, introductions, preludes, preliminaries, preambles, prologues, and prolegomena, have always been written, it seems, in view of their own self-effacement. Upon reaching the end of the *pre-* (which presents and precedes, or rather forestalls, the presentative production, and, in order to put before the reader's eyes what is not yet visible, is obliged to speak, predict, and predicate), the route which has been covered must cancel itself out. But this subtraction leaves a mark of erasure, a *remainder* which is added to the subsequent text and which cannot be completely summed up within it. Such an operation thus appears contradictory, and the same is true of the interest one takes in it.

But does a preface exist?

On the one hand—this is logic itself—this residue of writing remains anterior and exterior to the development of the content it announces. Preceding what ought to be able to present itself on its own, the preface falls like an empty husk, a piece of formal refuse, a moment of dryness or loquacity, sometimes both at once. From a point of view which can only, ultimately, be that of the science of logic, Hegel thus disqualifies the preface. Philosophical exposition has as its essence the capacity and even the duty to do without a preface. This is what distinguishes it from empirical discourses (essays, conversations, polemics), from particular philosophical sciences, and from exact sciences, whether mathematical or empirical. Hegel keeps coming back to this with unflagging insistence in the "foreword"'s which open his treatises (prefaces to each edition, introductions, etc.) Even before the *Introduction* (*Einleitung*) to the *Phenomenology of Spirit* (a circular anticipation of the critique of sensible certainty and of the origin of phenomenality) has announced "the presentation of appearing knowledge" (*die Darstellung des erscheinenden Wissens*), a *Preface* (*Vorrede*) will already have warned us against its own status as a fore-word:

> It is customary to preface a work (*Schrift*) with an explanation of the author's aim, why he wrote the book, and the relationship in which he believes it to stand to other earlier or contemporary treatises on the

---

1925). The "mystic writing-pad," which I am here calling a "magic slate," is a child's writing toy composed of a stiff dark waxed surface covered by a thin opaque sheet protected by a transparent piece of cellophane. Marks are made when pressure is exerted through all three layers, making the opaque layer take on the dark color of the waxed surface. When the top two layers are detached from the wax, the mark disappears, but the wax surface retains a furrow. The "magic slate," like the psychic apparatus, thus exhibits the capacity both to retain an imprint (memory) and to clear itself for the receipt of new marks (perception). Derrida has discussed this comparison of the psyche to a writing device in "Freud and the Scene of Writing" (in *Writing and Difference*, pp. 196–231).

same subject. In the case of a philosophical work, however, such an explanation seems not only superfluous but, in view of the nature of the subject-matter, even inappropriate and misleading (*sondern um der Natur der Sache willen sogar unpassend und zweckwidrig zu sein*). For whatever might appropriately be said about philosophy in a preface—say a historical *statement* of the main drift and the point of view, the general content and results, a string of random assertions and assurances about truth—none of this can be accepted as the way in which to expound philosophical truth. Also, since philosophy moves essentially in the element of universality, which includes within itself the particular, it might seem that here more than in any of the other sciences the subject-matter or thing itself (*die Sache selbst*), even in its complete nature, were expressed in the aim and the final results, the execution (*Ausführung*) being by contrast really the unessential factor (*eigentlich das Unwesentliche sei*).[13]

The preface to a philosophical work thus runs out of breath on the threshold of science. It is the site of a kind of chit-chat external to the very thing it appears to be talking about. This gossipy small talk of history reduces *the thing itself* (here the concept, the meaning of thought in the act of thinking itself and producing itself in the element of universality) to the form of a particular, finite object, the sort of object that determinate modes of knowledge—empirical descriptions or mathematical sciences—are incapable of producing spontaneously through their own workings and must therefore, for their part, *introduce* from the outside and define as a given:

> On the other hand, in the ordinary view of anatomy, for instance (say, the knowledge of the parts of the body regarded as inanimate), we are quite sure that we do not as yet possess the thing itself, the content of this science, but must in addition exert ourselves to know the particulars. Further, in the case of such an aggregate of information, which has no right to bear the name of Science, an opening talk (*Konversation*) about aim and other such generalities is usually conducted in the same historical and non-conceptual (*begrifflosen*) way in which the content itself (these nerves, muscles, etc.) is spoken of. In the case of philoso-

13. TN. *Hegel's Phenomenology of Spirit*, tr. A. V. Miller (New York: Oxford University Press, 1977), p. 1. The translation has occasionally been modified (e.g. the translation of *der Begriff* has been changed from "the Notion" to "the concept," and that of *die Sache selbst* has been changed (here and in note 15) from "the subject matter" or "the real issue" to "the thing itself") to bring it closer to the French translation Derrida is using. Derrida's interpolations from the German have been added.

phy, on the other hand, this would give rise to the incongruity that along with the employment of such a method its inability to grasp the truth would also be demonstrated. (*Phenomenology*, p. 1)

This preface to a philosophical text thus explains to us that, for a philosophical text as such, a preface is neither useful nor even possible. Does the preface take place, then? Where would it take place? How does this preface (the negative of philosophy) erase itself? In what mode does it come to predicate? A negation of negation? A denial? Is it left high and dry by the philosophical process which acts for itself as its own *presentation*, as the very domestic retinue of its own exposition (*Darstellung*)? ("The inner necessity that knowing should be science (*das Wissen Wissenschaft sei*) lies in its nature, and only the systematic exposition (*Darstellung*) of philosophy itself provides it." *Ibid.* p. 3.) Or is the prologue already carried away, beyond itself, in the movement which is located *in front of* it and which seems to follow it only for having *in truth* preceded it? Isn't the preface both negated and internalized in the presentation of philosophy by itself, in the self-production and self-determination of the concept?

But if something were to remain of the prolegomenon once inscribed and interwoven, something that would not allow itself to be sublated [*relevé*] in the course of the philosophical presentation, would that something necessarily take the form of that which *falls away* [*la tombée*]? And what about such a fall? Couldn't it be read otherwise than as the excrement of philosophical essentiality———not in order to sublate it back into the latter, of course, but in order to learn to take it differently into account?

Yes—if—Hegel writes beyond what he wants to say, each page of the preface comes unglued from itself and is forthwith divided: *hybrid* or *bifacial*. (Dissemination generalizes the theory and practice of the *graft* without a body proper, of the *skew* without a straight line, of the *bias* without a front.) The preface that Hegel *must* write, in order to denounce a preface that is both impossible and inescapable, must be assigned two locations and two sorts of scope. It belongs both to the inside and to the outside of the concept. But according to a process of mediation and dialectical reappropriation, the inside of speculative philosophy sublates *its own* outside as a moment of its negativity. The prefatory moment is necessarily opened up by the critical gap between the logical or scientific development of philosophy and its empiricist or formalist lag. This, indeed, is a lesson of Hegel's to be maintained, if possible, beyond Hegelianism: the essential complicity between empiricism and formalism. If the foreword is indispensable, it is because the prevailing culture still imposes both formalism and empiricism; that culture must be fought, or rather "formed" (*gebildet*) better, cultivated more carefully. The necessity of prefaces belongs to the *Bildung*. This struggle appears to be external to philosophy since it takes place rather in a didactic setting than within the self-presentation of a concept. But it is internal to philosophy to the extent that, as the Preface also says, the exteriority of the negative (falsehood, evil, death) still belongs to the process of truth and must leave its trace upon it. [14]

Thus, after defining the *internal necessity* of the self-presentation of the concept, Hegel identifies its *external necessity*, the necessity that takes time into account as the existence (*Dasein*) of the concept. But it is at first only a question of the necessity of time as a *universal* form of sensibility. One must then go on to recognize the gap between this formal notion of time, the general matrix in which the concept is present, and the empirical or historical determination of time, that of *our time*, for example:

> But the *external* necessity, so far as it is grasped in a general way, setting aside accidental matters of person and motivation, is the same as the inner, or in other words it lies in the shape (*Gestalt*) in which time sets forth the sequential existence of its moments (*wie die Zeit das Dasein ihrer Momente vorstellt*). To show that now is the propitious time (*an der Zeit*) for philosophy to be elevated to the status of a Science would therefore be the only true justification of any effort that has this aim, for to do so would demonstrate the necessity of the aim, would indeed at the same time be the accomplishing of it. (P. 3–4)

But since *our time* is not exactly, not simply propitious for such an elevation (*Erhebung*), since it is not yet quite the right time (*an der Zeit*), since the time, at any rate, is not equal to itself, it is still necessary to prepare it and make it join up with itself by didactic means; and if one judges that the time *has* come, one must make others aware of it and introduce them to what is already *there*; better yet: one must bring the being-there back to the concept of which it is the temporal, historical presence (*Dasein*) or, in a circular fashion, introduce the concept into its own being-there. A certain spacing between concept and being-there, between concept and existence, between thought and time, would thus constitute the rather unqualifiable lodging of the preface.

14. "Against this view it must be maintained that truth is not a minted coin that can be given and pocketed ready-made." "Out of this distinguishing, of course, comes identity, and this resultant identity is the truth. But it is not truth as if the disparity had been thrown away, like dross from pure metal, not even like the tool which remains separate from the finished vessel; disparity, rather, as the negative, the self (*Selbst*), is itself still directly present (*vorhanden*) in the True as such" (*Phenomenology*, pp. 22–23).

Time is the time of the preface; space—whose time *will have been* the Truth—is the space of the preface. The preface would thus occupy the entire *location* and *duration* of the book.

When the double necessity, both internal and external, *will have been* fulfilled, the preface, which will in a sense have introduced it as one makes an introduction to the (true) beginning (of the truth), will no doubt have been raised to the status of philosophy, will have been internalized and sublated into it. It will also, simultaneously, have *fallen away* of its own accord and been left "in its appropriate place in ordinary conversation."[15] A double topography, a double face, an overwritten erasure. What is the *status* of a text when it *itself* carries itself away and marks itself down? Is it a dialectical contradiction? A negation of negation? A labor of the negative and a process that works in the service of meaning? Of the being-abreast-of-itself of the concept?

You do not yet know whether what is written here, had you already read it, is not just a moment in the Hegelian preface.

Hegel's preface elaborates a critique of prefatory formality as it critiques mathematism and formalism in general. It is one and the same critique. As a discourse external to the concept and to the thing itself, as a machine devoid of meaning or life, as an *anatomical* structure, the preface always has some affinity with the procedure of mathematics. ("In mathematical cognition, insight is an activity external to the thing" . . . "Its purpose or concept" is a "relationship that is unessential, lacking the concept." P. 25.) Launched in the *Preface* to the *Phenomenology of Spirit*, the condemnation of the foreword is redoubled in the *Introduction* to the *Science of Logic*. Redoubled: shall it be said that it comes to repeat the preface to the *Phenomenology* or that it actually preceded the latter, conditioning it from the very beginning? Shall it be said—this is the traditional problem—that the entire *Phenomenology of Spirit* is in fact a preface introducing the *Logic*?[16] But

15. "From its very beginning, culture (*Bildung*) must leave room for the earnestness of life in its concrete richness; this leads the way to an experience of the thing itself (*in die Erfahrung der Sache selbst hineinführt*). And even when the thing itself has been penetrated to its depths by serious speculative effort, this kind of knowing and judging (*Beurteilung*) will still retain its appropriate place in ordinary conversation (*Konversation*)" (p. 3).

16. One ought here to reread very rigorously a number of sections from the Greater *Logic*: the *Preface*, the *Introduction*, and from Book One, that unclassifiable development preceding Section One called "With What Must the Science begin?" [*Hegel's Science of Logic*, trans. A. V. Miller, London: George Allen & Unwin, 1969. The translation has occasionally been slightly modified according to the needs of Derrida's exposition, and Derrida's interpolations from the German have been added.] Through the speculative concepts of method, beginning (abstract or concrete), ground, result, and presupposition, etc., the relations between logic and the phenomenology of spirit are there reinstalled in their endless circle. Each of the two develops and presupposes the other: the example determined by the

like any preface, this one can rightfully have been written only after the fact. It is *in truth* an endless postface; and this can be read especially in the preliminaries; it is from the end of the line, from the viewpoint of absolute

---

whole envelops the whole, etc. For example: a) "This spiritual movement which, in its simple undifferentiatedness, gives itself its own determinateness and in its determinateness its equality with itself, which therefore is the immanent development of the concept, this movement is the absolute method of knowing and at the same time is the immanent soul of the content itself. I maintain that it is only through this self-construing method (*auf diesem sich selbst konstruirenden Wege*) that philosophy is able to be an objective, demonstrated science. It is in this way that I have tried to expound (*darzustellen*) consciousness in the *Phenomenology of Spirit*. Consciousness is spirit as a concrete knowing, a knowing, too, in which externality is involved; but the development of this object, like the development of all natural and spiritual life, rests solely on the nature of the pure essentialities which constitute the content of logic. (Consciousness, as spirit in its manifestation which in its progress frees itself from its immediacy and external concretion, attains to the pure knowing which takes as its object those same pure essentialities as they are in and for themselves. They are pure thoughts, spirit thinking its own essential nature. Their self-movement is their spiritual life and is that through which philosophy constitutes itself and of which it is the presentation (*Darstellung*).

"In the foregoing there is indicated the relation of the science which I call the *Phenomenology of Spirit*, to logic. As regards the external relation, it was intended that the first part of the *System of Science* which contains the *Phenomenology* should be followed by a second part containing logic and the two concrete (*realen*) sciences, the Philosophy of Nature and the Philosophy of Spirit, which would complete the System of Philosophy. But the necessary expansion which logic itself has demanded has induced me to have this part published separately; it thus forms the first sequel to the Phenomenology of Spirit" (*Preface to the First Edition*, pp. 28–29).

b) "In the *Phenomenology of Spirit* I have exhibited (*dargestellt*) consciousness in its movement onwards from the first immediate opposition of itself and the object to absolute knowing. The path (*Weg*) of this movement goes through every form of the *relation of consciousness to the object* and has the *concept of science* for its result (*Resultate*). This concept therefore (apart from the fact that it emerges (*hervorgeht*) within logic itself) needs no justification here because it has received it in that work; and it cannot be justified in any other way than by this emergency (*Hervorbringung*) in consciousness, all the forms of which are resolved into this concept as into their truth. To establish or explain the concept of science in a ratiocinative [*räsonierende*: the word Hegel regularly uses to define the discursive mode of prefaces] manner can at most achieve this, that a general idea of the concept is presented to our thinking (*vor der Vorstellung*) and a historical knowledge (*historische Kenntnis*) of it is produced; but a definition of science—or more precisely of logic—has its proof solely in the already mentioned necessity of its emergence (*Hervorgangs*)" (*Introduction*, pp. 48–49).

c) "Hitherto philosophy had not found its method; it regarded with envy the systematic structure of mathematics and, as we have said, borrowed it or had recourse to the method of sciences which are only amalgams of given material (*Stoffe*), empirical propositions and thoughts—or even resorted to a crude rejection of all method. However, the exposition of what alone can be the true method of philosophical science falls within the treatment of logic itself; for the method is the consciousness of the form (*Form*) of the inner self-movement of the content of logic. In the *Phenomenology of Spirit* I have expounded an example of this method in application to a more concrete object, namely to consciousness" (*Introduction*, pp. 53–54).

knowledge, that the two books open and reciprocally envelop each other in a single volume. The preface to phenomenology is written from out of the end of logic. The self-presentation of the concept is the *true* preface to all prefaces. *Written* prefaces are phenomena external to the concept, while the concept (the being-abreast-of-itself of absolute logos) is the true *pre-face*, the essential *pre-dicate* of all writings.

The form of this movement is dictated by the Hegelian concept of *method*. Just as the *Introduction* (which follows the *Preface*) to the *Phenomenology of Spirit* critiques that critique of knowledge which treats the latter as an *instrument* or a *milieu*, so also the *Introduction* to the *Science of Logic* rejects the classical concept of method: an initial set of definitions of rules external to the operations, hollow preliminaries, an itinerary assigned beforehand to the actual route taken by knowledge. This is a critique *analogous* to the one Spinoza addressed to the Cartesian concept of method. If the path of science is itself science, then method is no longer a preliminary, external reflection; it is the production and the structure of the whole of science as the latter exposes itself in logic. Hence, either the preface already belongs to this exposition of the whole, engages it and is engaged in it, in which case the preface has no specificity and no textual place of its own, being merely a part of philosophical discourse; or else the preface escapes this in some way, in which case it is nothing at all: a textual form of vacuity, a set of empty, dead signs which have *fallen*, like the mathematical relation, outside the living concept. Then it is nothing but a mechanical, hollow *repetition*, without any internal link with the content it claims to announce.[17]

But why is *all this* explained precisely *in prefaces*? What is the status of this third term which cannot *simply*, as a *text*, be either inside philosophy or outside it, neither in the markings, nor in the marchings, nor in the margins, of the book? This term that is never sublated by the dialectical method without leaving a remainder? That is neither a pure form, completely empty, since it *announces* the path and the semantic production of the concept, nor a content, a moment of meaning, since it remains external to the logos of which it indefinitely feeds the critique, if only through the

---

17. This formal repetition without any link with the content, this purely "rhetorical" ornament, was something condemned by "good rhetoric" well before Hegel. This very condemnation was already a *topos*. But the rules of the genre had to reach a certain technical perfection and a certain procedural absurdity. The Latin authors confected prefaces any of which could be used to introduce a number of different books. Cicero confides to Atticus that he has set aside a whole collection of preambles, thinking they might come in handy some day.

How is such a repetition possible? What (is the story) about this *remainder*? Such is the question posed in and by the outwork [*hors-livre*].

gap between ratiocination and rationality, between empirical history and conceptual history? If one sets out from the oppositions form/content, signifier/signified, sensible/intelligible, one cannot comprehend the writing of a preface. But in thus *remaining*, does a preface *exist*? Its spacing (the preface to a rereading) diverges in (the) place of the χώρα.

We have come to a remarkable theshold [*limen*]of the text: what can be read of dissemination. *Limes*: mark, march, margin. Demarcation. Marching order: quotation: **"Now—this question also announced itself, explicitly, as the question of the liminal."**

> (From the *Preface* to the *Phenomenology of Spirit*) It might seem necessary at the outset to say more about the *method* of this movement, i.e. of Science. But its concept is already to be found in what has been said, and its proper exposition (*eigentliche Darstellung*) belongs to Logic, or rather it *is* Logic. For the method is nothing but the structure set forth in its pure essentiality. We should realize, however, that the system of ideas concerning philosophical method is yet another set of beliefs that belongs to a bygone culture. If this comment sounds boastful or revolutionary (*renommistich oder revolutionär*)—and I am far from adopting such a tone [the preface is thus signed "I"]—it should be noted that current opinion itself has already come to view the scientific regime bequeathed by mathematics as quite *old-fashioned*—with its explanations, divisions, axioms, sets of theorems, its proofs, principles, deductions, and conclusions from them. (P. 28)

The fascination exerted by the formal model of mathematics would thus seem to have guided the classical philosophers in their concept of method, in their *methodology*, in their discourse on method or their rules for the direction of the mind.[18] This ill-arranged formalism would in sum consist in imposing upon the presentation of truth a set of epigraphs that are either intolerable to truth or that truth should produce on its own; such a formalism blinds one to the path of truth and to the living historicity of

---

18. This time the *path* in question is not only that of Descartes. The critique is also directed at Spinoza. The *Introduction* to *Logic* makes this clear, referring us to the *Preface* to the *Phenomenology of Spirit*: "Pure mathematics, too, has its method which is appropriate for its abstract objects and for the quantitative form in which alone it considers them. I have said what is essential in the preface to the *Phenomenology of Spirit* about this method and, in general, the subordinate form of scientific method which can be employed in mathematics; but it will also be considered in more detail in the logic itself. *Spinoza*, *Wolf*, and others have let themselves be misled in applying it also to philosophy and in taking the external course followed by non-conceptual quantity (*den äusserlichen Gang der begrifflosen Quantität*) for the course of the concept, a procedure which is absolutely contradictory" (p. 53).

method as it exposes itself and engenders itself in the *Logic*. It is there, in the *Logic*, that the preface must and can disappear. Hegel had already said as much in the *Preface* to the *Phenomenology of Spirit*. Why does he nevertheless *repeat* it in the *Introduction* to the *Science of Logic*? What can be said here about this textual "event"? about this digraph?

> In no science is the need to begin with the thing itself (*von der Sache selbst*), without preliminary reflections (*ohne vorangehende Reflexionen*), felt more strongly than in the science of logic. In every other science the subject matter and the scientific method are distinguished from each other; also the content does not make an absolute beginning but is dependent on other concepts and is connected on all sides with other material (*Stoffe*). These other sciences are, therefore, permitted to speak of their ground and its context and also of their method, only as premises taken for granted. (*Logic*, p. 43.)

The *Introduction* to the *Logic* is subtitled "General Concept of Logic." The *preface* must be distinguished from the *introduction*. They do not have the same function, nor even the same dignity, in Hegel's eyes, even though the problem they raise in their relation to the philosophical corpus of exposition is analogous. The Introduction (*Einleitung*) has a more systematic, less historical, less circumstantial link with the logic of the book. It is *unique*; it deals with general and essential architectonic problems; it presents the general concept in its division and in its self-differentiation. The Prefaces, on the other hand, are multiplied from edition to edition and take into account a more empirical historicity; they obey an occasional necessity that Hegel defines, of course, *in a preface*: the *Preface* to the *Second Edition* of the *Science of Logic*.[19] And yet—this is why the problems are, as we said earlier, *analogous*—the *Introduction*, too, should disappear, should (shall) have disappeared, along with the Prefaces, in Logic. The *Introduction* only remains

19. 1831: He reminds us that if Plato, as word would have it, had to revise his *Republic* seven times, a modern philosopher, dealing with a more difficult subject matter, a more profound principle, a richer kind of material, ought to revise his exposition seventy-seven times. Which requires a great deal of leisure. "However, the author, in face of the magnitude of the task, has had to content himself with what it was possible to achieve in circumstances of external necessity, of the inevitable distractions caused by the magnitude and many-sidedness of contemporary affairs" (*Logic*, p. 42). Hegel also alludes to the "deafening chatter" that interferes with the work of knowing. But he was never so distracted by it that he failed to perceive certain of its effects, for example the following: "Thus they have the category in which they can place any apparently significant philosophy, and through which they may at the same time set it aside; this they call a fashion-philosophy" (*Hegel's Lectures on the History of Philosophy*, trans. E. S. Haldane and Frances H. Simson, London: Routledge & Kegan Paul, 1892, p. 42).

insofar as this absolutely *universal* philosophical science must provisionally, considering the prevailing lack of culture, introduce itself as a *particular* philosophical science. For the only legitimate place for an Introduction, within the system, is to open a *particular* philosophical science, *Esthetics* or the *History of Philosophy*, for example. The Introduction there acts to link the determinate generality of those derivative, dependent discourses with the absolute, unconditional generality of logic. Hegel thus by no means contradicts himself when, in his *Lectures* on esthetics or on the history of philosophy, he posits the necessity of an introduction.[20]

The liminal space is thus opened up by an inadequation between the form and the content of discourse or by an incommensurability between the signifier and the signified. As soon as one tries to reduce its mass [*bloc*] to a single surface, the protocol always becomes a formal instance. In all societies, the chief of protocol is a functionary of formalism. The inadequation between form and content should erase itself, however, in speculative logic, which, in contrast to mathematics, is at once the production and the presentation of its own content: "Logic, on the contrary, cannot presuppose any of these forms of reflection and laws of thinking, for these constitute part of its own content and have first to be established within the science. But not only the account of scientific method, but even the concept itself of the science as such belongs to its content, and in fact constitutes its final result" (*Logic*, p. 43).

---

20. This involves a certain treatment of *paleonymy*: "The circumstance mentioned makes it in no science so necessary as in the history of Philosophy to commence with an Introduction, and in it correctly to define, in the first place, the subject of the history about to be related. For it may be said, How should we begin to treat a subject, the name of which is certainly mentioned often enough, but of whose nature we as yet know nothing? . . . But in fact, when the concept of Philosophy is established, not arbitrarily but in a scientific way, such treatment becomes the science of Philosophy itself. For in this science the peculiar characteristic is that its concept forms the beginning in appearance merely, and it is only the whole treatment of the science that is the proof, and indeed we may say the finding of its concept; and this is really a result of that treatment.

"In this Introduction the concept of the science of Philosophy, of the subject of its history, has thus likewise to be set forth. At the same time, though this Introduction professes to relate to the history of Philosophy only, what has just been said of Philosophy on the whole, also holds good. What can be said in this Introduction is not so much something which may be stated beforehand, as what can be justified or proved in the treatment of the history. These preparatory explanations are for this reason only, not to be placed in the category of arbitrary assumptions. But to begin with stating what in their justification are really results, can only have the interest which may be possessed by a summary, given in advance, of the most general contents of a science. It must serve to set aside many questions and demands which might, from our ordinary prejudices, arise in such a history" (*Lectures on the History of Philosophy*, p. 4vi). Similar remarks are to be found in the Introduction to the *Lectures on Aesthetics*.

Its content is its final result: logic has as its object nothing other than scientificity in general, the very concept of science, thought as such inasmuch as it conceives, knows, and thinks itself. If logic needs no lemma, it is because, beginning with conceptual thought, it must also end with conceptual thought, and because it does not at first know all there is to know about scientificity, the concept of which will also be its ultimate acquisition. And yet that ultimate acquisition must *already* be its premise; it must announce from the first, abstractly, what it can only know at the end, in order that even in its exordium it move already *in* the element of its own content and need not borrow any formal rules from any other science. Whence the necessity of setting in motion the following proposition, which contradicts itself *immediately* if it is understood according to a noncircular linearity:

> What logic is cannot be stated beforehand (*voraussagen*), rather does this knowledge of what it is first emerge as the final outcome (*ihr Letztes*) and consummation (*Vollendung*) of the whole exposition (*ihre ganze Abhandlung*). Similarly, it is essentially within the science that the subject matter of logic, namely, *thought* or more specifically *conceptualizing* thought (*das begreifende Denken*) is considered; the concept of logic has its genesis in the course (*Verlauf*) of the exposition and cannot therefore be premised (*vorausgeschickt*). (*Logic*, p. 43)

Thus, Hegel must rescind the logical, scientific character of an Introduction to Logic at the very moment that, within the act of proposing one (but what is the textual operation of such a proposal?), he advances *there* that Logic cannot be preceded by any lemma or prolemma. He denies the logical character of his Introduction in conceding that it is but a concession, that it *remains*, like classical philosophy, external to its content, a mere formality designed to remove itself on its own initiative:

> Consequently, what is premised in this Introduction is not intended, as it were, to establish the concept of logic or to justify its method scientifically in advance, but rather by the aid of some reasoned (*räsonierendem*) and historical explanations and reflections to make more accessible to ordinary thinking the point of view from which this science is to be considered. (*Ibid.*, p. 43)

The constraint to which the Introduction yields remains, of course, accidental: one must correct the historical error into which philosophers of both former and latter days have allowed themselves to stray. Entering into conflict with them, Hegel marches out into their territory, which is also that of lemmatism, mathematism, and formalism. But this error being a form of negativity that cannot be avoided or eliminated (like the philosophical "conversation" it prescribes), we find it thought out, internalized, sublated by the movement of the concept, and in its turn negated and absorbed as an integral part of the logical text. The necessity of this movement sounds paradoxical or contradictory only if it is observed from the exteriority of a formalist instance. This contradiction is rather the very movement of speculative dialectics in its discursive progression. It constructs the concept of the preface according to the Hegelian values of negativity, sublation, presupposition, ground, result, circularity, etc., or according to the opposition between certainty and truth. The signifying *pre-cipitation*, which pushes the preface to the front, makes it seem like an empty form still deprived of what it wants to say; but since it is ahead of itself, it finds itself predetermined, in its text, by a semantic *after-effect*. But such indeed is the essence of speculative production: the signifying precipitation and the semantic after-effect are here *homogeneous* and *continuous*. Absolute knowledge is *present* at the zero point of the philosophical exposition. Its teleology has determined the preface as a postface, the last chapter of the *Phenomenology of Spirit* as a foreword, the *Logic* as an Introduction to the *Phenomenology of Spirit*. This point of ontoteleological fusion reduces both precipitation and after-effect to mere appearances or to sublatable negativities.

Hegel is thus at once as close and as foreign as possible to a "modern" conception of the text or of writing: nothing precedes textual generality absolutely. There is no preface, no program, or at least any *program* is already a pro*gram*, a moment of the text, reclaimed by the text from its own exteriority. But Hegel brings this generalization about by saturating the text with meaning, by *teleologically* equating it with its *conceptual tenor*, by reducing all absolute dehiscence between writing and wanting-to-say [*vouloir-dire*], by erasing a certain occurrence of the break between *anticipation* and *recapitulation*: a shake of the head.

If the preface appears inadmissible today, it is on the contrary because no possible heading can any longer enable anticipation and recapitulation to meet and to merge with one another. To lose one's head, no longer to know where one's head is, such is perhaps the effect of dissemination. If it would be ludicrous today to attempt a preface that really was a preface, it is because we *know* semantic saturation to be impossible; the signifying precipitation introduces an excess facing [*un débord*] ("that part of the lining which extends beyond the cloth," according to Littré) that cannot be mastered; the semantic after-effect cannot be turned back into a teleological anticipation and into the soothing order of the future perfect; the gap between the empty "form," and the fullness of "meaning" is structurally irremediable, and any formalism, as well as any thematicism, will be impotent to dominate that structure. They will miss it in their very attempt to master it. The generalization of the grammatical or the textual hinges on the disappearance, or rather the reinscription, of the semantic horizon, even when—especially when—it comprehends difference or plurality. In diverging from polysemy, comprising both more and less than the latter, dissemination interrupts the circulation that transforms into an origin what is actually an after-effect of meaning.

But the question of meaning has barely been opened and we have not yet finished with Hegel. We *know*, said we, a minute ago. But we know something here which is no longer anything, with a knowledge whose form can no longer be recognized under this old name. The treatment of paleonymy here is no longer a raising or a regaining of consciousness.

No doubt Hegel, too, allows for the insistence[21] of a certain gap between the form and content. That is, between what he calls certainty and what he calls truth. Isn't *The Phenomenology of Spirit* precisely the history of such discrepancies? The recital of an infinite preface? While criticizing formalism, mathematism, scientism—which are always the errors of a philosopher—Hegel steers clear of rejecting the necessity for formal, mathematical, or scientific (in the restricted sense of the term) moments. He takes care not to fall into the opposite errors: empiricism, intuitionism, prophetism. The complicity among these symmetrical failings chooses to take up residence in prefaces as its favorite spot. But it is still up to a preface to unmask that complicity, according to the overflow of a re-mark (a preface on prefaces, a preface within a preface) of which dissemination must problematize the formal rules and the abyssal movement; there occurs a completely different reinscription of "dead space and the equally lifeless numerical Unit," altogether other and *hence* very similar, a reinscription that *redoubles* the *Preface* to the *Phenomenology of Spirit*:

> Truth is its own self-movement, whereas the method just described [the mathematical method] is the mode of cognition that remains external to the material (*Stoffe*). Hence it is peculiar to mathematics, and must be left to that science, which, as we have noted, has for its principle the relationship of magnitude, a relationship alien to the concept (*begrifflose Verhältnis der Grösze*), and for its material (*Stoffe*)

21. TN. The word *insistence* is to be understood in its etymological sense of "standing firm in" (*in + sistere*).

dead space and the equally lifeless numerical Unit. This method, too,
in a looser form, i.e. more blended with the arbitrary and the
accidental, may retain its place, as in conversation (*Konversation*), or in
a piece of historical instruction designed rather to satisfy curiosity
(*Neugierde*) than to produce knowledge (*Erkenntnis*), which is about
what a preface (*Vorrede*) amounts to. . . . But we have already pointed
out that, once the necessity of the concept has banished the slipshod
style of conversational discussion (*den losen Gang der räsonierenden
Konversation*) and along with it the pedantry and pomposity of science,
they are not to be replaced by the non-method (*Unmethode*) of presenti-
ment (*des Ahnens*) and inspiration (*Begeisterung*), or by the arbitrariness
of prophetic utterance, both of which despise not only scientific
pomposity, but scientific procedure of all kinds. (Pp. 28–29)

The speculative dialectic must overcome the oppostion between form
and content, just as it must overcome all dualism or duplicity, without
ceasing to be scientific. It must *scientifically* think out the opposition
between science and its other.

It is not enough to arrive at triplicity in general, however, in order to
attain the speculative element of the concept. Formalism, too, can
accommodate triplicity: corrupt it, fix it in a *schema* or a *table of terms*, tear it
out of the life of the concept. The immediate target here is Schelling's
philosophy of nature:

> Of course, the *triadic* form (*Triplicität*) must not be regarded as
> scientific when it is reduced to a lifeless schema (*leblosen Schema*), to a
> mere shadow (*zu einem eigentlichen Schemen*), and when scientific orga-
> nization is degraded into a table of terms (*Tabelle*). Kant rediscovered
> this triadic form by instinct, but in his work it was still lifeless and
> uncomprehended (*unbegriffene*); since then it has, however, been raised
> to its absolute significance, and with it the true (*wahrhafte*) form
> (*Form*) in its true content has been presented, so that the concept of
> Science has emerged. This formalism of which we have already spoken
> generally and whose style we wish to describe in more detail, imagines
> that it has comprehended and expressed the nature and life of a form
> (*Gestalt*) when it has endowed it with some determination of the
> schema as a predicate. The predicate may be subjectivity or objectiv-
> ity, or, say, magnetism, electricity, etc., contraction or expansion,
> east or west, and the like. Such predicates can be multiplied to
> infinity, since in this way each determination or form can again be
> used as a form or moment in the case of an other, and each can

gratefully perform the same service for an other. In this sort of circle of reciprocity one never learns what the thing itself is, nor what the one or the other is. In such a procedure, sometimes determinations of sense are picked up from everyday intuition, and they are supposed, of course, to *mean* something different from what they say; sometimes what is in itself meaningful (*Bedeutende*), e.g. pure determinations of thought like Subject, Object, Substance, Cause, Universal, etc.— these are used just as thoughtlessly and uncritically as we use them in everyday life, or as we use ideas like strength and weakness, expansion and contraction; the metaphysics is in the former case as unscientific as are our sensuous representations in the latter.

Instead of the inner life and self-movement (*Selbstbewegung*) of its existence, this kind of simple determinateness of intuition—which means here sense-knowledge—is predicated in accordance with a superficial analogy, and this external, empty application of the formula (*Formel*) is called a "construction" (*Konstruktion*). This formalism is just like any other. (Pp. 29–30)

The static classification of dual oppositions and of third terms, taxonomical inscriptions, all varieties of anatomical thinking—i.e. the thinking of the preface, as we now know—content themselves with labeling inert, finite products. Schelling's philosophy of nature contains only a semblance of dialectical triplicity. From the outside, in a prefabricated "construction," such philosophy applies simple oppositions, formulas prescribed once and for all: somewhat as in a well-kept pharmacy[22] or grocery store, or

22. A "Chinese" pharmacy, perhaps, such as Mao Tse-tung alludes to in a very Hegelian stage of his argumentation against formalism, the "fifth indictment against stereotyped Party writing": "arrang(ing) items under a complicated set of headings, as if starting a Chinese pharmacy. Go and take a look at any Chinese pharmacy, and you will see cabinets with numerous drawers, each bearing the name of a drug—toncal, foxglove, rhubarb, saltpetre. . . indeed, everything that should be there. This method has been picked up by our comrades. In their articles and speeches, their books and reports, they use first the big Chinese numerals, second the small Chinese numerals, third the characters for the twelve earthly branches, and then capital A, B, C, D, then small a, b, c, d, followed by the Arabic numerals, and what not! How fortunate that the ancients and foreigners created all these symbols for us so that we can start a Chinese pharmacy without the slightest effort. For all its verbiage, an article that bristles with such symbols, that does not pose, analyse or solve problems and that does not take a stand for or against anything is devoid of real content and nothing but a Chinese pharmacy. I am not saying that such symbols as the ten celestial stems, etc., should not be used, but that this kind of approach to problems is wrong. The method borrowed from the Chinese pharmacy, which many of our comrades are very fond of, is really the most crude, infantile and philistine of all. It is a formalist method, classifying things according to their external features instead of their internal relations. If one takes a conglomeration of concepts that are not internally related and arranges them into an article,

even in a museum of natural history where one can find collected, classed, and exhibited all manner of dead limbs and cold bones, skins dried like parchments, anatomical plates, and other tableaux and displays that pin down the living to death:

> What results from this method of labeling all . . . is a synoptic table like a skeleton with scraps of paper stuck all over it, or like the rows of closed and labeled boxes in a grocer's stall (*in einer Gewürzkrämerbude*). It is as easy to read off as either of these; and just as all the flesh and blood has been stripped from this skeleton, and the no longer living "essence" [*Sache*] has been packed away in the boxes (*Büchsen*), so in the report the living essence of the matter [*Wesen der Sache*] has been stripped away or boxed up dead.
>
> To exhibit the realm of thought philosophically, that is, in its own immanent activity or, what is the same, in its necessary development, had therefore to be a fresh undertaking, one that had to be started right from the beginning; but this traditional material, the familiar forms of thought, must be regarded as an extremely important source (*Vorlage*), indeed as a necessary condition and as a presupposition to be gratefully acknowledged even though what it offers is only here and there a meagre shred or a disordered heap of dead bones. (*Logic*, Preface to Second Edition, p. 31)

In contrast to this triplicity of death, the speculative dialectic favors the living triplicity of the concept, which remains beyond the grasp of any arithmetic or of any numerology. "The number three makes its appearance in a deeper sense in religion as the Trinity and in philosophy as the Concept. In general, the numerical form of expression is too thin and inadequate to present true concrete unity. The Spirit is certainly a trinity, but it cannot be added up or counted. Counting is a bad procedure." (*Lectures on the History of Philosophy*).

Another way of working with *numbers*, dissemination sets up a pharmacy in which it is no longer possible to count by ones, by twos, or by threes; in which everything starts with the dyad. The dual opposition (remedy/poison, good/evil, intelligible/sensible, high/low, mind/matter, life/

---

speech or report simply according to the external features of things, then one is juggling with concepts and may also lead others to indulge in the same sort of game, with the result that they do not use their brains to think over problems and probe into the essence of things, but are satisfied merely to list phenomena in ABCD order. What is a problem? A problem is a contradiction in a thing. Where one has an unresolved contradiction, there one has a problem." *Selected Works of Mao Tse-tung* (Peking: Foreign Languages Press, 1967), III, 60–61.

death, inside/outside, speech/writing, etc.) organizes a conflictual, hierarchically structured field which can be neither reduced to unity, nor derived
from a primary simplicity, nor dialectically sublated or internalized into a
third term. The "three" will no longer give us the ideality of the speculative
solution but rather the effect of a strategic re-mark, a mark which, by phase
and by simulacrum, refers the name of one of the two terms to the absolute
outside of the opposition, to that absolute otherness which was marked—
once again— in the exposé of *differance*. Two/four, and the "closure of
metaphysics" can no longer take, can indeed never have taken, the form of a
circular line enclosing a field, a finite culture of binary oppositions, but
takes on the figure of a totally different partition. Dissemination *displaces*
the three of ontotheology along the angle of a certain re-folding [*re-
ploiement*]. A Crisis of *versus*:[23] these marks can no longer be summed up or
"decided" according to the two of binary oppositions nor sublated into the
three of speculative dialectics (for example "differance," "gramme,"
"trace," "broach/breach" [*entamer*], "de-limitation," "pharmakon," "supplement," "hymen," "mark-march-margin," and others; the movement of
these marks pervades the whole of the space of writing in which they occur,
hence they can never be enclosed within any finite taxonomy, not to speak of
any lexicon as such);[24] they *destroy* the trinitarian horizon. They destroy it
textually: they are the marks of dissemination (and not of polysemy) in that
they cannot be pinned down at any one *point* by the concept or the tenor of a
signified. They "add" a fourth term the more or the less. "**Even though it is
only a triangle open on its fourth side,the splayed square loosens up the obsidionality of the triangle and the circle which in their ternary rhythm (Oedipus,
Trinity, Dialectics) have always governed metaphysics. It loosens them up; that is,
it de-limits them, reinscribes them, re-cites them.**" The writing of such a story
belongs neither to the inside nor to the outside of the triangle; this is
something the consequences of which we have hardly begun to measure.

The opening of the square, the supplementary four (neither a cross nor a
closed square), the more or less which disjoins dissemination from

23. TN. *Crise du versus* is reminiscent of Mallarmé's *Crise de vers* (*Crisis of Verse*), which
Derrida will discuss at length in "The Double Session."
24. TN. Because Derrida's discourse operates a displacement of traditional binary
logic, it tends to amass and foreground a series of terms like those listed here which contain
within themselves skewed contradictions and which render undecidable any proposition in
which they occur. It is therefore tempting for translators and other prefacers to try to
facilitate the reader's entrance into Derrida's writing by constructing a "lexicon" of such
terms. Derrida is here both inviting and warning against such a procedure, which, while it
points up Derrida's neologistic innovations, reinscribes the effects of those innovations
within a finite, pointillistic topology.

polysemy, are regularly and explicitly associated with castration ("**castration—always at stake—**"): but with a certain *outside* of castration (a fall with no return and with no restricted economy) which could no longer be taken up and comprehended within the logocentric, sublimating field of talking truth, law, signification, full speech, the symbolic order, the intersubjective dialectic, or even the intersubjective triad.[25] If dissemination cannot *simply* be equated with the castration it *entails* or *entrains* (one should soon become (en)trained in reading this word), this is not only because of its "affirmative" character but also because, at least up to now, according to a necessity that is anything but accidental, the concept of castration has been metaphysically interpreted and arrested. The lack, the void, the break, etc., have been given the value of a signified or, which amounts to the same, of a transcendental signifier: the self-presentation of truth (veiled/unveiled) as *Logos*.

It is here that the question of psychoanalysis comes into play: it tests itself *practically* against a text which, able to "begin" only with four, can no longer, anywhere, except by simulacrum, be closed, mastered, encircled.

Dissemination endlessly opens up a *snag* in writing that can no longer be mended, a spot where neither meaning, however plural, nor *any form of presence* can pin/pen down [*agrapher*] the trace. Dissemination treats— doctors—that *point* where the movement of signification would regularly come to *tie down* the play of the trace, thus producing (a) history. The security of each point arrested in the name of the law is hence blown up. It is—at least—at the risk of such a blowup that dissemination has been broached/breached. With a detour through/of writing one cannot get over.[26]

25. TN. The reference here is to the psychoanalytical theories of Jacques Lacan, whose writings Derrida has discussed at length in "*Le facteur de la verité*" (*Poetique* 21, 1975; reprinted in *La Carte postale*, Paris: Flammarion, 1980; translated as "The Purveyor of Truth" by Willis Domingo, James Hulbert, Moshe Ron, and Marie-Rose Logan in *Yale French Studies* 52, 1975). For a detailed analysis of the encounter between Lacan and Derrida, see my "The Frame of Reference: Poe, Lacan, Derrida," in *The Critical Difference* (Baltimore: Johns Hopkins University Press, 1981).

26. TN. This paragraph—one of the most untranslatable in the entire book—both proposes and enacts the *differance* wrought by dissemination. The original French is: "La dissémination ouvre, sans fin, cet *accroc* de l'écriture qui ne se laisse plus recoudre, le lieu où ni le sens, fût-il pluriel, ni *aucune forme de présence* n'agraphe plus la trace. La dissémination traite—sur lit—le *point* où le mouvement de la signification viendrait régulièrement *lier* le jeu de la trace en produisant ainsi l'histoire. Saute la sécurité de ce point arrêté au nom de la loi. C'est—du moins—au risque de ce faire sauter que s'entamait la dissémination. Et le détour d'une écriture dont on ne revient pas." Behind the word "point" lies Lacan's notion of the *point de capiton* [in upholstery or quilting, a stitch], by which he translates the Greek word *lekton*, which he is substituting for the Saussurian notion of the "signified." (See Lacan's

This question can no longer be dissociated from a restaging of *arithmos* and of "counting" as a "bad procedure." Nor from a rereading of the *rythmos* of Democritus, which stands as a kind of writing that philosophy has never been able to reckon with, since it is rather *out of* the prior existence and restless exteriority of that writing that philosophy is able to arise and account for itself: it forms a written preface, in a sense, and one which discourse as such can no longer envelop in its circulation, in that circle where the speculative impossiblity and the speculative necessity of the prolegomenon meet.

The written preface (the slate [*bloc*] of the protocol), the outwork, then becomes a fourth text. Simulating the postface,[27] the recapitulation and

---

presentation to the first volume of his *Ecrits* republished by Seuil in a collection called, interestingly enough, "Points.") While Lacan's theory, according to Derrida, aims to "pin down" the history of a subject, dissemination is what produces an irreducible snag in that project.

27. According to the logic of sublation, the postface provides the truth both of the preface (always stated after the fact) and of the entire discourse (produced out of absolute knowledge). The *simulacrum* of a postface would therefore consist of feigning the final revelation of the meaning or functioning of a given stretch of language.

This operation can be dragged out in laboriousness and impatience whenever he who, *having writ, stops writing*, and forces himself to adequately rejoin the fact of his past text so as to unveil its underlying procedure or its fundamental truth. Witness the boredom experienced by Henry James while writing the prefaces to his complete works at the end of his life. Witness Theophile Gautier's exclamation: "For a long time now people have been inveighing against the uselessness of prefaces—yet they keep on writing them." Witness Flaubert's irritation toward his "three prefaces" in which he could see nothing but the unproductive hollowness of criticism. And it is indeed true that, according to its classical conception, the preface represents the *critical* instance of the text, wherever it may operate ("How eager I am to be finished with *Bovary*, *Anubis*, and my three *prefaces*, so that I can plunge into a new period, and throw myself into 'pure beauty'!" (to Louis Bouilhet, August 23, 1853). "Ah! how impatient I am to be rid of Bovary, Anubis, and my three prefaces (that is to say the only three times, which really amount to one, I will ever write criticism)! How eager I am to be done with all this so I can throw myself into a subject that is *vast* and *clean-cut*" (to Louise Colet, August 26, 1853). (*Préface à la vie d'écrivain* [*Preface to the life of a writer*], a selection of letters presented by Geneviève Bollème)).

But the simulacrum can also be play-acted: while pretending to turn around and look backward, one is also in fact starting over again, adding an extra text, complicating the scene, opening up within the labyrinth a supplementary digression, which is also a false mirror that pushes the labyrinth's infinity back forever in mimed—that is, endless— speculation. It is the textual *restance* of an operation, which can be neither opposed nor reduced to the so-called "principal" body of a book, to the supposed referent of the postface, nor even to its own semantic tenor. Dissemination would propose a certain theory—to be followed, also, as a marching order quite ancient in its form—of *digression*, written for example in the margins of *A Tale of a Tub*, or taking up where the "trap" described by the Second Preface to *La Nouvelle Héloïse* leaves off.

(Outwork would then, for example, be the hystero-colic sketch of an *appendix*, highly differentiated in its structure (dissemination describes or—to be more precise—*illustrates* recurrent anticipation, the auto-motion of the concept, it is another text entirely, but at the same time, as an "attendant discourse," it is the "double" of what it goes beyond.

Speculative philosophy thus proscribes the preface as empty form and as signifying precipitation; it prescribes it, on the other hand, insofar as it is in the preface that meaning *announces itself*, philosophy being always already

---

the act of appending, from one end to the other) to all possible treatises (treatments, rather, and so strangely contemporaneous to their own practice) on the *post-scriptum*: the P.S.'s to *Comment j'ai écrit certains de mes livres*, to *Ecce Homo* (Why I Write Such Good Books, which intersects with the "belated preface" to *The Dawn of Day* or with a certain foreword to *The Joyful Wisdom* ("Perhaps more than one preface (*nicht nur eine Vorrede*) would be necessary for this book; and after all it might still be doubtful whether any one could be brought nearer (*näher gebracht*) to the *experiences* (*Erlebnisse*) in it by means of prefaces, without having himself experienced (*erlebt*) something similar (*etwas Ähnliches*)" [trans. Thomas Common (New York: Russell & Russell, 1964), p. 1]), to the *Concluding Unscientific Postscripts to the Philosophical Fragments, A Mimic-Pathetic-Dialectic Composition, An Existential Contribution*, by "Johannes Climacus" [S. Kierkegaard, trans. David S. Swanson (Princeton: Princeton University Press, 1944)], to his foreword and to his *Introduction* ("You will perhaps remember, dear reader, that near the end of the *Philosophical Fragments* there appeared a certain remark which might look like the promise of a sequel. Viewed as a promise, indeed, the remark in question ["if I ever write a sequel"] was in the highest degree tentative, and at the farthest possible remove from a solemn engagement . . . . Such being the nature of the promise, it seems quite suitable that its fulfillment should be relegated to a *Postscript*. The author can scarcely be charged with having indulged in the feminine practice of saying the most important thing (if there is anything important in connection with the whole matter) as an after-thought, in a note at the end . . . . For it is ridiculous to treat everything as if the System were complete, and then to say at the end, that the conclusion is lacking. If the conclusion is lacking at the end, it is also lacking in the beginning . . . . But in a scientific structure the absence of a conclusion has retroactive power to make the beginning doubtful and hypothetical, which is to say: unsystematic. So at least from the standpoint of dialectical fearlessness. But our dialectician has not yet acquired it . . . . The scholarly introduction draws the attention away by its erudition. . . . . . The rhetorical address serves to distract by intimidating the dialectician" [pp. 13-18]), and finally to his "Appendix" (where it is explained that thus "the book is superfluous," that "the book has not only a Conclusion but a Revocation. More than that no one can require, either before or after" [pp. 546-47] and that "to write a book and revoke it is something else than not writing it at all" [p. 548]), and to his "First and Last Declaration" (which relates the problem of the *pseudonymity* or *polynymity* to that of "the author of the preface of the book" [p. 551]), to the "Appendix" to Der *Jubelsenior* by Jean-Paul (who hardly needs to be identified as the master of the double) (*Prodromus Galeatus* [in Werke, Munich: Carl Hanser Verlag, 1962]. "A preface should be nothing but a longer title. The present one should in my opinion confine itself to an elucidation of the word Appendix, nothing more" [p. 311] . . . . "The first and oldest Appendix mentioned in literary history is found at the end of my *Biographischen Belustigen*; it is commonly known that this was written by the creator of this literary genre himself, namely myself. The second Appendix that our literature has produced is printed in this book and appears immediately following this Preface. Now, since I have furnished the example of the Appendix, and since I remain like the Academy and the living model laid out on the table, the estheticians have an easy task drawing a theory, a salutory order and a useful formula for this genre out of existing Appendices; they can model their *legislative* domain

engaged in the Book.²⁸ This "contradiction" necessarily leaves protocolic traces, blocks of writing in the Hegelian text, for example the whole scriptural apparatus that opens the chapter on sensible certainty and whose strange functioning we shall analyze elsewhere. But the contradiction is dissipated when, at the end of the preface, which is also the end of history and the beginning of philosophy, the domain of conceptual apriority no longer knows any bounds. It is at the end of a famous preface that Hegel describes the strange "after-ness" of the concept and of philosophical a priority, the belatedness that succeeds in effacing itself *as it poses itself*:

after my *creative* power . . ." [pp. 412–13] . . . "Digressions are never of the essence in the novel, but they should never be treated as inessential in the Appendix. In the former they are stagnant refuse; in the latter they are a mosaic in the floor, a poetic Asaroton; thus the Ancients put straw, bones and such-like in the mosaics; in a word, they had the room for the sake of putting refuse there" [pp. 413–14]), and after this "hasty poetics of the appendix," which is also an analysis of excrement, after all the "promised digressions," to the "Appendix to the Appendix or My Christmas Eve" ("I do not believe that an author writes anything more willingly than his preface and his postscript: there he can write on and on about himself, which pleases him, and about his work, which delights him above all else. Out of the prison and slave-galley of his book he has leapt into these two pleasure camps, these two recreation places . . . . Is that not the reason why the book-binders put a blank sheet before the preface and one after the end, like vacancy signs on a door, indicating that the next page is also unoccupied and open to whatever scribbling comes along. However, these empty spaces enclosing the garden of the book are also the wilderness which must separate one book from another—as great empty expanses separate the realms of the Teutons, or those of the North Americans, or the solar systems. Also, no one will find fault with me if I save my preliminaries and my conclusions—for I sharpen myself in preparation for these from the moment I write the title—if I save them for certain days, utopian days" [p. 545] . . . . "Many arguments could be put forth supporting and strengthening the view that I had set aside this Appendix to the Appendix, like a preserved fruit, for the first holiday. In particular it could be said that I had cleverly waited for Christmas Day, so as to have my Christmas joy, as if I were my own son . . ." [p. 546])).

28. Cf. Kojève, *Introduction à la lecture de Hegel*; J.-M. Rey, "Kojève ou la fin de l'histoire," *Critique* No. 264; and E. Clémens, "L'histoire (comme) inachèvement," R.M.M. No. 2, 1971. It should be specified that Feuerbach had already examined in terms of *writing* the question of the Hegelian *presupposition* and of the textual residue. An entire systematic and differentiated reading would be necessary of his whole *Zur Kritik der Hegelschen Philosophie* (1839) [*Kleinere Schriften II*, (Berlin: Akademie Verlag, 1970, pp. 32–33] . . . "the exposition was supposed to *presuppose nothing*, that is, to leave no residue inside us, to empty us and drain us out completely . . ." [p. 22]. Since that cannot be effected, Feuerbach in his turn, as if expecting the favor to be returned, accuses Hegel of "speculative empiricism" and of formalism, then even of "pretense" and of "game-playing." What is of interest here, beyond each of these terms, is the necessity of the exchange and of the opposition. "But precisely for this reason with Hegel also—aside from the wonderfully scientific rigor of his development—the proof of the absolute has in essence and in *principle* only a *formal* significance. Hegelian philosophy presents a contradiction between truth and scientific spirit, between the essential and the formal, between *thought* and *writing*. *Formally*, the absolute idea is certainly not presupposed, but in essence it is" [p. 29] . . . . "The estrangement (*Entäusserung*) of the idea is, so to speak, only a *pretense*; it makes believe, but it

One word more about giving instructions (*das Belehren*) as to what the
world ought to be. Philosophy in any case always comes on the scene
too late to give any. As the thought (*Gedanke*) of the world, it appears
only when actuality is already there cut and dried after its process of
formation has been completed. The teaching of the concept, which is
also history's inescapable lesson, is that it is only when actuality is
mature that the ideal first appears over against the real and that the
ideal apprehends this same real world in its substance and builds it up
for itself into the shape of an intellectual realm. When philosophy
paints its grey on grey, then has a shape of life grown old. By
philosophy's grey on grey it cannot be rejuvenated but only understood. The owl of Minerva spreads its wings only with the falling of
the dusk.

But it is time to close this preface (*Vorwort*). After all, as a preface
(*als Vorwort*), its only business has been to make some external and
subjective remarks about the standpoint of the book it introduces. If a
topic is to be discussed philosophically, it spurns any but a scientific
and objective treatment, and so too if criticisms (*Widerrede*) of the
author take any form other than a scientific discussion of the thing
itself, they count only as a personal epilogue (*Nachwort*) and as a
capricious assertion, and he must treat them with indifference.[29]

The end of the preface, if such an end is possible, is the moment at which
the order of exposition (*Darstellung*) and the sequential unfolding of the
concept, in its self-movement, begin to overlap according to a sort of a
priori synthesis: there would then be no more discrepancy between produc-

---

is not in earnest; it is *playing*. The conclusive proof is the beginning of the *Logic*, whose
beginning should be the beginning of philosophy in general. Beginning as it does with
Being, is a mere formalism, because Being is not the true beginning, the true first term; one
could just as easily begin with the absolute Idea, for even before he *wrote* the *Logic*, that is,
even before he gave his ideas a scientific form of communication, the absolute Idea was
already a certainty for Hegel, an immediate truth." . . . "To Hegel the *thinker* the absolute
Idea was an absolute certainty; to Hegel the *writer*, it was a *formal* uncertainty" [p. 30].

What would *prohibit*—for such is the question—reading the Hegelian *text* as an immense
game of writing, a powerful and thus imperturbable simulacrum, yielding the undecidable
signs of its pretence only in the sub-text, the floating fable of its prefaces and its footnotes?
Hegel in person, after all, could have let himself get caught up in this. By inversion and
chiasmus from here on, Feuerbach cuts across Hegel and summons him back, unseasonably,
to the gravity of philosophy and history: "The philosopher must bring into the *text* of
philosophy that which Hegel relegates to footnotes: that part of man which does *not*
philosophize, which is *against* philosophy and *resists* abstract thought" [p. 254].

29. TN. *Hegel's Philosophy of Right*, trans. T. M. Knox (Oxford: Clarendon Press,
1942), pp. 12–13. The translation has been slightly modified, and Derrida's interpolations
from the German have been added.

tion and exposition, only a *presentation* of the concept by itself, in its own words, in its own voice, in its logos. No more anteriority or belatedness of form, no more exteriority of content; tautology and heterology would be coupled together in the speculative proposition. The analytic procedure and the synthetic procedure would mutually envelop each other. The concept is then enriched a priori by its own determination without going outside of itself, or through perpetual returns to itself, within the element of self-presence. The effective determination of the "real" unites with "ideational" reflection in the immanent law of the same development.

If Marx found himself obliged to defend himself from the Hegelian apriorism and idealism his critics were quick to accuse him of, it was precisely because of his *method of presentation*. His defense has an essential relation to his concept and practice of the preface.

Let us recall the explanation he gives in the *Afterword* (*Nachwort*) to the second German edition of *Capital* (January 1873). It is hardly insignificant that it should be just before his most famous paragraphs on the reversal of Hegelian dialectics that Marx proposes what he considers to be the decisive distinction between *method of presentation* and *method of inquiry*. This distinction alone would disrupt the *resemblance* between the form of his own discourse and the form of Hegel's presentation, a resemblance that had led certain reviewers who "shriek out at 'Hegelian sophistics' " astray. But one cannot undo this resemblance without transforming—along with the oppositions form/matter or content (*Form/Stoff*) and ideality/materiality (*Ideelle/Materielle*)—the concepts of reflection and anticipation, i.e. the relation between the beginning and the development, between introduction and process. This relation is not the same in discourse as it is in the real; it is not the same in the discourse of *research* as it is in the *presentation* of the *result* after the fact. It is around this valuation of the result (the "ground" is the "result" for Hegel)[30] that the entire debate revolves.

> *The European Messenger* of St. Petersburg, in an article dealing exclusively with the method of *"Das Kapital"* (May 1972 issue, pp. 427–26), finds my method of inquiry (*Forschungsmethode*) severely realistic, but my method of presentation (*Darstellungsmethode*), unfortunately, German-dialectical (*deutsch-dialektisch*). It says: "At first sight, if the judgment is based on the external form of the presentation (*Form der Darstellung*) of the subject, Marx is the most ideal of ideal philosophers (*der grösste Idealphilosoph*), always in the German, i.e. the bad sense of

---

30. Cf. the beginning of the "Theory of Being" in the Greater Logic. On this problem and on the "leap" involved in this result, cf. also Heidegger, *Identity and Difference*.

the word. But in point of fact he is infinitely more realistic than all his fore-runners in the work of economic criticism. He can in no sense be called an idealist."

. . . Whilst the writer pictures what he takes to be my actual method (*wirkliche Methode*), in this striking and (as far as concerns my own application of it) generous way, what else is he picturing but the dialectic method? Of course the method of presentation (*Darstellungsweise*) must differ in form (*formell*) from that of inquiry (*Forschungsweise*). The latter has to appropriate the material (*Stoff*) in detail, to analyze its different forms of development, to trace out their inner connection. Only after this work is done, can the actual movement (*wirkliche Bewegung*) be adequately described. If this is done successfully, if the life of the subject matter (*Stoff*) is ideally reflected as in a mirror (*spiegelt sich ideell wider*), then it may appear as if we had before us a mere a priori construction (*Konstruktion*).

My dialectic method is not only fundamentally (*der Grundlage nach*) different from the Hegelian, but is its direct opposite (*direktes Gegenteil*). To Hegel, the life-process of the human brain, i.e., the process of thinking (*Denkprozesz*), which, under the name of "the Idea," he even transforms into an independent subject (*in ein selbstständiges subjekt*), is the demiurgos of the real world, and the real world is only the external, phenomenal form of "the Idea." With me, on the contrary, the ideal (*ideelle*) is nothing else than the material world (*Materielle*) transposed (*umgesetzte*) by the human mind, and translated (*übersetzte*) into forms of thought.[31]

If, instead of engaging our steps toward *the fundamental* debate in its classical form (What can be said here of the concepts of method, reflection, presupposition, ground, result, the real world, etc.? From a Hegelian point of view, is the *Afterword*'s argumentation the *Widerrede* of an empirical realism that, in positing the absolute exteriority of the real to the concept, of effective determination to the process of presentation, would necessarily end up as a formalism, or even as an idealist criticism indefinitely confined to its own preface? etc.), we appear to be limiting ourselves to "textual" indications, it is because we have now arrived at the point where the relation between the "text"—in the narrow, classical sense of the term—and the

31. *Capital*, trans. Samuel Moore and Edward Aveling (New York: International Publishers, 1967), pp. 17–19 [with Derrida's interpolations from the German]. What follows these remarks in Marx's text is well known. Cf. also Althusser's *Avertissement* in the Garnier-Flammarion edition (Paris, 1969), esp. pp. 18–23, and Philippe Sollers, "Lénine et le matérialisme philosophique," in *Tel Quel* 43.

"real" is being played out, and because the very concepts of text and of extratext, the very transformation of the relation between them and of the preface we are engaged in, the practical and theoretical problematic of that transformation, are at stake. The new kind of text that retains and seems to limit us here is in fact the infinite excess facing [*débord*] of its classical representation. This lining fringe, this extra edge, this de-limitation, invites a rereading of the form of our relation to Hegel's logic and to all that can be subsumed therein. The breakthrough toward radical otherness (with respect to the philosophical concept—of the concept) always takes, *within philosophy*, the *form* of an a posteriority or an empiricism.³² But this is an effect of the specular nature of philosophical reflection, philosophy being incapable of inscribing (comprehending) what is outside it otherwise than through the appropriating assimilation of a negative image of it, and dissemination is written on the back—the *tain* —of that mirror. Not on its inverted specter. Nor in the triadic symbolic order of its sublimation. The question is to find out what it is that, written under the mask of empiricism, turning speculation upside down, *also does something else* and renders a Hegelian sublation [*relève*] of the preface impracticable. This question calls for prudent, differentiated, slow, stratified readings. It will have to concern itself, for example, with the motif of the "beginning" in Marx's text. While Marx recognizes, as does Hegel in his Greater *Logic*, the fact that "every beginning is difficult, holds in all sciences" (*Preface* to the first edition of *Capital*, 1867), he has an entirely different relation to the writing of his introductions. What he seeks to avoid is formal *anticipation*. So does Hegel, of course. But here, the expected "result," which must precede and condition the introduction, is not a pure determination of the concept, much less a "ground."

Is this simply because of its status as what Hegel would have called a *particular science*? And is political economy a "regional" science here?³³

In any event, the prefatory form can no longer easily be *internalized* in the logical apriority of the book and in its *Darstellung*.

> The present part consists of the first two chapters. The entire material lies before me in the form of monographs, which were not written for

---

32. On empiricism as the *philosophical* form or mask of the heterological breaching [*frayage*], cf. for example *Writing and Difference* pp. 151 ff; *Of Grammatology*, "The Exorbitant: Question of Method" pp. 162 ff; and "*La Différance*" in *Théorie d'ensemble*, coll. "Tel Quel" p. 45.

33. But it is the whole scheme of the subordination of the sciences, and then of the regional ontologies, to a general or fundamental onto-logic that is perhaps here being thrown into confusion. Cf. *Of grammatology*, p. 21.

publication but for self-clarification at widely separated periods; their remoulding into an integrated whole according to the plan I have indicated will depend upon circumstances.

A general introduction (*allgemeine Einleitung*), which I had drafted, is omitted, since on further consideration it seems to me confusing to anticipate results which still have to be substantiated, and the reader who really wishes to follow me will have to decide to advance from the particular to the general. A few brief remarks regarding the course of my study of political economy may, however, be appropriate here. . . . These studies led partly of their own accord to apparently quite remote subjects on which I had to spend a certain amount of time. But it was in particular the imperative necessity of earning my living which reduced the time at my disposal. My collaboration, continued now for eight years, with the *New York Tribune* . . .[34]

The development is so little modeled upon a law of conceptual immanence, so hard to anticipate, that it must bear the visible marks of its revisions, alterations, extensions, reductions, partial anticipations, plays of footnotes, etc. The *Preface* to the first edition of *Capital* (1867) exhibits, precisely, the work of transformation to which the earlier "presentation of the subject-matter" has been submitted, the quantitative and qualitative heterogeneity of the developments, and the entire historical scene in which the book is inscribed.[35]

Thus is sketched out the dissymmetrical space of a postscript to the Great Logic. A space at once general and infinitely differentiated. No doubt as apparently dependent and derivative as a postscript can be, it is nonetheless

34. TN. Preface to *A Contribution to the Critique of Political Economy*, trans. S. W. Ryazanskaya (New York: International Publishers, 1970), pp. 19, 23. Derrida's interpolation from the German has been added.

35. "The work, the first volume of which I now submit to the public, forms the continuation of my *Zur Kritik der Politischen Oekonomie* (*A Contribution to the Critique of Political Economy*) published in 1859. The long pause between the first part and the continuation is due to an illness of many years' duration that again and again interrupted my work.

"The substance of that earlier work is summarized in the first three chapters of this volume. This is done not merely for the sake of connexion and completeness. The presentation of the subject-matter is improved (*Die Darstellung ist verbessert*). As far as circumstances in any way permit, many points only hinted at in the earlier book are here worked out more fully, whilst, conversely, points worked out fully there are only touched upon in this volume. The sections on the history of the theories of value and of money are now, of course, left out altogether. The reader of the earlier work will find, however, in the notes to the first chapter additional sources of reference relative to the history of those theories.

"Every beginning is difficult, holds in all sciences (*aller Anfang ist schwer, gilt in jeder Wissenschaft*)" (p. 7).

a force of historical no-return, resistant to any circular recomprehension within the anamnesic domesticity (*Erinnerung*) of Logos, which would recover and proclaim truth in the fullness of its speech.

We are in an uneven chiasmus. In Hegel's reason for disqualifying the preface (its formal exteriority, its signifying precipitation, its textuality freed from the authority of meaning or of the concept, etc.), how can we avoid recognizing the very question of writing, in the sense that is being analyzed here? The preface then becomes necessary and structurally interminable, it can no longer be described in terms of a speculative dialectic: it is no longer merely an empty form, a vacant significance, the pure empiricity of the non-concept, but a completely other structure, a more powerful one, capable of accounting for effects of meaning, experience, concept, and reality, reinscribing them without this operation's being the inclusion of any ideal *"begreifen."* Inversely, isn't the type of preface that always in fact imposes itself on Hegel (that movement through which the concept already announces itself, precedes itself in its own *telos*, establishes the text within the element of its meaning from the outset), isn't this what in our eyes today makes those prefaces appear archaic, academic, contrary to the necessity of the text, written in an outworn rhetoric suspect in its reduction of the chain of writing to its thematic effects or to the formality of its articulations? If dissemination is without a preface, this is not in order that some sort of inaugural production, some self-presentation can be opened up; quite the contrary, it is because dissemination marks the essential limits shared by rhetoric, formalism, and thematicism, as well as those of the system of their exchange.

On the one hand, the preface is ruled out but it must be written: so that it can be integrated, so that its text can be erased in the logic of the concept which cannot *not* presuppose itself. On the other hand (almost the same), the preface is ruled out but it is still being written in that it is already made to function as a moment of the relaunched text, as something that belongs to a textual economy that no concept can anticipate or sublate. "Moment" and "to belong" therefore can no longer designate here a simple inclusion within some ideal interiority of writing. To allege that there is no absolute outside of the text is not to postulate some ideal immanence, the incessant reconstitution of writing's relation to itself. What is in question is no longer an idealist or theological operation which, in a Hegelian manner, would suspend and sublate what is outside discourse, logos, the concept, or the idea. The text *affirms* the outside, marks the limits of this speculative operation, deconstructs and reduces to the status of "effects" all the predicates through which speculation appropriates the outside. If there is no-

thing outside the text, this implies, with the transformation of the concept
of text in general, that the text is no longer the snug airtight inside of an
interiority or an identity-to-itself (even if the motif of "outside or bust" may
sometimes play a reassuring role: a certain kind of inside can be terrible),
but rather a different placement of the effects of opening and closing.

In either case, the preface is a fiction ("Here is the cynical Alcidamas,
writing this preface for laughs"). But in the first case, fiction is in the service
of meaning, truth is (the truth of) fiction, the fictive arranges itself on a
hierarchy, it itself negates and dissipates itself as accessory to the concept.
In the other case, outside of any mimetologism, fiction affirms itself as a
simulacrum and, through the work of this textual feint, disorganizes all the
oppositions to which the teleology of the book ought violently to have
subordinated it.

Such would be, for example, the play of the "hybrid preface," the
"renegade's preface" to the *Songs of Maldoror*. Through a supplementary
simulacrum, the sixth Song *presents itself* as the effective body of the text, the
real operation for which the first five Songs would only have been the
didactic preface, the "synthetic" exposition, the "frontispiece," the façade
one sees from the front before penetrating further, the picture engraved on
the cover of the book, the representative forefront giving advance notice of
"the preliminary explanation of my future poetics," and the "statement of
the thesis."

Where, in the topography of the text, can we situate this strange
declaration, this performance that has *already ceased* being part of the preface
and *doesn't yet* belong to the "analytic" part that seems to be getting under
way?

> The first five songs have not been useless; they were the frontispiece to
> my work, the foundation of the structure, the preliminary explanation
> of my future poetics: and I owed it to myself, before strapping up my
> suitcase and setting off for the lands of the imagination, to warn
> sincere lovers of literature with a rapid sketch, a clear and precise
> general picture, of the goal I had resolved to pursue. Consequently, it
> is my opinion that the synthetic part of my work is now complete and
> has been adequately paraphrased. In this part you learnt that I had set
> myself the task of attacking man and Him who created man. For the
> moment, and for later, you need to know no more. New considera-
> tions seem to me superfluous, for they would only repeat, admittedly
> in a fuller, but identical, form, the statement of the thesis which will
> have its first exposition at the end of this day. It follows from the

preceding remarks that from now on my intention is to start upon the analytic part; so true, indeed, is this that only a few minutes ago I expressed the ardent wish that you should be imprisoned in the sudoriferous glands of my skin in order to prove the sincerity of what I am stating with full knowledge of the facts. It is necessary, I know, to underpin with a large number of proofs the argument of my theorem; well, these proofs exist and you know that I do not attack anyone without good reason. I howl with laughter.[36]

All this is going on precisely at the end of a preface, in the twilight, between life and death, and the final Song will still rise up "at the end of this day." And will constitute the "first development" of a stated "thesis." In resorting to the two modes of mathematical proof, analysis and synthesis, in order to sport with the opposition, Lautréamont parodically switches them around and, grappling with them in the manner of Descartes,[37] rejoins the

36. TN. Comte de Lautreamont, *Maldoror and Poems*, trans. Paul Knight (Penguin, 1978), p. 212.

37. The following text by Descartes can be compared not only to the sixth Song, but also to the distinction drawn in the postscript of *Capital*, between the *method of inquiry* and the *method of presentation*: "The method of proof is two-fold, one being analytic, the other synthetic. Analysis shows the true way by which a thing was methodically derived, as it were effect from cause, so that, if the reader care to follow it and give sufficient attention to everything, he understands the matter no less perfectly and makes it as much his own as if he had discovered it himself. But it contains nothing to incite belief in an inattentive or hostile reader; for if the very least thing brought forward escapes his notice, the necessity of the conclusions is lost. . . . Synthesis contrariwise employs an opposite procedure, one in which the search goes as it were from effect to cause (though often here the proof itself is from cause to effect to a greater extent than in the former case). It does indeed clearly demonstrate its conclusions, and it employs a long series of definitions, postulates, axioms, theorems, and problems, so that if one of the conclusions that follow is denied, it may at once be shown to be contained in what has gone before. Thus the reader, however hostile and obstinate, is compelled to render his assent. Yet this method is not so satisfactory as the other and does not equally well content the eager learner, because it does not show the way in which the matter taught was discovered." ["Reply to Objections II," in *Philosophical Works of Descartes*, trans. Elizabeth S. Haldene and G. R. T. Ross (Cambridge: Cambridge University Press, 1911, 1977), II, 48–49.]

The synthetic path, a didactic procedure and secondary preface, is enforced only to overcome the "presuppositions . . . to which we have since our earliest years been accustomed. . . . This is why my writing took the form of Meditation rather than that of Philosophical Disputations or theorems and problems of a geometer; so that hence I might by this very fact testify that I had no dealings except with those who will not shrink from joining me in giving the matter attentive care and meditation. . . . And yet . . . I append here something in the synthetic style . . . ." [*Ibid.* pp. 50–51].

Unlike the *Meditations*, the *Principles of Philosophy* follow the synthetic order. Its Preface ("Author's Letter to the Translator [into French, the Abbé Claude Picot] of the book, which may here serve as Preface") recommends that the book "first of all be run through in its entirety like a novel," but a total of three times [*ibid.* I, 207–209].

constraints and the *topos* of the "vicious circle." The preface, a synthetic
mode of exposition, a discourse of themes, theses, and conclusions, here as
always precedes the analytic text of invention, which will *in fact* have come
before it but which cannot, for fear of remaining unreadable, present or
teach itself on its own. Yet the preface that must make the text intelligible
cannot in turn offer itself to the reader without his having first made his
actual infinite way through the desolate swamp ("his rugged and treacherous way across the desolate swamps of these sombre and poison-filled
pages," p. 29). The preface can become a discourse on method, a treatise on
poetics, a set of formal rules, only after the forging of the irruptive track of a
method that is actually *put in practice* as a path that breaks ground and
constructs itself as it goes along, without a predetermined itinerary.
Whence the artifice of a preface "which will not perhaps appear natural
enough" (p. 213) and which in any event will never be simply crossed out.[38]
Rather, it launches (into) another preface to a new novel:

> I shall not retract one of my words; but, telling what I have seen, it
> will not be difficult for me, with no other object than truth, to justify
> them. Today I am going to fabricate a little novel of thirty pages; the
> estimated length will, in the event, remain unchanged. Hoping to see
> the establishment of my theories quickly accepted one day by some
> literary form or another, I believe I have, after some groping attempts,
> at last found my definitive formula. It is the best: since it is the novel!
> This hybrid preface has been set out in a fashion which will not
> perhaps appear natural enough, in the sense that it takes, so to speak,
> the reader by surprise, and he cannot well see quite what the author is
> trying to do with him; but this feeling of remarkable astonishment,
> from which one must generally endeavor to preserve those who spend
> their time reading books and pamphlets, is precisely what I have made
> every effort to produce. In fact, I could do no less, in spite of my good
> intentions: and only later, when a few of my novels have appeared, will
> you be better able to understand the preface of the fuliginous ren-
> egade.
>   Before I begin, I must say that I find it absurd that it should be
> necessary (I do not think that everyone will share my opinion, if I am
> wrong) for me to place beside me an open inkstand and a few sheets of
> unspitballed paper [*papier non mâché*]. In this way I shall be enabled to

---

38. "Alexander Dumas the younger will never, absolutely never, make a speech at a
school prize-day. He does not know what morality is. It makes no compromises. If he did, he
would have to cross out, in a single stroke, every word he has written up to now, starting
with his absurd prefaces" (*Poems*, p. 257).

begin the sixth song in the series of instructive poems which I am eager to produce. Dramatic episodes of unrelenting usefulness! Our hero perceived that by frequenting caves and taking refuge in inaccessible places, he was transgressing the laws of logic, and committing a vicious circle. [Pp. 212–13; translation slightly modified]

The demonstration will follow: Maldoror escapes the circle by emerging from a certain cave, from "the depths of my beloved cave" (p. 40), no longer toward the light of truth, but according to an entirely other topology where the outlines of the preface and of the "main" text are blurred. Propagating the poisons, reconstructing the squares, analyzing the stones, passing through the columns and gratings,[39] forks and trellises of the *Songs of*

39. *Gratings*: "In the wall that enclosed the yard, on the west side, diverse openings had been parsimoniously cut out and closed off by gratings." . . . "From time to time the grate of an opening would rise up with a creak, as if by the ascending impetus of a hand doing violence to the nature of the iron . . . while his leg was still caught in the twists of the grate . . ." " . . . a few minutes later, I arrived in front of a grate whose solid bars were tightly criss-crossed. I wanted to peep inside through this thick screen. At first I could see nothing . . ." " . . . sometimes it would try, showing one of its tips in front of the grating . . ." " . . . And I glued my eye to the grate more intensely than ever!" (repeated seven times) "He said I had to be attached to a trellis . . ." Etc.

Columns: "My magnificent palace is built with walls of silver, columns of gold . . ." " . . . They flutter about the columns, like thick waves of black hair." "Don't speak of my spinal column, since it's a sword." " . . . I would feel sorry for the man of the column." Etc.

Squares: "The froth from my square mouth" " . . . But the order that surrounds you, represented notably by the perfect regularity of the square, the friend of Pythagorus, is even grander." " . . . Two enormous towers could be seen in the valley; I said so at the beginning. If you multiplied them by two, you came out with four . . . but I could never quite make out the necessity for this arithmetic operation." " . . . That is why I no longer go back through that valley where the two units of the multiplicand are standing!" " . . . I tore out a whole muscle from my left arm, for I no longer knew what I was doing, I was so moved by that quadruple misfortune. I, who thought that that was excremental matter." " . . . This bed, which draws to its breast the dying faculties, is but a tomb composed of squared pine planks . . . Finally, four enormous stakes nail the sum of all the members to the mattress." " . . . The squares are formed and immediately fall, never to rise again." " . . . It is nonetheless true that the crescent-shaped draperies no longer get the expression of their definitive symmetry from the quaternary number: go and see for yourself if you don't want to believe me." Etc.

Stones: "The stone would like to escape the laws of gravity." " . . . You, take a stone and kill her." " . . . I took a large stone . . . the stone bounced up as high as six churches." " . . . When I'm on the prowl . . . lonely as a stone in the middle of the road." " . . . When the shepherd boy David struck the giant Goliath on the forehead with a stone flung from his sling-shot . . ." " . . . The stone, unable to disperse its vital principles, shoots itself up into the air as if by gunpowder, and falls back down to sink solidly into the ground. Sometimes the peasant dreamer spots an aerolith vertically cleaving through space, heading downward toward a field of corn. He doesn't know where the stone comes from. You now possess, clear and succinct, the explanation of this phenomenon." " . . . He is not resigned, and goes to get, from the parvis of the miserable pagoda, a flat pebble with a sharp, tapered edge. He pitches it forcefully into the air . . . the chain is cut through the middle, like grass by a scythe, and the cult object falls to the ground, spilling its oil on the flagstones . . ." " . . . shoving the

Maldoror, dissemination also displaces a whole ontospeleology, another name for mimetology: not mimesis, an enigma of redoubtable power, but an interpretation of mimesis that misapprehends and distorts the logic of the double and of all that has elsewhere been called the supplement to (at) the origin, underivable repetition, duplicity with nothing coming before

---

immovable granite with my foot, I defied death . . . and threw myself like a cobblestone into the mouth of space." ". . . At night, with its propitious darkness, they leaped from the porphyry-crested craters of the underwater currents, leaving far behind them the pebbly chamber pot where the constipated anus of the human cockatoos bestirs itself, until they could no longer make out the suspended silhouette of the filthy planet." ". . . Nude as a stone, he threw himself upon the girl's body and lifted up her dress . . ." ". . . The children pelted her with stones as though she were a grackle." ". . . Its efforts were useless; the walls were built with freestone, and, when it hit the wall, I saw it bend back like a steel blade and bounce like a rubber ball." ". . . his face, condemned by the circumstances to an absence of natural expression, looked like the stony concretion of a stalactite." ". . . What I have left to do is break this mirror, to shatter it with a rock . . ." ". . . I had fallen asleep on the cliff . . ." ". . . that woman . . . so as to drag her, with your tarsi, through valleys and roadways, over brambles and stones . . ." ". . . Do you know that, when I think of the iron ring hidden under the stone by the hand of a maniac, an invisible shiver runs through my hair?" ". . . I went to bring back the ring I had buried beneath the stone . . ." ". . . If death arrests the fantastic leanness of my shoulders' two long arms, engaged in the lugubrious crushing of my literary gypsum, I would at least like the mourning reader to say to himself: 'I have to do him justice. He has greatly cretinized me' " ". . . the morning apparition of the rhythmic kneading of an icosahedral sack against its chalky parapet!" Etc.

Poisons: "The desolate swamps of these sombre, poison-filled pages . . ." ". . . my breath emits a poisonous exhalation . . ." ". . . With this poisoned weapon you lent me, I brought down off his pedestal, built by the cowardice of man, the Creator himself!" ". . . for lack of a type of sap fulfilling the simultaneous conditions of nutriciousness and absence of venomous matter." ". . . Victorious, I beat off the ambushes of the hypocritical poppy." ". . . Recognition had entered like a poison into the heart of the crowned madman!" Etc. [All translations of passages quoted in this note are mine.—Trans.]

And if one later sought to understand this network in the form of a "this is that," one would lose just about everything in the expectation: neither a pre-face nor a pre-dicate. A toothing stone, cornerstone, stumbling block, all, in the very vestibule of *Dissemination*, but also even before that, will have provisioned the trap, glutting the gorgonized reader's examination. So many stones! But *what is* the stone, the stoniness of the stone? Stone is the phallus. Is this any answer? Is this saying anything if the phallus is in fact the divestment of the thing? And what if, occupying no center, having no natural place, following *no path of its own*, the phallus has no meaning, eludes any dialectical sublimation (*Aufhebung*), extracts the very movement of signification, the signifier/signified relation, from any *Aufhebung*, in one direction or the other, both types amounting ultimately to the same? And what if the "assumption" or denial of castration should also, strangely enough, amount to the same, as one can *affirm*? In that case, apotropaics would always have more than one surprise up its sleeve. In this connection, it would be well to slate for a rereading Freud and the scene of writing, the procedure that opens and closes it, the signification of the phallus, the short analysis of *Das Medusenhaupt* ("To decapitate = to castrate. The terror of Medusa is thus a terror of castration that is linked to the sight of something." Freud goes on to explain that what turns to stone does so for and in front of the Medusa's severed head, for and in front of the mother insofar as she reveals her genitals. "The hair upon Medusa's head is frequently

it, etc. ("Imagine that mirrors (shadows, reflections, phantasms, etc.) would no longer be *comprehended* within the structure of the ontology and myth of the cave—which also situates the screen and the mirror—but would rather envelop it totally, producing here and there a particular, extremely determinate effect. The entire hierarchy described by the *Republic*, in its cave and in its line, would once again find itself at stake and in question in the theater of *Numbers*. Without occupying it entirely, the Platonic moment inhabits the fourth surface.")

Dissemination question: what "is going on," according to what time, what space, what structure, what becomes of the "event" when "I write," "I place beside me an open inkstand and a few sheets of unspitballed paper," or "I am going to write," "I have written": about writing, against writing, in writing; or else, I preface, I write for or against the preface, this is a preface, this is not a preface? What's the story with this autography of pure loss and without a signature? And how is it that this performance displaces such force in going without truth?

The structure of the feint describes here, as always, an extra turn.

The sixth Song would thus seem to push the preceding Songs back into the past of a discursive preface (ars poetica, methodology, didactic presentation). The first five Songs would not be part of the generative text, the text that is at once practical and "analytical." But in thus reversing itself, this schema also, according to the same logic, displaces the opposition between pre-text and text. It complicates the boundary line that ought to run

---

represented in works of art in the form of snakes, and these once again are derived from the castration complex. It is a remarkable fact that, however frightening they may be in themselves, they nevertheless serve actually as a mitigation of the horror, for they replace the penis, the absence of which is the cause of the horror (*dessen Fehlen die Ursache des Grauens ist*). This is a confirmation of the technical rule according to which a multiplication of penis symbols signifies castration (*Vervielfältigung der Penissymbole bedeutet Kastration*). The sight of Medusa's head makes the spectator stiff with terror, turns him to stone. Observe that we have here once again the same origin from the castration complex and the same transformation of affect! For becoming stiff (*das Starrwerden*) means an erection. Thus in the original situation it offers consolation to the spectator: he is still in possession of a penis, and the stiffening reassures him of the fact. . . . If Medusa's head takes the place of a representation (*Darstellung*) of the female genitals, or rather if it isolates their horrifying effects from their pleasure-giving ones, it may be recalled that displaying the genitals is familiar in other connections as an apotropaic act. What arouses horror in oneself will produce the same effect upon the enemy against whom one is seeking to defend oneself. We read in Rabelais of how the Devil took to flight when the woman showed him her vulva. The erect male organ also has an apotropaic effect, but thanks to another mechanism. To display the penis (or any of its surrogates) is to say: 'I am not afraid of you. I defy you. I have a penis.' Here, then, is another way of intimidating the Evil Spirit" [*Standard Edition*, XVIII, 273–74]), and the rest. In lapidary fashion, one could lay out the infinitely opened and turned-back series of these equivalents: stone—tomb—erect—stiff—dead, etc. Dissemination would always arrive on the scene to threaten signification.

between the text and what seems to lie beyond its fringes, what is classed as the *real*. Along with an ordered extension of the concept of text, dissemination inscribes a different law governing effects of sense or reference (the interiority of the "thing," reality, objectivity, essentiality, existence, sensible or intelligible presence in general, etc.), a different relation between writing, in the metaphysical sense of the word, and its "outside" (historical, political, economical, sexual, etc.). The sixth Song is not presented merely as the long-awaited text of the *real* analytical discovery, the record of the real investigation. It also gives itself as the *exit* from a certain text *into the real*. At the end of the fifth Song, this breaking through, this risky protrusion of the head from its hole, from its corner, is prescribed by the spider sequence: "We are no longer in the narrative . . . Alas! We have now come to reality . . ." It is an instance both of death and of awakening. The very place marked off for the preface. The exit from the narrative is nonetheless inscribed in a corner of the narrative and forecasts the coming novel. The text of the irruption out of writing at the end of the sixth Song ("Go and see for yourself . . .") repeats, one through the guise of the other, the instant of death and the instant of awakening. Let us return to the spider without a web (to spin):

> Every night, at the hour when sleep has reached its highest degree of intensity, an old spider of the large species slowly protrudes its head from a hole in the ground at one of the intersections of the angles of the room. . . . He is hoping that the present night (hope with him!) will see the last performance of the immense suction; for his only wish is that his torturer should put an end to his existence; death, that is all he asks. Look at this old spider of the large species, slowly protruding its head from a hole in the ground at one of the intersections of the room. We are no longer in the narrative. It listens carefully to hear if any rustling sound is still moving its mandibles in the atmosphere. Alas! We have now come to reality as far as the tarantula is concerned and, though one could perhaps put exclamation marks at the end of each sentence; that is perhaps not a reason for dispensing with them altogether! (Pp. 202–3, 204)

A spider emerging "from the depths of its nest," a headstrong dot that transcribes no dictated exclamation but rather intransitively performs its own writing (later on, you will read in this the inverted figure of castration), the text comes out of its hole and lays its menace bare: it passes, in one fell swoop, to the "real" text and to the "extratextual" reality. Within the encompassing tissue of the Songs (you are reading a piece of writing here and all this is producing (itself in) a text), two exteriorities heterogeneous to each other seem to succeed each other, to replace each other, but finally they end up covering the entire field with marks.

The staging of a title, a first sentence, an epigraph, a pretext, a preface, a single germ, will never make a beginning. It *was* indefinitely dispersed.

It is thus that the triangle of texts is *fractured*.

Out-text, the whole of the first five Songs, followed by real text. Out-text, the sixth Song, even the Poetry; exit *into* the real. There is nothing but text, there is nothing but extratext, in sum an "unceasing preface"[40] that undoes the philosophical representation of the text, the received opposition between the text and what exceeds it. The space of dissemination does not merely place the *plural* in effervescence; it shakes up an endless contradiction, marked out by the undecidable syntax of *more*. In practical terms, we might perhaps now reread the "nothing was real *any more/ any more* real." ("When I awake, the razor, making its way through the neck, will prove that nothing was any more, in fact, real.")

This is the protocol indispensable to any reelaboration of the problem of "ideology," of the specific inscription of each text (this time in the narrowest regional sense of the term) within the fields commonly referred to as fields of "real" causality (history, economics, politics, sexuality, etc.). The *theoretical* elaboration, at least, if one could remain within such a circumscription, ought to suspend or at any rate to complicate, with great caution, the naive opening that once linked the text to *its* thing, referent, or reality, or even to some last conceptual or semantic instance. Every time that, in order to hook writing precipitously up with some reassuring outside or in order to make a hasty break with idealism, one might be brought to ignore certain recent theoretical attainments (the critique of the transcendental signified in all its forms; deconstruction, the displacement and subordination of effects of sense or reference along with all that would preside over any logocentric, expressivist, mimetological concept and practice of writing; the reconstruction of the textual field out of the workings of intertextuality or of infinite referral from trace to trace; the reinscription, within the differential field, of the spacing of theme effects, substance effects, content

40. "Indeed, the scriptural function is now going to appear to be capable of controlling both the body and the outside world in which that body appears; immediately announcing the retroactive, encompassing effect of the *Poetry*, it will apparently be written immediately into the three dimensions of a volume linked to the future (and it will already become what it is: the "preface to a future book," a book projected forward in time as an unceasing preface, a non-book preceding any book whatever, indefinitely put off, a definitive departure from the book, that prison of the speaking era)." Sollers, "La science de Lautréamont," in *Logiques*, pp. 279–80.

effects, or effects of sensible or intelligible presence, wherever they might intervene, etc.), one would all the more surely regress into idealism, with all of what, as we have just pointed out, cannot but link up with it, singularly in the figures of empiricism and formalism.

In the reediting of the Book.

As a double derived from some primal unit, as image, imitation, expression, representation, the book has its origin, which is also its model, outside itself: the "thing itself" or that determination of what exists that is called "reality," as it is or as it is perceived, lived, or thought by the one who describes or inscribes. Reality present, then, or reality represented, this alternative is itself derived from a prior model. The Model of the Book, the Model Book, doesn't it amount to the absolute adequation of presence and representation, to the *truth* (*homoiosis* or *adaequatio*) of the thing and of the thought about the thing, in the sense in which truth first emerges in divine creation before being reflected by finite knowledge? Nature, God's Book, appeared to the medieval mind to be a written form consonant with divine thought and speech, true to God's attentive understanding[*entende-ment*, lit. "hearing"] as Logos, the truth that speaks and that hears itself speak, the locus of archetypes, the relay point of the *topos noetos* or the *topos ouranios*. A writing that was representative and true, adequate to its model and to itself, Nature was also an ordered totality, the volume of a book weighty with meaning, giving itself to the reader, which must also mean the hearer, as if it were a spoken word, passing from ear to ear and from mind to mind [*d'entendement à entendement*]. "The eye listens" (Claudel) when the book has as its vocation the proffering of divine logos.

This reminder—this quotation—ought simply to reintroduce us into the question of the preface, of the double inscription or double-jointedness of such a text: its semantic envelopment within the Book—the representative of a Logos or Logic (ontotheology and absolute knowledge)—and the left-overness [*restance*] of its textual exteriority, which should not be confused with its physical thickness.

This reminder ought also to introduce us into the question of the preface as *seed*. According to the χ (The chiasmus) (which can be considered a quick thematic diagram of dissemination), the preface, as *semen*, is just as likely to be left out, to well up and get lost as a seminal differance, as it is to be reappropriated into the sublimity of the father. As the preface to a book, it is the word of a father assisting and admiring[41] his work, answering for his

41. For this reason it is considered seemly in classical rhetoric to advise against prefaces, with their conceit, their complacency; the narcissistic admiration of the father for the son. "*Prefaces* are another stumbling-block; the *self* is detestable," said Pascal. . . . "Your book will have to speak for itself, if it comes to be read by the masses" (Voltaire). Writing on the

son, losing his breath in sustaining, retaining, idealizing, reinternalizing, and mastering his seed. The scene would be acted out, if such were possible, between father and son alone: autoinsemination, homoinsemination, reinsemination. Narcissism is the law, is on a par with the law. It is the paternal figure of the Platonic *boētheia* that will still lord it over the stage: the prolegomenon will *present itself* as a *moral* instance and will be written only so as to resuscitate a spoken word.[42] One that proclaims and manifests itself presently. Prefaces have often served as manifestos for various schools.

The effacement or sublimation of seminal differance is the movement through which the left-overness [*restance*] of the outwork gets internalized and domesticated into the ontotheology of the great Book. The point of general resistance, marked here, for example, by the name "Mallarmé," can always be retrospectively carried off in the guise of homonymy. Once again we confront the business of the old name, of onymism in general, of the false identity of the mark, all of which dissemination must disturb at the root.

What Mallarmé was still projecting under the old name of Book would have been, "had it existed" [*existât-il*], entirely different. Out (of the) book

---

Didactic Genre, Condillac, in *De l'art d'écrire*, describes the "abuse of prefaces": "Prefaces are another source of abuses. There all the ostentatiousness of an author reveals itself, as he ridiculously exaggerates the worth of his subject. It is quite reasonable to describe the point at which those who have written before us have left a science on which we hope to shed new light. But talking on of one's work, of one's sleepless nights, of the obstacles that had to be overcome; sharing with the public all the ideas one has had; not contenting oneself with a first preface but adding another to every book, to every chapter; giving the story of all the attempts made without success; indicating numerous means of resolving each question, when there is only one which can and will be used: this is the art of fattening a book to bore one's reader. If everything useless were removed from these works, almost nothing would remain. It is as though these authors wanted to write only the prefaces to the subjects they proposed to examine: they finish having forgotten to resolve the questions they have raised" [*Oeuvres complètes* (Paris: Lecointe et Durey, 1821), pp. 446–47]. Condillac then proposes "pruning back prefaces and all the "words which are dispensable." Pruning, trimming: if dissemination also *cuts* into the text, it is rather to produce forms which would often *resemble* those which Condillac—and all of the rhetoric and philosophy that he represents here— wishes to cut back so severely. And what of grafting-by-quotation in this French-style garden: Is it prohibited? Is it to flourish? Should the *topos* be pruned? Is classicism merely a branch of the baroque without knowing it? Condillac repeats La Bruyère who himself repeats someone else . . . "If one removes from many moral works the foreword, the dedication, the preface, the table of contents, the acknowledgements, there are scarcely enough pages left to be called a book" (La Bruyère, *Les Caractères*, "Des ouvrages de l'esprit"). Etc.

42. But it would be even better—and these two wishes are not contradictory—for the spoken word to resuscitate itself, for discourse, as is stated in the *Phaedrus*, to answer itself, to answer for itself. It would thus become its own father, and the preface would become useless: "It is quite useless for an author to defend in his preface a book which cannot answer for itself to the public" (Locke). One notices the extent to which the essential didacticism of the classical preface maintains a moralistic discourse. "My sole fault," Baudelaire was to say, "has been to count on universal intelligence, and not to write a preface setting out my literary principles and dealing with the very important question of Morality."

[*Hors-livre*]. Nevertheless Claudel came afterward. The play of *dissemination*, as one might have suspected, often has occasion to call upon him. And here we find grouped together everything of which dissemination will, word for word, have changed the sign:

> We have come out of that fatal torpor, that downtrodden attitude of spirit faced with matter, that fascination with quantity. We know that we are made to dominate the world and not the world to dominate us. The sun has come back to the sky, we have stripped off the curtains and thrown the padded furniture, the white elephants, and the "pallid bust of Pallas" out the window. We know that the world is indeed a text and that it speaks to us, humbly and joyously, of its own absence, but also of the eternal presence of someone else, namely, its Creator. Not only the writing, but the writer, not only the dead letter, but the living spirit, and not a magic cryptoglyph, but the Word in which all things are proffered. God! We know from the *Writ*—that is, Writing par excellence, the Holy Writ—that *we are a certain creaturely beginning*, that *we see all things darkly*, *as in a glass* (Igitur's mirror, to be exact), that *the world is a book written inside and out* (that book of which Igitur sought to make a facsimile) and that *visible things are made to lead us to the knowledge of invisible things*. With what attention shouldn't we therefore not only look at them but also study and question them! And how thankful we should be to philosophy and science for having placed at our disposal so many admirable tools to that end! Nothing can now stand in the way of our pursuing, with infinitely multiplying means, one hand on the Book of Books, the other on the Universe, that great symbolic inquiry that was for twelve centuries the occupation of the Fathers of Faith and Art.[43]

Thenceforth all finite books would become opuscules modeled after the great divine opus, so many arrested speculations, so many tiny mirrors catching a single grand image. The ideal form of this would be a book of total science, a book of absolute knowledge that digested, recited, and substantially ordered all books, going through the whole cycle of knowledge. But since truth is already constituted in the reflection and relation of God to himself, since truth already knows itself to *speak*, the *cyclical* book will also be a *pedagogical* book. And its preface, propaedeutic. The authority of the encyclopedic model, a unit analogous for man and for God, can act in very devious ways according to certain complex mediations. It stands, moreover, as a *model* and as a normative concept: which does not, however,

43. *Positions et Propositions* (Paris: Gallimard, 1928), pp. 205–7 (emphasis in original).

exclude the fact that, within the practice of writing, and singularly of so-called "literary" writing, certain forces remain foreign or contrary to it or subject it to violent reexamination. And this since time immemorial, although the modalities of such subversiveness are always different and cannot be reduced to the same. As for the encyclopedic enterprise, as it is explicitly formulated in the Middle Ages after a long history of preparatory work (Vitruvius, Seneca, Posidonius, etc.), it is thoroughly theological in essence and in origin, despite the fact that a group of so-called atheists participated in one great Encyclopedia that was particularly ignorant and unconscious of its roots.

Hegel declares the completion of philosophy. He writes a *Science of Logic* (the Greater Logic), the production of absolute knowledge, preceded by two Prefaces and an Introduction in which he explains the uselessness, even the danger, of forewords. But he also writes an *Encyclopedia of Philosophical Sciences* that coordinates all regions of knowledge. Of which, part, but the *first* part, is made up of a *Science of Logic* (the Lesser Logic), substantially identical to the Greater Logic which it thus inscribes within the ordered writing of the encyclopedic volume. The latter is no doubt the last of its kind in history to deserve the name; the philosophical encyclopedia, which conveys the organic and rational unity of knowledge, is not, in contrast to what is sold today under that title, an empirical aggregate of contents. Enriched with three prefaces (of which the second was of particular importance), Hegel's *Encylopedia* opens with an Introduction that explains—once again—that philosophy "misses an advantage enjoyed by the other sciences. It cannot like them rest the existence of its objects on the natural admissions of consciousness, nor can it assume that its method of cognition, either for starting or for continuing, is one already accepted." It must therefore produce, out of its own interiority, both its object and its method. "Such an explanation, however, is itself a lesson in philosophy, and properly falls within the scope of the science itself. A preliminary attempt to make matters plain would only be unphilosophical, and consist of a tissue of assumptions, assertions, and inferential pros and cons, i.e. of dogmatism without cogency, as against which there would be an equal right of counter-dogmatism. . . . But to seek to know before we know is as absurd as the wise resolution of Scholasticus, not to venture into the water until he had learned to swim."[44]

44. *Hegel's Logic: Being Part One of the Encyclopedia of the Philosophical Sciences*, trans. William Wallace (Oxford: Oxford University Press, 1975), pp. 3, 14. The same theme returns at the beginning of the Logic: the "preliminary notions" (Vorbegriffe) are as good as *definitions* "derived from a survey of the whole system, to which accordingly they are subsequent" (ibid. p. 25).

If the preliminary explanation is absolutely prior to the encyclopedic circle, then it stays outside it and explains nothing. It is not philosophical and in the extreme remains impossible. If on the other hand it is engaged within the philosophic circle, it is no longer a *pre*-liminary operation: it belongs to the actual movement of the method and to the structure of objectivity. Engenderer and consumer *of itself*, the concept relieves [*relève*] its preface and plunges into itself. The Encyclopedia gives *itself* birth. The conception of the concept is an autoinsemination.[45]

This return of the theological seed to itself internalizes its own negativity and its own difference to itself. The Life of the Concept is a necessity that, in *including* the dispersion of the seed, in making that dispersion work to the profit of the Idea, *excludes* by the same token all loss and all haphazard productivity. The exclusion is an inclusion.[46] In contrast to the seminal differance thus repressed, the truth that speaks (to) itself within the logocentric circle is the discourse of what *goes back to the father*.[47]

45. *Life*, the essential philosophical determination both of the concept and of the spirit, is necessarily described according to the general traits of vegetal or biological life, which is the particular object of the philosophy of nature. This analogy or this metaphoricity, which poses formidable problems, is only possible following the organicity of encyclopedic logic. From this perspective one can read all the analyses of the "return-into-self" of the "seed" (§ 347 and § 348), of the "internal chance" ("The animal is able to *move itself* to a certain extent, because like light, which is ideality severed from gravity, its subjectivity is a liberated time, which as it is removed from the real nature of externality, spontaneously *determines its place* [according to an internal chance]. The animal's *vocal faculty* is bound up with this, for as the *actual ideality of soul*, animal *subjectivity* dominates the abstract ideality of time and space, and displays its autonomous movement as a free vibration *within itself*" (§ 351).), of "lack" and "generation" (§ 369), and in general of the *syllogism* of life, the life of the spirit as truth and death (termination) of the natural life that bears within itself, in its finitude, "the original disease . . . and the inborn germ of death." "Subjectivity is the Concept, and implicitly therefore, it constitutes the absolute *being-in-self* of *actuality*, as well as concrete universality. Through this sublation of the *immediacy* of its reality, subjectivity has coincided with itself. The last *self-externality* of nature is sublated, so that the Concept, which in nature has implicit being, has become for itself" (§ 375 and § 376) [*Hegel's Philosophy of Nature*, trans. M. J. Petry (London: George Allen & Unwin, 1970), III, 83, 91, 102, 172, 209–11.]
Is the preface the *nature* of logos? The natural life of the concept?
46. The primal division of the self-judging of the Idea (*das Sich-Urteilen der Idee*) occurs (third syllogism) as a Being-with-the-self and for-the-self of the Idea as absolute Mind. The latter "eternally sets itself to work, engenders and enjoys itself . . ." (*sich . . . betätigt, erzeugt und geniesst*), like the God of Aristotle in the final epigraph of the *Encyclopedia* (Aristotle, *Metaphysics*, XI, 7) (*Hegel's Philosophy of Mind*, trans. William Wallace, Oxford: Oxford University Press, 1894, p. 197).
47. (The) Logic (is part of what) goes back to the (dead — more than ever) father, as well as to law and to logos: sublation itself. Logic is *true* and constitutes the truth of logocentrism, of logocentric culture and of the logocentric concept of culture. I have demonstrated (cf. "Le Puits et la pyramide, Introduction à la sémiologie de Hegel" [1968], in *Hegel et la Pensée moderne*, Paris; P.U.F., 1971) how sublation organizes, effecting itself therein, the relations

This is why Hegel never investigates in terms of writing the living circulation of discourse. He never interrogates the *exteriority*, or the repetitive autonomy, of that textual *remainder*[48] constituted for example by a preface, even while it is semantically sublated within the encyclopedic logic. He problematizes the preface along the lines of the meaning of the word: the will-to-say, pre-diction, fore-word (*pre-fari*) of the prologue or prolegomenon, which is *conceived* (like a living thing) and proclaimed from out of the last act of its epilogue. Within discourse, logos remains abreast of itself. What ought, however, to prohibit considering writing (here the pro-gramme, the pre-scription, the pre-text) as the simple empirical husk of the concept is the fact that this husk (for it is not a question of raising it from that condition but of questioning it otherwise) is *coextensive* with the whole life of the discourse. But above all, this coextension does not amount to some sort of equivalence or pair of doubles. Or at least the structure of such doubling can no longer be taken for granted. A certain exteriority

---

between signifier and signified in Hegelian dialectics. The signifier is sublated (*aufgehoben*) in the process of meaning (the signified). To stand this *Aufhebung* of the opposition signifier/signified on its head would be to leave or put back in place the truth of the phallocentric dialectic: the very rightness of reason which it is certainly not a question here of proving wrong. Nor is there any question of disproving Freud when he profoundly states that there is only one libido (why not?) and that it is *therefore* masculine (from then on, why? a question of shared common sense). On this subject, see the *Ecrits* of Jacques Lacan (passim and especially pp. 554, 692–95, 732, [Paris: Seuil, 1966]), [trans. Alan Sheriden, New York: Norton, 1977, pp. 197, 287–91,–].

As for "feminine sexuality" (and not just the problem posed in those terms, with its evident link to the problem of phallocentrism, and its less evident relation to the problematics of that metalanguage which becomes possible again and reoccupies the position that had, through feint, appeared to have been abandoned, from the moment one signifier finds itself *privileged* there), dissemination reads, if one looks closely, as a sort of womb (and, what is more, a theoretical one, just to see). Just beyond this anatomy of the preface, it will perhaps be perceived that the *same denial* is at work when the *Greater Logic* places prefaces in parentheses as when, in psychoanalytic phallocentrism, the same is done with anatomy. A very specific interest continues to instill or to find in these things what it claims to be able to do without.

48. How is one to account for the fact that Hegel's prefaces — the philosophical "more" and "less" —are repeatable, and *remain readable* in themselves up to a certain point, even in the absence of that logic from which they are supposed to derive their status? What would happen if one were to publish all of Hegel's prefaces together in a separate volume, like James's in *The Art of the Novel*? what if Hegel had written nothing but prefaces? or what if, instead of placing them outside the work as an hors d'œuvre, he had inserted them here or there, for instance in the *middle* (as in *Tristram Shandy*) of the *Greater Logic*, between *objective logic* and *subjective logic*, or anywhere else? The fact that all readability would not be thereby destroyed or all meaning-effects cancelled out "means," among other things, that it is part of the *remainder*-structure of the letter, which has no path of its own, to always be capable of missing its destination.

repeats itself in it, insists, plays beyond the bounds of any speculative syllogism, gets set on all its marks.

It is with an *almost* identical aim and result that Novalis, in his *Encyclopedia*[49] (is it meaningless that his enterprise should have remained scattered in its first fruits? shredded around its pointed seeds?), explicitly poses the question of the *form* of the total book as a *written* book: an exhaustive taxonomical writing, a hologram that would order and classify knowledge, *giving place* to literary writing. "Everything must be encyclopedized." "Encyclopedistics" will be "a kind of scientific grammar" [IV-817] written according to a plurality of modes, "fragments, letters, poems, rigorous scientific studies" [IV-948], each piece of the book to be dedicated to friends. The literal, the literary, and even the epistolary will find their lodging and their order of production in the biological body of this romantic encyclopedia ("Goethean manner of treating the sciences—my project" [IV-968]). For the order of the book, in the eyes of the author of "Pollen," must be at once organicist and tabular, germinal and analytical.

The question of the genetic pro-gram or the textual preface can no longer be eluded. Which does not mean that Novalis does not *in the final analysis* reinstall the seed in the *logos spermatikos*[50] of philosophy. Postface and preface alike will return to the status of Biblical moments. Comprehended *a priori* within the volumen. Thus:

---

49. Fragments published [in French] under the title *L'Encyclopédie* (trans. Maurice de Gandillac, Paris: Minuit, 1966). [The figures in brackets are Gandillac's references: the roman numeral refers to the Wasmuth edition of Novalis's *Fragmente* (vol. 3 of *Werke, Briefe, Dokumente*, Heidelberg, 1957); the arabic numeral refers to the system used in the Kluckholm edition (Leipzig: Bibliographisches Institut A.G., 1929).]

50. "Poetry is part of the philosophical technique. The philosophical predicate — expresses *everywhere ipso-finalization* — and indirect ipso-finalization" [IV - 892]. "Philosophy is rightly nostalgia — the aspiration to be *at home everywhere* [IV-566]. It is for this reason that the *philosophy of the seed*, conceived as an enrichment in the return-to-self, is always substantialist, and also derives from a romantic metaphorism and a myth of semantic depth, from that ideology which Bachelard analyzes (when he isn't giving in to it himself) in *La Formation de l'esprit scientifique* [*The Formation of the Scientific Spirit*], in reference to sperm and to gold. (A seminal *différance*: not only the seed, but the egg.) The treatment which they undergo in dissemination should break away from all mythological panspermism and all alchemical metallurgy. It is rather a question of broaching an articulation with the movement of genetic science and with the genetic movement of science, wherever science should take into account, more than metaphorically, the problems of writing and difference, of seminal differance (cf. *Of Grammatology*, p. 9). Elliptically, we cite this sentence by Freud, which should always be kept in mind: "All our provisional ideas in psychology will presumably some day be based on an organic substructure" ("On Narcissism: An Introduction," in *Standard Edition*, trans. James Strachey, [London: Hogarth Press, 1957], XIV, 78).

Table of contents—index of names—the outline is also an index. Does one begin with the *index*? [IV-790]

Relations between the title, the outline, and the table of contents. Necessity of a *postface*. [II-336]

ENCYCLOPEDISTICS. How will the philosophical copperplate tables be constituted? Therein already belong the table of categories— Fichte's theoretical system—Dyanology—the tables of the logic of *Maas*—Bacon's table of the sciences, etc. Tabulations, etc.

$$a = a$$
$$+ a \parallel - a$$
$$+ a \,\#\, - a$$

Geographical—geognostic—*minerological*—chronological—mathematical—technological—*chemical*—economic [*Cameralistische*]— political—galvanic—physical—artistic—physiological—musical— heraldic—numismatic—statistical—philological—grammatical— psychological—literary—*philosophical* copperplate tables. The *Outlines* that precede some books are already a kind of table— (Alphabets)—Indexes are *specialized* dictionaries and encyclopedias. (Geometry, for example, set out in huge tableau—arithmetic—algebra, etc.) Any possible *literary*, artistic, and *world* history must be capable of being expressed in a series of tables. (The less a book is fit to be put into a table, the less it is good.) [IV-244]

PHILOLOGY. What should a *preface*, a *title*, an *epigraph*, an *outline*— an *introduction*—a *note*,—a text, an *appendix* (tables, etc), an *index*, be—and how should they be ordered and classified? The outline is the combining formula of the index—the text is the execution. The preface is a poetic overture—or a notice to the reader, as well as to the binder. The epigraph is the *musical theme*. The usage of the book—the philosophy of its reading is given in the preface. The title is the *name*. A doubled and clarified *title*. (History of the title.) Definition and classification of the name. [IV-751]

ENCYCLOPEDISTICS. My book must contain the critical metaphysics of the review, of literary writing, of experimentation and observation, of reading, speaking, etc. [IV-758]

History itself is *prescribed*. Its development, its violence, even its discontinuities should not *disconcert* this musical volume, this encyclopedia which is also a "general bass or theory of composition." And in the general organization of this writing, the "literary," too, is assigned a province and a genesis of its own. It is a Bible, then, as tabular space but also as seminal reason *explaining itself*, ambitious to render an exhaustive account, one with nothing left out, of its own genetic production, its order and usage. (Dissemination *also* explains itself ("**the apparatus explains itself** ") but quite differently. As the heterogeneity and absolute exteriority of the seed, seminal differance does constitute itself into a program, but it is a program that cannot be formalized. For reasons that *can* be formalized. The infinity of its code, its rift, then, does not take a form saturated with self-presence in the encyclopedic circle. It is attached, so to speak, to the incessant falling of a *supplement to the code*. Formalism no longer fails before an empirical richness but before a queue or *tail*. Whose *self*-bite is neither specular nor symbolic.)

But what does the non-completion of Novalis's Encyclopedia signify about completeness as such? Is it an empirical accident?

> My book should become a scientific Bible—a model both real and ideal—and the germ of all books. [IV-758]
>
> PHILOLOGY. The index and the outline should be worked out first—then the text—then the introduction and preface—then the title.— All the sciences make up *one book*. Some belong to the index, some to the Outline, etc.
>
> . . . The description of the Bible is properly my undertaking —or better, the *theory of the Bible*—the art of the Bible and the theory of nature. (The raising of a book to the level of the Bible.)
>
> The fully executed Bible is a *complete, perfectly organized library*— the plan [*Schema*] of the Bible is at the same time the plan of the library. The authentic *plan*—the authentic *formula*—indicates at the same time its own genesis—its own usage, etc. (complete *file* concerning the use of each item—along with its instructions and description) [IV-771]
>
> Perfectly finished books make courses unnecessary. The book is Nature inscribed on a staff (like music) and *completed*. [IV-784]

The last word is *underlined* by Novalis. The book is nature inscribed on a staff: there is a total overlap between nature and the volume, a musical identity of the whole of being with the encyclopedic text. This proposition seems at first to draw on the ancient resources of the traditional metaphor ("reading the great book of the world," etc.). But this identity is not *given*: nature without the book is somehow incomplete. If the whole of what *is* were really one with the whole of the inscription, it would be hard to see how they would make two: nature *and* the Bible, being *and* the book. It would be particularly hard to understand the possibility of adding them together or the place where they might be conjoined. Wouldn't we have to choose here between the *is* [*est*] as copula (the book *is* nature) and the *and* [*et*] as conjunction? And in order that the predicative coupling be possible, a mute conjunction must enable us to think conjointly, together (*cum*) as set, the book *and* nature. That the sense of this coupling by the *is* should be one of fulfillment, a fulfilling productivity that comes not to repeat but to complete nature through writing, would mean that nature is somewhere incomplete, that it lacks something needed for it to be what it is, that it has to be supplemented. Which can be done by nature alone, since nature is all. The book comes to add itself to nature (an additive supplement translated by the conjunction *and*), but through this addition it must also complete nature, fulfill its essence (a complementary, vicarious supplement [= that which supplants] expressed by the copula *is*). The closure of the library articulates itself and turns on this hinge: the logic, or rather the graphics, of the supplement.

With the appearance of a book that, even if it passes for nature's double, is added to it in that duplication of the simulacrum, there is broached or breached a scientific or literary text that goes beyond the always-already-constitutedness of meaning and of truth within the theo-logico-encyclopedic space, of self-fertilization with no limen. Dissemination, soliciting *physis* as *mimesis*, places philosophy *on stage* and its book *at stake* [*en jeu*].[51]

51. And through another literal permutation of the signifier (the likes of which one must here begin to practice), at *the* stake [*en feu*]. The process of consuming or consummating, as through the hymen, never begins nor ends. Which makes its identity flow out *ex-pensively* [*se dé-pense*]. "The library at Alexandria can be burnt down. There are forces above and beyond papyrus: we may temporarily be deprived of our ability to discover these forces, but their energy will not be suppressed" (Antonin Artaud, *The Theater and Its Double*, trans. Mary C. Richards [New York: Grove Press, 1958], p. 10).

Festivals and fireworks, expenditure, consumption and the simulacrum; one would be quite naive to attribute to these, with a passion already speaking of itself, the innocence, sterility, and impotence of a *form*. At the end of *Music and Letters*, which constantly brings literature back to the festival, is it the simulacrum that must rise up from the ground, or the ground itself that must be changed into a simulacrum? There would be no festival, no literature, no simulacrum, if we could in all security answer that question: "Go and mine these substructions, when obscurity offends their perspective, no — line up rows of lanterns there, in order to see: the point is that your thoughts demand of the ground a simulacrum" (p. 654).

And in order to propagate this;

"What is that for —

"For play [*à un jeu*].

"In view that a superior attraction as of a void, we have the right, drawing it from ourselves through boredom with respect to things if they were to be established solid and preponderant — should dementedly detach them to the point of filling itself with them and

The adventurous excess of a writing that is no longer directed by any knowledge does not abandon itself to improvisation. The accident or throw of dice that "opens" such a text does not contradict the rigorous necessity of its formal assemblage. The game here is the unity of chance and rule, of the program and its leftovers or extras. This *play* will still be called *literature* or *book* only when it exhibits its negative, atheistic face (the insufficient but indispensable phase of reversal), the final clause of that age-old project, which is henceforth located along the edge of the closed book: the achievement dreamed of, the conflagration achieved. Such are Mallarmé's programmatic notes in view of the Book. The reader should now know as of this manifesto that those notes will form the object of the present treatise.

To recognize the fullness and self-presence of nature: "We know, captives of an absolute formula that, of course, there is nothing but what is. . . . Nature takes place; it can't be added to." If one confined oneself to this captivity, a captivity of formulas and absolute knowledge, one would be incapable of thinking anything that could be added to the whole, whether to fulfill it or to think it *as such*, not even its image or mimetic double, which would still be part of the whole within the great book of nature.

But if the formula for this absolute knowledge can be thought about and put in question, the whole is treated then by a "part" bigger than itself; this is the strange subtraction of a *remark* whose theory is borne by dissemination and which constitutes the whole, necessarily, as a *totality-effect*.

On this condition, "literature" *comes out* of the book. Mallarmé's Book issues from *The* Book. It is possible to discern without any doubt the features of the most visible filiation marking it as a descendant of the Bible. A diagram, at least, of Novalis's. But by affirmed simulacrum and theatrical staging, by the break-in of the re-mark, it has *issued out* of the book: it escapes it beyond return, no longer sends it back its image, no longer constitutes an object finished and *posed*, reposing in the bookcase of a *bibliothèque*.

---

also endowing them with resplendences, across the vacant space, in festivals solitary and at will" (p. 647).

These notes, in a postscript to that lecture, and even on the genre of the lecture: ". . . In view that a superior attraction . . .

"Pyrotechnical no less than metaphysical, this point of view; but a sort of fireworks, at the height and on the example of thought, makes ideal enjoyment light up with bloom" (p. 655).

A supplementary reading would make it apparent: the point is to work to set up or dismantle a scaffold, a scaffolding. We will need one in order to substitute, for the time of a lapse, Mallarmé's lustre for Plato's sun.

The beyond of literature — or nothing.

Any decipherment must be redoubled thereby. For example, consider these medallions, which have already been in circulation a long time:

At bottom, you see, the world is made to end up as a beautiful book [p. 872]. . . . I have always dreamed and attempted something else, with an alchemist's patience, ready to sacrifice all vanity and satisfaction, just as, long ago, they used to burn their furniture and the beams from their rafters to feed the furnace of the Philosopher's Stone [*Grand Oeuvre*]. What? it's hard to say: a book, plainly, in many volumes, a book that would truly be a book, architectural and premeditated, and not a collection of chance inspirations, no matter how marvelous . . . I'll go even further and say: *the* Book, convinced that at bottom there is but one, attempted unaware by whoever has written, even the Geniuses. The Orphic explanation of the Earth, which is the poet's sole duty and the literary game par excellence; for the very rhythm of the book, which then would be impersonal and alive right down to its pagination, juxtaposes itself with the equations of this dream, or Ode . . . I am possessed by this and perhaps I will succeed; not in composing this work in its entirety (one would have to be I don't know who for that!) but in showing one fragment of it executed, in making its glorious authenticity at some point scintillate, and in pointing to the whole of the rest, for which one life is not enough. Proving by the portions accomplished that this book exists, that I have known what I haven't been able to do. (Letter to Verlaine, November 16, 1885. The same letter speaks of "anonymous . . . work," "in which the Text would be speaking of itself and without the voice of an author").

Or this, which will have preluded, in passing, according to the logic of the *corner* and the *veil*, the improbable place of dissemination:

I believe that Literature, recaptured at its source which is Art and Science, will provide us with a Theater, whose shows [*représentations*] will be the true modern cult; a Book, an explication of man, adequate to our loveliest dreams. I believe all this is written down in nature in a way that allows only those interested in seeing nothing to close their eyes. That work exists; everyone has attempted it without knowing it; there is not a single genius or clown that has not recovered a trace of it without knowing it. To demonstrate this, to lift a corner of the veil from off what such a poem can be, is, in an isolation, my pleasure and my torture. (Pp. 875–76)

My torture, my pleasure.

In the book, "seeing nothing," "without knowing it," "without knowing it" (twice). A unilateral interpretation would conclude that Nature (the
world in its entirety) and the Book (the voluminous binding of all writing)
were one. If this oneness were not a given, it would simply have to be
reconstituted. Its teleological program, internalized and reassimilated by
the circle of its unfolding, would leave for a prefatory aside only the place of
illusion and the time for provisions. As though—right here—the preface
could be calmly installed in the ample presence of its future perfect, in the
mode of that *attending discourse* whose definition you will have read later on.

And yet, beneath the form of its protocolic block, the preface is everywhere; it is bigger than the book. "Literature" also indicates—practically—the beyond of everything: the "operation" is the inscription that
transforms the whole into a part requiring completion or supplementation.
This type of supplementarity opens the "literary game" in which, along
with "literature," the figure of the author finally disappears. "Yes, Literature exists and, if you will, alone, excepting everything [*à l'exception de tout*].
An accomplishment, at least, for which no name could be better chosen" (p.
646).

This accomplishment or fulfillment operates a shift in Novalis's encyclopedic complement. No doubt literature, too, seems to aim toward the
filling of a lack (a hole) in a whole that should not itself in its essence be
missing (to) itself. But literature is also the *exception to everything*: at once the
exception in the whole, the want-of-wholeness in the whole, and the
exception to everything, that which exists by itself, alone, with nothing
else, in exception to all. A part that, within *and* without the whole, marks
the wholly other, the other incommensurate with the whole.

Which cuts literature short: it doesn't exist, since there is nothing
outside the whole. It does exist, since there is an "exception to everything,"
an outside of the whole, that is, a sort of subtraction without lack. And
since it exists, all alone, the all is nothing, the nothing is all ("nothing was
any more, in fact, real"). This extra nothing, this nothing the more, or
more the less, exposes the order of meaning (of that which *is*), even
polysemous meaning, to the disconcerting law of dissemination. It gives
place, out of the protocol of "literary" practice, to a new problematics of
meaning and being.[52]

52. "It is, yes, relative to this very word, *it is* . . ." (Letter to Viélé-Griffin, August 8,
1891). Once again, to muffle the blow that follows, the question of the preface is indeed the
question of being, set on stage on the scaffold or the "planks of the prefacers" (p. 364). A
question of the Nature-Book as Logos, the circle of the epilogue and the prolegomenon. The
Preface to "Vathek": ". . . causes one not to want to hear another word of the Preface, eager to

The beyond of the whole, another name for the text insofar as it resists all ontology (in whatever manner the latter might determine that which is [*l'étant*] in its being [*être*] and presence), is not a *primum movens*. Nevertheless, from out of the "inside" of the system where it marks the effects of an empty inscribed column, it imprints upon the whole a movement of fiction.

It beats out the rhythm of both pleasure and repetition, according to a multiple *cut* or *cup* [*coupe*].

What should be read through this syntagm: the mark "cuts"; or the cut/cup of "Mallarmé"?

Dissemination produces (itself in) that: a cut/cup of pleasure.

To be obtained in the break between the two parts of each of the three texts.

And, right here, all pretext aside:

> But there is, here I intervene with assurance, something, very little, *a mere nothing*, let's expressly say, *which exists*, for example *equal to the text* . . . (p. 638, Mallarmé's italics).
>
> We know, captives of an absolute formula that, of course, there is nothing but what is. However, incontinent(ly) to put aside, under a pretext, the lure, would point up our inconsequence, denying the pleasure that we wish to take: for that *beyond* is its agent, and its motor might I say were I not loath to operate, in public, the impious dismantling of (the) fiction and consequently of the literary mechanism, so as to display the principal part or nothing. But, I venerate how, by some flimflam, we project, toward a height both forbidden and thunderous! the conscious lacks in us (of) what, above, bursts out.
>
> What is that for—
>
> For play. (P. 647)

Without that nothing, which especially is equal to the text, a pleasure is denied or put aside in the cut/cup we wish to take. But in that nothing the cup is once again unfit to drink. Where does pleasure take *place* if it is practically literary in essence? If the foreplay, the "bonus of seduction," the

---

find out for oneself. . . . But stop, and I deny that right. . . . A halt precipitated by your wishes, which would perhaps be the naturalization of the book, would notably be lacking the prolegomena needed to add pomp, if you do not wait" (p. 555). The Preface to *Un coup de dés*: "I would prefer that this Note be not read at all or that, once read, it be forgotten; it teaches the skillful Reader little that lies beyond his penetration: but it might disturb the newcomer obliged to apply his eye to the first words of the Poem so that the following words, disposed as they are, carry him on to the last, the whole without newness except a spacing out of reading."

No more than *Igitur*, then, *Un coup de dés* will not have been a book.

"preliminary pleasure" (*Vorlust*), the formal moment of literature, reaches satisfaction only at the *end* of pleasure, then the climax of pleasurable fulfillment [*jouissance*] would never be anything but the instance of seduction, the supplementary bonus of nothing else. Pleasure would always be a formal, threshold phenomenon. Null and endless, a repression both lifted and maintained. The graphics of the hymen, coming back to question all couples, all conceptual oppositions, particularly those that Freud has just held out to us.

The "conscious lacks" (there is an indefinite oscillation here, fit for its system, though always leaning a bit to one side: the noun can become an adjective and the verb a noun) come(s) extra. Between the same, the lack of excess, the recoupment, the supplement and/or complement: "*Only*, we should know that *verse would not exist*: it, philosophically remunerates the (de)fault of the existing languages, a superior complement" (p. 364).

The necessity of the "well-meditated cut." "With free verse (toward it I won't repeat myself) in prose with well-meditated cuts" (p. 655).

To break off here, perhaps, for the "external seal" and the "final kick [*coup final*]", the kick-off [*coup d'envoi*].

Coupe réglée: "A regularly repeated sampling." *Coupe sombre ou d'ensemencement*: "An operation consisting in the removal of some of the trees from a grove so that the remaining trees can sow the ground with the seeds they produce and which disseminate themselves naturally."

The *coupe claire*, the *coupe définitive*, and the *coupe à tire et à aire* will also be practiced.[53]

To break off here, clear-headedly and for kicks. The preface then inscribes the necessity of the figures of its face, its cut-off, its form, and the power of metaphorical representation that one would be quite imprudent to attribute to it.[54]

---

53. TN. These expressions, along with many of those in the preceding paragraphs, are found in Littré's definitions of the word *coupe* (and the word *coup*). The *coupe claire* is "an operation that consists of removing some of the standing trees from a forest so that the young saplings will gradually adjust to the light." The *coupe définitive* is "an operation that consists of removing the last remaining old trees when the new planting is vigorous enough to withstand the rigors of the weather." The *coupe à tire et à aire* is "an operation that removes everything, without leaving anything behind."

54. For example: "Love before marriage [*l'hymen*] is like a much too short preface at the head of an endless book" (Petit Senn).

A putting in play and at stake without prelude, of what remains to be prepared for a *coup*.

Then if one went to see for oneself, one would run across by chance, enmeshed in some corner, the lowdown about *la coupe or/livre*.[55]

55. TN. The expression *la coupe or/livre* plays on the following expressions: (1) *la coupe d'or*: a gold cup, a sports trophy (cf. the expressions "final kick" and "kick-off," above, and Mallarmé's frequent use of the word *jeu*: "game" or "play"); (2)the homonym *Hors livre*: Outwork, etc., the "title" of this "preface"; and (3) the words *or* and *livre*, "gold" and "book," both of which will figure prominently in "The Double Session."

Plato's Pharmacy

First version published in *Tel Quel*, nos 32 and 33, 1968.

Kolaphos:[1] blow to the cheek, knock, slap . . . (*kolaptō*). *Kolaptō*: 1. to go into, penetrate, *esp., said of birds*, to peck . . . *hence*, to slash open with the beak . . . *by anal., said of a horse striking the ground with his hoof.* 2. *by extension*, to notch, engrave: *gramma eis aigeiron* [poplar] Anth. 9, 341, or *kata phloiou* [bark], Call. fr. 101, an inscription on a poplar or on the bark of a tree (R. *Klaph*; cf. R. *Gluph*, to hollow out, scratch).

A text is not a text unless it hides from the first comer, from the first glance, the law of its composition and the rules of its game. A text remains, moreover, forever imperceptible. Its law and its rules are not, however, harbored in the inaccessibility of a secret; it is simply that they can never be booked, in the *present*, into anything that could rigorously be called a perception.

And hence, perpetually and essentially, they run the risk of being definitively lost. Who will ever know of such disappearances?

The dissimulation of the woven texture can in any case take centuries to undo its web: a web that envelops a web, undoing the web for centuries; reconstituting it too as an organism, indefinitely regenerating its own tissue behind the cutting trace, the decision of each reading. There is always a surprise in store for the anatomy or physiology of any criticism that might think it had mastered the game, surveyed all the threads at once, deluding itself, too, in wanting to look at the text without touching it, without laying a hand on the "object," without risking—which is the only chance of entering into the game, by getting a few fingers caught—the addition of some new thread. Adding, here, is nothing other than giving to read. One must manage to think this out: that it is not a question of embroidering upon a text, unless one considers that to know how to embroider still means to have the ability to follow the given thread. That is, if you follow me, the hidden thread. If reading and writing are one, as is easily thought these days, if reading *is* writing, this oneness designates neither undifferentiated

---

1. TN. It should be noted that the Greek word κολαφος, which here begins the essay on Plato, is the last word printed in Littré's long definition of the French word *coup*, with which the *Hors-livre* has just playfully left off.

(con)fusion nor identity at perfect rest; the *is* that couples reading with writing must rip apart.

One must then, in a single gesture, but doubled, read and write. And that person would have understood nothing of the game who, at this [*du coup*], would feel himself authorized merely to add on; that is, to add any old thing. He would add nothing: the seam wouldn't hold. Reciprocally, he who through "methodological prudence," "norms of objectivity," or "safe-guards of knowledge" would refrain from committing anything of himself, would not read at all. The same foolishness, the same sterility, obtains in the "not serious" as in the "serious." The reading or writing supplement must be rigorously prescribed, but by the necessities of a *game*, by the logic of *play*, signs to which the system of all textual powers must be accorded and attuned.

I

To a considerable degree, we have already said all we *meant to say*. Our lexicon at any rate is not far from being exhausted. With the exception of this or that supplement, our questions will have nothing more to name but the texture of the text, reading and writing, mastery and play, the paradoxes of supplementarity, and the graphic relations between the living and the dead: within the textual, the textile, and the histological. We will keep within the limits of this *tissue*: between the metaphor of the *histos*[2] and the question of the *histos* of metaphor.

Since we have already said everything, the reader must bear with us if we continue on awhile. If we extend ourselves by force of play. If we then *write* a bit: on Plato, who already said in the *Phaedrus* that writing can only repeat (itself), that it "always signifies (*sēmainei*) the same" and that it is a "game" (*paidia*).

1. Pharmacia

Let us begin again. Therefore the dissimulation of the woven texture can in any case take centuries to undo its web. The example we shall propose of this will not, seeing that we are dealing with Plato, be the *Statesman*, which will have come to mind first, no doubt because of the paradigm of the weaver, and especially because of the paradigm of the paradigm, the example of the example—writing—which immediately precedes it.[3] We will come back to that only after a long detour.

2. "*Histos: anything set upright*, hence: I. *mast*. II. *beam* of a loom, which stood upright, instead of lying horizontal as in our looms (except in the weaving methods used by the Gobelins and in India) to which the threads of the warp are attached, hence: 1. *loom*; 2. *the warp fixed to the loom*, hence, *the woof*; 3. *woven cloth, piece of canvas*; 4. by anal. *spider web*; or *honeycomb of bees*. III. *rod, wand, stick*. IV. by anal. *shinbone, leg.*"

3. "*Stranger*: It is difficult, my dear Socrates, to demonstrate anything of real importance without the use of examples. Every one of us is like a man who sees things in a dream and

We will take off here from the *Phaedrus*.[4] We are speaking of the *Phaedrus*
that was obliged to wait almost twenty-five centuries before anyone gave up
the idea that it was a badly composed dialogue. It was at first believed that
Plato was too young to do the thing right, to construct a well-made object.
Diogenes Laertius records this "they say" (*logos* [sc. *esti*], *legetai*) according
to which the *Phaedrus* was Plato's first attempt and thus manifested a certain
juvenile quality (*meirakiōdēs ti*).[5] Schleiermacher thinks this legend can be
corroborated by means of a ludicrous argument: an aging writer would not
have condemned writing as Plato does in the *Phaedrus*. This argument is not
merely suspect in itself: it lends credit to the Laertian legend by basing itself

---

thinks that he knows them perfectly and then wakes up, as it were, to find he knows nothing.
Young Socrates: What do you mean by this? *Stranger*: I have made a real fool of myself by
choosing this moment to discuss our strange human plight where the winning of knowledge
is concerned. *Young Socrates*: What do you mean? *Stranger*: Example, my good friend, has
been found to require an example. *Young Socrates*: What is this? Say on and do not hesitate for
my sake. *Stranger*: I will—in fact, I must, since you are so ready to follow. When young
children have only just learned their letters . . . (*hotan arti grammatōn empeiroi gignōntai . . .*)"
(277*d–e*, trans. Skemp). And the description of the interweaving (*sumplokē*) in writing
necessitates recourse to the paradigm in grammatical experience, and then progressively
leads to the use of this procedure in its "kingly" form and to the example or paradigm of
weaving.

4. TN. The basic English-language of Plato's dialogues to which I shall refer is *The
Collected Dialogues of Plato* (ed. Edith Hamilton and Huntington Cairns), Bollingen Series
LXXI (Princeton, N.J.: Princeton University Press, 1961). The dialogues have been
translated by the following: Hugh Tredennick (*Apology, Crito, Phaedo*); Benjamin Jowett
(*Charmides, Laches, Menexenus, Lesser Hippias, Cratylus, Timaeus, Greater Hippias*); J. Wright
(*Lysis*); Lane Cooper (*Euthyphro, Ion*); W. D. Woodhead (*Gorgias*); W. K. C. Guthrie
(*Protagoras, Meno*); W. H. D. Rouse (*Euthydemus*); R. Hackforth (*Phaedrus, Philebus*);
Michael Joyce (*Symposium*); Paul Shorley (*Republic*); F. M. Cornford (*Theaetetus, Parmenides,
Sophist*); J. B. Skemp (*Statesman*); A. E. Taylor (*Critias, Laws, Epinomis*); L. A. Post (*Letters*).
I have also consulted and sometimes partially adopted the renditions given in the
following: *Phaedrus*, trans. W. C. Helmbold and W. G. Rabinowitz (Indianapolis: Bobbs-
Merrill Educational Publishing, The Library of Liberal Arts, 1956); *Gorgias*, trans. W.
Hamilton (Baltimore: Penguin Books, 1960); *Apology, Crito, Phaedo, Symposium, Republic*,
trans. Benjamin Jowett, in *Dialogues of Plato* (New York: Washington Square Press, 1951);
Republic, trans. F. M. Cornford (New York & London: Oxford University Press, 1941); *The
Laws*, trans. Trevor J. Saunders (New York: Penguin Books, 1970).
In addition, I have occasionally modified the wording or word order of the Platonic texts
in order to bring them into line with the parenthetical Greek inserts. Some minor
adjustments have also been made when it seemed necessary to achieve a closer parallel to the
French version with which Derrida is working.
The paranthetical numbers given after the quotations are the standard references to the
Stephanus edition of Plato's works, traditionally reproduced in all translations.
5. On the history of interpretations of the *Phaedrus* and the problem of its composition, a
rich, detailed account can be found in L. Robin's *La Théorie platonicienne de l'amour*, 2d ed.
(Paris: Presses Universitaires de France, 1964), and in the same author's Introduction to the
Budé edition of the *Phaedrus*.

on a second legend. Only a blind or grossly insensitive reading could indeed have spread the rumor that Plato was *simply* condemning the writer's activity. Nothing here is of a single piece and the *Phaedrus* also, in its own writing, plays at saving writing—which also means causing it to be lost—as the best, the noblest game. As for the stunning hand Plato has thus dealt himself, we will be able to follow its incidence and its payoff later on.

In 1905, the tradition of Diogenes Laertius was reversed, not in order to bring about a recognition of the excellent composition of the *Phaedrus* but in order to attribute its faults this time to the senile impotence of the author: "The *Phaedrus* is badly composed. This defect is all the more surprising since it is precisely there that Socrates defines the work of art as a living being. But the inability to accomplish what has been well conceived is precisely a proof of old age."[6]

We are no longer at that point. The hypothesis of a rigorous, sure, and subtle form is naturally more fertile. It discovers new chords, new concordances; it surprises them in minutely fashioned counterpoint, within a more secret organization of themes, of names, of words. It unties a whole *sumplokē* patiently interlacing the arguments. What is magisterial about the demonstration affirms itself and effaces itself at once, with suppleness, irony, and discretion.

This is, in particular, the case—and this will be our supplementary thread—with the whole last section (274*b* ff.), devoted, as everyone knows, to the origin, history, and value of writing. That entire hearing of the *trial of writing* should some day cease to appear as an extraneous mythological fantasy, an appendix the organism could easily, with no loss, have done without. In truth, it is rigorously called for from one end of the *Phaedrus* to the other.

Always with irony. But what can be said of irony here? What is its major sign? The dialogue contains the only "rigorously original Platonic myths: the fable of the cicadas in the *Phaedrus*, and the story of Theuth in the same dialogue."[7] Interestingly, Socrates' first words, in the opening lines of the conversation, had concerned "not bothering about" mythologemes (229*c*–230*a*). Not in order to reject them absolutely, but, on the one hand, not bothering them, leaving them alone, making room for them, in order to free them from the heavy serious naïveté of the scientific "rationalists," and

---

6. H. Raeder, *Platons philosophische Entwickelung* (Leipzig, 1905). A critique of this view, "Sur la composition du *Phèdre*," by E. Bourguet, appeared in the *Revue de Métaphysique et de Morale*, 1919, p. 335.

7. P. Frutiger, *Les Mythes de Platon* (Paris: Alcan, 1930).

on the other, not bothering *with* them, in order to free *oneself* for the relation
with oneself and the pursuit of self-knowledge.

To give myths a send-off: a salute, a vacation, a dismissal; this fine
resolution of the *khairein*, which means all that at once, will be twice
interrupted in order to welcome these "two Platonic myths," so "rigorously
original." Both of these myths arise, moreover, in the opening of a question
about the status of writing. This is undoubtedly less obvious—has anyone
ever picked up on it?—in the case of the cicada story. But it is no less
certain. Both myths follow upon the same question, and they are only
separated by a short space, just time enough for a detour. The first, of
course, does not answer the question; on the contrary, it leaves it hanging,
marks time for a rest, and makes us wait for the reprise that will lead us to
the second.

Let us read this more closely. At the precisely calculated center of the
dialogue—the reader can count the lines—the question of *logography* is
raised (257c). Phaedrus reminds Socrates that the citizens of greatest
influence and dignity, the men who are the most free, feel ashamed
(*aiskhunontai*) at "speechwriting" and at leaving *sungrammata* behind them.
They fear the judgment of posterity, which might consider them "sophists"
(257d). The logographer, in the strict sense, is a *ghost writer* who composes
speeches for use by litigants, speeches which he himself does not pronounce, which he does not attend, so to speak, in person, and which
produce their effects in his absence. In writing what he does not speak, what
he would never say and, in truth, would probably never even think, the
author of the written speech is already entrenched in the posture of the
sophist: the man of non-presence and of non-truth. Writing is thus already
on the scene. The incompatibility between the *written* and the *true* is clearly
announced at the moment Socrates starts to recount the way in which men
are carried out of themselves by pleasure, become absent from themselves,
forget themselves and die in the thrill of song (259c).

But the issue is delayed. Socrates still has a neutral attitude: writing is
not in itself a shameful, indecent, infamous (*aiskhron*) activity. One is
dishonored only if one writes in a dishonorable manner. But what does it
mean to write in a dishonorable manner? and, Phaedrus also wants to know,
what does it mean to write beautifully (*kalōs*)? This question sketches out
the central nervure, the great fold that divides the dialogue. Between this
question and the answer that takes up its terms in the last section ("But
there remains the question of propriety and impropriety in writing, that is
to say the conditions which make it proper or improper. Isn't that so?"

274*b*), the thread remains solid, if not easily visible, all through the fable of the cicadas and the themes of psychagogy, rhetoric, and dialectics.

Thus Socrates begins by sending myths off; and then, twice stopped before the question of writing, he invents two of them—not, as we shall see, entirely from scratch, but more freely and spontaneously than anywhere else in his work. Now, the *khairein*, in the *Phaedrus'* opening pages, *takes place in the name of truth*. We will reflect upon the fact that the myths come back from vacation at the time and in the name of writing.

The *khairein* takes place *in the name of truth*: that is, in the name of knowledge of truth and, more precisely, of truth in the knowledge of the self. This is what Socrates explains (230*a*). But this imperative of self-knowledge is not first felt or dictated by any transparent immediacy of self-presence. It is not perceived. Only interpreted, read, deciphered. A hermeneutics *assigns* intuition. An inscription, the *Delphikon gramma*, which is anything but an oracle, prescribes through its silent cipher; it signifies as one signifies an order—autoscopy and autognosis. The very activities that Socrates thinks can be contrasted to the hermeneutic adventure of myths, which he leaves to the sophists (229*d*).

And the *khairein* takes *place* in the name of truth. The *topoi* of the dialogue are never indifferent. The themes, the topics, the (common-)places, in a rhetorical sense, are strictly inscribed, comprehended each time within a significant site. They are dramatically staged, and in this theatrical geography, unity of place corresponds to an infallible calculation or necessity. For example, the fable of the cicadas would not have taken place, would not have been recounted, Socrates would not have been incited to tell it, if the heat, which weighs over the whole dialogue, had not driven the two friends out of the city, into the countryside, along the river Ilissus. Well before detailing the genealogy of the genus cicada, Socrates had exclaimed, "How welcome and sweet the fresh air is, resounding with the summer chirping of the cicada chorus" (230*c*). But this is not the only counterpoint-effect required by the space of the dialogue. The myth that serves as a pretext for the *khairein* and for the retreat into autoscopy can itself only arise, during the first steps of this excursion, at the sight of the Ilissus. Isn't this the spot, asks Phaedrus, where Boreas, according to tradition, carried off Orithyia? This riverbank, the diaphanous purity of these waters, must have welcomed the young virgins, or even drawn them like a spell, inciting them to play here. Socrates then mockingly proposes a learned explanation of the myth in the rationalistic, physicalist style of the *sophoi*: it was while she was playing with Pharmacia (*sun Pharmakeiai paizousan*) that the boreal wind (*pneuma*

Boreou) caught Orithyia up and blew her into the abyss, "down from the rocks hard by," "and having thus met her death was said to have been seized by Boreas . . . For my part, Phaedrus, I regard such theories as attractive no doubt, but as the invention of clever, industrious people who are not exactly to be envied" (229*d*).

This brief evocation of Pharmacia at the beginning of the *Phaedrus*—is it an accident? An hors d'œuvre? A fountain, "perhaps with curative powers," notes Robin, was dedicated to Pharmacia near the Ilissus. Let us in any case retain this: that a little spot, a little stitch or mesh (*macula*) woven into the back of the canvas, marks out for the entire dialogue the scene where that *virgin* was cast into the abyss, surprised by death *while playing with Pharmacia*. Pharmacia (*Pharmakeia*) is also a common noun signifying the administration of the *pharmakon*, the drug: the medicine and/or poison. "Poisoning" was not the least usual meaning of "pharmacia." Antiphon has left us the logogram of an "accusation of poisoning against a mother-in-law" (*Pharmakeias kata tēs mētryias*). Through her games, Pharmacia has dragged down to death a virginal purity and an unpenetrated interior.

Only a little further on, Socrates compares the written texts Phaedrus has brought along to a drug (*pharmakon*). This *pharmakon*, this "medicine," this philter, which acts as both remedy and poison, already introduces itself into the body of the discourse with all its ambivalence. This charm, this spellbinding virtue, this power of fascination, can be—alternately or simultaneously—beneficent or maleficent. The *pharmakon* would be a *substance*—with all that that word can connote in terms of matter with occult virtues, cryptic depths refusing to submit their ambivalence to analysis, already paving the way for alchemy—if we didn't have eventually to come to recognize it as antisubstance itself: that which resists any philosopheme, indefinitely exceeding its bounds as nonidentity, nonessence, nonsubstance; granting philosophy by that very fact the inexhaustible adversity of what funds it and the infinite absence of what founds it.

Operating through seduction, the *pharmakon* makes one stray from one's general, natural, habitual paths and laws. Here, it takes Socrates out of his proper place and off his customary track. The latter had always kept him inside the city. The leaves of writing act as a *pharmakon* to push or attract out of the city the one who never wanted to get out, even at the end, to escape the hemlock. They take him out of himself and draw him onto a path that is properly an *exodus*:

> *Phaedrus*: Anyone would take you, as you say, for a foreigner being
> shown the country by a guide, and not a native—you never leave

town to cross the frontier nor even, I believe, so much as set foot outside the walls.

Socrates: You must forgive me, dear friend; I'm a lover of learning, and trees and open country won't teach me anything, whereas men in the town do. Yet you seem to have discovered a drug[8] for getting me out (*dokeis moi tēs emēs exocou to pharmakon hēurēkenai*). A hungry animal can be driven by dangling a carrot or a bit of greenstuff in front of it; similarly if you proffer me speeches bound in books (*en bibliois*) I don't doubt you can cart me all round Attica, and anywhere else you please. Anyhow, now that we've got here I propose for the time being to lie down, and you can choose whatever posture you think most convenient for reading, and proceed (230*d–e*).

It is at this point, when Socrates has finally stretched out on the ground and Phaedrus has taken the most comfortable position for handling the text or, if you will, the *pharmakon*, that the discussion actually gets off the ground. A spoken speech—whether by Lysias or by Phaedrus in person—a speech proffered *in the present, in the presence* of Socrates, would not have had the same effect. Only the *logoi en bibliois*, only words that are deferred, reserved, enveloped, rolled up, words that force one to wait for them in the form and under cover of a solid object, letting themselves be desired for the space of a walk, only hidden letters can thus get Socrates moving. If a speech could be purely present, unveiled, naked, offered up in person in its truth, without the detours of a signifier foreign to it, if at the limit an undeferred *logos* were possible, it would not seduce anyone. It would not draw Socrates, as if under the effects of a *pharmakon*, out of his way. Let us get ahead of ourselves. Already: writing, the *pharmakon*, the going or leading astray.

In our discussion of this text we have been using an authoritative French translation of Plato, the one published by Guillaume Budé. In the case of the *Phaedrus*, the translation is by Léon Robin. We will continue to refer to it, inserting the Greek text in parentheses, however, whenever it seems opportune or pertinent to our point. Hence, for example, the word *pharmakon*. In this way we hope to display in the most striking manner the regular, ordered polysemy that has, through skewing, indetermination, or overdetermination, but without mistranslation, permitted the rendering of the same word by "remedy," "recipe," "poison," "drug," "philter," etc. It will also be seen to what extent the malleable unity of this concept, or rather its rules and the strange logic that links it with its signifier, has been dis-

---

8. TN. Hackforth translates "recipe"; Helmbold & Rabinowitz, "remedy."

persed, masked, obliterated, and rendered almost unreadable not only by
the imprudence or empiricism of the translators, but first and foremost by
the redoubtable, irreducible difficulty of translation. It is a difficulty
inherent in its very principle, situated less in the passage from one language
to another, from one philosophical language to another, than already, as we
shall see, in the tradition between Greek and Greek; a violent difficulty in
the transference of a nonphilosopheme into a philosopheme. With this
problem of translation we will thus be dealing with nothing less than the
problem of the very passage into philosophy.

The *biblia* that will draw Socrates out of his reserve and out of the space in
which he is wont to learn, to teach, to speak, to dialogue—the sheltered
enclosure of the city—these *biblia* contain a text written by "the ablest
writer of our day" (*deinotatos ōn tōn nun graphein*). His name is Lysias.
Phaedrus is keeping the text or, if you will, the *pharmakon*, hidden under
his cloak. He needs it because he has not learned the speech by heart. This
point is important for what follows, the problem of writing being closely
linked to the problem of "knowing by heart." Before Socrates had stretched
out on the ground and invited Phaedrus to take the most comfortable
position, the latter had offered to reconstitute, without the help of the text,
the reasoning, argument, and design of Lysias' speech, its *dianoia*. Socrates
stops him short: "Very well, my dear fellow, but you must first show me
what it is that you have in your left hand under you cloak, for I surmise that
it is the actual discourse (*ton logon auton*)" (228*d*). Between the invitation
and the start of the reading, while the *pharmakon* is wandering about under
Phaedrus' cloak, there occurs the evocation of Pharmacia and the send-off of
myths.

Is it after all by chance or by harmonics that, even before the overt
presentation of writing as a *pharmakon* arises in the middle of the myth of
Theuth, the connection between *biblia* and *pharmaka* should already be
mentioned in a malevolent or suspicious vein? As opposed to the true
practice of medicine, founded on science, we find indeed, listed in a single
stroke, empirical practice, treatments based on recipes learned by heart,
mere bookish knowledge, and the blind usage of drugs. All that, we are
told, springs out of *mania*: "I expect they would say, 'the man is mad; he
thinks he has made himself a doctor by picking up something out of a book
(*ek bibliou*), or coming across a couple of ordinary drugs (*pharmakiois*),
without any real knowledge of medicine'" (268*c*).

This association between writing and the *pharmakon* still seems external;
it could be judged artificial or purely coincidental. But the intention and
intonation are recognizably the same: one and the same suspicion envelops

in a single embrace the book and the drug, writing and whatever works in an occult, ambiguous manner open to empiricism and chance, governed by the ways of magic and not the laws of necessity. Books, the dead and rigid knowledge shut up in *biblia*, piles of histories, nomenclatures, recipes and formulas learned by heart, all this is as foreign to living knowledge and dialectics as the *pharmakon* is to medical science. And myth to true knowledge. In dealing with Plato, who knew so well on occasion how to treat myth in its archeo-logical or paleo-logical capacity, one can glimpse the immensity and difficulty of this last opposition. The extent of the difficulty is marked out—this is, among a hundred others, the example that retains us here—in that the truth—the original truth—about writing as a *pharmakon* will at first be left up to a myth. The myth of Theuth, to which we now turn.

Up to this point in the dialogue, one can say that the *pharmakon* and the grapheme have been beckoning to each other from afar, indirectly sending back to each other, and, as if by chance, appearing and disappearing together on the same line, for yet uncertain reasons, with an effectiveness that is quite discrete and perhaps after all unintentional. But in order to lift this doubt and on the supposition that the categories of the voluntary and the involuntary still have some absolute pertinence in a reading—which we don't for a minute believe, at least not on the textual level on which we are now advancing—let us proceed to the last phase of the dialogue, to the point where Theuth appears on the scene.

This time it is without indirection, without hidden mediation, without secret argumentation, that writing is proposed, presented, and asserted as a *pharmakon* (274e).

In a certain sense, one can see how this section could have been set apart as an appendix, a superadded supplement. And despite all that calls for it in the preceding steps, it is true that Plato offers it somewhat as an amusement, an hors d'œuvre or rather a dessert. All the subjects of the dialogue, both themes and speakers, seem exhausted at the moment the supplement, writing, or the *pharmakon*, are introduced: "Then we may feel that we have said enough both about the art of speaking and about the lack of art (*to men tekhnēs te kai atekhnias logōn*)"[9] (274b). And yet it is at this moment of general exhaustion that the question of writing is set out.[10] And, as was foreshad-

9. Here, when it is a question of *logos*, Robin translates *tekhnē* by "art." Later, in the course of the indictment, the same word, this time pertaining to writing, will be rendered by "technical knowledge" [*connaissance technique*].

10. While Saussure, in his *Course in General Linguistics*, excludes or settles the question of writing in a sort of preliminary excursus or hors d'oeuvre, the chapter Rousseau devotes to

owed earlier by the use of the word *aiskhron* (or the adverb *aiskhrōs*), the question of writing opens as a question of morality. It is truly *morality* that is at stake, both in the sense of the opposition between good and evil, or good and bad, and in the sense of mores, public morals and social conventions. It is a question of knowing what is done and what is not done. This moral disquiet is in no way to be distinguished from questions of truth, memory, and dialectics. This latter question, which will quickly be engaged as *the* question of writing, is closely associated with the morality theme, and indeed develops it by affinity of essence and not by superimposition. But within a debate rendered very real by the political development of the city, the propagation of writing and the activity of the sophists and speechwriters, the primary accent is naturally placed upon political and social proprieties. The type of arbitration proposed by Socrates plays within the opposition between the values of seemliness and unseemliness (*euprepeia/ aprepeia*): "But there remains the question of propriety and impropriety in writing, that is to say the conditions which make it proper or improper. Isn't that so?" (274*b*).

Is writing seemly? Does the writer cut a respectable figure? Is it proper to write? Is it done?

Of course not. But the answer is not so simple, and Socrates does not immediately offer it on his own account in a rational discourse or *logos*. He lets it be heard by delegating it to an *akoē*, to a well-known rumor, to hearsay evidence, to a fable transmitted from ear to ear: "I can tell you what our forefathers have said about it, but the truth of it is only known by tradition. However, if we could discover that truth for ourselves, should we still be concerned with the fancies of mankind?" (274*c*).

The truth of writing, that is, as we shall see, (the) nontruth, cannot be discovered in ourselves by ourselves. And it is not the object of a science, only of a history that is recited, a fable that is repeated. The link between writing and myth becomes clearer, as does its opposition to knowledge, notably the knowledge one seeks in oneself, by oneself. And at the same time, through writing or through myth, the genealogical break and the estrangement from the origin are sounded. One should note most especially that what writing will later be accused of—repeating without knowing— here defines the very approach that leads to the statement and determina-

---

writing in the *Essay on the Origin of Languages* is also presented, despite its actual importance, as a sort of somewhat contingent supplement, a makeup criterion, "another means of comparing languages and of judging their relative antiquity." The same operation is found in Hegel's *Encyclopedia*; cf. "Le Puits et la pyramide," (1-1968) in *Hegel et la pensée moderne*, (Paris: Presses Universitaires de France, 1970, coll. "Epiméthée.").

tion of its status. One thus begins by repeating without knowing—through a myth—the definition of writing, which is to repeat without knowing. This kinship of writing and myth, both of them distinguished from *logos* and dialectics, will only become more precise as the text concludes. Having just repeated without knowing that writing consists of repeating without knowing, Socrates goes on to base the demonstration of his indictment, of his *logos*, upon the premises of the *akoē*, upon structures that are readable through a fabulous genealogy of writing. As soon as the myth has struck the first blow, the *logos* of Socrates will demolish the accused.

2. The Father of Logos

The story begins like this:

> *Socrates*: Very well. I heard, then, that at Naucratis in Egypt there lived one of the old gods of that country, the one whose sacred bird is called the ibis; and the name of the divinity was Theuth. It was he who first invented numbers and calculation, geometry and astronomy, not to speak of draughts and dice, and above all writing (*grammata*). Now the King of all Egypt at that time was Thamus who lived in the great city of the upper region which the Greeks call the Egyptian Thebes; the god himself they call Ammon. Theuth came to him and exhibited his arts and declared that they ought to be imparted to the other Egyptians. And Thamus questioned him about the usefulness of each one; and as Theuth enumerated, the King blamed or praised what he thought were the good or bad points in the explanation. Now Thamus is said to have had a good deal to remark on both sides of the question about every single art (it would take too long to repeat it here); but when it came to writing, Theuth said, "This discipline (*to mathēma*), my King, will make the Egyptians wiser and will improve their memories (*sophōterous kai mnēmonikōterous*): my invention is a recipe (*pharmakon*) for both memory and wisdom." But the King said . . . etc. (274c–e).

Let us cut the King off here. He is faced with the *pharmakon*. His reply will be incisive.

Let us freeze the scene and the characters and take a look at them. Writing (or, if you will, the *pharmakon*) is thus presented to the King. Presented: like a kind of present offered up in homage by a vassal to his lord

(Theuth is a demigod speaking to the king of the gods), but above all as a finished work submitted to his appreciation. And this work is itself an art, a capacity for work, a power of operation. This *artefactum* is an art. But the value of this gift is still uncertain. The value of writing—or of the *pharmakon*—has of course been spelled out to the King, but it is the King who will give it its value, who will set the price of what, in the act of receiving, he constitutes or institutes. The king or god (Thamus represents[11] Ammon, the king of the gods, the king of kings, the god of gods. Theuth says to him: *Ō basileu*) is thus the other name for the origin of value. The value of writing will not be itself, writing will have no value, unless and to the extent that god-the-king approves of it. But god-the-king nonetheless experiences the *pharmakon* as a product, an *ergon*, which is not his own, which comes to him from outside but also from below, and which awaits his condescending judgment in order to be consecrated in its being and value. God the king does not know how to write, but that ignorance or incapacity only testifies to his sovereign independence. He has no need to write. He speaks, he says, he dictates, and his word suffices. Whether a scribe from his secretarial staff then adds the supplement of a transcription or not, that consignment is always in essence secondary.

From this position, without rejecting the homage, the god-king will depreciate it, pointing out not only its uselessness but its menace and its mischief. Another way of not receiving the offering of writing. In so doing, god-the-king-that-speaks is acting like a father. The *pharmakon* is here presented to the father and is by him rejected, belittled, abandoned, disparaged. The father is always suspicious and watchful toward writing.

Even if we did not want to give in here to the easy passage uniting the figures of the king, the god, and the father, it would suffice to pay systematic attention—which to our knowledge has never been done—to the permanence of a Platonic schema that assigns the origin and power of speech, precisely of *logos*, to the paternal position. Not that this happens especially and exclusively in Plato. Everyone knows this or can easily imagine it. But the fact that "Platonism," which sets up the whole of Western metaphysics in its conceptuality, should not escape the generality of this structural constraint, and even illustrates it with incomparable subtlety and force, stands out as all the more significant.

11. For Plato, Thamus is doubtless another name for Ammon, whose figure (that of the sun king and of the father of the gods) we shall sketch out later for its own sake. On this question and the debate to which it has given rise, see Frutiger, *Mythes*, p. 233, n. 2, and notably Eisler, "Platon und das ägyptische Alphabet," *Archiv für Geschichte der Philosophie*, 1922; Pauly-Wissowa, *Real-Encyclopädie der classischen Altertumswissenschaft* (art. Ammon); Roscher, *Lexikon der griechischen und römischen Mythologie* (art. Thamus).

Not that logos *is* the father, either. But the origin of logos is *its father*. One could say anachronously that the "speaking subject" is the *father* of his speech. And one would quickly realize that this is no metaphor, at least not in the sense of any common, conventional effect of rhetoric. *Logos* is a son, then, a son that would be destroyed in his very *presence* without the present *attendance* of his father. His father who answers. His father who speaks for him and answers for him. Without his father, he would be nothing but, in fact, writing. At least that is what is said by the one who says: it is the father's thesis. The specificity of writing would thus be intimately bound to the absence of the father. Such an absence can of course exist along very diverse modalities, distinctly or confusedly, successively or simultaneously: to have lost one's father, through natural or violent death, through random violence or patricide; and then to solicit the aid and attendance, possible or impossible, of the paternal presence, to solicit it directly or to claim to be getting along without it, etc. The reader will have noted Socrates' insistence on the misery, whether pitiful or arrogant, of a *logos* committed to writing: ". . . It always needs its father to attend to it, being quite unable to defend itself or attend to its own needs" (275e).

This misery is ambiguous: it is the distress of the orphan, of course, who needs not only an attending presence but also a presence that will attend to its needs; but in pitying the orphan, one also makes an accusation against him, along with writing, for claiming to do away with the father, for achieving emancipation with complacent self-sufficiency. From the position of the holder of the scepter, the desire of writing is indicated, designated, and denounced as a desire for orphanhood and patricidal subversion. Isn't this *pharmakon* then a criminal thing, a poisoned present?

The status of this orphan, whose welfare cannot be assured by any attendance or assistance, coincides with that of a *graphein* which, being nobody's son at the instant it reaches inscription, scarcely remains a son at all and no longer *recognizes* its origins, whether legally or morally. In contrast to writing, living *logos* is alive in that it has a living father (whereas the orphan is already half dead), a father that is *present*, *standing* near it, behind it, within it, sustaining it with his rectitude, attending it in person in his own name. Living *logos*, for its part, recognizes its debt, lives off that recognition, and forbids itself, thinks it can forbid itself patricide. But prohibition and patricide, like the relations between speech and writing, are structures surprising enough to require us later on to articulate Plato's text between a patricide prohibited and a patricide proclaimed. The deferred murder of the father and rector.

The *Phaedrus* would already be sufficient to prove that the responsibility for *logos*, for its meaning and effects, goes to those who attend it, to those who are present with the presence of a father. These "metaphors" must be tirelessly questioned. Witness Socrates, addressing Eros: "If in our former speech Phaedrus or I said anything harsh against you, blame Lysias, the father of the subject (*ton tou logou patera*)" (275*b*). *Logos*—"discourse"—has the meaning here of argument, line of reasoning, guiding thread animating the spoken discussion (the *Logos*). To translate it by "subject" [*sujet*], as Robin does, is not merely anachronistic. The whole intention and the organic unity of signification is destroyed. For only the "living" discourse, only a spoken word (and not a speech's theme, object, or subject) can have a father; and, according to a necessity that will not cease to become clearer to us from now on, the *logoi* are the children. Alive enough to protest on occasion and to let themselves be questioned; capable, too, in contrast to written things, of responding when their father is there. They are their father's responsible presence.

Some of them, for example, descend from Phaedrus, who is sometimes called upon to sustain them. Let us refer again to Robin, who translates *logos* this time not by "subject" but by "argument," and disrupts in a space of ten lines the play on the *tekhnē tō logōn*. (What is in question is the *tekhnē* the sophists and rhetors had or pretended to have at their disposal, which was at once an art and an instrument, a recipe, an occult but transmissible "treatise," etc. Socrates considers the then classical problem in terms of the opposition between persuasion [*peithō*] and truth [alētheia] [260 *a*].)

> *Socrates*: I agree—if, that is, the arguments (*logoi*) that come forward to speak for oratory should give testimony that it is an art (*tekhnē*). Now I seem, as it were, to hear some arguments advancing to give their evidence that it tells lies, that it is not an art at all, but an artless routine. "Without a grip on truth," says the Spartan, "there can be no genuine art of speaking (*tou de legein*) either now or in the future."
>
> *Phaedrus*: Socrates, we need these arguments (*Toutōn dei tōn logōn, ō Sōkrates*). Bring the witnesses here and let's find out what they have to say and how they'll say it (*ti kai pōs legousin*).
>
> *Socrates*: Come here, then, noble brood (*gennaia*), and convince Phaedrus, father of such fine children (*kallipaida te Phaidron*), that if he doesn't give enough attention to philosophy, he will never become a competent speaker on any subject. Now let Phaedrus answer (260e-261*a*).

It is again Phaedrus, but this time in the *Symposium*, who must speak first because he is both "head of the table" and "father of our subject" (*patēr tou logou*) (177*d*).

What we are provisionally and for the sake of convenience continuing to call a metaphor thus in any event belongs to a whole system. If *logos* has a father, if it is a *logos* only when attended by its father, this is because it is always a being (*on*) and even a certain species of being (the *Sophist*, 260*a*), more precisely a *living* being. *Logos* is a *zōon*. An animal that is born, grows, belongs to the *phusis*. Linguistics, logic, dialectics, and zoology are all in the same camp.

In describing *logos* as a *zōon*, Plato is following certain rhetors and sophists before him who, as a contrast to the cadaverous rigidity of writing, had held up the living spoken word, which infallibly conforms to the necessities of the situation at hand, to the expectations and demands of the interlocutors present, and which sniffs out the spots where it ought to produce itself, feigning to bend and adapt at the moment it is actually achieving maximum persuasiveness and control.[12]

Logos, a living, animate creature, is thus also an organism that has been engendered. An *organism*: a differentiated body *proper*, with a center and extremities, joints, a head, and feet. In order to be "proper," a written discourse *ought* to submit to the laws of life just as a living discourse does. Logographical necessity (*anangkē logographikē*) ought to be analogous to biological, or rather zoological, necessity. Otherwise, obviously, it would have neither head nor tail. Both *structure* and *constitution* are in question in the risk run by *logos* of losing through writing both its tail and its head:

> *Socrates*: And what about the rest? Don't you think the different parts of the speech (*ta tou logou*) are tossed in hit or miss? Or is there really a cogent reason for starting his second point in the second place? And is that the case with the rest of the speech? As for myself, in my ignorance, I thought that the writer boldly set down whatever happened to come into his head. Can you explain his arrangement of the topics in the order he has adopted as the result of some principle of composition, some logographic necessity?

---

12. The association *logos-zōon* appears in the discourse of Isocrates *Against the Sophists* and in that of Alcidamas *On the Sophists*. Cf. also W. Süss, who compares these two discourses line by line with the *Phaedrus*, in *Ethos: Studien zur älteren griechischen Rhetorik* (Leipzig, 1910), pp. 34 ff) and A. Diès, "Philosophie et rhétorique," in *Autour de Platon* (Paris: Garbriel Beauchesne, 1927) I, 103.

Phaedrus: It's very kind of you to think me capable of such an accurate insight into his methods.

Socrates: But to this you will surely agree: every discourse (*logon*), like a living creature (*ōsper zōon*), should be so put together (*sunestanai*) that it has its own body and lacks neither head nor foot, middle nor extremities, all composed in such a way that they suit both each other and the whole (264*b–c*).

The organism thus engendered must be well born, of noble blood: "*gennaia!*," we recall, is what Socrates called the *logoi*, those "noble creatures." This implies that the organism, having been engendered, must have a beginning and an end. Here, Socrates' standards become precise and insistent: a speech must have a beginning and an end, it must begin with the beginning and end with the end: "It certainly seems as though Lysias, at least, was far from satisfying our demands: it's from the end, not the beginning, that he tries to swim (on his back!) upstream through the current of his discourse. He starts out with what the lover ought to say at the very end to his beloved!" (264*a*). The implications and consequences of such a norm are immense, but they are obvious enough for us not to have to belabor them. It follows that the spoken discourse behaves like someone attended in origin and present in person. *Logos*: "*Sermo tanquam persona ipse loquens*," as one Platonic Lexicon puts it. [13] Like any person, the *logos-zōon* has a father.

But what is a father?

Should we consider this known, and with this term—the known—classify the other term within what one would hasten to classify as a metaphor? One would then say that the origin or cause of *logos* is being compared to what we know to be the cause of a living son, his father. One would understand or imagine the birth and development of *logos* from the standpoint of a domain foreign to it, the transmission of life or the generative relation. But the father is not the generator or procreator in any "real" sense prior to or outside all relation to language. In what way, indeed, is the father/son relation distinguishable from a mere cause/effect or generator/engendered relation, if not by the instance of logos? Only a power of speech can have a father. The father is always father to a speaking/living being. In other words, it is precisely *logos* that enables us to perceive and investigate something like paternity. If there were a simple metaphor in the

---

13. Fr. Ast, *Lexique platonicien*. Cf. also B. Parain, *Essai sur le logos platonicien* (Paris: Gallimard, 1942), p. 211; and P. Louis, *Les Métaphores de Platon* (Paris: Les Belles Lettres, 1945), pp. 43–44.

expression "father of logos," the first word, which seemed the more familiar, would nevertheless receive more meaning *from* the second than it would transmit *to* it. The first familiarity is always involved in a relation of cohabitation with *logos*. Living-beings, father and son, are announced to us and related to each other within the household of *logos*. From which one does not escape, in spite of appearances, when one is transported, by "metaphor," to a foreign territory where one meets fathers, sons, living creatures, all sorts of beings that come in handy for explaining to anyone that doesn't know, by comparison, what *logos*, that strange thing, is all about. Even though this hearth is the heart of all metaphoricity, "father of logos" is not a simple metaphor. To have simple metaphoricity, one would have to make the statement that some living creature incapable of language, if anyone still wished to believe in such a thing, has a father. One must thus proceed to undertake a general reversal of all metaphorical directions, no longer asking whether *logos* can have a father but understanding that what the father claims to be the father of cannot go without the essential possibility of *logos*.

A *logos indebted* to a father, what does that mean? At least how can it be read within the stratum of the Platonic text that interests us here?

The figure of the father, of course, is also that of the good (*agathon*). Logos *represents* what it is indebted to: the father who is also chief, capital, and good(s). Or rather *the* chief, *the* capital, *the* good(s). *Patēr* in Greek means all that at once. Neither translators nor commentators of Plato seem to have accounted for the play of these schemas. It is extremely difficult, we must recognize, to respect this play in a translation, and the fact can at least be explained in that no one has ever raised the question. Thus, at the point in the *Republic* where Socrates backs away from speaking of the good in itself (VI, 506e), he immediately suggests replacing it with its *ekgonos*, its son, its offspring:

> . . . let us dismiss for the time being the nature of the good in itself, for to attain to my present surmise of that seems a pitch above the impulse that wings my flight today. But what seems to be the offspring (*ekgonos*) of the good and most nearly made in its likeness I am willing to speak if you too wish it, and otherwise to let the matter drop.
>
> Well, speak on, he said, for you will duly pay me the tale of the parent another time.
>
> I could wish, I said, that I were able to make and you to receive the payment, and not merely as now the interest (*tokous*). But at any rate receive this interest and the offspring of the good (*tokon te kai ekgonon autou tou agathou*).

Tokos, which is here associated with *ekgonos*, signifies production and the product, birth and the child, etc. This word functions with this meaning in the domains of agriculture, of kinship relations, and of fiduciary operations. None of these domains, as we shall see, lies outside the investment and possibility of a *logos*.

As product, the *tokos* is the child, the human or animal brood, as well as the fruits of the seed sown in the field, and the interest on a capital investment: it is a *return* or *revenue*. The distribution of all these meanings can be followed in Plato's text. The meaning of *patēr* is sometimes even inflected in the exclusive sense of financial capital. In the *Republic* itself, and not far from the passage we have just quoted. One of the drawbacks of democracy lies in the role that capital is often allowed to play in it: "But these money-makers with down-bent heads, pretending not even to see the poor, but inserting the sting of their money into any of the remainder who do not resist, and harvesting from them in interest as it were a manifold progeny of the parent sum (*tou patros ekgonous tokous pollaplasious*), foster the drone and pauper element in the state" (555*e*).

Now, about this father, this capital, this good, this origin of value and of appearing beings, it is not possible to speak simply or directly. First of all because it is no more possible to look them in the face than to stare at the sun. On the subject of this bedazzlement before the face of the sun, a rereading of the famous passage of the *Republic* (VII, 515*c* ff) is strongly recommended here.

Thus will Socrates evoke only the visible sun, the son that resembles the father, the *analogon* of the intelligible sun: "It was the sun, then, that I meant when I spoke of that offspring of the Good (*ton tou agathou ekgonon*), which the Good has created in its own image (*hon tagathon egennēsen analogon heautōi*), and which stands in the visible world in the same relation to vision and visible things as that which the good itself bears in the intelligible world to intelligence and to intelligible objects" (508*c*).

How does *Logos* intercede in this *analogy* between the father and the son, the *nooumena* and the *horōmena*?

The Good, in the visible-invisible figure of the father, the sun, or capital, is the origin of all *onta*, responsible for their appearing and their coming into *logos*, which both assembles and distinguishes them: "We predicate 'to be' of many beautiful things and many good things, saying of them severally that they *are*, and so define them in our speech (*einai phamen te kai diorizomen tōi logōi*)" (507 *b*).

The good (father, sun, capital) is thus the hidden illuminating, blinding source of *logos*. And since one cannot speak of that which enables one to speak (being forbidden to speak of it or to speak to it face to face), one will speak only of that which speaks and of things that, with a single exception, one is constantly speaking of. And since an account or reason cannot be given of what *logos* (account or reason: *ratio*) is accountable or owing *to*, since the capital cannot be counted nor the chief looked in the eye, it will be necessary, by means of a discriminative, diacritical operation, to count up the plurality of interests, returns, products, and offspring: "Well, speak on (*lege*), he said, for you will duly pay me the tale of the parent another time—I could wish, I said, that I were able to make and you to receive the payment, and not merely as now the interest. But at any rate receive this interest and the offspring of the good. Have a care, however, lest I deceive you unintentionally with a false reckoning (*ton logon*) of the interest (*tou tokou*)" (507*a*).

From the foregoing passage we should also retain the fact that, along with the account (*logos*) of the supplements (to the father-good-capital-origin, etc.), along with what comes above and beyond the One in the very movement through which it absents itself and becomes invisible, thus requiring that its place be supplied, along with differance and diacriticity, Socrates introduces or discovers the ever open possibility of the *kibdēlon*, that which is falsified, adulterated, mendacious, deceptive, equivocal. Have a care, he says, lest I deceive you with a false reckoning of the interest (*kibdēlon apodidous ton logon tou tokou*). *Kibdēleuma* is fraudulent merchandise. The corresponding verb (*kibdēleuō*) signifies "to tamper with money or merchandise, and, by extension, to be of bad faith."

This recourse to *logos*, from fear of being blinded by any direct intuition of the face of the father, of good, of capital, of the origin of being in itself, of the form of forms, etc., this recourse to logos as that which *protects us from the sun*, protects us under it and from it, is proposed by Socrates elsewhere, in the *analogous* order of the sensible or the visible. We shall quote at length from that text. In addition to its intrinsic interest, the text, in its official Robin translation, manifests a series of slidings, as it were, that are highly significant.[14] The passage in question is the critique, in the *Phaedo*, of "physicalists":

> Socrates proceeded:—I thought that as I had failed in the contempla-
> tion of true existence (*ta onta*), I ought to be careful that I did not lose
> the eye of my soul; as people may injure their bodily eye by observing

14. I am indebted to the friendship and alertness of Francine Markovits for having brought this to my attention. This text should of course be placed alongside those of books VI and VII of the *Republic*.

and gazing on the sun during an eclipse, unless they take the precaution of only looking at the image (*eikona*) reflected in the water, or in some analogous medium. So in my own case, I was afraid that my soul might be blinded altogether if I looked at things with my eyes or tried to apprehend them with the help of the senses. And I thought that I had better have recourse to the world of *idea* (*en logois*) and seek there the truth of things. . . . So, basing myself in each case on the idea (*logon*) that I judged to be the strongest . . ." (99*d*–100*a*).

Logos is thus a *resource*. One must *turn* to it, and not merely when the solar source is *present* and risks burning the eyes if stared at; one has also to turn away toward *logos* when the sun seems to withdraw during its eclipse. Dead, extinguished, or hidden, that star is more dangerous than ever.

We will let these yarns of suns and sons spin on for a while. Up to now we have only followed this line so as to move from *logos* to the father, so as to tie speech to the *kurios*, the master, the lord, another name given in the *Republic* to the good-sun-capital-father (508*a*). Later, within the same tissue, within the same texts, we will draw on other filial filaments, pull the same strings once more, and witness the weaving or unraveling of other designs.

3. The Filial Inscription:
Theuth, Hermes, Thoth, Nabû, Nebo

Universal history continued to unroll, the all-too-human gods whom Xenophanes had denounced were demoted to figures of poetic fiction, or to demons—although it was reported that one of them, Hermes Trismegistus, had dictated a variable number of books (42 according to Clement of Alexandria; 20,000 according to Iamblicus; 36,525 according to the priests of Thoth—who is also Hermes) in the pages of which are written all things. Fragments of this illusory library, compiled or concocted beginning in the third century, go to form what is called the *Corpus Hermeticum*...
  —Jorge Luis Borges, "The Fearful Sphere of Pascal"

A sense of fear of the unknown moved in the heart of his weariness, a fear of symbols and portents, of the hawk-like man whose name he bore soaring out of his captivity on osier woven wing, of Thoth, the god of writers, writing with a reed upon a tablet and bearing on his narrow ibis head the cusped moon.
  —James Joyce, *A Portrait of the Artist as a Young Man*

Another school declares that *all time* has already transpired and that
our life is only the crepuscular and no doubt falsified and mutilated
memory or reflection of an irrecoverable process. Another, that the
history of the universe—and in it our lives and the most tenuous
detail of our lives—is the scripture produced by a subordinate god
in order to communicate with a demon. Another, that the universe
is comparable to those cryptographs in which not all the symbols
are valid . . .

—Jorge Louis Borges, "Tlön, Uqbar, Orbis Tertius"

Our intention here has only been to sow the idea that the spontaneity,
freedom, and fantasy attributed to Plato in his legend of Theuth were
actually supervised and limited by rigorous necessities. The organization of
the myth conforms to powerful constraints. These constraints coordinate as
a system certain rules that make their presence known, sometimes in what
is empirically partitioned off for us as "Greek language" or "culture," and
sometimes, from without, in "foreign mythology." From which Plato has
not simply borrowed, nor borrowed a simple element: the identity of a
character, Thoth, the god of writing. One cannot, in fact, speak—and we
don't really know what the word could mean here anyway—of a borrowing,
that is, of an addition contingent and external to the text. Plato had to make
his tale conform to structural laws. The most general of these, those that
govern and articulate the oppositions speech/writing, life/death, father/
son, master/servant, first/second, legitimate son/orphan-bastard, soul/
body, inside/outside, good/evil, seriousness/play, day/night, sun/moon,
etc., also govern, and according to the same configurations, Egyptian,
Babylonian, and Assyrian mythology. And others, too, no doubt, which we
have neither the intention nor the means to situate here. In concerning
ourselves with the fact that Plato has not merely *borrowed* a *simple* element,
we are thus bracketing off the problem of factual genealogy and of the
empirical, effective communication among cultures and mythologies.[15]
What we wish to do here is simply to point to the internal, structural
necessity which alone has made possible such communication and any
eventual contagion of mythemes.

15. We can here only refer the reader to all the existing studies of the communications
between Greece and the East or Middle East. Such scholarship abounds. On Plato, his
relations with Egypt, the hypothesis of his voyage to Heliopolis, the testimony of Strabo and
Diogenes Laertius, one can find the references and essential documentation in Festugière's
Révélation d'Hermès Trismégiste (Paris: J. Gabalda, 1944–54), vol. 1; R. Godel's *Platon à
Héliopolis d'Egypte* (Paris: Les Belles Lettres, 1956); and S. Sauneron's *Les Prêtres de l'ancienne
Egypte* (Paris: Le Seuil, 1957).

Plato, of course, does not describe Theuth as a character. Not a single concrete characteristic is attributed to him, neither in the *Phaedrus* nor in the very brief allusion in the *Philebus*. That is at least how things appear. But in looking more closely, one comes to recognize that the situation he occupies, the content of his speeches and operations, and the relations among the themes, concepts, and signifiers in which his interventions are engaged, all organize the features of a strongly marked figure. The structural analogy that relates these features to other gods of writing, and mainly to the Egyptian Thoth, can be the effect neither of a partial or total borrowing, nor of chance or Plato's imagination. And in the simultaneous insertion, so rigorous and closely fit, of these traits into the systematic arrangement of Plato's philosophemes, this meshing of the mythological and the philosophical points to some more deeply buried necessity.

No doubt the god Thoth had several faces, belonged to several eras, lived in several homes.[16] The discordant tangle of mythological accounts in which he is caught should not be neglected. Nevertheless, certain constants can be distinguished throughout, drawn in broad letters with firm strokes. One would be tempted to say that these constitute the permanent identity of this god in the pantheon, if his function, as we shall see, were not precisely to work at the subversive dislocation of identity in general, starting with that of theological regality.

What then, are the pertinent traits for someone who is trying to reconstitute the structural resemblance between the Platonic and the other mythological figures of the origin of writing? The bringing out of these traits should not merely serve to determine each of the significations within the play of thematic oppositions as they have been listed here, whether in Plato's discourse or in a general configuration of mythologies. It must open onto the general problematic of the relations between the mythemes and the philosophemes that lie at the origin of western *logos*. That is to say, of a history— or rather, of History—which has been produced in its entirety in the *philosophical* difference between *mythos* and *logos*, blindly sinking down into that difference as the natural obviousness of its own element.

In the *Phaedrus*, the god of writing is thus a subordinate character, a second, a technocrat without power of decision, an engineer, a clever, ingenious servant who has been granted an audience with the king of the gods. The king has been kind enough to admit him to his counsel. Theuth presents a *tekhnē* and a *pharmakon* to the king, father, and god who speaks or commands with his sun-filled voice. When the latter has made his sentence

16. Cf. Jacques Vandier, *La Religion égyptienne* (Paris: Presses Universitaires de France, 1949), esp. pp. 64–65.

known, when he has let it drop from on high, when he has *in the same blow* prescribed that the *pharmakon* be dropped, Theuth will not respond. The forces present wish him to remain in his place.

Doesn't he have the same place in Egyptian mythology? There too, Thoth is an engendered god. He often calls himself the son of the god-king, the sun-god, Ammon-Ra: "I am Thoth, the eldest son of Ra."[17] Ra (the sun) is god the creator, and he engenders through the mediation of the word.[18] His other name, the one by which he is in fact designated in the *Phaedrus*, is Ammon. The accepted sense of this proper name: the hidden.[19] Once again we encounter here a hidden sun, the father of all things, letting himself be represented by speech.

The configurative unity of these significations—the power of speech, the creation of being and life, the sun (which is also, as we shall see, the eye), the self-concealment—is conjugated in what could be called the history of the egg or the egg of history. The world came out of an egg. More precisely, the living creator of the life of the world came out of an egg: the sun, then, was at first carried in an eggshell. Which explains a number of Ammon-Ra's characteristics: he is also a bird, a falcon ("I am the great falcon, hatched from his egg"). But in his capacity as origin of everything, Ammon-Ra is also the origin of the egg. He is designated sometimes as the bird-sun born from the primal egg, sometimes as the originary bird, carrier of the first egg. In this case, and since the power of speech is one with the power of creation, certain texts speak of "the egg of the great cackler." It would make no sense here to ask the at once trivial and philosophical

17. Cf. S. Morenz, *La Religion égyptienne* (Paris: Payot, 1962), p. 58. This formulation is noteworthy, according to Morenz, through its use of the first person. "This rarity seems remarkable to us because such formulae are common in the hymns composed in Greek which involve the Egyptian goddess Isis ("I am Isis," etc.); there is thus good reason to wonder whether this does not point to some extra-Egyptian origin of these hymns."

18. Cf. S. Sauneron, p. 123: "The initial god had only to *speak* to create; and the beings and things evoked were born through his voice," etc.

19. Cf. Morenz, p. 46, and S. Sauneron, who provides the following account: "What his name signifies exactly, we do not know. But it was pronounced in the same way as another word meaning 'to hide,' 'to conceal oneself,' and the scribes played on that assonance so as to define Ammon as the great god who masks his real countenance before his children. . . . Some went even further than that: Hecataeus of Abdera records a sacerdotal tradition according to which this name (Ammon) is supposed to be the expression used in Egypt to call someone. . . . It is indeed true that the word *amoini* means 'come,' 'come to me'; it is a fact, furthermore, that certain hymns begin with the words *Amoini Amoun* . . . 'Come to me, Ammon.' The similarity of sound alone between these two words made the priests suspect that there was some intimate link between them—to see therein an explanation of the divine name: thus, in addressing the primordial god . . . as an invisible, hidden being, they invite and exhort him, calling him Ammon, to show himself to them and unmask himself" (p. 127).

question of "the chicken or the egg," of the logical, chronological, or ontological priority of the cause over the effect. This question has been magnificently answered by certain sarcophagi: "O Ra, who art in thy egg." If we add that this egg is also a "hidden egg,"[20] we shall have constituted but also opened up the system of these significations.

The subordination of Thoth, the ibis, eldest son of the original bird, is marked in several ways: in the Memphitic doctrine, for example, Thoth is the executor, through language, of Horus' creative project.[21] He bears the signs of the great sun-god. He interprets him as a spokesman, a standard-bearer. And like his Greek counterpart, Hermes, whom Plato moreover never mentions, he occupies the role of messenger-god, of clever intermediary, ingenious and subtle enough to steal, and always to steal away. The signifier-god. Whatever he has to enounce or inform in words has already been thought by Horus. Language, of which he is depositary and secretary, can thus only represent, so as to transmit the message, an already formed divine thought, a fixed design.[22] The message itself is not, but only represents, the absolutely creative moment. It is a second and secondary word. And when Thoth is concerned with the spoken rather than with the written word, which is rather seldom, he is never the absolute author or initiator of language. On the contrary, he introduces difference into language and it is to him that the origin of the plurality of languages is attributed.[23] (Later, we will ask, turning back to Plato and to the *Philebus*, whether differentiation is really a second step and whether this "secondarity" is not the emergence of the grapheme as the very origin and possibility

20. Cf. Morenz, pp. 232–33. The paragraph that is about to end here will have marked the fact that this pharmacy of Plato's also brings into play [*entraîne*] Bataille's text, inscribing within the story of the egg the sun of the accursèd part [*la part maudite*]; the whole of that essay, as will quickly become apparent, being itself nothing but a reading of *Finnegans Wake*.

21. Cf. Vandier, p. 36: "These two gods Horus and Thoth were said to have been associates in the creative act, Horus representing the thought that conceives and Thoth the speech that executes" (p. 64). Cf. also A. Erman, *La Religion des Egyptiens* (Paris: Payot), p. 118.

22. Cf. Morenz, pp. 46–47; and Festugière, pp. 70–73. As a messenger, Thoth is consequently also an interpreter, *hermēneus*. This is one, among numerous others, of the features of his resemblance with Hermes. Festugière analyzes this in chapter 4 of his book.

23. J. Černý cites a hymn to Thoth beginning in the following terms: "Hail to thee, Moon-Thoth, who made different the tongue of one country from another." Černý had thought this document unique, but soon discovered that Boylan (*Thoth: The Hermes of Egypt* [London, 1922]) had quoted (p. 184) another analogous papyrus ("you who distinguished [or separated] the tongue of country from country") and still another (p. 197) ("you who distinguished the tongue of every foreign land"). Cf. J. Černý, "*Thoth as Creator of Languages,*" *Journal of Egyptian Archaeology* 34 (1948): 121 ff; S. Saunerson, *La Différenciation des langues d'après la tradition égyptienne*, Bulletin de l'Institut français d'Archéologie orientale du Caire (Cairo, 1960).

of *logos* itself. In the *Philebus*, Theuth is evoked indeed as the author of difference: of differentiation within language and not of the plurality of languages. But it is our belief that at their root the two problems are inseparable.)

As the god of language second and of linguistic difference, Thoth can become the god of the creative word only by metonymic substitution, by historical displacement, and sometimes by violent subversion.

This type of substitution thus puts Thoth *in Ra's place* as the moon takes the place of the sun. The god of writing thus supplies the place of Ra, supplementing him and supplanting him in his absence and essential disappearance. Such is the origin of the moon as supplement to the sun, of night light as supplement to daylight. And writing as the supplement of speech. "One day while Ra was in the sky, he said: *'Bring me Thoth,'* and Thoth was straightway brought to him. The Majesty of this god said to Thoth: *'Be in the sky in my place, while I shine over the blessed of the lower regions. . . You are in my place, my replacement, and you will be called thus: Thoth, he who replaces Ra.'* Then all sorts of things sprang up thanks to the play of Ra's words. He said to Thoth: *'I will cause you to embrace (ionh) the two skies with your beauty and your rays'*—and thus the moon (*ioh*) was born. Later, alluding to the fact that Thoth, as Ra's replacement, occupies a somewhat subordinate position: *'I will cause you to send (hôb) greater ones than yourself*— and thus was born the Ibis (*hib*), the bird of Thoth."[24]

This process of substitution, which thus functions as a pure play of traces or supplements or, again, operates within the order of the pure signifier which no reality, no absolutely external reference, no transcendental sig- nified, can come to limit, bound, or control; this substitution, which could be judged "mad" since it can go on infinitely in the element of the linguistic permutation of substitutes, of substitutes for substitutes; this unleashed chain is nevertheless not lacking in violence. One would not have under- stood anything of this "linguistic" "immanence" if one saw it as the peaceful milieu of a merely fictional war, an inoffensive word-play, in contrast to some raging *polemos* in "reality." It is not in any reality foreign to the "play of words" that Thoth also frequently participates in plots, perfidious intrigues, conspiracies to usurp the throne. He helps the sons do away with the father, the brothers do away with the brother that has become king. Nout, cursed by Ra, no longer disposed of a single date, a single day of the calendar on which she could give birth. Ra had blocked from her all time, all the days and periods there were for bringing a child into the world. Thoth, who also had a power of calculation over the institution of the

24. Erman, pp. 90–91.

calendar and the march of time, added the five epagomenic days. This supplementary time enabled Nout to produce five children: Haroeris, Seth, Isis, Nephtys and Osiris, who would later become king in the place of his father Geb. During the reign of Osiris (the sun-king), Thoth, who was also his brother,[25] "initiated men into arts and letters," and "created hiero-glyphic writing to enable them to fix their thoughts."[26] But later, he participates in the plot led by Seth, Osiris' jealous brother. The famous legend of the death of Osiris is well known: tricked into being shut up in a trunk the size of his body, he is dismembered, and his fourteen parts are scattered to the winds. After many complications, he is found and reassem-bled by his wife Isis, all except for the phallus, which has been swallowed by an Oxyrhynchus fish.[27] This does not prevent Thoth from acting with the cleverest and most oblivious opportunism. Isis, transformed into a vulture, lies on the corpse of Osiris. In that position she engenders Horus, "the child-with-his-finger-in-his-mouth," who will attack his father's murder-er. The latter, Seth, tears out Horus' eye while Horus rips off Seth's testicles. When Horus can get his eye back, he offers it to his father—and this eye is also the moon: Thoth, if you will—and the eye brings Osiris back to life and potency.

In the course of the fight, Thoth separates the combatants and, in his role of god-doctor-pharmacist-magician, sews up their wounds and heals them of their mutilation. Later, when the eye and testicles are back in place, a trial is held, during which Thoth turns on Seth whose accomplice he had nevertheless once been, and confirms as true the words of Osiris.[28]

As a substitute capable of doubling for the king, the father, the sun, and the word, distinguished from these only by dint of representing, repeating, and masquerading, Thoth was naturally also capable of totally supplanting them and appropriating all their attributes. He is added as the essential attribute of what he is added to, and from which almost nothing distin-guishes him. He differs from speech or divine light only as the revealer from the revealed. Barely.[29]

---

25. Ibid. p. 96.
26. Vandier, p. 51.
27. Ibid. p. 52.
28. Erman, p. 101
29. Thus it is that the god of writing can become the god of creative speech. This is a structural possibility derived from his supplementary status and from the logic of the supplement. The same can also be seen to occur in the evolution of the history of mythology. Festugière, in particular, points this out: "Thoth, however, does not remain content with this secondary rank. At the time when the priests in Egypt were forging cosmogonies in which the local clergy of each area sought to give the primary role to the god it honored, the

But before, as it were, his adequacy of replacement and usurpation, Thoth is essentially the god of writing, the secretary of Ra and the nine gods, the hierogrammate and the hypomnetographer.[30] Now, it is precisely by pointing out, as we shall see, that the *pharmakon* of writing is good for *hypomnēsis* (re-memoration, recollection, consignation) and not for the *mnēmē* (living, knowing memory) that Thamus, in the *Phaedrus*, condemns it as being of little worth.

In later episodes of the Osiris cycle, Thoth also becomes the scribe and bookkeeper of Osiris, who, it should not be forgotten, is then considered his brother. Thoth is represented as the model and patron of scribes, so important to the chancelleries of the Pharaohs: "while the sun god is the universal master, Thoth is his top functionary, his vizir, who stands near him in his ship in order to submit his reports."[31] As "Master of the books," he becomes, by dint of consigning them, registering them, keeping account of them, and guarding their stock, the "master of divine words."[32] His female counterpart writes, too: her name, Seshat, doubtless means *she-who-writes*. "Mistress of libraries," she records the exploits of the kings. The first goddess versed in the art of engraving, she marks the names of the kings on a tree in the temple of Heliopolis, while Thoth keeps account of the years on a notched pole. There is also the famous scene of the royal intitulation reproduced on the bas-reliefs of numerous temples: the king is seated beneath a persea-tree while Thoth and Seshat inscribe his name on the leaves of a sacred tree.[33] And also the scene of the last judgment: in the underworld, opposite Osiris, Thoth records the weight of the heart-souls of the dead.[34]

For it goes without saying that the god of writing must also be the god of death. We should not forget that, in the *Phaedrus*, another thing held

---

theologians of Hermopolis, who were competing with those of the Delta and of Heliopolis, elaborated a cosmogony in which the principal share fell to Thoth. Since Thoth was a magician, and since he knew of the power of sounds which, when emitted properly, unfailingly produce their effect, it was by means of voice, of speech, or rather, incantation, that Thoth was said to have created the world. Thoth's voice is thus creative: it shapes and creates; and, condensing and solidifying into matter, it becomes a being. Thoth becomes identified with his breath; his exhalation alone causes all things to be born. It is not impossible that these Hermopolitan speculations may offer some similarity with the *Logos* of the Greeks—at once Speech, Reason, and Demiurge—and with the *Sophia* of the Alexandrian Jews; perhaps the Priests of Thoth even underwent, well before the Christian era, the influence of Greek thought, but this cannot be solidly affirmed" (p. 68).

30. Ibid.; cf. also Vandier, passim, and Erman, passim.
31. Erman, p. 81.
32. Ibid.
33. Vandier, p. 182.
34. Vandier, pp. 136–37; Morenz, p. 173; Festugière, p. 68.

against the invention of the *pharmakon* is that it substitutes the breathless sign for the living voice, claims to do without the father (who is both living and life-giving) of *logos*, and can no more answer for itself than a sculpture or inanimate painting, etc. In all the cycles of Egyptian mythology, Thoth presides over the organization of death. The master of writing, numbers, and calculation does not merely write down the weight of dead souls; he first counts out the days of life, *enumerates* history. His arithmetic thus covers the events of divine biography. He is "the one who measures the length of the lives of gods and men."[35] He behaves like a chief of funereal protocol, charged in particular with the dressing of the dead.

Sometimes the dead person takes the place of the scribe. Within the space of such a scene, the dead one's place [*la place du mort*; also = the dummy, in bridge] then falls to Thoth. One can read on the pyramids the celestial history of one such soul: " '*Where is he going?*' asks a great bull threatening him with his horn" (we should note in passing that another name for Thoth, Ra's nocturnal representative, is the "bull among the stars"). " '*He's going full of vital energy to the skies, to see his father, to contemplate Ra,*' and the terrifying creature lets him pass." (The books of the dead, placed in the coffin next to the corpse, contained in particular formulas enabling him to "go out into the light of day" and see the sun. The dead person must see the sun: death is the prerequisite, or even the experience, of that face-to-face encounter. One thinks of the *Phaedo*.) God the father welcomes him into his bark, and "it even happens that he lets off his own celestial scribe and puts the dead man *in his place*, so that *he judges, arbitrates, and gives orders to one who is greater than himself.*"[36] The dead man can also simply be identified with Thoth: "he is simply called a god; he is Thoth, *the strongest of the gods.*"[37]

The hierarchical opposition between son and father, subject and king, death and life, writing and speech, etc., naturally completes its system with that between night and day, West and East, moon, and sun. Thoth, the "nocturnal representative of Ra, the bull among the stars,"[38] turns toward the west. He is the god of the moon, either as identified with it or as its protector.[39]

The system of these traits brings into play an original kind of logic: the figure of Thoth is opposed to its other (father, sun, life, speech, origin or

35. Morenz, pp. 47–48.
36. Erman, p. 249.
37. Ibid. p. 250.
38. Ibid. p. 41.
39. Boylan, pp. 62–75; Vandier, p. 65; Morenz, p. 54; Festugière, p. 67.

orient, etc.), but as that which at once supplements and supplants it. Thoth extends or opposes by repeating or replacing. By the same token, the figure of Thoth takes shape and takes its shape from the very thing it resists and substitutes for. But it thereby opposes *itself*, passes into its other, and this messenger-god is truly a god of the absolute passage between opposites. If he had any identity—but he is precisely the god of nonidentity—he would be that *coincidentia oppositorum* to which we will soon have recourse again. In distinguishing himself from his opposite, Thoth also imitates it, becomes its sign and representative, obeys it and *conforms* to it, replaces it, by violence if need be. He is thus the father's other, the father, and the subversive movement of replacement. The god of writing is thus at once his father, his son, and himself. He cannot be assigned a fixed spot in the play of differences. Sly, slippery, and masked, an intriguer and a card, like Hermes, he is neither king nor jack, but rather a sort of *joker*, a floating signifier, a wild card, one who puts play into play.

This god of resurrection is less interested in life or death than in death as a repetition of life and life as a rehearsal of death, in the awakening of life and in the recommencement of death. This is what *numbers*, of which he is also the inventor and patron, mean. Thoth repeats everything in the addition of the supplement: in adding to and doubling as the sun, he is other than the sun and the same as it; other than the good and the same, etc. Always taking a place not his own, a place one could call that of the dead or the dummy, he has neither a proper place nor a proper name. His propriety or property is impropriety or inappropriateness, the floating indetermination that allows for substitution and play. *Play*, of which he is also the inventor, as Plato himself reminds us. It is to him that we owe the games of dice (*kubeia*) and draughts (*petteia*) (274*d*). He would be the mediating movement of dialectics if he did not also mimic it, indefinitely preventing it, through this ironic doubling, from reaching some final fulfillment or eschatological reappropriation. Thoth is never present. Nowhere does he appear in person. No being-there can properly be *his own*.

Every act of his is marked by this unstable ambivalence. This god of calculation, arithmetic, and rational science[40] also presides over the occult sciences, astrology and alchemy. He is the god of magic formulas that calm the sea, of secret accounts, of hidden texts: an archetype of Hermes, god of cryptography no less than of every other -graphy.

---

40. Morenz, p. 95. Another of Thoth's companions is Maat, goddess of truth. She is also "daughter of Ra, mistress of the sky, she who governs the double country, the eye of Ra which has no match." Erman, in the page devoted to Maat, notes: ". . . . one of her insignia, God knows why, was a vulture feather" (p. 82).

Science and magic, the passage between life and death, the supplement to evil and to lack: the privileged domain of Thoth had, finally, to be medicine. All his powers are summed up and find employment there. The god of writing, who knows how to put an end to life, can also heal the sick. And even the dead.[41] The steles of Horus on the Crocodiles tell of how the king of the gods sends Thoth down to heal Harsiesis, who has been bitten by a snake in his mother's absence.[42]

The god of writing is thus also a god of medicine. Of "medicine": both a science and an occult drug. Of the remedy and the poison. The god of writing is the god of the *pharmakon*. And it is writing as a *pharmakon* that he presents to the king in the *Phaedrus*, with a humility as unsettling as a dare.

41. Vandier, pp. 71 ff. Cf. especially Festugière, pp. 287 ff. where a number of texts on Thoth as the inventor of magic are assembled. One of them, which particularly interests us, begins: "A formula to be recited *before the sun*: 'I am Thoth, inventor and creator of philters and letters, etc.' " (292).

42. Vandier, p. 230. Cryptography, medicinal magic, and the figure of the serpent are in fact intertwined in an astonishing folk tale transcribed by G. Maspéro in *Les Contes populaires de l'Egypte ancienne* (Paris: E. Guilmoro, 1911). It is the tale of Satni-Khamois and the mummies. Satni-Khamois, the son of a king, "spent his days running about the metropolis of Memphis so as to read the books written in sacred script and the books of the *Double House of Life*. One day a nobleman came along and made fun of him. −'Why are you laughing at me?' The nobleman said: − 'I am not laughing at you; but can I help laughing when you spend your time here deciphering writings that have no powers? If you really wish to read effective writing, come with me; I will send you to the place where you will find the book which Thoth himself has written with his own hand and which will place you just below the gods. There are two formulas written in it: if you recite the first, you will charm the sky, the earth, the world of night, the mountains, the waters; you will understand what the birds of the sky and the reptiles are all saying, as they are; you will see the fish, for a divine force will make them rise to the surface of the water. If you read the second formula, even if you are in the grave you will reassume the form you had on earth; even shall you see the sun rising in the sky, and its cycle, and the moon in the form it has when it appears.' Satni cried; 'By my life! let me know what you wish and I will have it granted you; but take me to the place where I can find the book!' The nobleman said to Satni: 'The book in question is not mine. It is in the heart of the necropolis, in the tomb of Nenoferkeptah, son of king Minebptah. . . . Take great heed not to take this book away from him, for he would have you bring it back, a pitchfork and a rod in his hand, a lighted brazier on his head. . . . ' Deep inside the tomb, light was shining out of the book. The doubles of the king and of his family were beside him, 'through the virtues of the book of Thoth.' . . . All this was repeating itself. Nenoferkeptah had already himself lived Satni's story. The priest had told him: 'The book in question is in the middle of the sea of Coptos, in an iron casket. The iron casket is inside a bronze casket; the bronze casket is inside a casket of cinnamon wood; the casket of cinnamon wood is inside a casket of ivory and ebony. The casket of ivory and ebony is inside a silver casket. The silver casket is inside a golden casket, and the book is found therein. [Scribe's error? the first version I consulted had consigned or reproduced it; a later edition of Maspéro's book pointed it out in a note: "The scribe has made a mistake here in his enumeration. He should have said: *inside* the iron casket is . . . etc." (Item left as evidence for a logic of inclusion).] And there is a schoene [in Ptolemy's day, equal to about 12,000 royal cubits of

4. The Pharmakon

This is the malady in them all for which law must find a pharmakon. Now it is a sound old adage that it is hard to fight against two enemies at once—even when they are enemies from opposite quarters. We see the truth of this in medicine and elsewhere.

Let us return to the text of Plato, assuming we have ever really left it. The word *pharmakon* is caught in a chain of significations. The play of that chain seems systematic. But the system here is not, simply, that of the intentions of an author who goes by the name of Plato. The system is not primarily that of what someone *meant-to-say* [*un vouloir-dire*]. Finely regulated communications are established, through the play of language, among diverse functions of the word and, within it, among diverse strata or regions of culture. These communications or corridors of meaning can sometimes be declared or clarified by Plato when he plays upon them "voluntarily," a

0.52m] of serpents, scorpions of all kinds, and reptiles around the casket in which the book lies, and there is an immortal serpent coiled around the casket in question. ' " After three tries, the imprudent hero kills the serpent, drinks the book dissolved in beer, and thus acquires limitless knowledge. Thoth goes to Ra to complain, and provokes the worst of punishments.

Let us note, finally, before leaving the Egyptian figure of Thoth, that he possesses, in addition to Hermes of Greece, a remarkable counterpart in the figure of Nabu, son of Marduk. In Babylonian and Assyrian mythology, "Nabu is essentially the son-god and, just as Marduk eclipses his father, Ea, we will see Nabu usurping Marduk's place." (E. Dhorme, *Les Religions de Babylonie et d'Assyrie* [Paris: Presses Universitaires de France], pp. 150 ff.) Marduk, the father of Nabu, is the sun-god. Nabu, "lord of the reed," "creator of writing," "bearer of the tables of the fates of the gods," sometimes goes ahead of his father from whom he borrows the symbolic instrument, the *marru*. "A votive object made of copper, uncovered in Susa, representing 'a snake holding in its mouth a sort of pall,' was marked with the inscription 'the marru of the god Nabu' " (Dhorme, p. 155). Cf. also M. David, *Les Dieux et le Destin en Babylonie* (Paris: P.U.F., 1949), pp. 86 ff.

One could spell out one by one the points of resemblance between Thoth and the biblical Nabu (Nebo).

word we put in quotation marks because what it designates, to content ourselves with remaining within the closure of these oppositions, is only a mode of "submission" to the necessities of a given "language." None of these concepts can translate the relation we are aiming at here. Then again, in other cases, Plato can *not* see the links, can leave them in the shadow or break them up. And yet these links go on working of themselves. In spite of him? thanks to him? in *his* text? *outside* his text? but then where? between his text and the language? for what reader? at what moment? To answer such questions in principle and in general will seem impossible; and that will give us the suspicion that there is some malformation in the question itself, in each of its concepts, in each of the oppositions it thus accredits. One can always choose to believe that if Plato did not put certain possibilities of passage into practice, or even interrupted them, it is because he perceived them but left them in the impracticable. This formulation is possible only if one avoids all recourse to the difference between conscious and unconscious, voluntary and involuntary, a very crude tool for dealing with relations in and to language. The same would be true of the opposition between speech—or writing—and language if that opposition, as is often the case, harked back to the above categories.

This reason alone should already suffice to prevent us from reconstituting the entire chain of significations of the *pharmakon*. No absolute privilege allows us absolutely to master its textual system. This limitation can and should nevertheless be displaced to a certain extent. The possibilities and powers of displacement are extremely diverse in nature, and, rather than enumerating here all their titles, let us attempt to produce some of their effects as we go along, as we continue our march through the Platonic problematic of writing.[43]

We have just sketched out the correspondence between the figure of Thoth in Egyptian mythology and a certain organization of concepts, philosophemes, metaphors, and mythemes picked up from what is called the Platonic text. The word *pharmakon* has seemed to us extremely apt for the task of tying all the threads of this correspondence together. Let us now reread, in a rendering derived from Robin, this sentence from the *Phaedrus*: "Here, O King, says Theuth, is a discipline (*mathēma*) that will make the Egyptians wiser (*sophōterous*) and will improve their memories (*mnēmonikōter-*

---

43. I take the liberty of referring the reader, in order to give him a preliminary, indicative direction, to the "Question of Method" proposed in *De la grammatologie* [translated by Gayatri Spivak as *Of Grammatology* (Baltimore: The Johns Hopkins University Press, 1976)]. With a few precautions, one could say that *pharmakon* plays a role *analogous*, in this reading of Plato, to that of *supplément* in the reading of Rousseau.

ous): both memory (*mnēmē*) and instruction (*sophia*) have found their remedy (*pharmakon*)."

The common translation of *pharmakon* by *remedy* [*remède*]—a beneficent drug—is not, of course, inaccurate. Not only can *pharmakon* really mean *remedy* and thus erase, on a certain surface of its functioning, the ambiguity of its meaning. But it is even quite obvious here, the stated intention of Theuth being precisely to stress the worth of his product, that he *turns* the word on its strange and invisible pivot, presenting it from a single one, the most reassuring, of its *poles*. This medicine is beneficial; it repairs and produces, accumulates and remedies, increases knowledge and reduces forgetfulness. Its translation by "remedy" nonetheless erases, in going outside the Greek language, the other pole reserved in the word *pharmakon*. It cancels out the resources of ambiguity and makes more difficult, if not impossible, an understanding of the context. As opposed to "drug" or even "medicine," *remedy* says the transparent rationality of science, technique, and therapeutic causality, thus excluding from the text any leaning toward the magic virtues of a force whose effects are hard to master, a dynamics that constantly surprises the one who tries to manipulate it as master and as subject.

Now, *on the one hand*, Plato is bent on presenting writing as an occult, and therefore suspect, power. Just like painting, to which he will later compare it, and like optical illusions and the techniques of *mimēsis* in general. His mistrust of the mantic and magic, of sorcerers and casters of spells, is well attested.[44] In the *Laws*, in particular, he reserves them terrible punishments. According to an operation we will have cause to remember later, he recommends that they be excluded—expelled or cut off—from the social arena. Expulsion and ostracism can even be accomplished at the same time, by keeping them in prison, where they would no longer be visited by free men but only by the slave that would bring them their food; then by depriving them of burial: "At death he shall be cast out beyond the borders without burial, and if any free citizen has a hand in his burial, he shall be liable to a prosecution for impiety at the suit of any who cares to take proceedings" (X, 909*b–c*).

On the other hand, the King's reply presupposes that the effectiveness of the *pharmakon* can be reversed: it can worsen the ill instead of remedy it. Or rather, the royal answer suggests that Theuth, by ruse and/or naïveté, has exhibited the reverse of the true effects of writing. In order to vaunt the

44. Cf. in particular *Republic* II, 364 ff; Letter VII, 333*e*. The problem is raised with copious and useful references in E. Moutsopoulos, *La Musique dans l'œuvre de Platon* (Paris: Presses Universitaires de France, 1959), pp. 13 ff.

worth of his invention, Theuth would thus have denatured the *pharmakon*, said the opposite (*tounantion*) of what writing is capable of. He has passed a poison off as a remedy. So that in translating *pharmakon* by *remedy*, what one respects is not what Theuth intended, nor even what Plato intended, but rather what the King says Theuth has said, effectively deluding either the King or himself. If Plato's text then goes on to give the King's pronouncement as the truth of Theuth's production and his speech as the truth of writing, then the translation *remedy* makes Theuth into a simpleton or a flimflam artist, *from the sun's point of view*. From that viewpoint, Theuth has no doubt played on the word, interrupting, for his own purposes, the communication between the two opposing values. But the King restores that communication, and the translation takes no account of this. And all the while the two interlocutors, whatever they do and whether or not they choose, remain within the unity of the same signifier. Their discourse plays within it, which is no longer the case in translation. *Remedy* is the rendition that, more than "medicine" or "drug" would have done, obliterates the virtual, dynamic references to the other uses of the same word in Greek. The effect of such a translation is most importantly to destroy what we will later call Plato's anagrammatic writing, to destroy it by interrupting the relations interwoven among different functions of the same word in different places, relations that are virtually but necessarily "citational." When a word inscribes itself as the citation of another sense of the same word, when the textual center-stage of the word *pharmakon*, even while it means *remedy*, cites, re-cites, and makes legible that which *in the same word* signifies, in another spot and on a different level of the stage, *poison* (for example, since that it not the only other thing *pharmakon* means), the choice of only one of these renditions by the translator has as its first effect the neutralization of the citational play, of the "anagram," and, in the end, quite simply of the very textuality of the translated text. It could no doubt be shown, and we will try to do so when the time comes, that this blockage of the passage among opposing values is itself already an effect of "Platonism," the consequence of something already at work in the translated text, in the relation between "Plato" and his "language." There is no contradiction between this proposition and the preceding one. Textuality being constituted by differences and by differences from differences, it is by nature absolutely heterogeneous and is constantly composing with the forces that tend to annihilate it.

One must therefore accept, follow, and analyze the composition of these two forces or of these two gestures. That composition is even, in a certain sense, the single theme of this essay. On the one hand Plato decides in favor of a logic that does not tolerate such passages between opposing senses of the same word, all the more so since such a passage would reveal itself to be something quite different from simple confusion, alternation, or the dialectic of opposites. And yet, on the other hand, the *pharmakon*, if our reading confirms itself, constitutes the original medium of that decision, the element that precedes it, comprehends it, goes beyond it, can never be reduced to it, and is not separated from it by a single word (or signifying apparatus), operating within the Greek and Platonic text. All translations into languages that are the heirs and depositaries of Western metaphysics thus produce on the *pharmakon* an *effect of analysis* that violently destroys it, reduces it to one of its simple elements by interpreting it, paradoxically enough, in the light of the ulterior developments it itself has made possible. Such an interpretative translation is thus as violent as it is impotent: it destroys the *pharmakon* but at the same time forbids itself access to it, leaving it untouched in its reserve.

The translation by "remedy" can thus be neither accepted nor simply rejected. Even if one intended thereby to save the "rational" pole and the laudatory intention, the idea of the *correct* use of the *science* or *art* of medicine, one would still run every risk of being deceived by language. Writing is no more valuable, says Plato, as a remedy than as a poison. Even before Thamus has let fall his pejorative sentence, the remedy is disturbing in itself. One must indeed be aware of the fact that Plato is suspicious of the *pharmakon* in general, even in the case of drugs used exclusively for therapeutic ends, even when they are wielded with good intentions, and even when they are as such effective. There is no such thing as a harmless remedy. The *pharmakon* can never be simply beneficial.

For two different reasons, and at two different depths. First of all because the beneficial essence or virtue of a *pharmakon* does not prevent it from hurting. The *Protagoras* classes the *pharmaka* among the things than can be both good (*agatha*) and painful (*aniara*) (354a). The *pharmakon* is always caught in the mixture (*summeikton*) mentioned in the *Philebus* (46a), examples of which are *hubris*, that violent, unbounded excess of pleasure that makes the profligate cry out like a madman (45e), and "relieving an itch by rubbing, and anything that can be treated by such a remedy (*ouk allēs deomena pharmaxeōs*)." This type of painful pleasure, linked as much to the malady as to its treatment, is a *pharmakon* in itself. It partakes of both good and ill, of the agreeable and the disagreeable. Or rather, it is within its mass that these oppositions are able to sketch themselves out.

Then again, more profoundly, even beyond the question of pain, the pharmaceutical remedy is essentially harmful because it is artificial. In this,

Plato is following Greek tradition and, more precisely, the doctors of Cos. The *pharmakon* goes against natural life: not only life unaffected by any illness, but even sick life, or rather the life of the sickness. For Plato believes in the natural life and normal development, so to speak, of disease. In the *Timaeus*, natural disease, like *logos* in the *Phaedrus*, is compared to a living organism which must be allowed to develop according to its own norms and forms, its specific rhythms and articulations. In disturbing the normal and natural progress of the illness, the *pharmakon* is thus the enemy of the living in general, whether healthy or sick. One must bear this in mind, and Plato invites us to do so, when writing is proposed as a *pharmakon*. Contrary to life, writing—or, if you will, the *pharmakon*—can only *displace* or even *aggravate* the ill. Such will be, in its logical outlines, the objection the king raises to writing: under pretext of supplementing memory, writing makes one even more forgetful; far from increasing knowledge, it diminishes it. Writing does not answer the needs of memory, it aims to the side, does not reinforce the *mnēmē*, but only *hypomnēsis*. And if, in the two texts we are now going to look at together, the formal structure of the argument is indeed the same; if in both cases what is supposed to produce the positive and eliminate the negative does nothing but *displace* and at the same time *multiply* the effects of the negative, leading the lack that was its cause to proliferate, the necessity for this is inscribed in the *sign pharmakon*, which Robin (for example) dismembers, here as remedy, there as drug. We expressly said the *sign pharmakon*, intending thereby to mark that what is in question is *indissociably* a signifier and a concept signified.

A) In the *Timaeus*, which spreads itself out, from its opening pages, in the space between Egypt and Greece as in that between writing and speech ("You Hellenes are never anything but children, and there is not an old man among you," whereas in Egypt "everything has been written down by us of old": *panta gegrammena* [22*b*, 23*a*]), Plato demonstrates that, among all the body's movements, the best is natural motion, which spontaneously, from within, "is produced in a thing by itself":

> Now of all motions that is the best which is produced in a thing by itself, for it is most akin to the motion of thought and of the universe, but that motion which is caused by others is not so good, and worst of all is that which moves the body, when at rest, in parts only and by some agency alien to it. Wherefore of all modes of purifying and reuniting the body the best is gymnastics; the next best is a surging motion, as in sailing or any other mode of conveyance which is not

fatiguing; the third sort of motion may be of use in a case of extreme necessity, but in any other will be adopted by no man of sense—I mean the purgative treatment (*tēs pharmakeutikēs katharseōs*) of physicians; for diseases unless they are very dangerous should not be irritated by medicines (*ouk erethisteon pharmakeiais*), since every form of disease is in a manner akin to the living being (*tēi tōn zōōn phusei*), whose complex frame (*sustasis*) has an appointed term of life. For not the whole race only, but each individual—barring inevitable accidents—comes into the world having a fixed span. . . . And this holds also of the constitution of diseases; if anyone regardless of the appointed time tries to subdue them by medicine (*pharmakeiais*), he only aggravates and multiplies them. Wherefore we ought always to manage them by regimen, as far as a man can spare the time, and not provoke a disagreeable enemy by medicines (*pharmakeuonta*) (89*a–d*)

The reader will have noted that:

1. The noxiousness of the *pharmakon* is indicted at the precise moment the entire context seems to authorize its translation by "remedy" rather than poison.

2. The natural illness of the living is defined in its essence as an *allergy*, a reaction to the aggression of an alien element. And it is necessary that the most general concept of disease should be allergy, from the moment the natural life of the body ought only to follow its own endogenous motions.

3. Just as health is auto-nomous and auto-matic, "normal" disease demonstrates its autarky by confronting the pharmaceutical aggression with *metastatic* reactions which displace the site of the disease, with the eventual result that the points of resistance are reinforced and multiplied. "Normal" disease defends itself. In thus escaping the supplementary constraints, the superadded pathogeny of the *pharmakon*, the disease continues to follow its own course.

4. This schema implies that the living being is finite (and its malady as well): that it can have a relation with its other, then, in the allergic reaction, that it has a limited lifetime, that death is already inscribed and prescribed within its structure, in its "constitutive triangles." ("The triangles in us are originally framed with the power to last for a certain time beyond which no man can prolong his life." Ibid.) The immortality and perfection of a living being would consist in its having no relation at all with any outside. That is the case with God (cf. *Republic* II, 381*b–c*). God has no allergies. Health and virtue (*hugieia kai aretē*), which are often associated in speaking of the body and, analogously, of the soul (cf. *Gorgias*, 479*b*), always proceed from

within. The *pharmakon* is that which, always springing up from without, acting like the outside itself, will never have any definable virtue of its own. But how can this supplementary parasite be excluded by maintaining the boundary, or, let us say, the triangle?

B) The system of these four features is reconstituted when, in the *Phaedrus*, King Thamus depresses and depreciates the *pharmakon* of writing, a word that should thus not too hastily be considered a metaphor, unless the metaphorical possibility is allowed to retain all its power of enigma. Perhaps we can now read the King's response:

> But the king said, "Theuth, my master of arts (*Ō tekhnikōtate Theuth*), to one man it is given to create the elements of an art, to another to judge the extent of harm and usefulness it will have for those who are going to employ it. And now, since you are father of written letters (*patēr ōn grammatōn*), your paternal goodwill has led you to pronounce the very opposite (*tounantion*) of what is their real power. The fact is that this invention will produce forgetfulness in the souls of those who have learned it because they will not need to exercise their memories (*lēthēn men en psuchais parexei mnēmēs ameletēsiai*), being able to rely on what is written, using the stimulus of external marks that are alien to themselves (*dia pistin graphēs exōthen hup' allotriōn tupōn*) rather than, from within, their own unaided powers to call things to mind (*ouk endothen autous huph' hautōn anamimnēskomenous*). So it's not a remedy for memory, but for reminding, that you have discovered (*oukoun mnēmēs, alla hupomnēseōs, pharmakon hēures*). And as for wisdom (*sophias de*), you're equipping your pupils with only a semblance (*doxan*) of it, not with truth (*alētheian*). Thanks to you and your invention, your pupils will be widely read without benefit of a teacher's instruction; in consequence, they'll entertain the delusion that they have wide knowledge, while they are, in fact, for the most part incapable of real judgment. They will also be difficult to get on with since they will be men filled with the conceit of wisdom (*doxosophoi*), not men of wisdom (*anti sophōn*)." (274e – 275b)

The king, the father of speech, has thus asserted his authority over the father of writing. And he has done so with severity, without showing the one who occupies the place of his son any of that paternal good will exhibited by Theuth toward his own children, his "letters." Thamus presses on, multiplies his reservations, and visibly wants to leave Theuth no hope.

In order for writing to produce, as he says, the "opposite" effect from what one might expect, in order for this *pharmakon* to show itself, with use, to be injurious, its effectiveness, its power, its *dunamis* must, of course, be ambiguous. As is said of the *pharmakon* in the *Protagoras*, the *Philebus*, the *Timaeus*. It is precisely this ambiguity that Plato, through the mouth of the King, attempts to master, to dominate by inserting its definition into simple, clear-cut oppositions: good and evil, inside and outside, true and false, essence and appearance. If one rereads the reasons adduced by the royal sentence, one will find this series of oppositions there. And set in place in such a way that the *pharmakon*, or, if you will, writing, can only go around in circles: writing is only apparently good for memory, seemingly able to help it from within, through its own motion, to know what is true. But in truth, writing is essentially bad, external to memory, productive not of science but of belief, not of truth but of appearances. The *pharmakon* produces a play of appearances which enable it to pass for truth, etc.

But while, in the *Philebus* and the *Protagoras*, the *pharmakon*, because it is painful, seems bad whereas it is beneficial, here, in the *Phaedrus* as in the *Timaeus*, it is passed off as a helpful remedy whereas it is in truth harmful. Bad ambiguity is thus opposed to good ambiguity, a deceitful intention to a mere appearance. Writing's case is grave.

It is not enough to say that writing is conceived out of this or that series of oppositions. Plato thinks of writing, and tries to comprehend it, to dominate it, on the basis of *opposition* as such. In order for these contrary values (good/evil, true/false, essence/appearance, inside/outside, etc.) to be in opposition, each of the terms must be simply *external* to the other, which means that one of these oppositions (the opposition between inside and outside) must already be accredited as the matrix of all possible opposition. And one of the elements of the system (or of the series) must also stand as the very possibility of systematicity or seriality in general. And if one got to thinking that something like the *pharmakon*—or writing—far from being governed by these oppositions, opens up their very possibility without letting itself be comprehended by them; if one got to thinking that it can only be out of something like writing—or the *pharmakon*—that the strange difference between inside and outside can spring; if, consequently, one got to thinking that writing as a *pharmakon* cannot simply be assigned a site within what it situates, cannot be subsumed under concepts whose contours it draws, leaves only its ghost to a logic that can only seek to govern it insofar as logic arises from it—one would then have to *bend* [*plier*] into strange contortions what could no longer even simply be called logic or discourse. All the more so if what we have just imprudently called a *ghost* can no longer be distinguished, with the same assurance, from truth, reality, living flesh, etc. One must accept the fact that here, for once, to leave a ghost behind will in a sense be to salvage nothing.

This little exercise will no doubt have sufficed to warn the reader: to come to an understanding with Plato, as it is sketched out in this text, is already to slip away from the recognized models of commentary, from the genealogical or structural reconstitution of a system, whether this reconstitution tries to corroborate or refute, confirm or "overturn," mark a return-to-Plato or give him a "send-off" in the quite Platonic manner of the *khairein*. What is going on here is something altogether different. That too, of course, but still completely other. If the reader has any doubt, he is invited to reread the preceding paragraph. Every model of classical reading is exceeded there at some point, precisely at the point where it attaches to the inside of the series—it being understood that this excess is not a *simple* exit *out* of the series, since that would obviously fall under one of the categories of the series. The excess—but can we still call it that?—is only a *certain* displacement of the series. And a certain *folding back* [*repli*]—which will later be called a *re-mark*—of opposition within the series, or even within its dialectic. We cannot qualify it, name it, comprehend it under a simple concept without immediately being off the mark. Such a functional displacement, which concerns differences (and, as we shall see, "simulacra") more than any conceptual identities signified, is a real and necessary challenge. It writes itself. One must therefore begin by reading it.

If writing, according to the king and under the sun, produces the opposite effect from what is expected, if the *pharmakon* is pernicious, it is because, like the one in the *Timaeus*, it doesn't come from around here. It comes from afar, it is external or alien: to the living, which is the right-here of the inside, to *logos* as the *zōon* it claims to assist or relieve. The imprints (*tupoi*) of writing do not inscribe themselves this time, as they do in the hypothesis of the *Theaetetus*, in the wax of the soul *in intaglio*, thus corresponding to the spontaneous, autochthonous motions of psychic life. Knowing that he can always leave his thoughts outside or check them with an external agency, with the physical, spatial, superficial marks that one lays flat on a tablet, he who has the *tekhnē* of writing at his disposal will come to rely on it. He will know that he himself can leave without the *tupoi*'s going away, that he can forget all about them without their leaving his service. They will represent him even if he forgets them; they will transmit his word even if he is not there to animate them. Even if he is dead, and only a *pharmakon* can be the wielder of such power, *over* death but also in cahoots with it. The *pharmakon* and writing are thus always involved in questions of life and death.

Can it be said without conceptual anachronism—and thus without serious interpretive error—that the *tupoi* are the representatives, the *physical* surrogates of the *psychic* that is absent? It would be better to assert that the written traces no longer even belong to the order of the *phusis*, since they are not alive. They do not grow; they grow no more than what could be sown, as Socrates will say in a minute, with a reed (*kalamos*). They do violence to the natural, autonomous organization of the *mnēmē*, in which *phusis* and *psuchē* are not opposed. If writing does belong to the *phusis*, wouldn't it be to that moment of the *phusis*, to that necessary movement through which its truth, the production of its appearing, tends, says Heraclitus, to take shelter in its crypt? "Cryptogram" thus condenses in a single word a pleonastic proposition.

If one takes the king's word for it, then, it is this life of the memory that the *pharmakon* of writing would come to hypnotize: fascinating it, taking it out of itself by putting it to sleep in a monument. Confident of the permanence and independence of its *types* (*tupoi*), memory will fall asleep, will not keep itself up, will no longer keep to keeping itself alert, present, as close as possible to the truth of what is. Letting itself get stoned [*médusée*] by its own signs, its own guardians, by the types committed to the keeping and surveillance of knowledge, it will sink down into *lēthē*, overcome by non-knowledge and forgetfulness.[45] Memory and truth cannot be separated. The movement of *alētheia* is a deployment of *mnēmē* through and through. A deployment of living memory, of memory as psychic life in its self-presentation to itself. The powers of *lēthē* simultaneously increase the domains of death, of nontruth, of nonknowledge. This is why writing, at least insofar as it sows "forgetfulness in the soul," turns us toward the inanimate and toward nonknowledge. But it cannot be said that its essence simply and *presently* confounds it with death or nontruth. For writing *has* no essence or value of its own, whether positive or negative. It plays within the simulacrum. It is in its type the mime of memory, of knowledge, of truth, etc. That is why men of writing appear before the eye of God not as wise men (*sophoi*) but in truth as fake or self-proclaimed wise men (*doxosophoi*).

45. We would here like to refer the reader in particular to the extremely rich text by Jean-Pierre Vernant (who deals with these questions with quite different intentions): "Aspects mythiques de la mémoire et du temps," in *Mythe et Pensée chez les Grecs* (Paris: Maspéro, 1965). On the word *tupos*, its relations with *perigraphē* and *paradeigma*, cf. A. von Blumenthal, *Tupos und Paradeigma*, quoted by P. M. Schuhl, in *Platon et l'art de son temps*, (Paris: Presses Universitaires de France, 1952), p. 18, n. 4.

This is Plato's definition of the sophist. For it is above all against sophistics that this diatribe against writing is directed: it can be inscribed within the interminable trial instituted by Plato, under the name of philosophy, against the sophists. The man who relies on writing, who brags about the knowledge and powers it assures him, this simulator unmasked by Thamus has all the features of a sophist: "the imitator of him who knows," as the *Sophist* puts it (*mimētēs tou sophou*, 268 c). He whom we would call the graphocrat is as much like the sophist Hippias as a brother. Like the Hippias we see in the *Lesser Hippias*, he boasts about knowing and doing all. And mainly—which Socrates twice, in two different dialogues, ironically pretends he has forgotten to include in his list—about having a better understanding than anyone else of mnemonics and mnemotechnics. This is indeed the power he considers his pride and joy:

> *Socrates*: Then in astronomy also, the same man will be true and false?
> *Hippias*: It would seem so.
> *Socrates*: And now, Hippias, consider the question at large about all
> the sciences, and see whether the same principle does not always
> hold. I know that in most arts you are the wisest (*sophōtatos*) of men,
> as I have heard you boasting in the Agora at the tables of the
> money-changers, when you were setting forth the great and envi-
> able stores of your wisdom. . . . Moreover, you told us that you had
> brought with you poems, epic, tragic, and dithyrambic, as well as
> prose writings of the most various kinds, and you said that your
> skill was also pre-eminent in the arts which I was just now mention-
> ing, and in the true principles of rhythm and harmony and of
> orthography. And, if I remember rightly, there were a great many
> other accomplishments in which you excelled. I have forgotten to
> mention your art of memory, which you regard as your special
> glory, and I dare say that I have forgotten many other things, but,
> as I was saying, only look to your own arts—and there are plenty of
> them—and to those of others, and tell me, having regard to the
> admissions which you and I have made, whether you discover any
> department of art or any description of wisdom or cunning,
> whichever name you use, in which the true and false are different
> and not the same. Tell me, if you can, of any. But you cannot.
> *Hippias*: Not without consideration, Socrates.
> *Socrates*: Nor will consideration help you, Hippias, as I believe, but
> then if I am right, remember what the consequence will be.
> *Hippias*: I do not know what you mean, Socrates.

> *Socrates*: I suppose that you are not using your art of memory . . .
> (368*a–d*).

The sophist thus sells the signs and insignia of science: not memory itself
(*mnēmē*), only monuments (*hypomnēmata*), inventories, archives, citations,
copies, accounts, tales, lists, notes, duplicates, chronicles, genealogies,
references. Not memory but memorials. He thus answers the demands of
the wealthy young men, and that is where he is most warmly applauded.
After admitting that his young admirers cannot stand to hear him speak of
the greater part of his knowledge (*Greater Hippias*, 285*c–d*), the sophist
must tell Socrates all:

> *Socrates*: What then are the subjects on which they listen to you with
> pleasure and applause? Pray enlighten me; I cannot see.
> *Hippias*: They delight in the genealogies of heroes and of men and in
> stories of the foundations of cities in olden times, and, to put it
> briefly, in all forms of antiquarian lore, so that because of them I
> have been compelled to acquire a thorough comprehension and
> mastery of all that branch of learning.
> *Socrates*: Bless my soul, you have certainly been lucky that the Lace-
> daemonians do not want to hear a recital of the list of our archons,
> from Solon downward; you would have had some trouble learning
> it.
> *Hippias*: Why? I can repeat fifty names after hearing them once.
> *Socrates*: I am sorry, I quite forgot about your mnemonic art . . .
> (285*d–e*).

In truth, the sophist only pretends to know everything; his "polymathy"
(*The Sophist*, 232*a*) is never anything but pretense. Insofar as writing *lends a
hand* to hypomnesia and not to live memory, it, too, is foreign to true
science, to anamnesia in its properly psychic motion, to truth in the process
of (its) presentation, to dialectics. Writing can only *mime* them. (It could be
shown, but we will spare ourselves the development here, that the problematic that today, and in this very spot, links writing with the (putting in)
question of truth—and of thought and speech, which are informed by
it—must necessarily exhume, without remaining at that, the conceptual
monuments, the vestiges of the battlefield (*champ de bataille*), the signposts
marking out the battle lines between sophistics and philosophy, and, more
generally, all the buttresses erected by Platonism. In many ways, and from
a viewpoint that does not cover the entire field, we are today on the eve of
Platonism. Which can also, naturally, be thought of as the morning after

Hegelianism. At that specific point, the *philosophia*, the *epistēmē* are not "overturned," "rejected," "reined in," etc., in the name of something like writing; quite the contrary. But they are, according to a relation that philosophy would call *simulacrum*, according to a more subtle excess of truth, assumed and at the same time displaced into a completely different field, where one can still, but that's all, "mime absolute knowledge," to use an expression coined by Bataille, whose name will enable us here to dispense with a whole network of references.)

The front line that is violently inscribed between Platonism and its closest other, in the form of sophistics, is far from being unified, continuous, as if stretched between two homogeneous areas. Its design is such that, through a systematic indecision, the parties and the party lines frequently exchange their respective places, imitating the forms and borrowing the paths of the opponent. These permutations are therefore possible, and if they are obliged to inscribe themselves within some common territory, the dissension no doubt remains internal and casts into absolute shadow some entirely-other of *both* sophistics *and* Platonism, some resistance having no common denominator with this whole commutation.

Contrary to what we have indicated earlier, there are also good reasons for thinking that the diatribe against writing is not aimed first and foremost at the sophists. On the contrary: sometimes it seems to proceed *from* them. Isn't the stricture that one should exercise one's memory rather than entrust traces to an outside agency the imperious and classical recommendation of the sophists? Plato would thus be appropriating here, once again, as he so often does, one of the sophists' argumentations. And here again, he will use it against them. And later on, after the royal judgment, Socrates' whole discourse, which we will take apart stitch by stitch, is woven out of schemes and concepts that issue from sophistics.

One must thus minutely recognize the crossing of the border. And be fully cognizant that this reading of Plato is at no time spurred on by some slogan or password of a "back-to-the-sophists" nature.

Thus, in both cases, on both sides, writing is considered suspicious and the alert exercise of memory prescribed. What Plato is attacking in sophistics, therefore, is not simply recourse to memory but, within such recourse, the substitution of the mnemonic device for live memory, of the prosthesis for the organ; the perversion that consists of replacing a limb by a thing, here, substituting the passive, mechanical "by-heart" for the active reanimation of knowledge, for its reproduction in the present. The boundary (between inside and outside, living and nonliving) separates not only speech from writing but also memory as an unveiling (re-)producing a presence from re-memoration as the mere repetition of a monument; truth as distinct from its sign, being as distinct from types. The "outside" does not begin at the point where what we now call the psychic and the physical meet, but at the point where the *mnēmē*, instead of being present to itself in its life as a movement of truth, is supplanted by the archive, evicted by a sign of re-memoration or of com-memoration. The space of writing, space *as* writing, is opened up in the violent movement of this surrogation, in the difference between *mnēmē* and *hypomnēsis*. The outside is already *within* the work of memory. The evil slips in within the relation of memory to itself, in the general organization of the mnesic activity. Memory is finite by nature. Plato recognizes this in attributing life to it. As in the case of all living organisms, he assigns it, as we have seen, certain limits. A limitless memory would in any event be not memory but infinite self-presence. Memory always therefore already needs signs in order to recall the non-present, with which it is necessarily in relation. The movement of dialectics bears witness to this. Memory is thus contaminated by its first substitute: *hypomnēsis*. But what Plato *dreams* of is a memory with no sign. That is, with no supplement. A *mnēmē* with no *hypomnēsis*, no *pharmakon*. And this at the very moment and for the very reason that he calls *dream* the confusion between the hypothetical and the anhypothetical in the realm of mathematical intelligibility (*Republic*, 533*b*).

Why is the surrogate or supplement dangerous? It is not, so to speak, dangerous in itself, in that aspect of it that can present itself as a thing, as a being-present. In that case it would be reassuring. But here, the supplement *is* not, is not a being (*on*). It is nevertheless not a simple nonbeing (*mē on*), either. Its slidings slip it out of the simple alternative presence/absence. *That* is the danger. And that is what enables the type always to pass for the original. As soon as the supplementary outside is opened, its structure implies that the supplement itself can be "typed," replaced by its double, and that a supplement to the supplement, a surrogate for the surrogate, is possible and necessary. Necessary because this movement is not a sensible, "empirical" accident: it is linked to the ideality of the *eidos* as the possibility of the repetition of the same. And writing appears to Plato (and after him to all of philosophy, which is as such constituted in this gesture) as that process of redoubling in which we are fatally (en)trained: the supplement of a supplement, the signifier, the representative of a representative. (A series whose first term or rather whose first structure does not yet—but we will do it later—have to be *kicked up* [*faire sauter*] and its irreducibility made apparent.) The structure and history of *phonetic* writing have of course played a decisive role in the determination of writing as the doubling of a sign, the sign of a sign. The signifier of a phonic signifier. While the phonic signifier would remain in animate proximity, in the living presence of *mnēmē* or *psuchē*, the graphic signifier, which reproduces it or imitates it, goes one degree further away, falls outside of life, entrains life out of itself and puts it to sleep in the type of its double. Whence the *pharmakon*'s two misdeeds: it dulls the memory, and if it is of any assistance at all, it is not for the *mnēmē* but for *hypomnēsis*. Instead of quickening life in the original, "in person," the *pharmakon* can at best only restore its monuments. It is a debilitating poison for memory, but a remedy or tonic for its external signs, its *symptoms*, with everything that this word can connote in Greek: an empirical, contingent, superficial event, generally a fall or collapse, distinguishing itself like an index from whatever it is pointing to. Your writing cures only the symptom, the King has already said, and it is from him that we know the unbridgable difference between the essence of the symptom and the essence of the signified; and that writing belongs to the order and exteriority of the symptom.

Thus, even though writing is external to (internal) memory, even though hypomnesia is not in itself memory, it affects memory and hypnotizes it in its very inside. That is the effect of this *pharmakon*. If it were purely external, writing would leave the intimacy or integrity of psychic memory untouched. And yet, just as Rousseau and Saussure will do in response to the same necessity, yet without discovering *other* relations between the intimate and the alien, Plato maintains *both* the exteriority of writing *and* its power of maleficent penetration, its ability to affect or infect what lies deepest inside. The *pharmakon* is that dangerous supplement[46] that breaks into the very thing that would have liked to do without it yet lets itself *at once* be breached, roughed up, fulfilled, and replaced, completed by the very trace through which the present increases itself in the act of disappearing.

If, instead of meditating on the structure that makes such supplementarity possible, if above all instead of meditating on the reduction by which "Plato-Rousseau-Saussure" try in vain to master it with an odd kind of "reasoning," one were to content oneself with pointing to the "logical contradiction," one would have to recognize here an instance of that kind of

46. TN. The expression "that dangerous supplement," used by Rousseau in his *Confessions* to describe masturbation, is the title of that chapter in *Of Grammatology* in which Derrida follows the consequences of the way in which the word *supplément*'s two meanings in French — "addition" and "replacement" — complicate the logic of Rousseau's treatment of sex, education, and writing. Writing, pedagogy, masturbation, and the *pharmakon* share the property of being — with respect to speech, nature, intercourse, and living memory — at once something secondary, external, and compensatory, and something that substitutes, violates, and usurps.

"kettle-logic" to which Freud turns in the *Traumdeutung* in order to illustrate the logic of dreams. In his attempt to arrange everything in his favor, the defendant piles up contradictory arguments: 1. The kettle I am returning to you is brand new; 2. The holes were already in it when you lent it to me; 3. You never lent me a kettle, anyway. Analogously: 1. Writing is rigorously exterior and inferior to living memory and speech, which are therefore undamaged by it. 2. Writing is harmful to them because it puts them to sleep and infects their very life which would otherwise remain intact. 3. Anyway, if one has resorted to hypomnesia and writing at all, it is not for their intrinsic value, but because living memory is finite, it already has holes in it before writing ever comes to leave its traces. Writing has no effect on memory.

The opposition between *mnēmē* and *hypomnēsis* would thus preside over the meaning of writing. This opposition will appear to us to form a system with all the great structural oppositions of Platonism. What is played out at the boundary line between these two concepts is consequently something like the major decision of philosophy, the one through which it institutes itself, maintains itself, and contains its adverse deeps.

Nevertheless, between *mnēmē* and *hypomnēsis*, between memory and its supplement, the line is more than subtle; it is hardly perceptible. On both sides of that line, it is a question of *repetition*. Live memory repeats the presence of the *eidos*, and truth is also the possibility of repetition through recall. Truth unveils the *eidos* or the *ontōs on*, in other words, that which can be imitated, reproduced, repeated in its identity. But in the anamnesic movement of truth, what is repeated must present itself as such, as what it is, in repetition. The true is repeated; it is what is repeated in the repetition, what is represented and present in the representation. It is not the repeater in the repetition, nor the signifier in the signification. The true is the presence of the *eidos* signified.

Sophistics—the deployment of hypomnesia—as well as dialectics—the deployment of anamnesia—both presuppose the possibility of repetition. But sophistics this time keeps to the other side, to the other face, as it were, of repetition. And of signification. What is repeated is the repeater, the imitator, the signifier, the representative, in the absence, as it happens, of *the thing itself*, which these appear to reedit, and without psychic or mnesic animation, without the living tension of dialectics. Writing would indeed be the signifier's capacity to repeat itself by itself, mechanically, without a living soul to sustain or attend it in its repetition, that is to say, without truth's *presenting itself* anywhere. Sophistics, hypomnesia, and writing would thus only be separated from philosophy, dialectics, anamnesis, and living speech by the invisible, almost nonexistent, thickness of that *leaf* between the signifier and the signified. The "leaf": a significant metaphor, we should note, or rather one taken from the signifier face of things, since the leaf with its recto and verso first appears as a surface and support for writing. But by the same token, doesn't the unity of this leaf, of the system of this difference between signified and signifier, also point to the inseparability of sophistics and philosophy? The difference between signifier and signified is no doubt the governing pattern within which Platonism institutes itself and determines its opposition to sophistics. In being inaugurated in this manner, philosophy and dialectics are determined in the act of determining their other.

This profound complicity in the break has a first consequence: the argumentation against writing in the *Phaedrus* is able to borrow all its resources from Isocrates or Alcidamas at the moment it turns their own weapons, "transposing" them,[47] against the sophists. Plato imitates the imitators in order to restore the truth of what they imitate: namely, truth itself. Indeed, only truth as the presence (*ousia*) of the present (*on*) is here discriminative. And its power to discriminate, which commands or, as you will, is commanded by the difference between signified and signifier, in any case remains systematically inseparable from that difference. And this discrimination itself becomes so subtle that eventually it separates nothing, in the final analysis, but the same from itself, from its perfect, almost indistinguishable double. This is a movement that produces itself entirely within the structure of ambiguity and reversibility of the *pharmakon*.

How indeed does the dialectician simulate him whom he denounces as a simulator, as the simulacrum-man? On the one hand, the sophists advised, as does Plato, the exercise of memory. But, as we have seen, it was in order to enable themselves to speak without knowing, to recite without judgment, without regard for truth, in order to give signs. Or rather in order to sell them. Through this economy of signs, the sophists are indisputably men of writing at the moment they are protesting they are not. But isn't Plato one, too, through a symmetrical effect of reversal? Not only because he is actually a writer (a banal argument we will specify later on) and cannot, whether *de facto* or *de jure*, explain what dialectics is without recourse to writing; not only because he judges that the repetition of the same is necessary in anamnesis; but also because he judges it indispensable as an inscription in the type. (It is notable that *tupos* applies with equal

47. We are here using Diès's word, referring to his study of *La transposition platonicienne*, more precisely to his first chapter, "la Transposition de la rhétorique," in *Autour de Platon* II, 400.

pertinence to the graphic impression and to the *eidos* as model. Among many other examples, cf. *Republic*, 402*d*). This necessity belongs to the order of the law and is posited by the *Laws*. In this instance, the immutable, petrified identity of writing is not simply added to the signified law or prescribed rule like a mute, stupid simulacrum: it assures the law's permanence and identity with the vigilance of a guardian. As another sort of guardian of the laws, writing guarantees the means of returning at will, as often as necessary, to that ideal object called the law. We can thus scrutinize it, question it, consult it, make it talk, without altering its identity. All this, even in the same words (notably *boētheia*), is the other side, exactly opposite, of Socrates' speech in the *Phaedrus*.

> *Clinias*: And, mark you, such argument will be a most valuable aid to intelligent legislation (*nomothesia*), because legal prescriptions (*prostagmata*), once put into writing (*en grammasi tethenta*), remain always on record, as though to challenge the question of all time to come. Hence we need feel no dismay if they should be difficult on a first hearing, since even the dull student may return to them for reiterated scrutiny. Nor does their length, provided they are beneficial, make it less irrational than it is impious, in my opinion at least, for any man to refuse such discourse his heartiest support (*to mē ou boēthein toutois tois logois*). (X, 891*a*. I am still quoting from an authorized translation,[48] including the Greek where pertinent, and leaving the reader to appreciate the usual effects of translation. On the relation between written and unwritten laws, see notably VII, 7935*b–c*).

The italicized Greek words amply demonstrate it: the *prostagmata* of the law can be *posited* only in writing (*en grammasi tethenta*). *Nomothesia* is engrammatical. The legislator is a writer. And the judge a reader. Let us skip to book XII: "He that would show himself a righteously equal judge must keep these matters before his eyes; he must procure books (*grammata*) on the subject, and must make them his study. There is, in truth, no study whatsoever so potent as this of law, if the law be what it should be, to make a better man of its student" (957*c*).

Inversely, symmetrically, the rhetors had not waited around for Plato in order to *translate writing into judgment*. For Isocrates,[49] for Alcidamas, *logos*

---

48. TN. Derrida is quoting from Diès; I am quoting from A. E. Taylor. Interestingly, another of these "effects of translation" is precisely the difficulty involved in translating a discussion of effects of translation.

49. If one holds, as does Robin, that the *Phaedrus* is, despite certain appearances, "an indictment against the rhetoric of Isocrates" (Introduction to the *Phaedrus*, Budé edition, p. clxxiii) and that the latter is more concerned, whatever he may say, with *doxa* than with

was also a living thing (*zōon*) whose vigor, richness, agility, and flexibility were limited and constrained by the cadaverous rigidity of the written sign. The type does not adapt to the changing givens of the present situation, to what is unique and irreplaceable about it each time, with all the subtlety required. While *presence* is the general form of what is, the *present*, for its part, is always different. But writing, in that it repeats itself and remains identical in the type, cannot flex itself in all senses, cannot bend with all the differences among presents, with all the variable, fluid, furtive necessities of psychagogy. He who speaks, in contrast, is not controlled by any preestablished pattern; he is better able to conduct his signs; he is there to accentuate them, inflect them, retain them, or set them loose according to the demands of the moment, the nature of the desired effect, the hold he has on the listener. In attending his signs in their operation, he who acts by vocal means penetrates more easily into the soul of his disciple, producing

epistēmē (p. clxviii), one will not be surprised by the title of his discourse, "Against the Sophists." Neither will one be amazed to find, for example, this passage, whose formal resemblance with Socrates' argumentation is blinding: "But it is not these sophists alone who are open to criticism, but also those who profess to teach political discourse (*tous politikous logous*). For the latter have no interest whatever in the truth, but consider that they are masters of an art if they can attract great numbers of students by the smallness of their charges . . . [One should note that Isocrates charged very high fees, and know what the price of truth was when it was speaking through his mouth] . . . For they are themselves so stupid and conceive others to be so dull that, although the speeches which they compose are worse than those which some laymen improvise, nevertheless they promise to make their students such clever orators that they will not overlook any of the possibilities which a subject affords. More than that, they do not attribute any of this power either to the practical experience or to the native ability of the student, but undertake to transmit the science of discourse (*tēn tōn logōn epistēmēn*) as simply as they would teach the letters of the alphabet. . . . But I marvel when I observe these men setting themselves up as instructors of youth who cannot see that they are applying the analogy of an art with hard and fast rules to a creative process. For, excepting these teachers, who does not know that the art of using letters remains fixed and unchanged, so that we continually and invariably use the same letters for the same purposes, while exactly the reverse is true of the art of discourse? For what has been said by one speaker is not equally useful for the speaker who comes after him; on the contrary, he is accounted most skilled in this art who speaks in a manner worthy of his subject and yet is able to discover in it topics which are nowise the same as those used by others. But the greatest proof of the difference between these two arts is that oratory is good only if it has the qualities of fitness for the occasion, propriety of style, and originality of treatment, while in the case of letters there is no such need whatsoever." The conclusion: one ought to pay in order to write. Men of writing should never be paid. The ideal would be that they would always put their pockets on the line. That they would pay, since they are in such need of the help of the masters of *logos*. "So that those who make use of such analogies (*paradeigmasin*: letters) ought more justly to pay out than to accept fees, since they attempt to teach others when they are themselves in great need of instruction" (*Kata tōn sophistōn* XIII, 9, 10, 12, 13 [trans. George Norlin, in *Isocrates*, Loeb Classical Library (New York: G.P. Putnam's Sons, 1929) II, 169–71.].

effects that are always unique, leading the disciple, as though lodged within him, to the intended goal. It is thus not its pernicious violence but its breathless impotence that the sophists held against writing. In contrast to this blind servant with its haphazard, clumsy movements, the Attic school (Gorgias, Isocrates, Alcidamas) extolled the force of living *logos*, the great master, the great power: *logos dunastēs megas estin*, says Gorgias in his *Encomium of Helen*. The dynasty of speech may be just as violent as that of writing, but its infiltration is more profound, more penetrating, more diverse, more assured. The only ones who take refuge in writing are those who are no better speakers than the man in the street. Alcidamas recalls this in his treatise "on those who write speeches" and "on the Sophists." Writing is considered a consolation, a compensation, a remedy for sickly speech.

Despite these similarities, the condemnation of writing is not engaged in the same way by the rhetors as it is in the *Phaedrus*. If the written word is scorned, it is not as a *pharmakon* coming to corrupt memory and truth. It is because *logos* is a more effective *pharmakon*. This is what Gorgias calls it. As a *pharmakon*, *logos* is at once good and bad; it is not at the outset governed exclusively by goodness or truth. It is only within this ambivalence and this mysterious indetermination of *logos*, and after these have been recognized, that Gorgias *determines* truth as a *world*, a structure or order, the counterpart (*kosmos*) of *logos*. In so doing he no doubt prefigures the Platonic gesture. But before such a determination, we are in the ambivalent, indeterminate space of the *pharmakon*, of that which in *logos* remains potency, potentiality, and is not yet the transparent language of knowledge. If one were justified in trying to capture it in categories that are subsequent to and dependent upon the history thus opened up, categories arising precisely *in the aftermath of decision*, one would have to speak of the "irrationality" of living *logos*, of its spellbinding powers of enchantment, mesmerizing fascination, and alchemical transformation, which make it kin to witchcraft and magic. Sorcery (*goēteia*), psychagogy, such are the "facts and acts" of speech, the most fearsome of *pharmaka*. In his *Encomium of Helen*, Gorgias used these very words to qualify the power of speech.

> Sacred incantations sung with words (*hai gar entheoi dia logōn epōidai*) are bearers of pleasure and banishers of pain, for, merging with opinion in the soul, the power of incantation is wont to beguile it (*ethelxe*) and persuade it and alter it by witchcraft (*goēteiai*). There have been discovered two arts of witchcraft and magic: one consists of errors of soul and the other of deceptions of opinion. . . . What cause then

prevents the conclusion that Helen similarly, against her will, might have come under the influence (*humnos*) of speech, just as if ravished by the force of the mighty? . . . For speech constrained the soul, persuading it which it persuaded, both to believe the things said and to approve the things done. The persuader, like a constrainer, does the wrong and the persuaded, like the constrained, in speech is wrongly charged.[50]

Persuasive eloquence (*peithō*) is the power to break in, to carry off, to seduce internally, to ravish invisibly. It is furtive force per se. But in showing that Helen gave in to the violence of speech (would she have yielded to a letter?), in disculpating this victim, Gorgias indicts *logos* in its capacity to lie. "By introducing some reasoning (*logismon*) into speech (*tōi logōi*)," he wishes "to free the accused of blame and, having reproved her detractors as prevaricators and proved the truth, to free her from their ignorance."

But before being reined in and tamed by the *kosmos* and order of truth, *logos* is a wild creature, an ambiguous animality. Its magical "pharmaceutical" force derives from this ambivalence, which explains the disproportion between the strength of that force and the inconsiderable thing speech seems to be:

> But if it was speech which persuaded her and deceived her heart, not even to this is it difficult to make an answer and to banish blame as follows. Speech is a powerful lord, which by means of the finest and most invisible body effects the divinest works: it can stop fear and banish grief and create joy and nurture pity.

Such persuasion entering the soul through speech is indeed a *pharmakon*, and that is precisely what Gorgias calls it:

> The effect of speech (*tou logou dunamis*) upon the condition of the soul (*pros tēn tēs psuchēs taxin*) is comparable (*ton auton de logon*) to the power of drugs (*tōn pharmakōn taxis*) over the nature of bodies (*tēn tōn somatōn phusin*). For just as different drugs dispel different secretions from the body, and some bring an end to disease and others to life, so also in the case of speeches, some distress, others delight, some cause fear, others make the hearers bold, and some drug and bewitch the soul with a kind of evil persuasion (*tēn psuchēn epharmakeusan kai exegoēteusan*).

50. [English translation by George Kennedy, in *The Older Sophists*, ed. R. K. Sprague (Columbia, S.C.: University of South Carolina Press, 1972), pp. 50–54.] On this passage of the *Encomium*, on the relations of *thelgō* and *peithō*, of charm and persuasion, on their use in Homer, Aeschylus, and Plato, see Diès, pp. 116–17.

The reader will have paused to reflect that the relation (the analogy) between the *logos*/soul relation and the *pharmakon*/body relation is itself designated by the term *logos*. The name of the relation is the same as that of one of its terms. The *pharmakon* is *comprehended* in the structure of *logos*. This comprehension is an act of both *domination* and *decision*.

5. The Pharmakeus

For if there were nothing any more to hurt us, we should have no need whatever of any assistance. And thus you see it would then be made apparent that it was only on account of evil that we felt regard and affection for good (*tagathon*), as we considered good to be a medicine (*pharmakon*) for evil, and evil to be a disease. But where there is no disease, there is, we are aware, no need of medicine (*ouden dei pharmakou*). This, then, it appears, is the nature of good. . . .
—Yes, he said, that would seem to be true.

—*Lysis*, 220c–d

But if this is the case, and if *logos* is already a penetrating supplement, then isn't Socrates, "he who does not write," also a master of the *pharmakon*? And in that way isn't he the spitting image of a sophist? a *pharmakeus*? a magician? a sorcerer? even a poisoner? and even one of those impostors denounced by Gorgias? The threads of these complicities are almost impossible to disentangle.

Socrates in the dialogues of Plato often has the face of a *pharmakeus*. That is the name given by Diotima to Eros. But behind the portrait of Eros, one cannot fail to recognize the features of Socrates, as though Diotima, in looking at him, were proposing to Socrates the portrait of Socrates (*Symposium*, 203c,d,e). Eros, who is neither rich, nor beautiful, nor delicate, spends his life philosophizing (*philosophōn dia pantos tou biou*); he is a fearsome sorcerer (*deinos goēs*), magician (*pharmakeus*), and sophist (*sophistēs*). A being that no "logic" can confine within a noncontradictory definition, an individual of the demonic species, neither god nor man, neither immortal nor mortal, neither living nor dead, he forms "the medium of the prophetic arts, of the priestly rites of sacrifice, initiation, and incantation, of divination and of sorcery (*thusias-teletas-epōdas-manteian*)" (202e).

In that same dialogue, Agathon accuses Socrates of trying to bewitch him, to cast a spell over him (*Pharmattein boulei me, ō Sōkrates*, 194a). The portrait of Eros by Diotima is placed between this exclamation and the portrait of Socrates by Alcibiades.

Who reminds us that Socrates' brand of magic is worked through *logos* without the aid of any instrument, through the effects of a voice without accessories, without the flute of the satyr Marsyas:

> And aren't you a piper as well? I should think you were—and a far more wonderful piper than Marsyas, who had only to put his flute to his lips to bewitch mankind. . . . His tunes will still have a magic power, and by virtue of their own divinity they will show which of us are fit subjects for divine initiation. Now the only difference, Socrates, between you and Marsyas is that you can get just the same effect without any instrument at all (*aneu organōn*)—with nothing but a few simple words (*psilois logois*[51]). . . ." (215*c–d*)

When confronted with this simple, organless voice, one cannot escape its penetration by stopping up one's ears, like Ulysses trying to block out the Sirens (216*a*).

The Socratic *pharmakon* also acts like venom, like the bite of a poisonous snake (217–18). And Socrates' bite is worse than a snake's since its traces invade the soul. What Socrates' words and the viper's venom have in common, in any case, is their ability to penetrate and make off with the most concealed interiority of the body or soul. The demonic speech of this thaumaturge (en)trains the listener in dionysian frenzy and philosophic *mania* (218*b*). And when they don't act like the venom of a snake, Socrates' pharmaceutical charms provoke a kind of *narcosis*, benumbing and paralyzing into aporia, like the touch of a sting ray (*narkē*):

> *Meno*: Socrates, even before I met you they told me that in plain truth you are a perplexed man yourself and reduce others to perplexity. At this moment I feel you are exercising magic and witchcraft upon me and positively laying me under your spell until I am just a mass of helplessness (*goēteueis me kai pharmatteis kai atekhnōs katepaideis, hōste meston aporias gegonenai*). If I may be flippant, I think that not only in outward appearance (*eidos*) but in other respects as well you are exactly like the flat stingray (*narkē*) that one meets in the sea. Whenever anyone comes into contact with it, it numbs him, and that is the sort of thing that you seem to be doing to me now. My mind and my lips are literally numb, and I have nothing to reply to you. . . . In my opinion you are well advised not to leave Athens and live abroad. If

51. "Bare, ungarnished voice, etc."; *psilos logos* also has the sense of abstract argument or simple affirmation without proof (cf. *Theaetetus*, 165*e*).

you behaved like this as a foreigner in another country, you would most likely be arrested as a wizard (*goēs*). (*Meno*, 80*a–b*)

Socrates arrested as a wizard (*goēs* or *pharmakeus*): that will have to wait.

What can be said about this *analogy* that ceaselessly refers the socratic *pharmakon* to the sophistic *pharmakon* and, proportioning them to each other, makes us go back indefinitely from one to the other? How can they be distinguished?

Irony does not consist in the dissolution of a sophistic charm or in the dismantling of an occult substance or power through analysis and questioning. It does not consist in undoing the charlatanesque confidence of a *pharmakeus* from the vantage point of some obstinate instance of transparent reason or innocent *logos*. Socratic irony precipitates out one *pharmakon* by bringing it in contact with another *pharmakon*. Or rather, it reverses the *pharmakon*'s powers and turns *its* surface over[52]—thus taking effect, being recorded and dated, in the act of *classing* the *pharmakon*, through the fact that the *pharmakon* properly consists in a certain inconsistency, a certain impropriety, this nonidentity-with-itself always allowing it to be turned against itself.

What is at stake in this overturning is no less than science and death. Which are consigned to a single type in the structure of the *pharmakon*, the one and only name for that potion that must be awaited. And even, in Socrates' case, deserved.

---

52. Alternately and/or all at once, the Socratic *pharmakon* petrifies and vivifies, anesthetizes and sensitizes, appeases and anguishes. Socrates is a benumbing stingray but also an animal that needles: we recall the bee in the *Phaedo* (91*c*); later we will open the *Apology* at the point where Socrates compares himself precisely to a gadfly. This whole Socratic configuration thus composes a bestiary. Is it surprising that the demonic inscribes itself in a bestiary? It is on the basis of this zoopharmaceutical ambivalence and of that other Socratic *analogy* that the contours of the *anthrōpos* are determined.

II

The use Socrates makes of the *pharmakon* does not have as its goal the guaranteeing of the *pharmakeus'* power. The technique of infiltration or paralysis can even eventually be turned against its user although one must always, in the symptomatological manner of Nietzsche, be careful to diagnose the *economy*, the investment and deferred benefit behind the sign of pure renunciation or the *bidding* of disinterested sacrifice.

The nakedness of the *pharmakon*, the blunt bare voice (*psilos logos*), carries with it a certain mastery in the dialogue, on the condition that Socrates overtly renounce its benefits: knowledge as power, passion, pleasure. On the condition, in a word, that he consent to die. The death of the body, at least: that is the price that must be paid for *alētheia* and the epistēmē, which are also powers.

The fear of death is what gives all witchcraft, all occult medicine, a hold. The *pharmakeus* is banking on that fear. Hence the Socratic pharmacy, in working to free us from it, corresponds to an operation of *exorcism*, in a form that could be envisaged and conducted from the side and viewpoint of God. After wondering whether some God had given men a drug to induce fear (*phobou pharmakon*), the Athenian of the *Laws* dismisses the idea: "Let's repeat the point we were making to the legislator: 'Agreed then: there is probably no such thing as a drug (*pharmakon*) to produce fear, either by gift or human contrivance (I leave quacks (*goētas*) out of account: they're beyond the pale). But is there a drink that will produce a lack of fear (*aphobias*) and stimulate overconfidence about the wrong thing at the wrong moment? What do we say to this?'" (649*a*).

It is the child in us that is afraid. The charlatans will all disappear when the "little boy within us" no longer fears death as he fears a *mormolukeion*, a scarecrow set up to frighten children, a bogeyman. And incantations must be redoubled daily in order to free the child from this fantasy: "*Cebes*: Probably even in us there is a little boy who has these childish terrors. Try to

120

persuade him not to be afraid of death as though it were a bogey.—What you should do, said Socrates, is to say a magic spell over him every day until you have charmed his fears away.—But, Socrates, said Simmias, where shall we find a magician (*epōdon*) who understands these spells now that you are leaving us?" (*Phaedo*, 77*e*). In the *Crito*, too, Socrates refuses to give in to the people who "conjure up fresh hordes of bogeys to terrify our childish minds, by subjecting us to chains and executions and confiscations of our property" (46*c*).

The counterspell, the exorcism, the antidote, is dialectics. In answer to Cebes, Socrates recommends seeking not only a magician but also—the surest incantation—training in dialectics: "Seek for him among all peoples, far and wide, sparing neither pains nor money; for there is no better way of spending your money. And you must seek among yourselves, too; for you will not find others better suited for the task" (*Phaedo*, 78*a–b*).

To seek "among yourselves" by mutual questioning and self-examination, to seek to know oneself through the detour of the language of the other, such is the undertaking presented by Socrates, who recalls the Delphic inscription (*tou Delphikou grammatos*), to Alcibiades as the antidote (*alexipharmakon*), the counterpotion. In the text of the *Laws* which we left off quoting earlier, when the necessity of the letter has been firmly laid down, the introjection or internalization of the *grammata* into the judge's soul—their most secure dwelling-place—is then prescribed as an antidote. Let us pick up the thread of the text again:

> He that would show himself a righteously equal judge must keep these matters before his eyes; he must procure books on the subject, and must make them his study. There is, in truth, no study whatsoever so potent as this of law, if the law be what it should be, to make a better man of its student—else 'twould be for nothing that the law which so stirs our worship and wonder bears a name so cognate with that of understanding [*nomos/nous*]. Furthermore, consider all other discourse, poesy with its eulogies and its satires, or utterances in prose, whether in literature or in the common converse of daily life, with their contentious disagreements and their too often unmeaning admissions. The one certain touchstone of all is the writings of the legislator (*ta tou nomothetou grammata*). *The good judge will possess those writings within his own soul* (*ha dei kektēmenon en hautōi*) *as antidotes* (*alexipharmaka*) *against other discourse*, and thus he will be the state's preserver as well as his own. He will secure in the good the retention and increase of their rectitude, and in the evil, or those of them whose

vicious principles admit remedy, will promote, so far as he can, conversion from folly, from profligacy, from cowardice, in a word, from all forms of wrong. As for those who are fatally attached to such principles, if our judges and their superiors prescribe death as a cure (*iama*) for a soul in that state, they will, as has been more than once said already, deserve the praise of the community for their conduct (XII, 957*c*–958*a*; emphasis mine).

Anamnesic dialectics, as the repetition of the *eidos*, cannot be distinguished from self-knowledge and self-mastery. Those are the best forms of exorcism that can be applied against the terrors of the child faced with death and the quackery of the bogeyman. Philosophy consists of offering reassurance to children. That is, if one prefers, of taking them out of childhood, of forgetting about the child, or, inversely, but by the same token, of speaking first and foremost *for* that little boy within us, of teaching him to speak—to dialogue—by displacing his fear or his desire.

One could play at classifying, within the weave of the *Statesman* (280*a* ff), that species of protection (*amunterion*) that is called dialectics and apprehended as a counter-poison. Among the things that can be called artificial (manufactured or acquired), the Stranger distinguishes those with the function of doing something (tending toward *poiein*) and those, called defenses (*amunteria*), with the function of preventing suffering (*tou me paskhein*). Among the latter, one can distinguish (1) *antidotes* (*alexipharmaka*), which can be either human or divine (and dialectics is from this perspective the very antidoteness of the antidote in general, before any possibility of dividing it up between the human and the divine. Dialectics is precisely the passage between the two) and (2) *problems* (*problemata*): what stands before one—obstacles, shelters, armor, shields, defenses. Leaving antidotes aside, the Stranger pursues the division of the *problemata*, which can function either as armaments or as fences. The *fences* (*phragmata*) are screens or protections (*alexeteria*) against storm and heat; these *protections* can be housings or coverings; *coverings* can be spread below (like rugs) or wrapped around, etc. The process of division goes on through the different techniques for manufacturing these wraps until it reaches the woven garment and the art of weaving: the *problematic* space of protection. This art would thus rule out, if one follows the divisions literally, all recourse to antidotes, and consequently, to that species of antidote or inverted *pharmakon* constituted by dialectics. The text excludes dialectics. And yet, it will nevertheless be necessary later to distinguish between two sorts of texture, if one bears in mind that dialectics is also an art of weaving, a science of the *sumploke*.

The dialectical inversion of the *pharmakon* or of the dangerous supplement makes death both acceptable and null. Acceptable because it is annulled. In making us welcome death, the immortality of the soul, which acts like an antibody, dissipates its terrifying fantasy. The inverted *pharmakon*, which scatters all the hobgoblins, is none other than the origin of the *epistēmē*, the opening to truth as the possibility of repetition and the submission of that "greed for life" (*epithumein zēn, Crito,* 53e) to law (the good, the father, the king, the chief, the capital, the sun, all of which are invisible). It is the laws themselves that, in the *Crito,* urge one not to "cling so greedily to life, at the price of violating the most stringent laws."

What indeed does Socrates say when Cebes and Simmias ask him to provide them with a magician? He urges them to practice the philosophic dialogue and seek its most worthy object: the truth of the *eidos* as that which is identical to itself, always the same as itself and therefore simple, incomposite (*asuntheton*), undecomposable, invariable (78c,e). The *eidos* is that which can always be repeated as *the same.* The ideality and invisibility of the *eidos* are its power-to-be-repeated. Now, law is always a law of repetition, and repetition is always submission to a law. In the personification of the Laws in the *Crito,* Socrates is called upon to accept both death and law *at once.* He is asked to recognize himself as the offspring, the son or representative (*ekgonos*) or even the slave (*doulos*) of the law that, in uniting his father and mother, made possible his birth. Violence is thus even more sacrilegious when it offends the law of the mother/country than when it wounds the father and mother (51c). This is why, say the Laws, Socrates must die in conformity with the law and within the confines of the city—Socrates, who was (almost) always reluctant to go outside:

> Are you so wise as to have forgotten that compared with your mother and father and all the rest of your ancestors your country is something far more precious, more venerable, more sacred, and held in greater honor both among gods and among all reasonable men? . . . Violence is a sin even against your country. . . . Socrates, we have substantial evidence that you are satisfied with us and with the state (*polis*). You would not have been so exceptionally reluctant to cross the borders of your country (*polis*) if you had not been exceptionally attached to it. You have never left the city to attend a festival or for any other purpose, except on some military expedition. You have never traveled abroad as other people do, and you have never felt the impulse to acquaint yourself with another country or constitution. You have been content with us and with our city (*polis*). You have definitely chosen

us, and undertaken to observe us in all your activities as a citizen.
(51a,c—51b-c)

The Socratic word does not wander, stays at home, is closely watched:
within autochthony, within the city, within the law, under the surveillance
of its mother tongue. This will take on its full significance further on, when
writing will be described as errancy as such, mute vulnerability to all
aggression. In nothing does writing reside.

The *eidos*, truth, law, the *epistēmē*, dialectics, philosophy—all these are
other names for that *pharmakon* that must be opposed to the *pharmakon* of
the Sophists and to the bewitching fear of death. It is *pharmakeus* against
pharmakeus, *pharmakon* against *pharmakon*. This is why Socrates heeds the
Laws as though, through their voices, he were under the power of an
initiatic spell, a sonorous spell, then, or rather, a phonic spell, one that
penetrates and carries away the inner courts of the soul. "That, my dear
friend Crito, I do assure you, is what I seem to hear them saying, just as a
Corybant seems to hear the strains of music, and the sound of their
arguments (*hē ēkhē toutōn tōn logōn*) rings so loudly in my head that I cannot
hear the other side" (54d). Those Corybants, that music, are evoked by
Alcibiades in the *Symposium* in his efforts to describe the effects of the
Socratic utterance: "the moment I hear him speak I am smitten with a kind
of sacred rage, worse than any Corybant, and my heart jumps into my
mouth" (215e).

The philosophical, epistemic order of *logos* as an antidote, as a force
inscribed within the general alogical economy of the pharmakon is not something
we are proposing here as a daring interpretation of Platonism. Let us,
rather, look at the prayer that opens the *Critias*: "I call on the god to grant
us that most effective medicine (*pharmakon teleōtaton*), that best of all
medicines (*ariston pharmakon*): knowledge (*epistēmēn*)." And one could also
consider the astonishing dramatic staging of the first act of the *Charmides*. It
should be followed moment by moment. Dazzled by the beauty of Charmides, Socrates wants above all to undress the soul of this young man who
loves philosophy. Charmides is sent for so that he can be presented to a
doctor (Socrates) who can relieve him of his headaches and his weakness.
Socrates accepts to pass himself off as a man who knows a cure for headaches.
There then ensues a "cloak" scene similar to the one in the *Phaedrus*,
involving a certain *pharmakon*:

> When Critias told him that I was the person who had the cure (*ho to
> pharmakon epistamenos*), he looked at me in an indescribable manner,
> and made as though to ask me a question. And all the people in the

palaestra crowded about us, and at that moment, my good friend, I glanced through the opening of his garment, and was inflamed by his beauty. Then I could no longer contain myself. . . . But still when he asked me if I knew the cure for the headache (*to tēs kephalēs pharmakon*) . . . I replied that it was a kind of leaf, which required to be accompanied by a charm (*epōdē de tis epi tōi pharmakōi*), and if a person would repeat the charm at the same time that he used the cure, he would be made whole, but that without the charm the leaf would be of no avail. —Then I will write out the charm from your dictation, he said (155*d* – 156*a*. Cf. also 175 – 176).[53]

But the head cannot be cured separately. Good doctors take care of "the whole," and it is by caring for the whole that they have been inspired by a Thracian physician, "one of the physicians of the Thracian king Zalmoxis who are said to be able even to give immortality," Socrates shows that the whole of the body can only be cured at the source—the soul—of all its goods and evils. "And the cure of the soul, my dear youth, has to be effected by the use of certain charms (*epōdais tisin*), and these charms are fair words, and by them temperance (*sōphrosunēn*) is implanted in the soul, and where temperance comes and stays, there health is speedily imparted, not only to the head, but to the whole body" (157*a*). And the discussion turns to the essence of temperance, the best *pharmakon*, the capital cure.

Philosophy thus opposes to its other this transmutation of the drug into a remedy, of the poison into a counterpoison. Such an operation would not be possible if the *pharmako-logos* did not already harbor within itself that complicity of contrary values, and if the *pharmakon* in general were not, prior to any distinction -making, that which, presenting itself as a poison, may turn out to be a cure, may retrospectively reveal itself in the truth of its curative power. The "essence" of the *pharmakon* lies in the way in which, having no stable essence, no "proper" characteristics, it is not, in any sense

---

53. The reader will have noted that this scene makes a strange, inverse and symmetrical pendant to the one in the *Phaedrus*. It is inverted in that the unit which, under the cloak, allowed a text and a *pharmakon* to (e)merge is *preinscribed* in the *Phaedrus* (the *pharmakon* is the text already written by "the ablest writer of our day"), and only *prescribed* in the *Charmides* (the prescription for the *pharmakon* Socrates recommends must be taken down under his dictation). The Socratic prescription here is oral, and speech accompanies the *pharmakon* as the condition of its effectiveness. Within the thickness and depth of this scene, one should reread, from the middle of the *Statesman*, the critique of the written medical prescription, the "*hypomnēmata graphein*" whose rigidity does not allow it to adapt to the specificity and the progress of the disease: this is an illustration of the political problem of written laws. Like the doctor who comes back to visit his patient, the legislator must be able to modify his initial prescriptions (294*a*–297*b*; see also 298*d*–*e*).

(metaphysical, physical, chemical, alchemical) of the word, a *substance*. The *pharmakon* has no ideal identity; it is aneidetic, firstly because it is not monoeidetic (in the sense in which the *Phaedo* speaks of the *eidos* as something simple, noncomposite: *monoeides*). This "medicine" is not a simple thing. But neither is it a composite, a sensible or empirical *suntheton* partaking of several simple essences. It is rather the prior medium in which differentiation in general is produced, along with the opposition between the *eidos* and its other; this medium is *analogous* to the one that will, subsequent to and according to the decision of philosophy, be reserved for transcendental imagination, that "art hidden in the depths of the soul," which belongs neither simply to the sensible nor simply to the intelligible, neither simply to passivity nor simply to activity. The element-medium will always be analogous to a mixed-medium. In a certain way, Plato thought about and even formulated this ambivalence. But he did so in passing, incidentally, discreetly: in connection with the union of opposites within virtue, not the union of virtue with its opposite:

> *Stranger*: But in those of noble nature from their earliest days whose nurture too has been all it should be, the laws can foster the growth of this common bond of conviction and only in these. This is the talisman (*pharmakon*) appointed for them by the design of pure intelligence. This most godlike bond alone can unite the elements of virtue which are diverse in nature and would else be opposing in tendency. (*Statesman*, 310*a*)

This pharmaceutical nonsubstance cannot be handled with complete security, neither in its being, since it has none, nor in its effects, the sense of which is always capable of changing. In this way, writing, touted by Theuth as a remedy, a beneficial drug, is later overturned and denounced by the king and then, in the king's place, by Socrates, as a harmful substance, a philter of forgetfulness. Inversely, and although in a less immediately readable manner, the hemlock, that potion which in the *Phaedo* is never called anything but a *pharmakon*,[54] is presented to Socrates as a poison; yet it is transformed, through the effects of the Socratic *logos* and of the philosophical demonstration in the *Phaedo*, into a means of deliverance, a way toward salvation, a cathartic power. The hemlock has an *ontological*

---

54. The opening lines of the dialogue are: "*Echecrates*: Were you there with Socrates yourself, Phaedo, when he drank the poison (*pharmakon*) in his cell?" (57*a*).

   Near the end of the dialogue: "*Socrates*: . . . I prefer to have a bath before drinking the poison (*pharmakon*), rather than give the women the trouble of washing me when I am dead" (115*a*). Cf. also 117*a*.

effect: it initiates one into the contemplation of the *eidos* and the immortality of the soul.[55] *That is how Socrates takes it.*

Is this crossed connection-making the result of mere artifice or play? There is certainly *play* in such a movement, and this chiasmus is authorized, even prescribed, by the ambivalence of the *pharmakon*. Not only by the polarity good/evil, but by the double participation in the distinct regions of the soul and the body, the invisible and the visible. This double participation, once again, does not mix together two previously separate elements; it refers back to a *same* that is not the identical, to the common element or medium of any possible dissociation. Thus, writing is *given* as the sensible, visible, spatial surrogate of the *mnēmē*; it later turns out to be harmful and benumbing to the invisible interior of the soul, memory and truth. Inversely, the hemlock is given as a poison that harms and benumbs the body. But it later turns out to be helpful to the soul, which it delivers from the body and awakens to the truth of the *eidos*. If the *pharmakon* is "ambivalent," it is because it constitutes the medium in which opposites are opposed, the movement and the play that links them among themselves, reverses them or makes one side cross over into the other (soul/body, good/evil, inside/ outside, memory/forgetfulness, speech/writing, etc.). It is on the basis of this play or movement that the opposites or differences are stopped by Plato. The *pharmakon* is the movement, the locus, and the play: (the production of) difference. It is the differance of difference. It holds in reserve, in its undecided shadow and vigil, the opposites and the differends that the process of discrimination will come to carve out. Contradictions and pairs of opposites are lifted from the bottom of this diacritical, differing, deferring, reserve. Already inhabited by differance, this reserve, even though it "precedes" the opposition between different effects, even though it preexists differences as effects, does not have the punctual simplicity of a *coincidentia oppositorum*. It is from this fund that dialectics draws its philosophemes. The *pharmakon*, without being anything in itself, always exceeds them in constituting their bottomless fund [*fonds sans fond*]. It keeps itself forever in reserve even though it has no fundamental pro-

---

55. One could therefore also consider the hemlock as a sort of *pharmakon* of immortality. Such an interpretation is invited by the ritual, ceremonial form with which the *Phaedo* closes (116*b–c*). In his *"Festin d'immortalité" (Esquisse d'une étude de mythologie comparée indo-européenne* 1924), G. Dumézil refers to certain "traces, in Athens, of a cycle of Theseus correlated with the *Thargelia*" (we will later have occasion to speak of a certain relation between the Thargelia and the birth and death of Socrates), and notes: "Neither Pherecydes nor Appollodorus has set down the rites that must have corresponded, in a certain district of Greece, to the story of the *pharmakon* of immortality desired by the *Giants*, and to that of the 'artificial Goddess,' *Athena*, who caused the Giants to lose their immortality" (p. 89).

fundity nor ultimate locality. We will watch it infinitely promise itself and endlessly vanish through concealed doorways that shine like mirrors and open onto a labyrinth. It is also this store of deep background that we are calling the *pharmacy*.

6. The Pharmakos

It is part of the rules of this game that the game should *seem to stop*. Then the *pharmakon*, which is older than either of the opposites, is "caught" by philosophy, by "Platonism" which is constituted by this apprehension, as a mixture of two pure, heterogeneous terms. And one could follow the word *pharmakon* as a guiding thread within the whole Platonic problematic of the mixture. Apprehended as a blend and an impurity, the *pharmakon* also acts like an aggressor or a housebreaker, threatening some internal purity and security. This definition is absolutely general and can be verified even in cases where such forced entries are valorized: the good remedy, Socratic irony, comes to disturb the intestinal organization of self-complacency. The purity of the inside can then only be restored if the *charges are brought home* against exteriority as a supplement, inessential yet harmful to the essence, a surplus that *ought* never to have come to be added to the untouched plenitude of the inside. The restoration of internal purity must thus reconstitute, *recite*—and this is myth as such, the *mythology* for example of a *logos* recounting its origin, going back to the eve of the pharma-kographic aggression—that to which the *pharmakon* should not have had to be added and attached like a *literal parasite*: a *letter* installing itself inside a living organism to rob it of its *nourishment* and to *distort* [like static, = "*bruit parasite*"] the pure audibility of a voice. Such are the relations between the writing supplement and the *logos-zōon*. In order to cure the latter of the *pharmakon* and rid it of the parasite, it is thus necessary to put the outside back in its place. To keep the outside out. This is the inaugural gesture of "logic" itself, of good "sense" insofar as it accords with the self-identity of *that which is*: being is what it is, the outside is outside and the inside inside. Writing must thus return to being what it *should never have ceased to be*: an accessory, an accident, an excess.

The cure by *logos*, exorcism, and catharsis will thus eliminate the excess. But this elimination, being therapeutic in nature, must call upon the very thing it is expelling, the very surplus it is *putting out*. The pharmaceutical operation must therefore *exclude itself from itself*.

What does this mean about what (it is) to write?

Plato does not make a show of the chain of significations we are trying progressively to dig up. If there were any sense in asking such a question, which we don't believe, it would be impossible to say to what extent he manipulates it voluntarily or consciously, and at what point he is subject to constraints weighing upon his discourse from "language." The word "language," through all that binds it to everything we are putting in question here, is not of any pertinent assistance, and to follow the constraints of a language would not exclude the possibility that Plato is playing with them, even if his game is neither representative nor voluntary. It is in the back room, in the shadows of the pharmacy, prior to the oppositions between conscious and unconscious, freedom and constraint, voluntary and involuntary, speech and language, that these textual "operations" occur.

Plato seems to place no emphasis on the word *pharmakon* at the point where writing's effects swerve from positive to negative, when poison, under the eyes of the king, appears as the truth of the remedy. It is not said that the *pharmakon* is the locus, the support, and the executor of this mutation. Later—we will come to this—while expressly comparing writing to painting, Plato will not explicitly put this judgment together with the fact that elsewhere he refers to painting as a *pharmakon*. For in Greek, *pharmakon* also means paint, not a natural color but an artificial tint, a chemical dye that imitates the chromatic scale given in nature.

Yet all these significations nonetheless appear, and, more precisely, all these words appear in the text of "Plato." Only the chain is concealed, and, to an inappreciable extent, concealed from the author himself, if any such thing exists. One can say in any event that all the "pharmaceutical" words we have been pointing out do actually make an "act of presence," so to speak, in the text of the dialogues. Curiously, however, there is another of these words that, to our knowledge, is never used by Plato. If we line it up with the series *pharmakeia-pharmakon-pharmakeus*, we will no longer be able to content ourselves with reconstituting a chain that, for all its hiddenness, for all it might escape Plato's notice, is nevertheless something that passes through certain discoverable *points of presence* that can be seen in the text. The word to which we are now going to refer, which is present in the language and which points to an experience that was present in Greek culture even in Plato's day, seems strikingly absent from the "Platonic text."

But what does *absent* or *present* mean here? Like any text, the text of "Plato" couldn't not be involved, at least in a virtual, dynamic, lateral manner, with all the words that composed the system of the Greek language. Certain forces of association unite—at diverse distances, with different strengths and according to disparate paths—the words "actually present" in a discourse with all the other words in the lexical system, whether or not they appear as "words," that is, as relative verbal units in such discourse. They communicate with the totality of the lexicon through their syntactic play and at least through the subunits that compose what we call a word. For example, "pharmakon" is already in communication with all the words from the same family, with all the significations constructed out of the same root, and these communications do not stop there. The textual chain we must set back in place is thus no longer simply "internal" to Plato's lexicon. But in going beyond the bounds of that lexicon, we are less interested in breaking through certain limits, with or without cause, than in putting in doubt the right to posit such limits in the first place. In a word, we do not believe that there exists, in all rigor, a Platonic text, closed upon itself, complete with its inside and its outside. Not that one must then consider that it is leaking on all sides and can be drowned confusedly in the undifferentiated generality of its element. Rather, provided the articulations are rigorously and prudently recognized, one should simply be able to untangle the hidden forces of attraction linking a present word with an absent word in the text of Plato. Some such force, given the *system* of the language, cannot *not* have acted upon the writing and the reading of this text. With respect to the weight of such a force, the so-called "presence" of a quite relative verbal unit—the word—while not being a contingent accident worthy of no attention, nevertheless does not constitute the ultimate criterion and the utmost pertinence.

The circuit we are proposing is, moreover, all the more legitimate and easy since it leads to a word that can, on one of its faces, be considered the synonym, almost the homonym, of a word Plato "actually" used. The word in question is *pharmakos* (wizard, magician, poisoner), a synonym of *pharmakeus* (which Plato uses), but with the unique feature of having been overdetermined, overlaid by Greek culture with another function. Another *role*, and a formidable one.

The character of the *pharmakos* has been compared to a scapegoat. The *evil* and the *outside*, the expulsion of the evil, its exclusion out of the body (and out) of the city—these are the two major senses of the character and of the ritual.

Harpocration, commenting on the word *pharmakos*, describes them thus: "At Athens they led out two men to be purifications for the city; it was at the Thargelia, one was for the men and the other for the women."[56] In

56. The principal sources that enable us to describe the ritual of the *pharmakos* are collected in W. Mannhardt's *Mythologische Forschungen* (1884). These sources are themselves referred to in particular by J. G. Frazer in *The Golden Bough* (New York: S. G. Phillips,

1959), pp. 540 ff; by J. E. Harrison in *Prolegomena to the Study of Greek Religion* (New York: Meridian, 1903), pp. 95 ff, and in *Themis, a Study of the Social Origins of Greek Religion* (1912, p. 416); by Nilsson in *History of Greek Religion* (1925), p. 27; and by P. M. Schuhl in *Essai sur la formation de la pensée grecque* (1934), pp. 36–37. One can also consult the chapter Marie Delcourt devotes to Oedipus in her *Légendes et culte des héros en Grèce* (1942), p. 101; see also by the same author, *Pyrrhos et Pyrrha: Recherches sur les valeurs du feu dans les légendes helléniques* (1965), p. 29, and especially *Oedipe ou la légende du conquérant* (1944), pp. 29–65.

This is doubtless the moment to point out, in connection with the clear necessity of bringing together the figures of Oedipus and the *pharmakos*, that, despite certain appearances, the discourse we are holding here is not in a strict sense a psychoanalytical one. This is true at least to the extent that we are drawing upon the same textual stores (Greek culture, language, tragedy, philosophy, etc.) which Freud had to begin by tapping and to which he never ceased to refer. It is precisely these stores, this fund, that we propose to interrogate here. This does not, however, mean that the distance we have thus taken with respect to a psychoanalytical discourse which might evolve naïvely within an insufficiently deciphered Greek text is of the same order as that maintained for example by Delcourt, *Légendes*, pp. 109, 113, etc.; or J. P. Vernant "Oedipe sans complexe," in *Raison présente* (1967).

After the first publication of this text, there appeared the remarkable essay by J. P. Vernant, "Ambiguïté et renversement: sur la structure énigmatique d'Oedipe-Roi" in *Echanges et Communications, mélanges offerts à Claude Lévi-Strauss* (The Hague: Mouton, 1970) [translated by Page du Bois as "Ambiguity and Reversal: On the Enigmatic Structure of *Oedipus Rex*", in *New Literary History* 10, no. 3 (1978)]. One can read, in particular, the following passage, which seems to confirm our hypothesis (cf. note 52): "How could the city admit into its heart one who, like Oedipus, 'has shot his bolt beyond the others' and has become *isotheos*? When it establishes ostracism, it creates an institution whose role is symmetrical to and the inverse of the ritual of the Thargelia. In the person of the ostracized, the city expels what in it is too elevated, what incarnates the evil which can come to it from above. In the evil of the *pharmakos*, it expels what is the vilest in itself, what incarnates the evil that menaces it from below. By this double and complementary rejection it delimits itself in relation to what is not yet known and what transcends the known: it takes the proper measure of the human in opposition on one side to the divine and heroic, on the other to the bestial and monstrous" [Eng. trans. pp. 491–92]. See also (notably on the *poikilon* which we will mention later) "La metis d'Antiloque," *Revue des Etudes grecques*, January/December 1967, and "La metis du renard et du poulpe," ibid. July/December 1969. An additional confirmation can be found in the *Oeuvres* of Marcel Mauss, which appeared in 1969. One can read the following:

"Moreover, all these ideas are double-faced. In other Indo-European languages, it is the notion of poison which is not certain. Kluge and the etymologists are right in comparing the *potio*, "Poison," series with *gift, gift* ["gift," which means "present" in English, means "poison" or "married" in other Germanic languages.—Trans.]. One can also read with interest the lively discussion by Aulus-Gellius (12) on the ambiguity of the Greek *pharmakon* and the Latin *venenum*. Indeed, the Lex Cornelia de Sicariis et veneficis, of which Cicero has fortunately preserved for us the actual "recitation," still specifies *venenum malum* (13). The magic brew, the delectable charm (14), can be either good or bad. The Greek *philtron* is not necessarily a sinister word, either, and the potion of friendship or love is only dangerous if the enchanter so desires."

(12) 12, 9, with apt quotations from Homer.

(13) *Pro Cluentio*, 148. In the Digesta, it is still recommended that one specify what sort of "venenum," "bonus sive malum," is intended.

(14) If the etymology linking *venenum* (see Walde, Lat. etym. Wört.) with Venus and the skr. *van, vanati* is correct, which seems probable.

(*"Gift-gift"* (1924), first published in *Mélanges offerts à Charles Andler par ses amis et élèves*, Istra, Strasbourg; in *Oeuvres* III, 50 (Editions de Minuit, 1969).)

general, the *pharmakoi* were put to death. But that, it seems,[57] was not the essential end of the operation. Death occurred most often as a secondary effect of an energetic fustigation. Aimed first at the genital organs.[58] Once the *pharmakoi* were cut off from the space of the city, the blows[59] were designed to chase away or draw out the evil from their bodies. Did they burn them, too, in order to achieve purification? In his *Thousand Histories*,

This brings us to *The Gift* [*L'Essai sur le don*], which refers to the above article: "(*Gift, gift: Mélanges. Ch. Andler*, Strasburg, 1924.) We asked why we do not examine the etymology of *gift* as coming from the Latin *dosis*, Greek δόσις, a dose (of poison). It would suppose that High and Low German had retained a scientific word for a common event, and this is contrary to normal semantic rules. Moreover, one would have to explain the choice of the word *Gift*. Finally, the Latin and Greek *dosis*, meaning poison, shows that with the Ancients as well there was association of ideas and moral rules of the kind we are describing.

"We compare the uncertainty of the meaning of *Gift* with that of the Latin *venenum* and the Greek φίλτρον and φάρμακον. Cf. also *venia, venus, venenum—vanati* (Sanskrit, to give pleasure) and *gewinnen* and win." [trans. Ian Cunnison (Glencoe, Ill.: Free Press, 1954), p. 127.]

57. Cf. Harrison, p. 104

58. "Similarly, the object of beating the human scapegoat on the genital organs with squills [a herbaceous, bulbous plant, sometimes grown for its pharmaceutical, esp. diuretic, properties] must have been to release his reproductive energies from any restraint or spell under which they might be laid by demoniacal or other malignant agency . . ." Frazer (1954 ed.), p. 541.

59. We recall the presumed etymology of *pharmakon/pharmakos*, detailed in E. Boisacq, *Dictionnaire étymologique de la langue grecque.* "*Pharmakon*: charm, philter, drug, remedy, poison. *Pharmakos*: magician, wizard, poisoner; the one sacrificed in expiation for the sins of a city (cf. Hipponax; Aristophanes), hence, rascal;* *pharmassō*: Attic, *-ttō*, work on or alter by means of a drug.

*Havers, *Indogermanische Forschungen* XXV, 375–92, on the basis of the relation *parempharaktos: parakekommenos*, derives *pharmakon* from *pharma*: "blow," and the latter from R. *bher*: to strike, cf. Lith. *buriu*, so that *pharmakon* can be said to signify: "that which pertains to an attack of demonic possession or is used as a curative against such an attack," given the common popular belief that illnesses are caused by the doings of demons and cured in the same way. Kretschmer Glotta III, 388 ff, objects that *pharmakon*, in epic, always designates a substance, an herb, a lotion, a drink, or other matter, but not the act of healing, charming, or poisoning; Havers' etymology adds only one possibility among others, for example the derivation from *pherō, pherma*, "*quod terra fert.*"

Cf. also Harrison, p. 108: ". . . *pharmakos* means simply 'magic-man.' Its Lithuanian cognate is *burin*, magic; in Latin it appears as *forma*, formula, magical spell; our *formulary* retains some vestige of its primitive connotation. *Pharmakon* in Greek means healing drug, poison, and dye, but all, for better or worse, are magical."

In his *Anatomy of Criticism* (New York: Atheneum, 1970), Northrop Frye sees in the figure of the *pharmakos* a permanent archetypal structure in Western literature. The exclusion of the *pharmakos*, who is, says Frye, "neither innocent nor guilty" (p. 41), is repeated from Aristophanes to Shakespeare, affecting Shylock as well as Falstaff, Tartuffe no less than Charlie Chaplin. "We meet a *pharmakos* figure in Hawthorne's Hester Prynne, in Melville's Billy Budd, in Hardy's Tess, in the Septimus of *Mrs. Dalloway*, in stories of persecuted Jews and Negroes, in stories of artists whose genius makes them Ishmaels of a bourgeois society" (p. 41, cf. also pp. 45–48, p. 148–49).

Tzetzes gives the following account, based on certain fragments by the satirical poet Hipponax, of the ceremony: "The (rite of the) *pharmakos* was a purification of this sort of old. If a calamity overtook the city by the wrath of God, whether it were famine or pestilence or any other mischief, they led forth as though to a sacrifice the most unsightly of them all as a purification and a remedy to the suffering city. They set the sacrifice in the appointed place, and gave him cheese with their hands and a barley cake and figs, and seven times they smote him with leeks and wild figs and other wild plants. Finally they burnt him with fire with the wood of wild trees and scattered the ashes into the sea and to the winds, for a purification, as I said, of the suffering city."

The city's body *proper* thus reconstitutes its unity, closes around the security of its inner courts, gives back to itself the word that links it with itself within the confines of the agora, by violently excluding from its territory the representative of an external threat or aggression. That representative represents the otherness of the evil that comes to affect or infect the inside by unpredictably breaking into it. Yet the representative of the outside is nonetheless *constituted*, regularly granted its place by the community, chosen, kept, fed, etc., in the very heart of the inside. These parasites were as a matter of course domesticated by the living organism that housed them at its expense. "The Athenians regularly maintained a number of degraded and useless beings at the public expense; and when any calamity, such as plague, drought, or famine, befell the city, they sacrificed two of these outcasts as scapegoats."[60]

The ceremony of the *pharmakos* is thus played out on the boundary line between inside and outside, which it has as its function ceaselessly to trace and retrace. *Intra muros/extra muros*. The origin of difference and division, the *pharmakos* represents evil both introjected and projected. Beneficial insofar as he cures—and for that, venerated and cared for—harmful insofar as he incarnates the powers of evil—and for that, feared and treated with caution. Alarming and calming. Sacred and accursed. The conjunction, the *coincidentia oppositorum*, ceaselessly undoes itself in the passage to decision or crisis. The expulsion of the evil or madness restores *sōphrosunē*.

These exclusions took place at critical moments (drought, plague, famine). *Decision* was then repeated. But the mastery of the critical instance requires that surprise be prepared for: by rules, by law, by the regularity of repetition, by fixing the date. This ritual practice, which took place in Abdera, in Thrace, in Marseilles, etc., was reproduced *every year* in Athens.

---

60. Frazer, (1954 ed.), pp. 540–41. Cf. also Harrison, p. 102.

And up through the fifth century. Aristophanes and Lysias clearly allude to it. Plato could not have been unaware of it.

The date of the ceremony is noteworthy: the sixth day of the Thargelia. That was the day of the birth of him whose death—and not only because a *pharmakon* was its direct cause—resembles that of a *pharmakos* from the inside: Socrates.

Socrates, affectionately called the *pharmakeus* in the dialogues of Plato; Socrates, who faced with the complaint (*graphē*) lodged against him, refused to defend himself, declined the logographic offer of Lysias, "the ablest writer of our time," who had proposed to ghost-write a defense for him; Socrates was born on the sixth day of the Thargelia. Diogenes Laertius testifies to this: "He was born on the sixth day of Thargelion, the day when the Athenians purify the city."

7. The Ingredients:
Phantasms, Festivals, and Paints

The rite of the *pharmakos*: evil and death, repetition and exclusion.

Socrates ties up into a system all the counts of indictment against the *pharmakon* of writing at the point at which he adopts as his own, in order to uphold it, interpret it, and make it explicit, the divine, royal, paternal, solar word, the capital sentence of Thamus. The worst effects of writing were only predicted by that word. The king's speech was not demonstrative; it did not pronounce knowledge—it pronounced itself. Announcing, presaging, cutting. It is a *manteia*, Socrates suggests (275*c*). The discourse of Socrates will hence apply itself to the task of translating that *manteia* into philosophy, cashing in on that capital, turning it to account, taking account of it, giving accounts and reasons, upholding the reasoning of that basileo-patro-helio-theological dictum. Transforming the *mythos* into *logos*.

What indeed would be the first thing a disdainful god would find to criticize in that which seems to lie outside his field of effectiveness? Its ineffectiveness, of course, its improductiveness, a productiveness that is only apparent, since it can only repeat what in truth is already there. This is why—Socrates' first argument—writing is not a good *tekhnē*, by which we should understand an art capable of engendering, pro-ducing, bringing forth: the clear, the sure, the secure (*saphes kai bebaion*). That is, the *alētheia* of the *eidos*, the truth of being in its figure, its "idea," its nonsensible visibility, its intelligible invisibility. The truth of what is: writing literally hasn't a damn sight to do with it. It has rather a blindness to do with it. Whoever might think he has pro-duced truth through a grapheme would only give proof of the greatest foolishness (*euētheia*). Whereas the sage Socrates knows that he knows nothing, that nitwit would not know that he already knows what he thinks he is learning through writing, and which he is only recalling to mind through the types. Not remembering, by anamnesis, the *eidos* contemplated before the fall of the soul into the body, but reminding himself, in a hypomnesic mode, of that of which he already has mnesic knowledge. Written *logos* is only a way for him who already knows (*ton eidota*) to remind himself (*hupomnēsai*) of the things writing is about (*ta gegrammena*) (275*d*). Writing thus only intervenes at a time when a subject of knowledge already possesses the signifieds, which are then only given to writing on consignment.

Socrates thus adopts the major, decisive opposition that cleaves the *manteia* of Thamus: *mnēmē/hupomnēsis*, the subtle difference between knowledge as memory and nonknowledge as rememoration, between two forms and two moments of repetition: a repetition of truth (*alētheia*) which presents and exposes the *eidos*; and a repetition of death and oblivion (*lēthē*) which veils and skews because it does not present the *eidos* but re-presents a presentation, repeats a repetition.[61]

Hupomnēsis, which is here what forecasts and shapes the thought about writing, not only does not coincide with memory, but can only be constructed as a thing dependent on memory. And consequently, on the presentation of truth. At the moment it is summoned to appear before the paternal instance, writing is determined within a problematic of knowing-remembering. It is thus from the start stripped of all its own attributes or path-breaking powers. Its path-breaking force is cut not by repetition but by the ills of repetition, by that which within repetition is doubled, redoubled, that which repeats repetition and in so doing, cut off from "good" repetition (which presents and gathers being within living memory), can always, left to itself, stop repeating itself. Writing would be pure repetition, dead repetition that might always be repeating nothing, or be unable *spontaneously* to repeat itself, which also means unable to repeat anything *but* itself: a hollow, cast-off repetition.

This pure repetition, this "bad" reissue, would thus be tautological. Written *logoi* "seem to talk to you as though they were intelligent, but if

61. It could be shown that all of Husserl's phenomenology is systematically organized around an analogous opposition between presentation and re-presentation (*Gegenwärtigung/Vergegenwärtigung*), and between primary memory (which is part of the originary "in an extended sense") and secondary memory. Cf. *La Voix et le phénomène {Speech and Phenomena}*.

you ask them anything about what they say, from a desire to be instructed, they go on telling you just the same thing forever (*hen ti sēmainei monon tauton aei*)" (275*d*). Pure repetition, absolute self-repetition, repetition of a self that is already reference and repetition, repetition of the signifier, repetition that is null or annulling, repetition of death—it's all one. Writing is not the living repetition of the living.

Which makes it similar to painting. And just as the *Republic*, in its condemnation of the imitative arts, links poetry and painting together; just as Aristotle's *Poetics* associates them under the single heading of *mimēsis*; so too Socrates here compares a piece of writing to a portrait, the *graphēma* to the *zōgraphēma*. "You know, Phaedrus, that's the strange (*deinon*) thing about writing, which makes it truly analogous to painting (*homoion zō-graphiai*). The painter's products stand before us as though they were alive (*hōs zōnta*), but if you question them, they maintain a most majestic (*semnōs*) silence. It is the same with written words. . . ." (275*d*).

The impotence to answer for itself, the unresponsiveness and irresponsi-bility of writing, is decried again by Socrates in the *Protagoras*. Bad public speakers, those who cannot answer "a supplementary question," are "like books: they cannot either answer or ask a question on their own account" (329*a*). That is why, says the Seventh Letter, "no intelligent man will ever be so bold as to put into language those things which his reason has contemplated, especially not into a form that is unalterable—which must be the case with what is expressed in written symbols" (343*a*; cf. also *Laws* XII, 968*d*).

What, in depth, are the resemblances underlying Socrates' statements that make writing homologous to painting? From out of what horizon arise their common silence, their stubborn muteness, their mask of solemn, forbidding majesty that so poorly hides an incurable aphasia, a stone deafness, a closedness irremediably inadequate to the demands of *logos*? If writing and painting are convoked together, summoned to appear with their hands tied, before the tribunal of *logos*, and to respond to it, this is quite simply because both are being *interrogated*: as the presumed repre-sentatives of a spoken word, as agents capable of speech, as depositaries or even fences for the words the court is trying to force out of them. If they should turn out not to be up to testifying in this hearing, if they turn out to be impotent to represent a live word properly, to act as its interpreter or spokesman, to sustain the conversation, to respond to oral questions, then bam! they are good for nothing. They are mere figurines, masks, simulacra.

Let us not forget that painting is here called *zōgraphia*, inscribed repre-sentation, a drawing *of the living*, a portrait of an animate model. The model for this type of painting is representative painting, which conforms to a live model. The word *zōgraphēma* is indeed sometimes shortened to *gramma* (*Cratylus*, 430*e* and 431*c*). Similarly, writing was supposed to paint a living word. It thus resembles painting to the extent that it is conceived—in this whole Platonic problematic, this massive and fundamental determination can be stated in a word—on the basis of the particular model of phonetic writing, which reigned in Greek culture. The signs of writing functioned within a system where they were supposed to represent the signs of voice. They were signs of signs.

Thus, just as painting and writing have faithfulness to the model as their model, the resemblance between painting and writing is precisely *resemblance itself*: both operations must aim above all at resembling. They are both apprehended as mimetic techniques, art being first determined as mimesis.

Despite this resemblance of resemblance, writing's case is a good deal more serious. Like any imitative art, painting and poetry are of course far away from truth (*Republic* X, 603*b*). But these two both have mitigating circumstances. Poetry imitates, but it imitates voice by means of voice. Painting, like sculpture, is silent, but so in a sense is its model. Painting and sculpture are arts of silence, as Socrates, the son of a sculptor who at first wanted to follow in his father's footsteps, very well knows. He knows this and says it in the *Gorgias* (450 *c–d*). The silence of the pictorial or sculptural space is, as it were, normal. But this is no longer the case in the scriptural order, since writing gives itself as the image of speech. Writing thus more seriously denatures what it claims to imitate. It does not even substitute an image for its model. It inscribes in the space of silence and in the silence of space the living time of voice. It displaces its model, provides no image of it, violently wrests out of its element the animate interiority of speech. In so doing, writing estranges itself immensely from the truth of the thing itself, from the truth of speech, from the truth that is open to speech.

And hence, from the king.

Let us recall the famous indictment of pictorial mimetics in the *Republic* (X, 597).[62] First, it is a question of banning poetry from the city, and this time, in contrast to what occurs in books II and III, for reasons linked essentially with its mimetic nature. The tragic poets, when they practice imitation, corrupt the minds of the listeners (*tēs tōn akouontōn dianoias*) if these do not possess an antidote (*pharmakon*, 595*a*). This counterpoison is "knowledge of the real nature of things" (*to eidenai auta hoia tungkhanei*

---

62. I shall study this passage from another viewpoint in a forthcoming text, "Entre deux coups de dés."

onta). If one considers that imitators and masters of illusion will later be presented as charlatans and thaumaturges (602*d*)—species of the genus *pharmakeus*—then once again ontological knowledge becomes a pharmaceutical force opposed to another pharmaceutical force. The order of knowledge is not the transparent order of forms and ideas, as one might be tempted retrospectively to interpret it; it is the antidote. Long before being divided up into occult violence and accurate knowledge, the element of the *pharmakon* is the combat zone between philosophy and its other. An element that is *in itself*, if one can still say so, *undecidable*.

Of course, in order to define the poetry of imitation, one has to know what imitation in general is. This is where that most *familiar* of examples comes in: the origin of the bed. Elsewhere, we will be able to take the time to inquire about the necessity governing the choice of this example and about the switch in the text that makes us slide insensibly from the table to the bed. The already made bed. In any case, God is the true father of the bed, of the clinical *eidos*. The carpenter is its "Demiurge." The painter, who is again called a zoographer, is neither its generator (*phutourgos*: author of the *phusis*—as truth—of the bed), nor its demiurge. Only its imitator. It is thus by three degrees that he is separated from the original truth, the *phusis* of the bed.

And hence, from the king.

"This, then, will apply to the maker of tragedies also, if he is an imitator and is in his nature at three removes from the king and the truth, as are all other imitators" (597*e*).

As for couching this *eidōlon* in written form, writing down the image that poetic imitation has already made, that would be equivalent to moving to a *fourth degree* of distance from the king, or rather, through a change of order or of element, wandering into an excessive estrangement from him, if Plato himself did not elsewhere assert, speaking of the imitative poet in general, that "he is always at an infinite remove from truth" (*tou de alēthous porrō panu aphestōta*) (605*c*). For in contrast to painting, writing doesn't even create a phantasm. The painter, of course, does not produce the being-true but the appearance, the *phantasm* (598*b*), that is, what is already a simulation of the copy (*Sophist*, 236*b*). In general, *phantasma* (the copy of a copy) has been translated as "simulacrum."[63] He who writes with the alphabet no longer

63. On the place and evolution of the concept of *mimēsis* in Plato's thought, we refer the reader primarily to V. Goldschmidt's *Essai sur le Cratyle* (1940) (esp. pp. 165 ff). What is made clear there is the fact that Plato did not always and everywhere condemn *mimēsis*. But one can at any rate conclude this: whether or not Plato condemns imitation, he poses the question of poetry by determining it as *mimēsis*, thus opening the field in which Aristotle's

even imitates. No doubt because he also, in a sense, imitates perfectly. He has a better chance of reproducing the voice, because phonetic writing decomposes it better and transforms it into abstract, spatial elements. This *de-composition* of the voice is here both what best conserves it and what best corrupts it. What imitates it perfectly because it no longer imitates it at all. For imitation affirms and sharpens its essence in effacing itself. Its essence is its nonessence. And no dialectic can encompass this self-inadequation. A perfect imitation is no longer an imitation. If one eliminates the tiny difference that, in separating the imitator from the imitated, by that very fact refers to it, one would render the imitator absolutely different: the imitator would become another being no longer referring to the imitated.[64] Imitation does not correspond to its essence, is not what it is —imitation— unless it is in some way at fault or rather in default. It is bad by nature. It is only good insofar as it is bad. Since (de)fault is inscribed within it, it has no nature; nothing is properly its own. Ambivalent, playing with itself by hollowing itself out, good and evil at once—undecidably, *mimēsis* is akin to the *pharmakon*. No "logic," no "dialectic," can consume its reserve even though each must endlessly draw on it and seek reassurance through it.

And as it happens, the technique of imitation, along with the production of the simulacrum, has always been in Plato's eyes manifestly magical, thaumaturgical:

> And the same things appear bent and straight to those who view them in water and out, or concave and convex, owing to similar errors of vision about colors, and there is obviously every confusion of this sort in our souls. And so scene painting (*skiagraphia*) in its exploitation of

Poetics, entirely subsumed under that category, will produce *the concept* of literature that reigned until the nineteenth century, up to but not including Kant and Hegel (not including them at least if *mimēsis* is translated as *imitation*).

On the other hand, Plato condemns under the name *phantasm* or *simulacrum* what is being advanced today, in its most radical exigency, as writing. Or at any rate that is what one can call, *within* philosophy and "mimetology," that which exceeds the conceptual oppositions within which Plato defines the phantasm. Beyond these oppositions, beyond the values of truth and nontruth, this excess (of) writing can no longer, as one might guess, be qualified simply as a simulacrum or phantasm. Nor can it indeed be named by the classical concept of writing.

64. "Let us suppose the existence of two objects (*pragmata*). One of them shall be Cratylus, and the other the image of Cratylus, and we will suppose, further, that some god makes not only a representation such as a painter would make of your outward form and color, but also creates an inward organization like yours, having the same warmth and softness, and into this infuses motion, and soul, and mind, such as you have, and in a word copies all your qualities, and places them by you in another form. Would you say that this was Cratylus and the image of Cratylus, or that there were two Cratyluses? *Cratylus*: I should say that there were two Cratyluses" (432*b–c*).

this weakness of our nature falls nothing short of witchcraft (*thaumato-poia*), and so do jugglery (*goēteia*) and many other such contrivances. (*Republic* X, 602c–d; cf. also 607c).[65]

The antidote is still the *epistēmē*. And since hybris is at bottom nothing but that excessive momentum that (en)trains being in(to) the simulacrum, the mask, the festival, there can be no antidote but that which enables one to remain *measured*. The *alexipharmakon* will be the science of measure, in every sense of the word. The text goes on:

But satisfactory remedies have been found for dispelling these illu-sions by measuring (*metrein*), counting (*arithmein*), and weighing (*histanai*). We are no longer at the mercy of an appearance (*phainomenon*) of difference in size and quantity and weight; the faculty which has done the counting and measuring or weighing takes control instead. And this can only be the work of the calculating or reasoning element (*tou logistikou ergon*) in the soul. (The word translated as "remedies" is the word used in the *Phaedrus* to qualify the attendance, the assistance [*boētheia*] that the father of living speech ought always to provide for writing, which is quite helpless in itself.)

The illusionist, the technician of sleight-of-hand, the painter, the writ-er, the *pharmakeus*. This has not gone unnoticed: ". . . isn't the word *pharmakon*, which means color, the very same word that applies to the drugs of sorcerers or doctors? Don't the casters of spells resort to wax figurines in pursuing their evil designs?"[66] Bewitchment [*l'envoûtement*] is always the effect of a *representation*, pictorial or scriptural, capturing, captivating the form of the other, par excellence his face, countenance, word and look, mouth and eye, nose and ears: the *vultus*.

The word *pharmakon*, then, also designates pictorial color, the material in which the *zōgraphēma* is inscribed. Turn to the *Cratylus*: in his exchange with Hermogenes, Socrates examines the hypothesis according to which names imitate the essence of things. He compares, in order to make a distinction between them, musical or pictorial imitation, on the one hand, and nominal imitation, on the other. What he does then is interesting to us not only because he refers to the *pharmakon* but also because another necessity imposes itself on him, one on which we will henceforth progres-sively attempt to shed some light: at the moment he takes up the question of the differential elements of nominal language, he is obliged, as is

65. On all these themes, see esp. P. M. Schuhl, *Platon et l'Art de son temps*.
66. Schuhl, p. 22. Cf. also *l'Essai sur la formation de la pensée grecque*, pp. 39 ff.

Saussure after him, to suspend the insistence on voice as sonority imitative of sounds (imitative music). If the voice names, it is through the differences and relations that are introduced among the *stoikheia*, the elements or letters (*grammata*). The same word (*stoikheia*) is used for both elements and letters. And one ought to reflect upon what here appears to be a conventional or pedagogical necessity: phonemes in general, vowels—*phōnēenta*[67] —and consonants, are designated by the letters that inscribe them.

> *Socrates*: . . . But how shall we further analyze them, and when does the imitator begin? Imitation of the essence is made by syllables and letters. Ought we not, therefore, first to separate the letters, just as those who are beginning rhythm first distinguish the powers of elementary sounds (*stoikheiōn*) and then of compound sounds, and when they have done so, but not before, proceed to the consideration of rhythms?
>
> *Hermogenes*: Yes.
>
> *Socrates*: Must we not begin in the same way with letters—first separating the vowels (*phōnēenta*), and then the consonants and mutes (*aphōna kai aphthonga*), into classes, according to the received distinctions of the learned, also the semivowels, which are neither vowels nor yet mutes, and distinguishing into classes the vowels themselves. And when we have perfected the classification of things, we shall give their names, and see whether, as in the case of letters, there are any classes to which they may all be referred, and hence we shall see their natures, and see, too, whether they have in them classes as there are in the letters. And when we have well considered all this, we shall know how to apply them to what they resemble, whether one letter is used to denote one thing, or whether there is to be an admixture of several of them, just as, in painting, the painter who wants to depict anything sometimes uses purple only, or any other color (*allo tōn pharmakōn*), and sometimes mixes up several colors, as his method is when he has to paint flesh color or anything of that kind—he uses a particular color (*pharmakou*) as his figures appear to require it. And so, too, we shall apply letters to the expression of objects, either single letters when required, or several letters, and so we shall form syllables, as they are called, and from syllables make nouns and verbs, and thus, at last, from the combination of nouns and verbs arrive at language,

---

67. Cf. also Philebus, 18*a*–*b*.

large and fair and whole, just as the painter used his paint (*tēi graphikēi*) to reproduce a living creature (*zōon*). (424*b* – 425*a*)

And further on:

Socrates: Very good, but if the name is to be like the thing, the letters out of which the first names are composed must also be like things. Returning to the image of the picture, I would ask how anyone could ever compose a picture which would be like anything at all, if there were not pigments (*pharmakeia*) in nature which resembled the things imitated, and out of which the picture is composed. (434*a–b*)

The *Republic* also calls the painter's colors *pharmaka* (420*c*). The magic of writing and painting is like a cosmetic concealing the dead under the appearance of the living. The *pharmakon* introduces and harbors death. It makes the corpse presentable, masks it, makes it up, perfumes it with its essence, as it is said in Aeschylus. *Pharmakon* is also a word for perfume. A perfume without essence, as we earlier called it a drug without substance. It transforms order into ornament, the cosmos into a cosmetic. Death, masks, makeup, all are part of the festival that subverts the order of the city, its smooth regulation by the dialectician and the science of being. Plato, as we shall see, is not long in identifying writing with festivity. And play. A certain festival, a certain game.

8. The Heritage of the Pharmakon:
Family Scene

We have now penetrated into another level of the Platonic reserves. This pharmacy is also, we begin to perceive, a theater. The theatrical cannot here be summed up in speech: it involves forces, space, law, kinship, the human, the divine, death, play, festivity. Hence the new depth that reveals itself to us will necessarily be another scene, on another stage, or rather another tableau in the unfolding of the play of writing. After the presentation of the *pharmakon* to the father, after the put-down of Theuth, Socrates takes the spoken word back to his own account. He seems to want to substitute *logos* for myth, discourse for theater, demonstration for illustration. And yet, within his very explanations, another scene slowly comes to light, less immediately visible than the preceding one, but, in its muffled latency, just as tense, just as violent as the other, composing with it, within the pharmaceutical enclosure, an artful, living organization of figures, displacements, repetitions.

This scene has never been read for what it is, for what is at once sheltered and exposed in its metaphors: its *family* metaphors. It is all about fathers and sons, about bastards unaided by any public assistance, about glorious, legitimate sons, about inheritance, sperm, sterility. Nothing is said of the mother, but this will not be held against us. And if one looks hard enough as in those pictures in which a second picture faintly can be made out, one might be able to discern her unstable form, drawn upside-down in the foliage, at the back of the garden. In the garden of Adonis, *eis Adōnidos kēpous* (276*b*).

Socrates has just compared the offspring (*ekgona*) of painting with those of writing. He has ridiculed their self-satisfied unsatisfactoriness, the solemn tautological monotony of the responses they give whenever we interrogate them. He goes on:

> And once a thing is put in writing, the composition, whatever it may be, drifts all over the place, getting into the hands not only of those who understand it, but equally of those who have no business with it; it doesn't know how to address the right people, and not address the wrong. And when it is ill-treated and unfairly abused it always needs its parent to come to its aid, being unable to defend itself or attend to its own needs. (275*e*)

The anthropomorphic or even animistic metaphor can doubtless be explained by the fact that what is written down is *speech* (*logos gegrammenos*). As a living thing, *logos* issues from a father. There is thus for Plato no such thing as a written thing. There is only a *logos* more or less alive, more or less distant from itself. Writing is not an independent order of signification; it is weakened speech, something not completely dead: a living-dead, a reprieved corpse, a deferred life, a semblance of breath. The phantom, the phantasm, the simulacrum (*eidōlon*, 276*a*) of living discourse is not inanimate; it is not insignificant; it simply signifies little, and always the same thing. This signifier of little, this discourse that doesn't amount to much, is like all ghosts: errant. It rolls (*kulindeitai*) this way and that like someone who has lost his way, who doesn't know where he is going, having strayed from the correct path, the right direction, the rule of rectitude, the norm; but also like someone who has lost his rights, an outlaw, a pervert, a bad seed, a vagrant, an adventurer, a bum. Wandering in the streets, he doesn't even know who he is, what his identity—if he has one—might be, what his name is, what his father's name is. He repeats the same thing every time he is questioned on the street corner, but he can no longer repeat his origin. Not to know where one comes from or where one is going, for a discourse with no guarantor, is not to know how to speak at all, to be in a state of infancy. Uprooted, anonymous, unattached to any house or country, this almost insignificant signifier is at everyone's disposal,[68] can be picked up by both the competent and the incompetent, by those who understand and know what to do with it [*ceux qui entendent et s'y entendent*] (*tois epaïousin*), and by those who are completely unconcerned with it, and who, knowing nothing about it, can inflict all manner of impertinence upon it.

At the disposal of each and of all, available on the sidewalks, isn't writing thus essentially democratic? One could compare the trial of writing with the trial of democracy outlined in the *Republic*. In a democratic society, there is no concern for competence: responsibilities are given to anyone at all. Magistracies are decided by lots (557*a*). Equality is equally dispensed to equal and unequal alike (558*c*). Excess, anarchy; the democratic man, with no concern for hierarchy, "establishes and maintains all his pleasures on a footing of equality, forsooth, and so lives turning over the guardhouse of his soul to each as it happens along until it is sated, as if it had drawn the lot for that office, and then in turn to another, disdaining none but fostering them all equally. . . . And he does not accept or admit into the guardhouse reason (*logon*) or truth (*alēthē*) when anyone tells him that some pleasures arise from honorable and good desires, and others from those that are base, and that we ought to practice and esteem the one and control and subdue the others, but he shakes his head at all such admonitions and avers that they are all alike and to be equally esteemed" (561*b—c*).

68. J. P. Vernant calls attention to such "democratization" of and through writing in classical Greece. "To this importance assumed by speech, which from that time forward became the instrument par excellence of political life, there also corresponds a change in the social significance of writing. In the kingdoms of the Near East, writing was the privilege and specialty of scribes. Writing enabled the royal administration to control the economic and social life of the State by keeping records of it. Its purpose was to constitute archives which were always kept more or less secret inside the palace. . . ." In classical Greece, "instead of being the exclusive privilege of one caste, the secret belonging to a class of scribes working for the palace of the king, writing becomes the 'common property' of all citizens, an instrument of publicity. . . .Laws had to be written down. . . . The consequences of this change in the social status of writing will be fundamental for intellectual history" (Vernant, *Mythe et Pensée*, pp. 151–52; cf. also pp. 52, 78, and *Les Origines de la pensée grecque*, pp. 43–44). Could it not be said, then, that Plato is continuing to think of writing from the viewpoint of the king, presenting it within the outmoded structures of the *basileia*? Structures which no doubt adhere to the mythemes informing his thought? But on the other hand, Plato believes in the need for written laws; and the suspicion against the occult virtues of writing would be aimed rather toward a non-"democratic" politics of writing. One must untangle all these threads and respect all these strata and discrepancies. In any event, the development of phonetic writing is inseparable from the movement of "democratization."

This errant democrat, wandering like a desire or like a signifier freed from *logos*, this individual who is not even perverse in a regular way, who is ready to do anything, to lend himself to anyone, who gives himself equally to all pleasures, to all activities—eventually even to politics or philosophy ("at another time seeming to occupy himself with philosophy, and frequently he goes in for politics and bounces up and says and does whatever enters his head" 561*d*)—this adventurer, like the one in the *Phaedrus*, simulates everything at random and is really nothing. Swept off by every stream, he belongs to the masses; he has no essence, no truth, no patronym, no constitution of his own. Moreover, democracy is no more a true constitution than the democrat has a character of his own: "I certainly think, said I, that he is a manifold man stuffed with the most excellent differences, and that like that city he is the fair and many-colored (*poikilon*) one whom many a man and woman would count fortunate in his life, as containing within himself the greatest number of patterns of constitutions and qualities" (561*e*). Democracy is orgy, debauchery, flea market, fair, "a bazaar (*pantopōlion*) of constitutions where one can choose the one to make one's own" (557*d*).

Whether it is seen as graphics or as politics, or, better—as the whole eighteenth century in France will do, especially Rousseau—as politicographics, such degradation can always be explained in terms of a bad relation between father and son (cf. 559*a*-560*b*). Desires, says Plato, should be raised like sons.

Writing is the miserable son. *Le misérable*. Socrates' tone is sometimes *categorical* and condemnatory—denouncing a wayward, rebellious son, an immoderation or perversion—and sometimes touched and condescending—pitying a defenseless living thing, a son abandoned by his father. In any event the son is *lost*. His impotence is truly that of an orphan[69] as much

69. The orphan is always, in the text of Plato—and elsewhere—the model of the persecuted creature. We had begun by stressing the affinity between writing and *mythos* created by their common opposition to *logos*. Orphanhood is perhaps another side of their kinship. *Logos* has a father; the father of a myth is almost impossible to find. Hence the need for assistance (*boētheia*) mentioned by the *Phaedrus* in connection with writing as an orphan. This also appears elsewhere: "*Socrates*: . . . And no one was left to tell Protagoras' tale, or yours either, about knowledge and perception being the same thing. *Theaetetus*: So it appears. *Socrates*: I fancy it would be very different if the author of the first story were still alive. He would have put up a good fight for his offspring. But he is dead, and here we are trampling on the orphan. Even its appointed guardians, like Theodorus here, will not come to the rescue (*boēthein*). However, we will step into the breach ourselves and see that it has fair play (*boēthein*). *Theodorus*: . . . I shall be grateful for any succor (*boētheis*) you can give him. *Socrates*: Very good, Theodorus. You shall see what my help (*boētheian*) will amount to . . ." (*Theaetetus*, 164*d*–165*a*).

as that of a justly or unjustly persecuted patricide. In his commiseration, Socrates sometimes gets quite carried away: alongside the living discourses persecuted and deprived of the aid of a logographer (this was the case with Socrates' own spoken words), there are also half-dead discourses—writings—persecuted for lack of the dead father's voice. Writing can thus be attacked, bombarded with unjust reproaches (*ouk en dikēi loidorētheis*) that only the father could dissipate—thus assisting his son—if the son had not, precisely, killed him.

In effect, the father's death opens the reign of violence. In choosing violence—and that is what it's all about from the beginning—and violence against the father, the son—or patricidal writing—cannot fail to expose himself, too. All this is done in order to ensure that the dead father, first victim and ultimate resource, not be there. Being-there is always a property of paternal speech. And the site of a fatherland.

Writing, the outlaw, the lost son. Plato, we recall, always associates speech and law, *logos* and *nomos*, and laws speak. In the personification in the *Crito*, they speak to Socrates directly. And in the tenth book of the *Republic*, they address themselves precisely to the father who has lost his son, they console him and urge him to resist his grief:

> When a good and reasonable man, said I, experiences such a stroke of fortune as the loss of a son or anything else that he holds most dear, we said, I believe, then too, that he will bear it more easily than the other sort. . . .Now is it not reason and law (*logos kai nomos*) that exhorts him to resist, while that which urges him to give way to his grief is the bare feeling itself (*auto to pathos*)?. . . The law declares (*legei pou ho nomos*) that it is best to keep quiet as far as possible in calamity. . . . (603e—604a—b)

What is the father? we asked earlier. The father is. The father is (the son lost). Writing, the lost son, does not answer this question—it writes (itself): (that) the father *is not*, that is to say, is not present. When it is no longer a spoken word fallen away from the father, writing suspends the question *what is*, which is always, tautologically, the question "what is the father?" and the reply "the father is what is." At that point a flap is produced that can no longer be thought about within the familiar opposition of father to son, speech to writing.

The time has come to recall the fact that Socrates, in the dialogues, plays the role of father, *represents* the father. Or the elder brother. We will see in a minute what the story is with the elder brother. And Socrates reminds the Athenians, like a father speaking to his children, that in killing him it is themselves they will hurt most. Let us listen to him in his prison cell. His ruse is infinite—and therefore naive or null (keep me alive—since I am already dead—for you):

> Remember my request to give me a hearing without interruption. . . . I assure you that if I am what I claim to be, and you put me to death, you will harm yourselves more than me. . . .If you put me to death, you will not easily find anyone to take my place. It is literally true, even if it sounds rather comical, that God has specially appointed me to this city, as though it were a large thoroughbred horse which because of its great size is inclined to be lazy and needs the stimulation of some stinging fly. It seems to me that God has attached me to this city to perform the office of such a fly, and all day long I never cease to settle here, there, and everywhere, rousing, persuading, reproving every one of you. You will not easily find another like me, gentlemen, and if you take my advice you will spare my life. I suspect, however, that before long you will awake from your drowsing, and in your annoyance you will take Anytus' advice and finish me off with a single slap, and then you will go on sleeping till the end of your days, unless God in his care for you sends someone to take my place (*epipempseie*). If you doubt whether I am really the sort of person who would have been sent to this city as a gift from God, you can convince yourselves by looking at it in this way. Does it seem natural that I should have neglected my own affairs and endured the humiliation of allowing my family to be neglected for all these years, while I busied myself all the time on your behalf, going to see each one of you privately like a father or an elder brother (*hōsper patera ē adelphon presbuteron*), and urging you to set your thoughts on goodness? (*Apology*, 30c–31b).

And what pushes Socrates to take the place [*suppleér*] of the father or elder brother toward the Athenians—a role in which he, too, will have to be replaced—is a certain voice. Which forbids, moreover, more than it bids; and which he obeys spontaneously, like the good horse in the *Phaedrus*, for whom the commands of the voice, of *logos*, suffice:

> The reason for this is what you have often heard me say before on many other occasions—that I am subject to a divine or supernatural experience [*phōnē*], which Meletus saw fit to travesty in his indictment (*ho dē kai en tēi graphēi epikōmōidōn Meletos egrapsato*). It began in my early childhood—a sort of voice (*phōnē*) which comes to me, and when it comes it always dissuades me from what I am proposing to do, and never urges me on. (31c–d)

As the bearer of this sign from God (*to tou theou sēmeion*, 40 *b*, *c* ; *to daimonion sēmeion*, *Republic* VI, 496*c*), Socrates thus takes voice from the father; he is the father's spokesman. And Plato writes *from out of his death*. All Plato's writing—and we are not speaking here about what it means, its intended content: the reparations of and to the father made against the *graphē* that decided his *death*—is thus, *when read from the viewpoint of Socrates' death*, in the situation of writing as it is indicted in the *Phaedrus*. These scenes enclose and fit into each other endlessly, abyssally. The pharmacy has no foundation.

Now, what about the accused? Up to now writing—written speech—has had no other status, as it were, than that of an orphan or moribund parricide. And while it becomes perverted in the course of its adventures by breaking with its origin, nothing has yet indicated that that origin was itself already bad. But it now appears that written discourse, in its "proper" meaning—that which is inscribed in sensible space—is deformed at its very birth. It is not well born: not only, as we have seen, because it is not entirely viable, but because it is not of good birth, of legitimate birth. It is not *gnēsios*. It is not exactly a commoner; it is a bastard. By the voice of its father it cannot be avowed, recognized. It is outside the law. After Phaedrus has agreed, Socrates goes on (276*a–b*):

> *Socrates*: But now tell me, is there another sort of discourse, that is brother to the written speech, but of unquestioned legitimacy (*adelphon gnēsion*)? Can we see how it originates, and how much better and more effective it is than the other?
>
> *Phaedrus*: What sort of discourse have you now in mind, and what is its origin?
>
> *Socrates*: The sort that goes together with knowledge and is written in the soul of the learner (*hos met'epistēmēs graphetai en tēi tou manthanontos psuchēi*), that can defend itself (*dunatos men amunai heautōi*), and knows to whom it should speak and to whom it should say nothing.
>
> *Phaedrus*: Do you mean the discourse of a man who really knows (*tou eidotos logon*), which is living and animate (*zōnta kai empsukhon*)? Would it be fair to call the written discourse only a kind of ghost (*eidōlon*) of it?
>
> *Socrates*: Precisely.

In its content, this exchange has nothing original about it. Alcidamas[70] said more or less the same thing. But it marks a sort of reversal in the

---

70. Cf. M. J. Milne, *A study in Alcidamas and his relation to contemporary sophistic* (1924) and P. N. Schuhl, *Platon et l'Art de son temps*, p. 49.

There is another allusion to the legitimate sons in 278*a*. On the opposition between

functioning of the argument. While presenting writing as a false brother—traitor, infidel, and simulacrum—Socrates is for the first time led to envision the brother of this brother, the legitimate one, as *another sort of writing*: not merely as a knowing, living, animate discourse, but as an *inscription* of truth in the soul. It is no doubt usually assumed that what we are dealing with here is a "metaphor." Plato—why not and so what?—thought so, too, perhaps, at the moment the history of this "metaphor" (inscription, imprint, mark, etc., in the wax of the mind or soul) was being engaged, or even inaugurated; a "metaphor" philosophy will never thereafter be able to do without, however uncritical its treatment might be. But it is not any less remarkable here that the so-called living discourse should suddenly be described by a "metaphor" borrowed from the order of the very thing one is trying to exclude from it, the order of its simulacrum. Yet this borrowing is rendered necessary by that which structurally links the intelligible to its repetition in the copy, and the language describing dialectics cannot fail to call upon it.

According to a pattern that will dominate all of Western philosophy, good writing (natural, living, knowledgeable, intelligible, internal, speaking) is opposed to bad writing (a moribund, ignorant, external, mute artifice for the senses). And the good one can be designated only through the metaphor of the bad one. Metaphoricity is the logic of contamination and the contamination of logic. Bad writing is for good a model of linguistic designation and a simulacrum of essence. And if the network of opposing predicates that link one type of writing to the other contains in its meshes all the conceptual oppositions of "Platonism"—here considered the dominant structure of the history of metaphysics—then it can be said that philosophy is played out in the play between two kinds of writing. Whereas all it wanted to do was to distinguish between writing and speech.

It is later confirmed that the conclusion of the *Phaedrus* is less a condemnation of writing in the name of present speech than a preference for one sort of writing over another, for the fertile trace over the sterile trace, for a seed that engenders because it is planted inside over a seed scattered wastefully outside: at the risk of *dissemination*. This, at least, is presumed by that. Before trying to account for this in terms of the general structure of Platonism, let us follow this movement.

The entrance of the *pharmakon* on the scene, the evolution of the magic powers, the comparison with painting, the politico-familial violence and

---

bastards and well-born sons (*nothoi/gnēsioi*), cf. notably, *Republic* (496*a*: "sophisms" have nothing "gnēsion" about them), and the *Statesman* (293*e*: "imitations" of constitutions are not "well born") Cf. also *Gorgias*, 513*b*; *Laws*, 741 *a*, etc.

perversion, the allusion to makeup, masks, simulacra—all this couldn't *not* lead us to games and festivals, which can never go without some sort of urgency or outpouring of sperm.

The reader will not be disappointed, provided he accepts a certain scansion of the text and agrees not to consider as mere rhetorical contingencies the terms of the analogy proposed by Socrates.

Here is the analogy: simulacrum-writing is to what it represents (that is, true writing—writing which is true because it is authentic, corresponds to its value, conforms to its essence, is the writing of truth in the soul of him who possesses the *epistēmē*) as weak, easily exhausted, superfluous seeds giving rise to ephemeral produce (floriferous seeds) are to strong, fertile seeds engendering necessary, lasting, nourishing produce (fructiferous seeds). On the one hand, we have the patient, sensible farmer (*ho noun ekhōn geōrgos*); on the other, the Sunday gardener, hasty, dabbling, and frivolous. On the one hand, the serious (*spoudē*); on the other, the game (*paidia*) and the holiday (*heortē*). On the one hand cultivation, agri-culture, knowledge, economy; on the other, art, enjoyment and unreserved spending.

> *Socrates*: . . . and now tell me this. If a sensible farmer[71] had some seeds to look after (*hōn spermatōn kēdoito*) and wanted them to bear fruit,

---

71. An analogous allusion to the farmer or husbandman is found in the *Theaetetus* (166a, ff); it is caught in a similar problematic, in the middle of the extraordinary defense Socrates puts in Protagoras' mouth, making him sound off about his four (non)truths, which are of the utmost importance to us here: it is a point at which all the corridors of this pharmacy intersect.

"*Socrates*: No doubt, then, Protagoras will make all the points we have put forward in our attempt to defend him, and at the same time will come to close quarters with the assailant, dismissing us with contempt. Your admirable Socrates, he will say, finds a little boy who is scared at being asked whether one and the same person can remember and at the same time not know one and the same thing. When the child is frightened into saying no, because he cannot foresee the consequence, Socrates turns the conversation so as to make a figure of fun of my unfortunate self. . . . For I do indeed assert that the truth is as I have written (*hōs gegrapha*). Each one of us is a measure of what is and of what is not, but there is all the difference in the world between one man and another (*murion mentoi diapherein heteron heterou antōi toutōi*). . . . In this statement (*logon*), again, don't set off in chase of words (*tōi rhēmati*), but let me explain still more clearly what I mean. Remember how it was put earlier in the conversation. To the sick man his food appears sour and is so; to the healthy man it is and appears the opposite. Now there is no call to represent either of the two as wiser—that cannot be—nor is the sick man to be pronounced unwise because he thinks as he does, or the healthy man wise because he thinks differently. What is wanted is a change (*metablēteon*) to the opposite condition, because the other state is better.

"And so too in education a change has to be effected from the worse condition to the better; only whereas the physician produces a change by means of drugs (*pharmakois*) the Sophist does it by discourse (*logois*). . . . And as for the wise (sophous), my dear Socrates, so far

would he with serious intent (*spoudēi*) plant them during the summer in a garden of Adonis,[72] and enjoy watching it produce fine fruit within eight days? If he did so at all wouldn't it be in a holiday spirit (*heortēs . . . Kharin*) just for fun (*paidias*)?[73] For serious purposes wouldn't he behave like a scientific farmer, sow his seeds in suitable soil, and be well content if they came to maturity within eight months? . . . And are we to maintain that he who has knowledge of what is just, honorable, and good has less sense than the farmer in dealing with his seeds? . . . Then it won't be with serious intent (*spoudēi*) that he will "write them in water" (*en hudati grapsei*, an expression equivalent to "writing in sand") or in that black fluid we call ink, using his pen to sow words (*melani speirōn dia kalamou meta logōn*) that can't either speak in their own support (*boēthein*) or teach the truth adequately. (276*b–c*)

---

from calling them frogs, I call them, when they have to do with the body, physicians, and when they have to do with plants, husbandmen. . . . In this way it is true both that some men are wiser (*sophóteroi*) than others and that no one thinks falsely. . . ."

72. "At the feasts of Adonis," notes Robin, "it was customary to grow, out of season, in a seashell, in a basket, in a vase, certain short-lived plants: offerings that symbolized the premature end of Aphrodite's beloved." Adonis, who was born in a tree—a metamorphosis of Myrrha—was loved and pursued by Venus, then hunted by Mars, who, jealous, changed into a boar, killed him with a wound in the thigh. In the arms of Venus who arrived too late, he became an anemone, an ephemeral spring flower. Anemone: that is, breath.

The opposition farmer/gardener (fruits/flowers; lasting/ephemeral; patience/haste; seriousness/play, etc.) can be juxtaposed to the theme of the double gift in the *Laws*:

"As to the fruit harvest, there must be an accepted general understanding to some effect as this. Two gifts are bestowed on us by the bounty of the goddess of harvest, one the 'ungarnered nursling of Dionysus' (*paidian Dionusiada*), the other destined for storage. So our law of fruits shall impose the following rules. If a man taste the common sort of fruit, whether grapes or figs, before Arcturus have brought round the season of vintage . . . he shall incur a fine in honor of Dionysus, of fifty drachmas" (VIII, 844*d–e*).

Within the problematic space that brings together, by opposing them, writing and agriculture, it could easily be shown that the paradoxes of the supplement as *pharmakon* and as writing, as engraving and as bastardy, etc., are the same as those of the graft [*greffe*], of the operation of grafting [*greffer*] (which means "engraving"), of the grafter [*greffeur*], of the *greffier* (a clerk of the court; a registrar), of the grafting-knife [*greffoir*], and of the scion [*greffon*]. [The sense of "graft" in English as political or financial corruption is not irrelevant here, either.—Trans.] It could also be shown that all the most modern dimensions (biological, psychical, ethical) of the problem of graft, even when they concern parts believed to be hegemonic and perfectly "proper" to what one thinks belongs to the individual (the intellect or head, the affect or heart, the desires or loins) are caught up and constrained within the graphics of the supplement.

73. Alcidamas, too, had defined writing as a game (*paidia*). Cf. Paul Friedlander, *Platon: Seinswahrheit und Lebenswirklichkeit*, part 1, chap. 5, and A. Diès, p. 427.

Sperm, water, ink, paint, perfumed dye: the *pharmakon* always penetrates like a liquid; it is absorbed, drunk, introduced into the inside, which
it first marks with the hardness of the type, soon to invade it and inundate it
with its medicine, its brew, its drink, its potion, its poison.

In liquid, opposites are more easily mixed. Liquid is the element of the
pharmakon. And water, pure liquidity, is most easily and dangerously
penetrated then corrupted by the *pharmakon*, with which it mixes and
immediately unites. Whence, among all the laws governing an agricultural
society, comes the one severely protecting water. Principally against the
pharmakon:

> Water, above all things, is exceptionally necessary for the growth of
> all garden produce, but is easily corrupted. It is not easy to affect the
> other contributory causes of the growth of products of the ground—
> the soil, the sunlight, the winds—by doctoring (*pharmakeusesin*),
> diverting, or intercepting the supply, but water can be tampered with
> in all these ways and the law must accordingly come to the rescue. So
> we shall meet the case by enacting as follows. If one man intentionally
> tampers with another's supply, whether of spring water or standing
> water, whether by way of drugging (*pharmakeiais*), of digging, or of
> abstraction, the injured party shall put the amount of damage on
> record, and proceed at law before the urban commissioners. A party
> convicted of putting poison (*pharmakeiais*) in the waters, shall, over
> and above the payment of the fine imposed, undertake the purification
> of the contaminated springs or reservoir in such fashion as the canon
> law may direct this purification to be performed in the individual case.
> (*Laws* VIII, 845*d–e*)

Writing and speech have thus become two different species, or values, of
the trace. One, writing, is a lost trace, a nonviable seed, everything in
sperm that overflows wastefully, a force wandering outside the domain of
life, incapable of engendering anything, of picking itself up, of regenerating itself. On the opposite side, living speech makes its capital bear fruit
and does not divert its seminal potency toward indulgence in pleasures
without paternity. In its seminar, in its seminary, it is in conformity with
the law. In it there is still a marked unity between *logos* and *nomos*. What is
the law in question? Here is how the Athenian states it:

> That was exactly my own meaning when I said I knew of a device for
> establishing this law of restricting procreative intercourse to its natu-
> ral function by abstention from congress with our own sex, with its
> deliberate murder of the race and its wasting of the seed of life on a

stony and rocky soil, where it will never take root and bear its natural fruit, and equal abstention from any female field whence you would desire no harvest. Once suppose this law perpetual and effective—let it be, as it ought to be, no less effective in the remaining cases than it actually is against incest with parents—and the result will be untold good. It is dictated, to begin with, by nature's own voice, leads to the suppression of the mad frenzy of sex, as well as marriage breach of all kinds, and all manner of excess in meats and drinks, and wins men to affection of their wedded wives. There are also numerous other blessings which will follow, if one can only compass the establishment of such a law. Yet should some young and lusty bystander of exuberant virility (*pollou spermatos mestos*) overhear us as we propose it, he might probably denounce our enactments as impracticable folly and make the air ring with his clamor. (*Laws* VIII, 838*e*–839*b*)

One could cite here both the writing *and* the pederasty of a young man named Plato. And his ambiguous relation to the paternal supplement: in order to make up for the father's death, he transgressed the law. He repeated the father's death. These two gestures contradict each other or cancel each other out. Whether it be a question of sperm or of writing, the transgression of the law is a priori subject to a law of transgression. Transgression is not thinkable within the terms of classical logic but only within the graphics of the supplement or of the *pharmakon*. Of that *pharmakon* which can *equally well* serve the seed of life and the seed of death, childbirth and abortion. Socrates was well aware of that:

> *Socrates*: Moreover, with the drugs (*pharmakia*) and incantations they administer, midwives can either bring on the pains of labor or allay them at their will, make a difficult labor easy, and at an early stage cause a miscarriage if they so decide.(*Theaetetus*, 149*c*–*d*)

The scene becomes more complicated: while condemning writing as a lost or parricidal son, Plato behaves like a son *writing* this condemnation, at once repairing and confirming the death of Socrates. But in this scene where we have remarked the apparent absence of the mother, Socrates is not really the father, either; only the *surrogate* father. This *accoucheur*, the son of a midwife, this intercessor, this go-between is neither a father, even though he takes the father's place, nor a son, even though he is the son's comrade or brother and obeys the paternal voice of God. Socrates is the supplementary relation between father and son. And when we say that Plato writes *from out of* the father's death, we are thinking not only of some event entitled "the death of Socrates" which, it is said, Plato did not attend (*Phaedo*, 59*b*: "I believe that Plato was ill"); but primarily of the sterility of the Socratic seed left to its own devices. Socrates knows that he will never be a son, nor a father, nor a mother. The knowledge the go-between needs for matchmaking should have been the same as the knowledge the midwife needs for delivering ("Consider the knowledge of that sort of plant or seed that should be sown in any given soil. Does that not go together with skill in tending and harvesting the fruits of the earth?" *Theaetetus*, 149e), if prostitution and transgression of the law had not kept them separate. If Socrates' art is still better than that of a matchmaker-midwife, it is no doubt because his task is to distinguish between apparent or false fruit (*eidōlon kai pseudos*) and true living fruit (*gonimon te kai alēthes*). But for the essential, Socrates shares the lot of the midwife: sterility. "I am so far like the midwife that I cannot myself give birth to wisdom. . . . Heaven constrains me to serve as a midwife, but has debarred me from giving birth." And let us recall the ambiguity of the Socratic *pharmakon*, both anxiogenic and tranquilizing: "My art has power to bring on these pangs or to allay them" (150a–151b).

The seed must thus submit to *logos*. And in so doing, it must do violence to itself, since the natural tendency of sperm is opposed to the law of *logos*: "The marrow . . . we have named semen. And the semen, having life and becoming endowed with respiration, produces in that part in which it respires a lively desire of emission, and thus creates in us the love of procreation. Wherefore also in men the organ of generation becoming rebellious and masterful, like an animal disobedient to reason (*tou logou*), and maddened with the sting of lust, seeks to gain absolute sway" (*Timaeus*, 91b).

One must here take care: at the moment Plato seems to be raising writing up by turning live speech into a sort of psychic *graphē*, he maintains this movement within a problematic of *truth*. Writing *en tēi psuchēi* is not pathbreaking writing, but only a writing of transmission, of education, of demonstration, or at best, of dis-covering, a writing of *alētheia*. Its order is didactic, maieutic, or at any rate elocutionary. Dialectical. This type of writing must be capable of sustaining itself in living dialogue, capable most of all of properly teaching the true, as it is *already* constituted.

This authority of truth, of dialectics, of seriousness, of presence, will not be gainsaid at the close of this admirable movement, when Plato, after having in a sense reappropriated writing, pushes his irony—and his seriousness—to the point of rehabilitating a certain form of play. Compared with other pastimes, playful hypomnesic writing, second-rate writing, is preferable, should "go ahead." Ahead of the other brothers, for there are even worse seeds in the family. Hence the dialectician will sometimes write, amass monuments, collect *hupomnēmata*, just for fun. But he will do so while still putting his products at the service of dialectics and in order to leave a trace (*ikhnos*) for whoever might want to follow in his footsteps on the pathway to truth. The dividing line now runs less between presence and the trace than between the dialectical trace and the nondialectical trace, between play in the "good" sense and play in the "bad" sense of the word.

> *Socrates*: He will sow his seed in literary gardens, I take it, and write when he does write by way of pastime (*paidias kharin*), collecting a store of reminders (*hupomnēmata*) both for his own memory, against the day "when age oblivious comes," and for all such as tread in his footsteps (*tauton ikhnos*), and he will take pleasure in watching the tender plants grow up. And when other men resort to other pastimes, regaling themselves with drinking parties and suchlike, he will doubtless prefer to indulge in the recreation I refer to.
>
> *Phaedrus*: And what an excellent one it is, Socrates! How far superior to the other sort is the recreation that a man finds in words (*en logois*), when he discourses about justice and the other topics you speak of.
>
> *Socrates*: Yes indeed, dear Phaedrus. But far more excellent, I think, is the serious treatment (*spoudē*) of them, which employs the art of dialectic. The dialectician selects a soul of the right type, and in it he plants and sows his words founded on knowledge (*phuteuēi te kai speirēi met' epistēmēs logous*), words which can defend '(*boēthein*) both themselves and him who planted them, words which instead of remaining barren contain a seed whence new words grow up in new characters (*en allois ēthesi*), whereby the seed is vouchsafed immortality, and its possessor the fullest measure of blessedness that man can attain unto. (276d–277a)

9. Play: From the Pharmakon to the Letter and from Blindness to the Supplement

"Kai tēi tēs spoudēs adelphēi paidiai"
—*Letter* VI, 323*d*

"Logos de ge ēn hē tēs sēs diaphorotētos hermēneia"
—*Theaetetus*, 209*a*

It has been thought that Plato simply condemned play. And by the same token the art of *mimēsis* which is only a type of play.[74] But in all questions involving play and its "opposite," the "logic" will necessarily be baffling. Play and art are lost by Plato as he saves them, and his logos is then subject to that untold constraint that can no longer even be called "logic." Plato does very well speak of play. He speaks in praise of it. But he praises play "in the best sense of the word," if this can be said without eliminating play beneath the reassuring silliness of such a precaution. The best sense of play is play that is supervised and contained within the safeguards of ethics and politics. This is play comprehended under the innocent, innocuous category of "fun." Amusement: however far off it may be, the common translation of *paidia* by *pastime* [*divertissement*] no doubt only helps consolidate the Platonic repression of play.

The opposition *spoudē/paidia* will never be one of simple symmetry. *Either* play is *nothing* (and that is its only *chance*); either it can give place to no activity, to no discourse worthy of the name—that is, one charged with truth or at least with meaning—and then it is *alogos* or *atopos. Or else* play begins to *be* something and its very presence lays it open to some sort of dialectical confiscation. It takes on meaning and works in the service of seriousness, truth, and ontology. Only *logoi peri ontōn* can be taken seriously. As soon as it comes into being and into language, play *erases itself as such*. Just as writing must erase itself as such before truth, etc. The point is that

74. Cf. *Republic*, 60*a–b* ff; *Statesman*, 288*c–d*; *Sophist*, 234 *b–c*; *Laws* II, 667*e–668a*; *Epinomis*, 975*d*, etc.

there *is* no *as such* where writing or play are concerned. Having no essence, introducing difference as the condition for the presence of essence, opening up the possibility of the double, the copy, the imitation, the simulacrum— the game and the *graphē* are constantly disappearing as they go along. They cannot, in classical affirmation, be affirmed without being negated.

Plato thus plays at taking play seriously. That is what we earlier called the stunning hand Plato has dealt himself. Not only are his writings defined as games,[75] but human affairs in general do not in his eyes need to be taken seriously. One thinks of the famous passage in the *Laws*. Let us reread it despite its familiarity, so as to follow the theological assumption of play into games, the progressive neutralization of the *singularity* of play:

> To be sure, man's life is a business which does not deserve to be taken too seriously (*megalēs men spoudēs ouk axia*); yet we cannot help being in earnest with it, and there's the pity. Still, as we are here in this world, no doubt, for us the becoming thing is to show this earnestness in a suitable way (*hēmin summetron*). . . . I mean we should keep our seriousness for serious things, and not waste it on trifles, and that, while God is the real goal of all beneficent serious endeavor (*makariou spoudēs*), man, as we said before,[76] has been constructed as a toy (*paignion*) for God, and this is, in fact, the finest thing about him. All of us, then, men and women alike, must fall in with our role and spend life in making our *play* as perfect as possible—to the complete inversion of current theory. . . . It is the current fancy that our serious work should be done for the sake of our play; thus it is held that war is serious work which ought to be well discharged for the sake of peace. But the truth is that in war we do not find, and we never shall find, either any real play or any real education worth the name, and *these* are the things I count supremely serious for such creatures as ourselves.

75. Cf. *Parmenides*, 137*b*; *Statesman*, 268*d*; *Timaeus*, 59*c–d*. On the context and historical background of this problematic of play, cf. notably Schuhl, pp. 61–63.

76. Cf. *Laws* I, 644*d–e*: "Let us look at the whole matter in some such light as this. We may imagine that each of us living creatures is a puppet made by gods, possibly as a plaything (*hōs paignion*) or possibly with some more serious purpose (*hōs spoudēi tini*). That, indeed, is more than we can tell, but one thing is certain. These interior states are, so to say, the cords, or strings, by which we are worked; they are opposed to one another, and pull us with opposite tensions in the direction of opposite actions, and therein lies the division of virtue from vice. In fact, so says our argument (*logos*) a man must always yield to one of these tensions without resistance, but pull against all the other strings—must yield, that is, to that golden and hallowed drawing of judgments (*tēn tou logismou agōgēn khrusēn kai hieran*) which goes by the name of the public law of the city. The others are hard and ironlike, it soft, as befits gold, whereas they resemble very various substances."

Let us henceforth keep hold of this rein called *khrusus* or *chrysology*.

Hence it is peace in which each of us should spend most of his life and spend it best. What, then, is our right course? We should pass our lives in the playing of games—*certain* games, that is, sacrifice, song, and dance—with the result of ability to gain heaven's grace, and to repel and vanquish an enemy when we have to fight him. . . . (803*b–e*)

Play is always lost when it seeks salvation in games. We have examined elsewhere, in "Rousseau's era,"[77] this disappearance of play into games. This (non)logic of play and of writing enables us to understand what has always been considered so baffling:[78] why Plato, while subordinating or condemning writing and play, should have written so much, presenting his writings, *from out of Socrates' death*, as games, *indicting* writing in writing, lodging against it that complaint (*graphē*) whose reverberations even today have not ceased to resound.

What law governs this "contradiction," this opposition to itself of what is said against writing, of a dictum that pronounces itself against itself as soon as it finds its way into writing, as soon as it writes down its self-identity and carries away what is proper to it *against* this ground of writing? This "contradiction," which is nothing other than the relation-to-self of diction as it opposes itself to scription, as it *chases* itself (away) in hunting down what is properly its *trap*—this contradiction is not contingent. In order to convince ourselves of this, it would already suffice to note that what seems to inaugurate itself in Western literature with Plato will not fail to re-edit itself at least in Rousseau, and then in Saussure. In these three cases, in these three "eras" of the repetition of Platonism, which give us a new thread to follow and other knots to recognize in the history of *philosophia* or the *epistēmē*, the exclusion and the devaluation of writing must somehow, in their very affirmation, come to terms with:

1. a generalized sort of writing and, along with it,

2. a "contradiction": the written proposal of logocentrism; the simultaneous affirmation of the being-outside of the outside and of its injurious intrusion into the inside;

3. the construction of a "literary" work. Before Saussure's *Anagrams*, there were Rousseau's; and Plato's work, outside and independent of its logocentric "content," which is then only one of its inscribed "functions," can be read in its anagrammatical texture.

Thus it is that the "linguistics" elaborated by Plato, Rousseau, and Saussure must both put writing out of the question and yet nevertheless

77. Cf. *Of Grammatology*.
78. The principal references are collected in Robin's *La Théorie platonicienne de l'amour*, pp. 54–59.

borrow from it, for fundamental reasons, all its demonstrative and theoretical resources. As far as the Genevans are concerned, we have tried to show this elsewhere. The case is at least equally clear for Plato.

Plato often uses the example of letters of the alphabet in order to come to grips with a problem. They give him a better grip on things; that is, he can use them to explain dialectics—but he never "comes to grips with" the writing he uses. His intentions are always apparently didactic and analogical. But they conform to a constant necessity, which is never thematized as such: what always makes itself apparent is the law of difference, the irreducibility of structure and relation, of proportionality, within analogy.

We noted earlier that *tupos* can designate with equal pertinence the graphic unit and the eidetic model. In the *Republic*, even before he uses the word *tupos* in the sense of model-form (*eidos*) Plato finds it necessary to turn to the example of the letter, still for apparently pedagogical ends, as a model that must be known before one can recognize its copies or icons reflected in water or in a mirror:

> It is, then, said I, as it was when we learned our letters and felt that we knew them sufficiently only when the separate letters did not elude us, appearing as a few elements in all the combinations that convey them, and when we did not disregard them in small things or great and think it unnecessary to recognize them, but were eager to distinguish them everywhere, in the belief that we should never be literate and letter-perfect till we could do this. . . . And is it not also true that if there are any likenesses of letters (*eikonas grammatōn*) reflected in water or mirrors, we shall never know them until we know the originals, but such knowledge belongs to the same art and discipline? (402a–b)

We have no doubt already been warned by the *Timaeus*: in all these *comparisons* with writing, we are not supposed to take the letters *literally*. The *stoikheia tou pantos*, the elements (or letters) of the whole are not assembled like syllables (48c). "They cannot reasonably be compared by a man of any sense even to syllables."[79] And yet, in the *Timaeus*, not only is the entire mathematical play of proportionalities based on a *logos* that can do without voice, God's calculation (*logismos theou*) (34a) being able to express itself in the silence of numbers; but, in addition, the introduction of the *different* and the *blend* (35a), the problematic of the *moving* cause and the *place*—the third irreducible class—the duality of paradigms (49a), all these things "require" (49a) that we define the origin of the world as a *trace*, that

79. As for the use of letters, in the context of a comparison between the *Timaeus* and the *Jafr*, the Islamic science of letters as a science of "permutation," cf. notably H. Corbin, *Histoire de la philosophie islamique*, (Paris: Nouvelle Revue Française), pp. 204ff.

is, a receptacle. It is a matrix, womb, or receptacle that is never and nowhere offered up in the form of presence, or in the presence of form, since both of these already presuppose an inscription within the mother. Here, in any case, the turns of phrase that are somewhat awkwardly called "Plato's metaphors" are exclusively and irreducibly scriptural. Let us, for example, point to a sign of this awkwardness in a certain preface to the *Timaeus*: "In order to conceive of place, one must always, through a process of abstraction that is almost unrealizable in practice, separate or detach an object from the 'place' it occupies. This abstraction, however difficult, is nevertheless imposed upon us by the very fact of change, since two different objects cannot coexist in the same place, and since, without changing place, a same object can become 'other.' But then, we find ourselves unable to represent 'place' itself except by metaphors. Plato used several quite different ones, which have greatly confused modern readers. The 'Place,' the 'locus,' 'that in which' things appear, 'that upon which' they manifest themselves, the 'receptacle,' the 'matrix,' the 'mother,' the 'nurse'—all these expressions make us think of space, which contains things. But later on it is a question of the 'impression-bearer,' the formless 'base,' the completely inodorous substance on which the perfume-maker can fix the scent, the soft gold on which the jeweller can impress many diverse figures" (Rivaud, Budé edition, p. 66). Here is the passage beyond all "Platonic" oppositions, toward the aporia of the originary inscription:

> . . . Then we made two classes; now a third must be revealed. The two sufficed for the former discussion. One, we assumed, was a pattern (*paradeigmatos*) intelligible and always the same, and the second was only the imitation of the pattern, generated and visible. There is also a third kind which we did not distinguish at the time, conceiving that the two would be enough. But now the argument seems to require that we should set forth in words another kind, which is difficult of explanation and dimly seen. What nature are we to attribute to this new kind of being? We reply that it is the receptacle, and in a manner the nurse (*hupodokhēn autēn hoion tithēnēn*), of all generation (*pasēs geneseōs*). . . . [This nurse] must be always called the same, for, inasmuch as she always receives all things, she never departs at all from her own nature and never, in any way or at any time, assumes a form like that of any of the things which enter into her; she is the natural recipient of all impressions (*ekmageion*), and is stirred and informed by them, and appears different from time to time by reason of them. But the forms which enter into and go out of her are the likenesses of eternal realities (*tōn ontōn aei mimēmata*) modeled within her after their

patterns (*tupōthenta*) in a wonderful and mysterious manner, which we will hereafter investigate. For the present we have only to conceive of three natures: first, that which is in process of generation; secondly, that in which the generation takes place; and thirdly, that of which the thing generated is a resemblance naturally produced. And we may liken the receiving principle to a mother, and the source or spring to a father, and the intermediate nature to a child, and may remark further that if the model is to take every variety of form, then the matter in which the model is fashioned will not be duly prepared unless it is formless and free from the impress of any of those shapes which it is hereafter to receive from without. . . . . Wherefore the mother and receptacle of all created and visible and in any way sensible things is not to be termed earth or air or fire or water, or any of their compounds, or any of the elements from which these are derived, but is an invisible and formless being which receives all things and in some mysterious way partakes of the intelligible, and is most incomprehensible (48*e*–51*b*; The *khōra* is big with everything that is disseminated here. We will go into that elsewhere).

Whence the recourse to dream a bit further on, as in that text of the *Republic* (533*b*) where it is a question of "seeing" what cannot simply be conceived in terms of the opposition between sensible and intelligible, hypothetical and anhypothetical, a certain *bastardy* whose notion (*nothos*) was probably not unknown to Democritus (cf. Rivaud; *Le Problème du devenir et la notion de la matière* . . . p. 310, n. 744):

And there is a third nature, which is space and is eternal, and admits not of destruction and provides a home for all created things, and is apprehended, when all sense is absent, by a kind of spurious reason (*logismōi tini nothōi: bastard* reasoning), and is hardly real—which we, beholding as in a dream, say of all existence that it must of necessity be in some place and occupy a space, but that what is neither in heaven nor in earth has no existence. Of these and other things of the same kind, relating to the true and waking reality of nature, we have only this dreamlike sense, and we are unable to cast off sleep and determine the truth about them. (52*b*–*c*)

Inscription is thus the *production of the son* and at the same time the constitution of *structurality*. The link between structural relations of proportionality on the one hand and literality on the other does not appear only in cosmogonic discourse. It can also be seen in political discourse, and in the discourse of linguistics.

In the political order, structure is a sort of writing. At the moment of ultimate difficulty, when no other pedagogical resource is available, when theoretical discourse cannot find any other way of formulating the order, the world, the *cosmos* of politics, Socrates turns to the grammatical "metaphor." The analogy of the "large letters" and "small letters" comes up in the famous text of the *Republic* (368c-e) at the point where "keen vision" is necessary, and where it seems to be lacking. Structure is read as a form of writing in an instance where the intuition of sensible or intelligible presence happens to fail.

The same thing occurs in the domain of linguistics. As in Saussure's *Course in General Linguistics*, the scriptural reference becomes absolutely indispensable at the point at which the principle of difference and diacriticity in general must be accounted for as the very condition of signification. This is how Theuth comes to make his second appearance on the Platonic scene. In the *Phaedrus*, the inventor of the *pharmakon* gave a long speech in person and presented his letters as credentials to the king. More concise, more indirect, more allusive, his other intervention seems to us just as philosophically remarkable. It occurs in the name not of the invention of graphics but of grammar, of the science of grammar as a science of differences. It is in the beginning of the *Philebus*: the debate is open on the relations between pleasure (*khairein*) and intelligence or prudence (*phronein*) (11d). The discussion soon founders on the problem of *limits*. And hence, as in the *Timaeus*, on the composition of the same and the other, the one and the multiple, the finite and the infinite. ". . . the men of old, who were better than ourselves and dwelt nearer the gods, passed on this gift in the form of a saying. All things, as it ran, that are ever said to be consist of a one and a many, and have in their nature a conjunction (*en hautois sumphuton*) of limit and unlimitedness (*peras de kai apeirian*)." Socrates opposes dialectics, the art of respecting the intermediate forms (*ta mesa*), to eristic, which immediately leaps toward the infinite (16c–17a). This time, in contrast to what happens in the *Phaedrus*, letters are charged with the task of introducing clarity (*saphēneia*) into discourse:

> *Protarchus*: I think I understand, more or less, part of what you say, Socrates, but there are some points I want to get further cleared up.
> *Socrates*: My meaning, Protarchus, is surely clear in the case of the alphabet; so take the letters of your school days as illustrating it.
> *Protarchus*: How do you mean?
> *Socrates*: The sound (*phōnē*) that proceeds through our mouths, yours and mine and everybody's, is one, isn't it, and also an unlimited variety?

Protarchus: To be sure.

Socrates: And we have no real understanding if we stop short at knowing it either simply as an unlimited variety, or simply as one. What makes a man "lettered" is knowing the number and the kinds of sounds. (17*a–b*)

After a detour through the example of musical intervals (*diastēmata*), Socrates goes back to letters in an effort to explain phonic intervals and differences:

Socrates: . . . We might take our letters again to illustrate what I mean now. . . . The unlimited variety of sound was once discerned by some god, or perhaps some godlike man; you know the story that there was some such person in Egypt called Theuth. He it was who originally discerned the existence, in that unlimited variety, of the vowels (*ta phōnēenta*)—not "vowel" in the singular but "vowels" in the plural—and then of other things which, though they could not be called articulate sounds, yet were noises of a kind. There were a number of them, too, not just one, and as a third class he discriminated what we now call the mutes (*aphōna*). Having done that, he divided up the noiseless ones or mutes (*aphthonga kai aphōna*) until he got each one by itself, and did the same thing with the vowels and the intermediate sounds; in the end he found a number of the things, and affixed to the whole collection, as to each single member of it, the name "letters" (*stoikheion*). It was because he realized that none of us could get to know one of the collection all by itself, in isolation from all the rest, that he conceived of "letter" as a kind of bond of unity (*desmon*) uniting as it were all these sounds into one, and so he gave utterance to the expression "art of letters," implying that there was one art that dealt with the sounds. (18*b–d*)

The scriptural "metaphor" thus crops up every time difference and relation are irreducible, every time otherness introduces determination and puts a system in circulation. The play of the other within being must needs be designated "writing" by Plato in a discourse which would like to think of itself as spoken in essence, in truth, and which nevertheless is written. And if it is written *from out of the death of Socrates*, this is no doubt the profound reason for it. From out of Socrates' death—that is, it would here be just as well to say, from out of the parricide in the *Sophist*. Without that violent eruption against the venerable paternal figure of Parmenides, against his thesis of the unity of being; without the disruptive intrusion of otherness and nonbeing, of nonbeing as other in the unity of being, writing and its play would not have been necessary. Writing is parricidal. Is it by chance that, for the Stranger in the *Sophist*, the necessity and inevitability of parricide, "plain enough, as they say, for even the blind (*tuphlōi*) to see" (one ought to say, *especially* for the blind to see), are the condition of possibility of a discourse on the false, the idol, the icon, the mimeme, the phantasm, and "the arts concerned with such things"? And thus, of writing? Writing is not named at this point but that does not prevent—on the contrary—its relation with all the aforementioned concepts from remaining systematic, and we have recognized it as such:

> *Stranger*: We shall find it necessary in self-defense to put to the question that pronouncement of father Parmenides (*Ton tou patros Parmenidou logon*), and establish by main force that what is not (*mē on*), in some respect has a being, and conversely that what is (*on*), in a way is not.
>
> *Theaetetus*: It is plain that the course of the argument requires us to maintain that at all costs (*Phainetai to toiouton diamakheteon en tois logois*).
>
> *Stranger*: Plain enough even for the blind to see, as they say. Unless these propositions are either refuted or accepted, anyone who talks of false statements or false judgment as being images or likenesses or copies or semblances, or of any of the arts concerned with such things, can hardly escape becoming a laughingstock by being forced to contradict himself.
>
> *Theaetetus*: Quite true.
>
> *Stranger*: That is why we must now dare to lay unfilial hands on that paternal pronouncement (*tōi patrikōi logōi*), or else, if some scruple holds us back, drop the matter entirely.
>
> *Theatetus*: As for that, we must let no scruple hinder us. (241*d*–242*a*)

This parricide, which opens up the play of difference and writing, is a frightening decision. Even for an anonymous Stranger. It takes superhuman strength. And one runs the risk of madness or of being considered mad in the well-behaved, sane, sensible society of grateful sons.[80] So the Stranger

---

80. It would be interesting to articulate with this analysis that passage from the *Laws* (VIII, 836*b*–*c*), in which a *pharmakon* is sought as a "protection (*diaphugēn*) against this peril," namely, pederasty. The Athenian wonders, without holding out much hope, what would happen "were one to follow the guidance of nature and adopt the law of the old days before Laius (*tēi phusei thēsei ton pro tou Laiou nomon*)—I mean, to pronounce it wrong that male should have to do carnally with youthful male as with female. . . ." Laius, to whom the oracle

is still afraid of not having the strength, not only to play the fool, but also to maintain a discourse that might—for real—be without head or tail; or, to put it another way, to set off on a path where he might not be able to avoid ending up walking on his head. In any event, this parricide will be just as decisive, cutting, and redoubtable as capital punishment. With no hope of return. One lays one's head, as well as one's chief, on the line. Thus, after having begged Theaetetus, without illusions, not to consider him a patricide (*patraloian*), the Stranger asks another favor:

> *Stranger*: In that case, for the third time, I have a small favor to ask.
> *Theaetetus*: You have only to mention it.
> *Stranger*: I believe I confessed just now that on this point the task of refutation has always proved too much for my powers, and still does so.
> *Theaetetus*: You did say that.
> *Stranger*: Well, that confession, I am afraid, may make you think me scatterbrained (*manikos*) when at every turn I shift my position to and fro (*para poda metabalōn emauton anō kai katō*). (242a–b)

The discourse, then, is off. Paternal *logos* is upside down. Is it then by chance if, once "being" has appeared as a *triton ti*, a third irreducible to the dualisms of classical ontology, it is again necessary to turn to the example of grammatical science and of the relations among letters in order to explain the interlacing that weaves together the system of differences (solidarity-exclusion), of kinds and forms, the *sumplokē tōn eidōn* to which "any discourse we can have owes its existence" (*ho logos gegonen hēmin*) (259e)? The *sumplokē*, too, of being and nonbeing (240c)? As far as the rules of concordance and discordance, of union and exclusion among different things are concerned, this *sumplokē* "might be said to be in the same case with the letters of the alphabet" (253a; cf. the *Statesman* where the "paradigm" of the *sumplokē* is equally *literal*, 278a–b).[81]

had predicted that he would be killed by his son, was also the representative of unnatural love. Cf. "*Oedipe*," in Delcourt, p. 103.

We also know that according to the *Laws*, there is no greater crime or sacrilege than the murder of the parents: such a murderer should be put to "repeated deaths" (IX, 869b). And even receive punishment worse than death, which is not the ultimate chastisement. "Hence we must make the chastisements for such crime here in this present life, if we can, no less stern than those of the life to come" (881b).

81. On the problem of the letters of the alphabet, particularly as it is treated in the *Statesman*, cf. V. Goldschmidt, *Le Paradigme dans la dialectique Platonicienne* (Paris: Presses Universitaires de France, 1947), pp. 61–67.

Grammatical science is doubtless not in itself dialectics. Plato indeed explicitly subordinates the former to the latter (253*b–c*). And, to him, this distinction can be taken for granted; but what, in the final analysis, justifies it? Both are in a sense sciences of language. For dialectics is also the science that guides us *"dia tōn logōn,"* on the voyage through discourses or arguments (253*b*). At this point, what distinguishes dialectics from grammar appears twofold: on the one hand, the linguistic units it is concerned with are larger than the word (*Cratylus*, 385*a*–393*d*); on the other, dialectics is always guided by an intention of *truth*. It can only be satisfied by the presence of the *eidos*, which is here both the signified and the referent: the thing itself. The distinction between grammar and dialectics can thus only in all rigor be established at the point where truth is fully present and fills the *logos*.[82] But what the parricide in the *Sophist* establishes is not only that any *full*, *absolute* presence of what *is* (of the being-present that most truly "is": the good or the sun that can't be looked in the face) is impossible; not only that any full intuition of truth, any truth-filled intuition, is impossible; but that the very condition of discourse—*true or false*—is the diacritical principle of the *sumplokē*. If truth is the presence of the *eidos*, it must always, on pain of mortal blinding by the sun's fires, come to terms with relation, nonpresence, and thus nontruth. It then follows that the absolute precondition for a rigorous difference between grammar and dialectics (or ontology) cannot in principle be fulfilled. Or at least, it can perhaps be fulfilled *at the root of the principle*, at the point of arche-being or arche-truth, but that point has been crossed out by the necessity of parricide. Which means, by the very necessity of *logos*. And that is the difference that prevents there being *in fact* any difference between grammar and ontology.

But now, what *is* the impossibility of any truth or of any full presence of being, of any fully-being? Or inversely, since such truth would be death as the absolute form of blindness, what is death as truth? Not *what is?* since the form of that question is produced by the very thing it questions, but how is

---

82. The structure of this problematic is entirely *analogous* in the *Logical Investigations* of Husserl. See *Speech and Phenomena*. One will also reread in a new way, since it is a matter of *sumplokē* and *pharmakon*, the end of the *Statesman*. In his work of weaving (*sumplokē*), the royal weaver will be able to interweave his web through the joining of the opposites of which virtue is composed. Literally, the *sumplokē*, the weaving, is *intrigued* with the *pharmakon*: "But in those of noble nature from their earliest days whose nurture too has been all it should be, the laws can foster the growth of this common bond of conviction (*kata phusin monois dia nomōn emphuesthai*). This is the talisman (*pharmakon*) appointed for them by the design of pure intelligence. This most godlike bond alone can unite the elements of goodness which are diverse in nature and would else be opposing in tendency." (310*a*).

the impossible plenitude of any absolute presence of the *ontōs on* written? How is it inscribed? How is the necessity of the multiplicity of genres and ideas, of relation and difference, prescribed? How is dialectics traced?

The absolute invisibility of the origin of the visible, of the good-sun-father-capital, the unattainment of presence or beingness in any form, the whole surplus Plato calls *epekeina tēs ousias* (beyond beingness or presence), gives rise to a structure of replacements such that all presences will be supplements substituted for the absent origin, and all differences, within the system of presence, will be the irreducible effect of what remains *epekeina tēs ousias*.

Just as Socrates supplements and replaces the father, as we have seen, dialectics supplements and replaces the impossible *noēsis*, the forbidden intuition of the face of the father (good-sun-capital). The withdrawal of that face both opens and limits the exercise of dialectics. It welds it irremediably to its "inferiors," the mimetic arts, play, grammar, writing, etc. The disappearance of that face is the movement of differance which violently opens writing or, if one prefers, which opens itself to writing and which writing opens for itself. All these "movements," in all these "senses," belong to the same "system." Also belonging to that same system are the proposition in the *Republic*, describing in nonviolent terms the inaccessibility of the father *epekeina tēs ousias*, and the patricidal proposal which, proffered by the Stranger, threatens the paternal *logos*. And which by the same token threatens the domestic, hierarchical interiority of the pharmacy, the proper order and healthy movement of goods, the lawful prescription of its controlled, classed, measured, labeled products, rigorously divided into remedies and poisons, seeds of life and seeds of death, good and bad traces, the unity of metaphysics, of technology, of well computed binarism. This philosophical, dialectical mastery of the *pharmaka* that should be handed down from legitimate father to well-born son is constantly put in question by a family scene that constitutes and undermines at once the passage between the pharmacy and the house. "Platonism" is both the general *rehearsal* of this family scene and the most powerful effort to master it, to prevent anyone's ever hearing of it, to conceal it by drawing the curtains over the dawning of the West. How can we set off in search of a different guard, if the pharmaceutical "system" contains not only, in a single stranglehold, the scene in the *Phaedrus*, the scene in the *Republic*, the scene in the *Sophist*, and the dialectics, logic, and mythology of Plato, but also, it seems, certain non-Greek structures of mythology? And if it is not certain that there are such things as non-Greek "mythologies"—the opposition *mythos/logos* being only authorized *following* Plato—into what general, unnamable necessity are we thrown? In other words, what does Platonism signify as repetition?

To repeat: the disappearance of the good-father-capital-sun is thus the precondition of discourse, taken this time as a moment and not as a principle of *generalized* writing. That writing (is) *epekeina tēs ousias*. The disappearance of truth as presence, the withdrawal of the present origin of presence, is the condition of all (manifestation of) truth. Nontruth is the truth. Nonpresence is presence. Differance, the disappearance of any origi-nary presence, is *at once* the condition of possibility *and* the condition of impossibility of truth. At once. "At once" means that the being-present *(on)* in its truth, in the presence of its identity and in the identity of its presence, is *doubled* as soon as it appears, as soon as it presents itself. *It appears, in its essence, as* the possibility of its own most proper non-truth, of its pseudo-truth reflected in the icon, the phantasm, or the simulacrum. What is is not what it is, identical and identical to itself, unique, unless it *adds to itself* the possibility of being *repeated* as such. And its identity is hollowed out by that addition, withdraws itself in the supplement that presents it.

The disappearance of the Face or the structure of repetition can thus no longer be dominated by the value of truth. On the contrary, the opposition between the true and the untrue is entirely comprehended, *inscribed*, within this structure or this generalized writing. The true and the untrue are both species of repetition. And there is no repetition possible without the *graphics of supplementarity*, which supplies, for the lack of a full unity, another unit that comes to relieve it, being enough the same and enough other so that it can replace by addition. Thus, on the one hand, repetition is that without which there would be no truth: the truth of being in the intelligible form of ideality discovers in the *eidos* that which can be re-peated, being the same, the clear, the stable, the identifiable in its equality with itself. And only the *eidos* can give rise to repetition as anamnesis or maieutics, dialectics or didactics. Here repetition gives itself out to be a repetition of life. Tautology is life only going out of itself to come home to itself. Keeping close to itself through *mnēmē*, *logos*, and *phōnē*. But on the other hand, repetition is the very movement of non-truth: the presence of what is gets lost, disperses itself, multiplies itself through mimemes, icons, phantasms, simulacra, etc. Through phenomena, already. And this type of repetition is the possibility of becoming-perceptible-to-the-senses: nonideality. This is on the side of non-philosophy, bad memory, hypomnesia, writing. Here, tautology is life going out of itself beyond return. Death rehearsal. Unreserved spending. The irreducible excess, through the play of the supplement, of any self-intimacy of the living, the good, the true.

These two types of repetition relate to each other according to the graphics of supplementarity. Which means that one can no more "separate" them from each other, think of either one apart from the other, "label" them, than one can in *the pharmacy* distinguish the medicine from the poison, the good from the evil, the true from the false, the inside from the outside, the vital from the mortal, the first from the second, etc. Conceived within this original reversibility, the *pharmakon* is the *same* precisely because it has no identity. And the same (is) as supplement. Or in differance. In writing. If he had *meant* to say something, such would have been the speech of Theuth making of writing as a *pharmakon* a singular present to the King.

But Theuth, it should be noted, spoke not another word.

The great god's sentence went unanswered.

. . . .

After closing the pharmacy, Plato went to retire, to get out of the sun. He took a few steps in the darkness toward the back of his reserves, found himself leaning over the *pharmakon*, decided to analyze.

Within the thick, cloudy liquid, trembling deep inside the drug, the whole pharmacy stood reflected, repeating the abyss of the Platonic phantasm.

The analyst cocks his ears, tries to distinguish between two repetitions. He would like to isolate the good from the bad, the true from the false.

He leans over further: they repeat each other.

Holding the *pharmakon* in one hand, the calamus in the other, Plato mutters as he transcribes the play of formulas. In the enclosed space of the pharmacy, the reverberations of the monologue are immeasurably amplified. The walled-in voice strikes against the rafters, the words come apart, bits and pieces of sentences are separated, disarticulated parts begin to circulate through the corridors, become fixed for a round or two, translate each other, become rejoined, bounce off each other, contradict each other, make trouble, tell on each other, come back like answers, organize their exchanges, protect each other, institute an internal commerce, take themselves for a dialogue. Full of meaning. A whole story. An entire history. All of philosophy.

"*hē ēkhē toutōn tōn logōn*... the sound of these arguments rings so loudly in my head that I cannot hear the other side."

In this stammering buzz of voices, as some philological sequence or other floats by, one can sort of make this out, but it is hard to hear: *logos* beds itself [*le logos s'aime lui-même* = logos loves itself; *s'aime* is a homonym for *sème*: to sow, as in a flower bed.—Trans.] . . . *pharmakon* means *coup* . . . "so that *pharmakon* will have meant: that which pertains to an attack of demoniac possession [*un coup démoniaque*] or is used as a curative *against* such an attack" . . . an armed enforcement of order [*un coup de force*] . . . a shot fired [*un coup tiré*] . . . a planned overthrow [*un coup monté*] . . . but to no avail [*un coup pour rien*] . . . like cutting through water [*un coup dans l'eau*] . . . *en udati grapsei* . . . and a stroke of fate [*un coup du sort*] . . . Theuth who invented writing . . . the calendar . . . dice . . . *kubeia* . . . the calendar trick [*le coup du calendrier*] . . . the unexpected dramatic effect [*le coup de théâtre*] . . . the writing trick [*le coup de l'écriture*] . . . the dice-throw [*le coup de dés*] . . . two in one blow [*le coup double*] . . . *kolaphos* . . . *gluph* . . . *colpus* . . . *coup* . . . glyph . . . scalpel . . . scalp . . . *khrusos* . . . *chrysolite* . . . *chrysology* . . .

Plato gags his ears [*Platon se bouche les oreilles; boucher* = to plug up; *bouche* = mouth. —Trans.] the better to hear-himself-speak, the better to see, the better to analyze.

He listens, means to distinguish, between two repetitions.

He is searching for gold. *Pollakis de legomena kai aei akouomena* . . . "Often repeated and constantly attended to for many years, it is at last with great effort freed from all alloy, like gold . . ." and the philosopher's stone. The "golden rule."

One ought to distinguish, between two repetitions.

—But they repeat each other, still; they substitute for each other . . .

—Nonsense: they don't replace each other, since they are added . . .

—Precisely . . .

One still has to take note of this. And to finish that Second Letter: ". . . Consider these facts and take care lest you sometime come to repent of having now unwisely published your views. It is a very great safeguard to learn by heart instead of writing . . . *to mē graphein all'ekmanthanein.* . . . It is impossible for what is written not to be disclosed. That is the reason why I have never written anything about these things . . . *oud'estin sungramma Platōnos ouden oud'estai*, and why there is not and will not be any written work of Plato's own. What are now called his . . . *Sōkratous estin kalou kai neou gegonotos* . . . are the work of a Socrates embellished and modernized. Farewell and believe. Read this letter now at once many times and burn it . . . ."

—I hope this one won't get lost. Quick, a duplicate . . . graphite . . . carbon . . . reread this letter . . . burn it. *Il y a là cendre*. And now, to distinguish, between two repetitions . . .

The night passes. In the morning, knocks are heard at the door. They seem to be coming from outside, this time . . .

Two knocks . . . four . . .

—But maybe it's just a residue, a dream, a bit of dream left over, an echo of the night . . . that other theater, those knocks from without . . .

TRANCE PARTITION (1)

"In regard to Nature, it is agreed that philosophy ought to know her as she is, that if the philosophers' stone (*der Stein der Weisen*) is hidden anywhere, it must at any rate be within Nature herself, that she contains her own reason within her. . . . the ethical world (*die sittliche Welt*), on the other hand, the State. . ."

"Innocence, therefore, is merely nonaction, like the mere being of a stone (*das Sein eines Steines*), not even that of a child."

Hegel

"The Moravian brothers put people to death by tickling. A somewhat similar torture was tried on women: they were polluted to death. . . .

" 'Most adorable philosopher!' I cried, throwing my arms around Braschi's neck, 'No one has ever given an explanation like yours of this important matter . . .'

" 'Let's go; it's late: didn't you say that the dawn must not find us in the midst of our impurities?' . . .

"We went into the church."

Sade

". . . Gullibility whipped up with blasphemy, this wordly black magic spreads, indeed, to literature, an object of study or criticism.

"A certain deference, better, toward the extinct laboratory of the philosophers' elixir, would consist of taking up again, without the furnace, the manipulations, poisons, cooled down into something other than precious stones, so as to continue simply through intelligence. Since there are only, in all, two pathways open to mental research, into which our need bifurcates — namely, esthetics on the one hand and political economy on the other — it is principally of the latter that alchemy was the glorious, hasty, and troubling precursor. Everything that once stood out, pure, for lack of meaning, prior to the current apparition of the crowd, should be restored to the social realm. The null stone, dreaming of gold, once called philoso-

{*continued on p. 286*}

The Double Session

First version published in *Tel Quel*, nos. 41 and 42, 1970. The text
was there accompanied by a preliminary editorial note, which we
here reproduce:
  "The title has been proposed by the editors. For reasons that will
become clear in the reading, this text did not present itself under
any title. It formed the occasion for two sessions (February 26 and
March 5, 1969) of the *Groupe d'Etudes théoriques*. The reader should
also know that at that time only the first part of "La Dissémination"
had been published (*Critique*, no. 261, February 1969).
  "Each participant had been handed a sheet on which a passage
from Plato's *Philebus* (38e–39e) and Mallarmé's *Mimique* (Pléiade, p.
310) had been printed. We are reproducing here the typography and
the topography of that handout. Is it pointless to add that a
blackboard stood covered with a series of framed and numbered
quotations? And that the room was lighted by a sumptuous, old-
fashioned lustre?[1] (Editor's note)"

1. TN. *Lustre*: "A decorative object, as a chandelier having glass pendants" (American
Heritage Dictionary).

SOCRATES: And if he had someone with him, he would put what he said to himself into actual speech addressed to his companion, audibly uttering those same thoughts, so that what before we called opinion (δόξαν) has now become assertion (λόγος).—PROTARCHUS: Of course.—SOCRATES: Whereas if he is alone he continues thinking the same thing by himself, going on his way maybe for a considerable time with the thought in his mind.—PROTARCHUS: Undoubtedly.—SOCRATES: Well now, I wonder whether you share my view on these matters.—PROTARCHUS: What is it?—SOCRATES: It seems to me that at such times our soul is like a book (Δοκεῖ μοι τότε ἡμῶν ἡ ψυχὴ βιβλίῳ τινὶ προσεοικέναι).—PROTARCHUS: How so?—SOCRATES: It appears to me that the conjunction of memory with sensations, together with the feelings consequent upon memory and sensation, may be said as it were to write words in our souls (γράφειν ἡμῶν ἐν ταῖς ψυχαῖς τότε λόγους). And when this experience writes what is true, the result is that true opinion and true assertions spring up in us, while when the internal scribe that I have suggested writes what is false (ψευδῆ δ᾽ ὅταν ὁ τοιοῦτος παρ᾽ ἡμῖν γραμματεὺς γράψῃ), we get the opposite sort of opinions and assertions. —PRO-TARCHUS: That certainly seems to me right, and I approve of the way you put it—SOCRATES: Then please give your approval to the presence of a second artist (δημιουργὸν) in our souls at such a time.—PROTARCHUS: Who is that?—SOCRATES: A painter (Ζωγράφον) who comes after the writer and paints in the soul pictures of these assertions that we make.—PROTARCHUS: How do we make out that he in his turn acts, and when?—SOCRATES: When we have got those opinions and assertions clear of the act of sight ('ὄψεως) or other sense, and as it were see in ourselves pictures or images (εἰκόνας) of what we previously opined or asserted. That does happen with us, doesn't it?—PROTARCHUS: Indeed it does.—SOCRATES: Then are the pictures of true opinions and assertions true, and the pictures of false ones false?—PROTARCHUS: Unquestionably.—SOCRATES: Well, if we are right so far, here is one more point in this connection for us to consider.—PROTARCHUS: What is that?—SOCRATES: Does all this necessarily befall us in respect of the present (τῶν ὄντων) and the past (τῶν γεγονότων), but not in respect of the future (τῶν μελλόντων)?—PROTARCHUS: On the contrary, it applies equally to them all.—SOCRATES: We said previously, did we not, that pleasures and pains felt in the soul alone might precede those that come through the body? That must mean that we have anticipatory pleasures and anticipatory pains in regard to the future.—PROTARCHUS: Very true.—SOCRATES: Now do those writings and paintings (γράμματά τε καὶ ξωγραφήματα), which a while ago we assumed to occur within ourselves, apply to past and present only, and not to the future?—PROTARCHUS: Indeed they do.—SOCRATES: When you say 'indeed they do', do you mean that the last sort are all expectations concerned with what is to come, and that we are full of expectations all our life long?—PROTARCHUS: Undoubtedly.—SOCRATES: Well now, as a supplement to all we have said, here is a further question for you to answer.

MIMIQUE

Silence, sole luxury after rhymes, an orchestra only marking with its gold, its brushes with thought and dusk, the detail of its signification on a par with a stilled ode and which it is up to the poet, roused by a dare, to translate! the silence of an afternoon of music; I find it, with contentment, also, before the ever original reappearance of Pierrot or of the poignant and elegant mime Paul Margueritte.

Such is this PIERROT MURDERER OF HIS WIFE composed and set down by himself, a mute soliloquy that the phantom, white as a yet unwritten page, holds in both face and gesture at full length to his soul. A whirlwind of naive or new reasons emanates, which it would be pleasing to seize upon with security: the esthetics of the genre situated closer to principles than any! (no)thing in this region of caprice foiling the direct simplifying instinct... This — "The scene illustrates but the idea, not any actual action, in a hymen (out of which flows Dream), tainted with vice yet sacred, between desire and fulfillment, perpetration and remembrance: here anticipating, there recalling, in the future, in the past, *under the false appearance of a present.* That is how the Mime operates, whose act is confined to a perpetual allusion without breaking the ice or the mirror: he thus sets up a medium, a pure medium, of fiction." Less than a thousand lines, the role, the one that reads, will instantly comprehend the rules as if placed before the stageboards, their humble depository. Surprise, accompanying the artifice of a notation of sentiments by unproffered sentences — that, in the sole case, perhaps, with authenticity, between the sheets and the eye there reigns a silence still, the condition and delight of reading.

<table>
<tr><td>I</td><td>

"exit in the
midst of the session
I feign to carry off
the 160—the play
—I bring it back—
and return it
to the cubbyholes
the other way around
only when it has become
a book again"[2]

</td><td>

"   ⌐ where it seems
—Such is the double session" [(192A)]

" . . . which
thus gives two sessions" [91(A)]

</td></tr>
</table>

"If it please some one, surprised by the scope, to incriminate . . . it will be (the) Language whose gambol this is.

—Words, of themselves, are exalted on many a facet known as the rarest or having value for the mind, the center of vibratory suspense; whoever perceives them independent of the ordinary sequence, projected, on the walls of a cave, as long as their mobility or principle lasts, being that which of discourse is not said: all of them quick, before becoming extinct or extinguished, to enter into a reciprocity of fires that is distant or presented on the bias as some contingency.

The debate—which the average necessary obviousness deflects into a detail, remains one for grammarians." (O.C. p. 386)

(II)

"In short

⌐ in place of a page that each would have—
          he will not
have it; I will keep all . . ." [121(A)]
    "identity between   ⌐ is this beginning
place and page   by the end? ⌐
session and volume . . ." (p. 138)   [94(A)]

(III)

"He has set foot in the antre; extracted the subtle remains" (O.C. 407).

"What inevitable treachery, however, in the fact of an evening of our existence lost in that antre of cardboard and painted canvas, or of genius: a Theater! if nothing is worth our taking an interest in it . . . The one, wholly intimate solemnities: to place the ivory knife in the darkness made by two joined pages of a volume: the other, luxurious, proud, and so specially Parisian: a *Premiere* in any spot at all . . ." (O.C. pp. 717–18).

(IV)

"He finds himself in a place—City—where   of which he would have set up the
                                                   festival—(wedding)
                        Th   Dr
The deed that ought to have brought him glory   is a crime: he stops in
time in this Operation;" . . . [169(A)]
                   operation
         "—the Hero
     extricates —the Hymn
(the maternal one) that creates him, and is
restored to the Th it was—" [4(A)]

(V)

2. *Le "Livre" de Mallarmé* [*Mallarmês "Book"*], edited by Jacques Scherer (Paris: Gallimard, 1957), p. 182. [Page numbers following quotations from Mallarmé refer either to *Le "Livre"* (generally recognizable by an accompanying (A) or (B), which, in Scherer's code, indicates the size of the manuscript page) or to the *Oeuvres complètes* (Paris: Pléiade, 1945). Because of the care with which Derrida examines the details of Mallarmé's writing, existing translations of Mallarmé have proved unusable. Moreover, many of the texts cited have never, to my knowledge, been translated. For these reasons, all translations of Mallarmé's works are my own.—Trans.]

These quotations on the blackboard are to be pointed to in silence. So that, while reading a text already written in black and white, I can count on a certain across-the-board index, standing all the while behind me, white on black. In the course of these crossings, it will always be a certain way of writing in white that should be remarked.

The double session (figure I), about which I don't quite have the gall to say plumb straight out that it is reserved for the question *what is literature*, this question being henceforth properly considered a quotation already, in which the place of the *what is* ought to lend itself to careful scrutiny, along with the presumed authority under which one submits anything whatever, and particularly literature, to the form of its inquisition—this double session, about which I will never have the militant innocence to announce that it is concerned with the question *what is literature*, will find its corner BETWEEN [*ENTRE*] literature and truth, between literature and that by which the question *what is? wants* answering.

This double session will itself have been picked up on a corner, in the middle or the suspense of the two parts of a text, of which only one is visible, readable for having at least been published, and of which the whole is grafted onto *Numbers* which will have to be counted in. In the eyes of some, the reference to this half-absent text will be obvious. In any case, it can be taken for granted that the session and the text are neither absolutely separate nor simply inseparable.

The place of interest, then, this corner between literature and truth, will form a certain angle. It will be a figure of folding back, of the angle ensured by a fold.

And now there is the *question of the title*.

This, among others that are just as decisive, is an extremely profound question raised by Goux, concerning "The still unthought thought about the network, a polynodal, nonrepresentative organization, a thought about the *text* . . . the text which nothing can *entitle*. Without title or chapter; without head(ing) or capital."[3]

Mallarmé knew this. Indeed, he had constructed this question, or rather undone it with a bifid answer, separating the question from itself, displacing it toward an essential *indecision* that leaves its very titles up in the air.

Which introduces us (in)to the corner that interests us: *on the one hand*, Mallarmé prescribes a *suspension* of the title, which—like the head, or capital, or the oracle—carries its head high, speaks in too high a voice, both

3. Jean-Joseph Goux, "Numismatiques II," in *Tel Quel* 36, p. 59.

because it raises its voice and drowns out the ensuing text, and because it is found high up on the page, the top of the page becoming the eminent center, the beginning, the command station, the chief, the archon. Mallarmé thus urges that the title be stilled. A discreet injunction, found in the burst of an active fragment, upon a certain short, sharp ridge. From this we will also retain evidence of a certain hymen, to which the fact of indecision will later cause us to return:

"*I prefer, faced with aggression, to retort that contemporaries don't know how to read—*

Unless it be in the newspaper; it dispenses, certainly, the advantage of not interrupting the chorus of preoccupations.

To read—

That practice—

To seek support, according to the page, upon the blank space, which inaugurates it, upon oneself, for an ingenousness, forgetful even of the title that would raise its voice too high: and, when, in a break—the slightest, disseminated—chance is aligned, conquered word by word, indefectibly the white blank returns, a moment ago gratuitous, certain now, to conclude that nothing beyond and to authenticate the silence—

Virginity which solitarily, before a transparency of the adequate eye, has, itself, as it were divided itself into its fragments of candor, the one and the other, nuptial proofs of the Idea.

The air or song beneath the text, conducting divination from here to there, applies its motif in the form of an invisible fleuron or tailpiece" (p. 386–87).

What resists the authority and presumption of the title, the plumbline and aplomb of the heading, is not merely the invisible tailpiece [*cul-de-lampe*] which, at the other extremity, and according to its definition in typographical terms, "serves to fill in a blank space on a page." What ruins the *"pious capital letter"* of the title and works toward the decapitation or ungluing of the text is the regular intervention of the blanks, the ordered return of the white spaces, the measure and order of dissemination, the law of spacing, the ρυθμός[4] (written character and cadence), the *"punctuation which, disposed upon white paper, already produces signification there"* (p. 655). The unfailing return, the periodic regularity of the white in the text ("*indefectibly the white blank returns . . .*") is re-marked in the *"virginity,"* the

---

4. On the meaning and the problematics of this word, see Emile Benveniste, "The Notion of 'Rhythm' in Its Linguistic Expression," in *Problems in General Linguistics*, trans. Mary E. Meek (Coral Gables, Fla: University of Miami Press, 1971); and K. Von Fritz, *Philosophie und sprachlicher Ausdruck bei Demokrit, Plato und Aristoteles* (Darmstadt, 1963), pp. 25 ff.

"*candor*," and the "*nuptial proofs of the Idea.*" Through these words, and the whiteness of a certain veil that is interposed or torn, we have already been introduced, gently, into a certain angle in which we are interested.

To *suspend* the title, then, is necessary, considering what the title dominates.

But the function of the title is not merely one of hierarchy. The title to suspend is also, by virtue of its place, suspended, in suspense or in suspension. Up above a text from which it expects and receives all—or nothing. Among other roles, this suspension occurs in the spot where Mallarmé has disposed the *lustre*, the innumerable lustres that hang over the stage of his texts.

The entitled, then, does not assign the capital of a type of writing; it ensures its suspense, along with its contours, its borders, its frame. It provides a first fold and draws a sort of womblike matrix of whiteness. Whence not only the painstaking care involved in the choice of titles (of which we will see several examples), but also, as far as the ungluing or decapitation is concerned, the "semantic reversal"[5] for which we will determine the law of indecision. Mallarmé recommends, then, that silence be imposed on the title but also that one draw upon it as upon the resources of a germinal or seminal blank. The function of the title sentences or generative sentences for Mallarmé has been recognized before. Robert G. Cohn devotes two chapters to it using the example of the *Throw of Dice.*[6] Writing to Maurice Guillemot,[7] Mallarmé *describes* the suspensive value of the title, or more precisely of the empty space it marks out at the top of the page. This letter has a claim on our interest for other motifs as well: for example, the motif of the singular practice of a *description* which is nothing less than a *representation*, notably when what seems to be in question is furniture, decor, and atmosphere (the description is of a kind of writing that describes itself, de-inscribes itself as it goes along, marking the angles and "*coilings*" or "*reprises*" that bring it back to itself; it is never simply a

5. In a different context, apropos of other examples, Jean-Pierre Richard analyzes what he calls precisely the "semantic reversal" of the theme of *la décollation* [ungluing/decapitation], in *L'Univers imaginaire de Mallarmé* [*Mallarmé's Imaginary Universe*] (Paris: Seuil, 1961), p. 199.

6. *L'Oeuvre de Mallarmé: Un coup de dés*, Librairie des Lettres, 1951. [Because R. G. Cohn's two books published in English on *Un coup de dés* (*Mallarmé's Un coup de dés: An Exegesis* and *Mallarmé's Masterwork: New Findings*) do not exactly correspond to this book originally published in French, I have translated the quotations from the French, using Cohn's corresponding English terminology where possible.—Trans.]

7. Quoted by Jacques Scherer, *L'Expression littéraire dans l'Oeuvre de Mallarmé* [*Literary Expression in the Works of Mallarmé*] (Paris: Droz, 1947), p. 79.

description of things); the motif too of a word I have never encountered anywhere else, not even in Mallarmé: syntaxer [*syntaxier*]. *"There is at Versailles a kind of wainscotting in scrollwork tracery, pretty enough to bring tears to the eyes; shells, coilings, curves, reprises of motifs. That is how the sentence I toss out on the paper first appears to me, in summary design, which I then review, purify, reduce, and synthesize. If one obeys the invitation proffered by the wide white space expressly left at the top of the page as if to mark a separation from everything, the already read elsewhere, if one approaches with a new, virgin soul, one then comes to realize that I am profoundly and scrupulously a syntaxer, that my writing is entirely lacking in obscurity, that my sentence is what it has to be, and to be forever . . ."*

The title will thus remain suspended, in suspension, up in the air, but glittering like a theater lustre of which the multiplicity of facets (figure II) can never be counted or reduced: *"Sole principle! and just as the lustre glistens, that is to say, itself, the prompt exhibition, under all its facets, of whatever, and our adamantine sight, a dramatic work shows the succession of exteriorities of the act without any moment's retaining any reality and that in the final analysis what happens is nothing . . . the perpetual suspense of a tear that can never be entirely formed nor fall (still the lustre) scintillates in a thousand glances . . ."* (p. 296).

Since we will later find ourselves bolstering up this absence of event, the imminent, visible configuration of its non(taking)-place (*"without any moment's retaining any reality and that in the final analysis what happens is nothing"*), in the syntax of the curtain, the screen, the veil, let us recall, from among the *Services* [*Offices*], the *Sacred Pleasure* [*Plaisir sacré*]. The bow or baton of the conductor—of the orchestra—waiting, depending, like a lifted quill, can also be illuminated by some such suspension or lustre *" . . . when the curtain is about to rise upon the desert magnificence of autumn. The imminent scattering of luminous fingering, which the foliage suspends, mirrors itself, then, in the pit of the readied orchestra.*

The conducting baton waits for a signal.

Never would the sovereign bow fall, beating out the first measure, if it were necessary at this special moment of the year that the lustre in the hall represent, with its multiple facets, any lucidity in the audience as to what they were doing there" (p. 388).

There might perhaps be suspended, over this double session, a title faceted thus

[*pronounce without writing,*]   THE "INTO" OF MALLARMÉ
[*four times*[8]   that is, THE "INTER" OF MALLARMÉ
                    that is, THE ANTRE OF MALLARMÉ
                    that is, THE IN-TWO OF "MALLARMÉ"[9]*

It is written as it is pronounced.

And the first of the two subtitles would then be suspended by two dots, according to the syntax that is written thus

[*write, this time,*]   Hymen: INTER Platonem et Mallarmatum[10]*
[*without pronouncing*

"*The speaker takes his seat*"[11]*

---

* Notes 9–11 appear on page 182.

8. Triumphantly, the opposition rushes in here with an objection, mobilized and marching forth in columns of *pressing business*: they will say *voilà*!, here is a play of the signifier that cannot be effected without being said aloud. Therefore it is no longer confind to the sole medium of that *writing* that has recently been grating on our ears.

For those who, lacking the ability to read, would be simple and hasty enough to content themselves with such an objection, let us very briefly go back over this: what is being pursued in the light of this lustre (and *is* indeed, in a sense, designed to grate on the ear) is a certain displacement of writing, a systematic transformation and generalization of its "concept." The old opposition between speech and writing no longer has any pertinence as a way of testing a text that deliberately deconstructs that opposition. Such a text is no more "spoken" than it is "written," no more *against* speech than *for* writing, in the metaphysical sense of these words. Nor is it *for* any third force, particularly any radicalism of the origin or of the center. The values of *archē* and *telos*, along with the history and transcendentality that are dependent upon them, constitute precisely the principal objects of this deconstructive critique. To repeat: "That is why it has never been a question of opposing a graphocentrism to a logocentrism, nor, in general, any center to any other center. . . . And even less a rehabilitation of what has always been called writing. It is not a question of returning to writing its rights, its superiority or its dignity . . ." [*Positions*, trans. A. Bass (Chicago: Chicago University Press, 1981), p. 12.]. And, since it is necessary to insist: ". . . which amounts, of course, to reforming the concept of writing . . . oral language already belongs to this [generalized] writing. But that presupposes a modification of the concept of writing. . . .Phonologism does not brook any objections as long as one conserves the colloquial concepts of speech and writing which form the solid fabric of its argumentation. Colloquial and quotidian conceptions, inhabited besides—uncontradictorily enough—by an old history, limited by frontiers that are hardly visible yet all the more rigorous by that very fact" [*Of Grammatology*, trans. Gayatri Chakravorty Spivak (Baltimore: Johns Hopkins University Press, 1976), pp. 55, 56].

It is thus an old word and an old concept of writing, along with all that is invested in it, that periodicals of every stripe have been claiming to turn against this critique, not without borrowing certain resources from it in their confusion. These reactions are obviously symptomatic and belong to a certain type. Freud recounts that when he was having trouble gaining acceptance for the possibility of masculine hysteria, he encountered, among those primary sorts of resistance which do not reveal mere foolishness or lack of culture, the resistance of a surgeon who *expressly* told him: "But, my dear colleague, how can you ·onounce such absurdities? *Hysteron* (sic) signifies 'uterus.' How then can a man be hysterical?"

This example is not insignificant. But others could be cited as well: the presumed origin of a concept or the imagined etymology of a word have often been held up against the process of their transformation, without any regard for the fact that what was being utilized was precisely the vulgar sign most heavily overladen with history and unconscious motivations.

This note, this reference, the choice of this example are placed here merely to herald a certain *out-of-placeness* of language: we are thus introduced into what is *supposed* to be found *behind* the hymen: the hystera (ὑστέρα), which exposes itself only by transference and simulacrum—by mimicry.

9. TN. In French: L'ANTRE DE MALLARMÉ [Mallarmé's antre]
L' "ENTRE" DE MALLARMÉ [Mallarmé's "between" or "enter"]
L'ENTRE-DEUX "MALLARME" [The go-between "Mallarmé" or
"Mallarmé" between two, neither fish nor fowl]

10. TN. In French: L'hymen: ENTRE Platon et Mallarmé. [The Hymen or marriage: BETWEEN Plato and Mallarmé.] Why Latin? On the one hand, the Latin makes it clear that the word "hymen" is to be read both as "membrane" and as "marriage." It also establishes the word "inter" as a pivot for wordplays in which "between is not playful enough. Then again, what *is* "between Plato and Mallarmé" if not precisely Latin? In using Latin to weasel out of a difficulty in translation, we thus, inadvertently but perhaps inevitably, find ourselves caught in one of the crucial hinges of Western philosophy: the textural rifts and drifts produced by the process of *translation* of the Greek philosophers, precisely, into Latin.

11. TN. In French: "*Le causeur s'assied.*" This is a quotation from a lecture by Mallarmé composed in memory of Villiers de l'Isle-Adam. The lecture begins: "A man accustomed to dreaming has come here to speak of another, who is dead.

Ladies and Gentlemen,
The Speaker takes his seat.
Does anyone really know what writing is? . . ."

On the page that each of you has (see figure III), a short text by Mallarmé, *Mimique*,[12] is embedded in one corner, sharing or completing it, with a segment from the *Philebus*,[13] which, without actually naming *mimēsis*, illustrates the mimetic system and even defines it, let us say in anticipation, as a system of *illustration*.

What is the purpose of placing these two texts there, and of placing them in that way, at the opening of a question about what goes (on) or doesn't go (on) *between* [*entre*] literature and truth? That question will remain, like these two texts and like this mimodrama, a sort of epigraph to some future development, while the thing entitled surveys (from a great height) an event, of which we will still be obliged, at the end of the coming session, to point to the absence.

Because of a certain fold that we shall outline, these texts, and their commerce, definitively escape any exhaustive treatment. We can nevertheless begin to mark out, in a few rough strokes, a certain number of motifs. These strokes might be seen to form a sort of frame, the enclosure or borders of a history that would precisely be that of a certain play between literature and truth. The history of this relationship would be organized by—I won't say by *mimēsis*, a notion one should not hasten to translate (especially by imitation), but by a certain interpretation of *mimēsis*. Such an interpretation has never been the act or the speculative decision of any one author at a given moment, but rather, if one reconstitutes the system, the whole of a history. *Inter Platonem et Mallarmatum*, between Plato and Mallarmé—whose proper names, it should be understood, are not real references but indications for the sake of convenience and initial analysis—a whole history has taken place. This history was also a history of literature if one accepts the idea that literature was born of it and died of it, the certificate of its birth as such, the declaration of its name, having coincided with its disappearance, according to a logic that the hymen will help us define. And this history, if it has any meaning, is governed in its entirety by the value of truth and by a certain relation, inscribed in the hymen in question, *between* literature and truth. In saying "this history, if it has any meaning," one seems to be admitting that it might not. But if we were to go to the end of this analysis, we would see it

12. TN. *Mimique*: "1. Adj. (a) Mimic. *Language mimique.*, (i) sign language; (ii) dumb show. (b) Z[oology]: Mimetic. 2. Subst. fem. (a) Mimic art; mimicry. (b) F[amiliar]: Dumb show." (Mansion's Shorter French and English Dictionary.)

13. TN. *Philebus*, trans. R. Hackforth, in *The Collected Dialogues of Plato*, ed. Edith Hamilton and Huntington Cairns, Bollingen Series LXXI (Princeton, N.J.: Princeton University Press, 1961), pp. 1118–19.

confirmed not only that this history has a meaning, but that the very concept of history has lived only upon the possibility of meaning, upon the past, present, or promised presence of meaning and of truth. Outside this system, it is impossible to resort to the concept of history without reinscribing it elsewhere, according to some specific systematic strategy.

True history, the history of meaning, is told in the *Philebus*. In rereading the scene you have before your eyes, you will have remarked four facets.

1. *The book is a dialogue or a dialectic*. At least it should be. The comparison of the soul to a book (*biblíōi*) comes up in such a way that the book appears only as a mode or instance of discourse (*logos*), namely, stilled, silent, internal discourse: not any "stilled ode" or "silence of an afternoon of music," as in *Mimique*, nor the "stilled voice," as in *Music and Letters*, but internalized speech. That is, in a word, thinking (*dianoia*) as it is defined in the *Theaetetus* and the *Sophist*: "Well, thinking and discourse are the same thing, except that what we call thinking is, precisely, the inward dialogue carried on by the mind with itself without spoken sound" (*Sophist*, 263e). " 'How do you describe that process of thinking (*dianoeisthai*)?' 'As a discourse that the mind carries on with itself about any subject it is considering. You must take this explanation as coming from an ignoramus, but I have a notion that, when the mind is thinking, it is simply talking to itself, asking questions and answering them, and saying yes or no' " (*Theaetetus*, 189e). According to the reasoning of the *Philebus*, first there was the *doxa*, the opinion, feeling, or evaluation that sprang up spontaneously within me and pertained to an appearance or semblance of truth, prior to any communication or discourse. Then when I proffered that *doxa* aloud, addressing it to a present interlocutor, it became discourse (*logos*). But from the instant this *logos* can have been formed, when the possibility of dialogue has come into being, it might happen, through an accident of circumstance, that I wouldn't have a partner handy: alone, then, I address this discourse to myself, I converse with myself in a sort of inward commerce. What I then hold is still a discourse but it is soundless, aphonic, private— which also means deprived: of its mouthpiece, its voice. Now, it is in connection with this deficient *logos*, this blank voice, this amputated dialogue—amputated of its vocal organ as well as of its other—that Socrates resorts to the "metaphor" of the book. Our soul then resembles a book not only for the obvious reason that it is a kind of *logos* and dialogue (and the book is thus only a species within the genus "dialogue"), but particularly because this reduced or mumbled conversation remains a false dialogue, a minor interchange, equivalent to a loss of voice. In this dialogue that has

run out of voice, the need for the book or for writing in the soul is only felt through lack of the presence of the other, through lack of any employment of the voice: the object is to reconstitute the presence of the other by substitution, and by the same token to repair the vocal apparatus. The metaphorical book thus has all the characteristics that, until Mallarmé, have always been assigned to the book, however these might have been belied by literary practice. The book, then, stands as a substitute for dialogue, as it calls itself, as it calls itself alive.

2. *The truth of the book is decidable.* This false dialogue constituted by the book is not necessarily a dialogue that is false. The psychic *volumen*, the book within the soul, can either be true or false according as the writer in us (*par hēmin grammateus*) says and, as a direct consequence, writes down things that are true or false. The value of the book as flattened-out *logos* is a function of, in proportion to, in a ratio (also *logos*) with, its truth. "When the internal scribe that I have suggested writes what is false we get the opposite sort of opinions and assertions." Psychic writing must in the last instance appear before the tribunal of dialectics and ontology. It is only worth its weight in truth, and truth is its sole standard of measurement. It is through recourse to the truth of that which is, of things as such, that one can always decide whether writing is or is not true, whether it is in conformity or in "opposition" to the true.

3.   *The value of the book (true/false) is not intrinsic to it.* A span of writing is worth nothing in itself; it is neither good nor bad, neither true nor false. This proposal of neutrality (neither/nor), when exported outside the Platonic context, can have some surprising effects, as we shall see in a moment. But as for the Platonic book, its truth or falsity only declares itself at the moment the writer transcribes an inner speech, when he copies into the book a discourse that has already taken place and stands in a certain relation of truth (of similarity) or falsity (dissimilarity) with things in themselves. If one steps outside the metaphorical instance of the book, one can say that the writer transcribes into the outer book, into the book in what is called its "proper" meaning, what he has previously engraved upon his psychic shell. It is with respect to that primary engraving that it is necessary to divide between the true and the false. The book, which copies, reproduces, imitates living discourse, is worth only as much as that discourse is worth. It can be worth less, to the extent that it is bereft of the *life* of *logos*; it can't be worth more. In this way, writing *in general* is interpreted as an imitation, a duplicate of the living voice or present *logos*. Writing in general is not, of

course, literary writing. But elsewhere, in the *Republic*, for example, poets are only judged and condemned for being imitators, mimes that do not practice "simple diegesis." The specific place of the poet can as such be judged according to whether or not he makes use, and in this or that way, of mimetic form.[14] The kind of poetry whose case is thus being heard cannot,

---

14. It is not possible for us to examine here the extremely complex system of Plato's concept of *mimēsis*. We will attempt elsewhere ("Between Two Throws of Dice") to reconstitute its network and its "logic" around three focal points.

a. *The double parricide/The parricidal double*. Homer, toward whom Plato directs numerous signs of filial respect, admiration, and gratitude, is cast out of the city, like every other mimetic poet, with all honors due to a being who is "holy and wondrous" (*hieron kai thaumaston*) (*Republic*, 398*a*), when he isn't being asked to "erase" from his text all the politically dangerous passages (386*c*). Homer, the blind old father, is condemned because he *practices* mimesis (or mimetic, rather than simple, diegesis). The other father, Parmenides, is condemned because he *neglects* mimesis. If violence must be done to *him*, it is because his *logos*, the "paternal thesis," would prohibit (one from accounting for) the proliferation of doubles ("idols, icons, likenesses, semblances"). The necessity for this parricide, we are told in this very connection (*Sophist* 241*d–e*), ought to be plain enough for even the blind (*tuphlōi*) to see.

b. *The double inscription of mimēsis*. It is impossible to pin *mimēsis* down to a binary classification or, more precisely, to assign a single place to the *technē mimētikē* within the "division" set forth in the *Sophist* (at the point at which a method and a paradigm are being sought in an effort to hunt down the Sophist in an organized manner). The mimetic form is *both* one of the three forms of "productive or creative art" (*technē poiētikē*) *and*, on the other branch of the fork, a form or procedure belonging among the acquisitive arts (*ktētikē*) (nonproductive, nonpoetic) used by the Sophist in his hunt for rich young men (218*d*– 233*b*ff). As a "wizard and imitator," the Sophist is capable of "producing" "likenesses and homonyms" of everything that exists (234*b–235a*). The Sophist mimes the poetic, which nevertheless itself comprises the mimetic; he produces production's double. But just at the point of capture, the Sophist still eludes his pursuers through a supplementary division, extended toward a vanishing point, between two forms of the mimetic (235*d*): the making of likenesses (the *eikastic*) or faithful reproduction, and the making of semblances (the *fantastic*), which simulates the eikastic, pretending to simulate faithfully and deceiving the eye with a simulacrum (a phantasm), which constitutes "a very extensive class, in painting (*zōgraphia*) and in imitation of all sorts." This is an aporia (236*e*) for the philosophical hunter, who comes to a stop before this bifurcation, incapable of continuing to track down his quarry; it is an endless escape route for that quarry (who is also a hunter), who will turn up again, after a long detour, in the direction of Mallarmé's *Mimique*. This mimodrama and the *double science* arising from it will have concerned only a certain obliterated history of the relations between philosophy and sophistics.

c. *Mimēsis, guilty or not guilty*. If we go back to *mimēsis* "prior" to the philosophical "decision," we find that Plato, far from linking the destiny of art and poetry to the structure of *mimēsis* (or rather to the structure of all of what people today often translate—in order to reject it—as re-presentation, imitation, expression, reproduction, etc.), disqualifies in *mimēsis* everything that "modernity" makes much of: the mask, the disappearance of the author, the simulacrum, anonymity, apocryphal textuality. This can be verified by reread-ing the passage in *The Republic* on simple narration and mimesis (393*a* ff). What is important for our purposes here is this "internal" duplicity of the *mimeisthai* that Plato wants to cut in two, in order to separate good *mimēsis* (which reproduces faithfully and truly yet is already

of course, be simply identified with what we call "literature." If, as we have precisely been tempted to think, literature is born/dead of a relatively recent break, it is nonetheless true that the whole history of the interpretation of the arts of letters has moved and been transformed within the diverse logical possibilities opened up by the concept of *mimēsis*. These are numerous, paradoxical, and disconcerting enough to have unleashed a rich system of combinations and permutations. Here is not the place for us to demonstrate this. Let us retain the schematic law that structures Plato's discourse: he is obliged sometimes to condemn *mimēsis* in itself as a process of duplication, whatever its model might be,[15] and sometimes to disqualify *mimēsis* only in function of the model that is "imitated," the mimetic operation in itself remaining neutral, or even advisable.[16] But in both cases, *mimēsis* is lined up alongside truth: either it hinders the unveiling of the thing itself by substituting a copy or double for what is; or else it works in the service of truth through the double's resemblance (*homoiōsis*). *Logos*, which is itself imitated by writing, only has value as truth; it is under this heading that Plato always interrogates it.

   4.   And finally, a fourth trait, to finish out the frame of this text: the element of the thus characterized book is the *image* in general (the icon or phantasm), the imaginary or the *imaginal*. If Socrates is able to *compare* the silent relation between the soul and itself, in the "mute soliloquy" (*Mimi-*

---

threatened by the simple fact of its duplication) from bad, which must be contained like madness (396*a*) and (harmful) play (396*e*).

   Here is an outline of this "logic": 1. *Mimēsis* produces a thing's double. If the double is faithful and perfectly like, no qualitative difference separates it from the model. Three consequences of this: (a) The double—the imitator—is nothing, is worth nothing in itself. (b) Since the imitator's value comes only from its model, the imitator is good when the model is good, and bad when the model is bad. In itself it is neutral and transparent. (c) If *mimēsis* is nothing and is worth nothing in itself, then it is nothing in value and being—it is in itself negative. Therefore it is an evil: to imitate is bad in itself and not just when what is imitated is bad. 2. Whether like or unlike, the imitator is something, since *mimēsis* and likenesses do exist. Therefore this nonbeing does "exist" in some way (*The Sophist*). Hence: (a) in adding to the model, the imitator comes as a supplement and ceases to be a nothing or a nonvalue. (b) In adding to the "existing" model, the imitator is not the same thing, and even if the resemblance were absolute, the resemblance is never absolute (*Cratylus*). And hence never absolutely true. (c) As a supplement that can take the model's place but never be its equal, the imitator is in essence inferior even at the moment it replaces the model and is thus "promoted." This schema (two propositions and six possible consequences) forms a kind of logical machine; it programs the prototypes of all the propositions inscribed in Plato's discourse as well as those of the whole tradition. According to a complex but implacable law, this machine deals out all the clichés of criticism to come.

   15. *Republic*, 395*b–c* and passim.
   16. Ibid. 396*c–d*.

que), to a book, it is because the book imitates the soul or the soul imitates the book, because each is the image or *likeness* of the other ("image" has the same root as *"imitari"*). Both of these likenesses, even before resembling each other, were in themselves already reproductive, imitative, and pictorial (in the representative sense of the word) in essence. *Logos* must indeed be shaped according to the model of the *eidos*;[17] the book then reproduces the *logos*, and the whole is organized by this relation of repetition, resemblance (*homoiōsis*), doubling, duplication, this sort of specular process and play of reflections where things (*onta*), speech, and writing come to repeat and mirror each other.

As of this point, the appearance of the painter is prescribed and becomes absolutely ineluctable. The way is paved for it in the scene from the *Philebus*. This other "demiurge," the *zōgraphos*, comes *after* the *grammateus*: "a painter, who comes after the writer and paints in the soul pictures of these assertions that we make." This collusion between painting (*zōgraphia*) and writing is, of course, constant. Both in Plato and after him. But painting and writing can only be images of each other to the extent that they are both interpreted as images, reproductions, representations, or repetitions of something alive, of living speech in the one case, and of animal figures in the other (*zōgraphia*). Any discourse about the relationship between literature and truth always bumps up against the enigmatic possibility of repetition, within the framework of the *portrait*.

What, in fact, is the painter doing here? He too is painting metaphorically, of course, and in the soul, just like the *grammateus*. But he comes along after the latter, retraces his steps, follows his traces and his trail. And he *illustrates* a book that is already written when he appears on the scene. He "paints in the soul pictures of these assertions." Sketching, painting, the art of space, the practice of spacing, the inscription written inside the outside (the outwork [*hors-livre*]), all these are only things that are added,

17. After showing in the *Cratylus* that nomination excluded *mimēsis*, that the form of a word could not, mimelike, resemble the form of a thing (423*a* ff), Socrates nevertheless maintains that, through another sort of resemblance, a non-sensible sort, the right name could be taken as an image of the thing in its "truth" (439*a* ff). And this thesis is not carried off in the ironic oscillations of the *Cratylus*. The priority of what is, in its truth, over language, like the priority of a model over its image, is as unshakable as absolute certainty. "Let us suppose that to any extent you please you can learn things through the medium of names, and suppose also that you can learn them from the things themselves. Which is likely to be the nobler and clearer way—to learn of the image (*ek tēs eikonos*), whether the image and the truth of which the image is the expression have been rightly conceived, or to learn of the truth (*ek tēs alētheias*) whether the truth and the image of it have been duly executed? . . . We may admit so such, that the knowledge of things is not to be derived from names. No, they must be studied and investigated in themselves" (trans. B. Jowett).

for the sake of illustration, representation, or decoration, to the book of the discourse of the thinking of the innermost man. The painting that shapes the images is a portrait of the discourse; it is worth only as much as the discourse it fixes and freezes along its surface. And consequently, it is also worth only as much as the *logos* capable of interpreting it, of reading it, of saying what it is-trying-to-say and what in truth it is being made to say through the reanimation that makes it speak.

But painting, that degenerate and somewhat superfluous expression, that supplementary frill of discursive thought, that ornament of *dianoia* and *logos*, also plays a role that seems to be just the opposite of this. It functions as a pure indicator of the essence of a thought or discourse defined as image, representation, repetition. If *logos* is first and foremost a faithful image of the *eidos* (the figure of intelligible visibility) of what is, then it arises as a sort of primary painting, profound and invisible. In that case painting in its usual sense, a painter's painting, is really only the painting of a painting. Hence it can reveal the essential picturality, the representativity, of *logos*. That is indeed the task assigned by Socrates to the *zōgraphos-dēmiourgos* in the *Philebus*: "How do we make out that he in his turn acts, and when?" asks Protarchus, and Socrates replies, "When we have got those opinions and assertions clear of the act of sight (*opseōs*), or other sense, and as it were see in ourselves pictures or images of what we previously opined or asserted." The painter who works after the writer, the worker who shapes his work after opinion and assertion, the artisan who follows the artist, is able, through an exercise of analysis, separation, and impoverishment, precisely to purify the pictorial, imitative, imaginal essence of thought. The painter, then, knows how to restore the naked image of the thing, the image as it presents itself to simple intuition, as it shows itself in its intelligible *eidos* or sensible *horaton*. He strips it of all that superadded language, of that legend that now has the status of a commentary, of an envelope around a kernel, of an epidermic canvas.

So that in psychic writing, between the *zōgraphia* and the *logos* (or *dianoia*) there exists a very strange relation: one is always the supplement of the other. In the first part of the scene, the thought that directly fixed the essence of things did not essentially need the illustrative ornament that writing and painting constituted. The soul's thinking was only intimately linked to *logos* (and to the proffered or held-back voice). Inversely, a bit further on, painting (in the metaphorical sense of psychic painting, of course, just as a moment ago it was a question of psychic writing) is what gives us the image of the thing itself, what communicates to us the direct intuition, the immediate vision of the thing, freed from the discourse that accompanied it, or even encumbered it. Naturally, I would like to stress once more, it is always the *metaphors* of painting and writing that are linked in this way back and forth: we recall that, on another plane, outside these metaphors, Plato always asserts that in their literal sense painting and writing are totally incapable of any intuition of the thing itself, since they only deal in copies, and in copies of copies.

If discourse and inscription (writing-painting) thus appear alternately as useful complements or as useless supplements to each other, now useful, now useless, now in one sense, now in another, this is because they are forever intertwined together within the tissue of the following complicities or reversibilities:

1.   They are both measured against the truth they are capable of.

2.   They are images of each other and that is why one can replace [*suppléer*] the other when the other is lacking.

3.   Their common structure makes them both partake of *mnēmē* and *mimēsis*, of *mnēmē* precisely by dint of participating in *mimēsis*. Within the movement of the *mimeisthai*, the relation of the mime to the mimed, of the reproducer to the reproduced, is always a relation to a *past present*. The imitated comes before the imitator. Whence the problem of time, which indeed does not fail to come up: Socrates wonders whether it would be out of the question to think that *grammata* and *zōgraphēmata* might have a relation to the future. The difficulty lies in conceiving that what is imitated could be still to come with respect to what imitates, that the image can precede the model, that the double can come before the simple. The overtures of "hope" (*elpis*), anamnesis (the future as a past present due to return), the preface, the anterior future (future perfect), all come to arrange things.[18]

It is here that the value of *mimēsis* is most difficult to master. A certain movement effectively takes place in the Platonic text, a movement one should not be too quick to call contradictory. On the one hand, as we have

18. Nothing in the above-mentioned logical program was to change when, following Aristotle, and particularly during the "age of classicism," the models for imitation were to be found not simply in nature but in the works and writers of Antiquity that had known how to imitate nature. One could find a thousand examples up to the Romantics (including the Romantics and often those well after them). Diderot, who nevertheless so powerfully solicited the mimetological "machine," especially in *Le Paradoxe sur le Comédien*, confirms upon the analysis of what he calls the "ideal imagined model" (supposedly non-Platonic) that all manner of reversals are included in the program. And, as for the logic of the future perfect: "Antoine Coypel was certainly a man of wit when he recommended to his fellow artists: 'Let us paint, if we can, in such a way that the figures in our paintings will be the living models of the ancient statues rather than that those statues be the originals of the figures we paint.' The same advice could be given to literati" ("Pensées détachées sur la peinture," in *Oeuvres esthétiques*, Garnier, ed. Vernière, p. 816).

just verified, it is hard to separate *mnēmē* from *mimēsis*. But on the other hand, while Plato often discredits *mimēsis* and almost always disqualifies the mimetic arts, he never separates the unveiling of truth, *alētheia*, from the movement of *anamnēsia* (which is, as we have seen, to be distinguished from *hypomnēsi.*).

What announces itself here is an internal division within *mimēsis*, a self-duplication of repetition itself; *ad infinitum*, since this movement feeds its own proliferation. Perhaps, then, there is always more than one kind of *mimēsis*; and perhaps it is in the strange mirror that reflects but also displaces and distorts one *mimēsis* into the other, as though it were itself destined to mime or mask *itself*, that history—the history of literature—is lodged, along with the whole of its interpretation. Everything would then be played out in the paradoxes of the supplementary double: the paradoxes of something that, added to the simple and the single, replaces and mimes them, both like and unlike, unlike because it is—in that it is—like, the same as and different from what it duplicates. Faced with all this, what does "Platonism" decide and maintain? ("Platonism" here standing more or less immediately for the whole history of Western philosophy, including the anti-Platonisms that regularly feed into it.) What is it that is decided and maintained in ontology or dialectics throughout all the mutations or revolutions that are entailed? It is precisely the *ontological*: the presumed possibility of a discourse about what is, the deciding and decidable *logos* of or about the *on* (being-present). That which is, the being-present (the matrix-form of substance, of reality, of the oppositions between matter and form, essence and existence, objectivity and subjectivity, etc.) is distinguished from the appearance, the image, the phenomenon, etc., that is, from anything that, presenting it *as* being-present, doubles it, re-presents it, and can therefore replace and de-present it. There is thus the 1 and the 2, the simple and the double. The double comes *after* the simple; it multiplies it as a *follow-up*. It follows, I apologize for repeating this, that the image *supervenes* upon reality, the representation upon the present in presentation, the imitation upon the thing, the imitator upon the imitated. First there is what is, "reality," the thing itself, in flesh and blood as the phenomenologists say; then there is, imitating these, the painting, the portrait, the zographeme, the inscription or transcription of the thing itself. Discernability, at least numerical discernability, between the imitator and the imitated is what constitutes order. And obviously, according to "logic" itself, according to a profound synonymy, what is imitated is more real, more essential, more true, etc., than what imitates. It is anterior and superior to it. One should constantly bear in mind, henceforth, the clinical paradigm of *mimēsis*, the order of the three beds in the *Republic* X (596a ff): the painter's, the carpenter's, and God's.

Doubtless this order will appear to be contested, even inverted, in the course of history, and on several occasions. But never have the absolute distinguishability between imitated and imitator, and the anteriority of the first over the second, been displaced by any metaphysical system. In the domain of "criticism" or poetics, it has been strongly stressed that art, as imitation (representation, description, expression, imagination, etc.), should not be "slavish" (this proposition scans twenty centuries of poetics) and that consequently, through the liberties it takes with nature, art can create or produce works that are more valuable than what they imitate. But all these derivative oppositions send us back to the same root. The extra-value or the extra-being makes art a richer kind of nature, freer, more pleasant, more creative: more natural. At the time of the great systematization of the classical doctrine of imitation, Desmaret, in his *Art of Poetry*, translates a then rather common notion:

> And Art enchants us more than nature does. . . .
> Not liking what is imitated, we yet love what imitates.

Whether one or the other is preferred (but it could easily be shown that because of the nature of the imitated/imitator relation, the *preference*, whatever one might say, can only go to the imitated), it is at bottom this order of appearance, the precedence [*pré-séance*] of the imitated, that governs the philosophical or critical interpretation of "literature," if not the operation of literary writing. This order of appearance is *the order of all appearance*, the very process of appearing in general. It is the order of truth. "Truth" has always meant two different things, the history of the essence of truth—the truth of truth—being only the gap and the articulation between the two interpretations or processes. To simplify the analyses made by Heidegger but without necessarily adopting the order of succession that he seems to recognize, one can retain the fact that the process of truth is *on the one hand* the unveiling of what lies concealed in oblivion (*alētheia*), the veil lifted or raised [*relevé*] from the thing itself, from that which *is* insofar as it is, presents itself, produces itself, and can even exist in the form of a determinable hole in Being; *on the other hand* (but this other process is prescribed in the first, in the ambiguity or duplicity of the presence of the present, of its *appearance*—that which appears *and* its appearing—in the *fold* of the present participle),[19] truth is agreement (*homoiōsis* or *adaequatio*), a relation of

19. Cf. Heidegger, "Moira," in *Early Greek Thinking*, trans. D. F. Krell and F. A. Capuzzi (New York: Harper & Row, 1975).

resemblance or equality between a re-presentation and a thing (unveiled, present), even in the eventuality of a statement of judgment.

Now, mimesis, all through the history of its interpretation, is always commanded by the process of truth:

1. either, even before it can be translated as imitation, *mimēsis* signifies the presentation of the thing itself, of nature, of the physis that produces itself, engenders itself, and appears (to itself) as it really is, in the presence of its image, its visible aspect, its face: the theatrical mask, as one of the essential references of the *mimeisthai*, reveals as much as it hides. *Mimēsis* is then the movement of the *phusis,* a movement that is somehow natural (in the nonderivative sense of this word), through which the *phusis*, having no outside, no other, must be doubled in order to make its appearance, to appear (to itself), to produce (itself), to unveil (itself); in order to emerge from the crypt where it prefers itself; in order to shine in its *alētheia*. In this sense, *mnēmē* and *mimēsis* are on a par, since *mnēmē* too is an unveiling (an un-forgetting), *alētheia*.

2. or else *mimēsis* sets up a relation of *homoiōsis* or *adaequatio* between two (terms). In that case it can more readily be translated as imitation. This translation seeks to express (or rather historically produces) the thought about this relation. The two faces are separated and set face to face: the imitator and the imitated, the latter being none other than the thing or the meaning of the thing itself, its manifest presence. A good imitation will be one that is true, faithful, like or likely, adequate, in conformity with the *phusis* (essence or life) of what is imitated; it effaces itself of its own accord in the process of restoring freely, and hence in a living manner, the freedom of true presence.

In each case, *mimēsis* has to follow the process of truth. The presence of the present is its norm, its order, its law. It is in the name of truth, its only reference—*reference* itself—that *mimēsis* is judged, proscribed or prescribed according to a regular alternation.

The invariable feature of this reference sketches out the closure of metaphysics: not as a border enclosing some homogeneous space but according to a noncircular, entirely other, figure. Now, this reference is discreetly but absolutely displaced in the workings of a certain syntax, whenever any writing both marks and goes back over its mark with an undecidable stroke. This double mark escapes the pertinence or authority of truth: it does not overturn it but rather inscribes it within its play as one of its functions or parts. This displacement does not take place, has not taken place once, as an *event*. It does not occupy a simple place. It does not take place *in* writing. This dis-location (is what) writes/is written. This redou-

bling of the mark, which is at once a formal break and a formal generalization, *is exemplified by the text of Mallarmé, and singularly by the "sheet" you have
before your eyes* (but obviously every word of this last proposition must by the
same token be displaced or placed under suspicion).

Let us reread *Mimique*. Near the center, there is a sentence in quotation
marks. It is not a citation, as we shall see, but the simulacrum of a citation
or explicitation:—*"The scene illustrates but the idea, not any actual action . . ."*

This is a trap: one might well be tempted to interpret this sentence and
the sequence that follows from it in a very classical way, as an "idealist"
reversal of traditional mimetology. One would then say: of course, the
mime does not imitate any actual thing or action, any reality that is already
given in the world, existing before and outside his own sphere; he doesn't
have to conform, with an eye toward verisimilitude, to some real or external
model, to some *nature*, in the most belated sense of the word. But the
relation of imitation and the value of adequation remain intact since it is
still necessary to imitate, represent, or "illustrate" the idea. But what is the
idea? one would proceed to ask. What is the ideality of the idea? When it is
no longer the *ontōs on* in the form of the thing itself, it is, to speak in a
post-Cartesian manner, the copy inside me, the representation of the thing
through thought, the ideality—*for* a subject—of what is. In this sense,
whether one conceives it in its "Cartesian" or in its "Hegelian" modification, the idea is the presence of what is, and we aren't yet out of Platonism.
It is still a matter of imitating (expressing, describing, representing,
illustrating) an *eidos* or *idea*, whether it is a figure of the thing itself, as in
Plato, a subjective representation, as in Descartes, or both, as in Hegel.

Of course. Mallarmé's text can be read this way and reduced to a brilliant
literary idealism. The frequent use of the word *Idea*—often enlarged and
hypostatized by a capital letter—and the story of the author's supposed
Hegelianism tend to invite such a reading. And that invitation has rarely
gone unanswered. But a reading here should no longer be carried out as a
simple table of concepts or words, as a static or statistical sort of punctuation. One must reconstitute a chain in motion, the effects of a network and
the play of a syntax. In that case *Mimique* can be read quite differently than
as a neo-idealism or a neo-mimetologism. The system of *illustration* is
altogether different there than in the *Philebus*. With the values that must be
associated with it, the *lustre* is reinscribed in a completely other place.

There is no imitation. The Mime imitates nothing. And to begin with,
he doesn't imitate. There is nothing prior to the writing of his gestures.
Nothing is prescribed for him. No present has preceded or supervised the
tracing of his writing. His movements form a figure that no speech

anticipates or accompanies. They are not linked with *logos* in any order of consequence. *"Such is this PIERROT MURDERER OF HIS WIFE composed and set down by himself, a mute soliloquy . . ."*

"Composed and set down by himself . . ." We here enter a textual labyrinth panelled with mirrors. The Mime *follows* no preestablished script, no program obtained elsewhere. Not that he improvises or lets himself go spontaneously: he simply does not obey any verbal order. His gestures, his gestural writing (and Mallarmé's insistence on describing the regulated gesture of dance or pantomime as a hieroglyphic inscription is legendary), are not dictated by any verbal discourse or imposed by any diction. The Mime inaugurates; he breaks into a white page: ". . . *a mute soliloquy that the phantom, white as a yet unwritten page, holds in both face and gesture at full length to his soul."*

The blank—the other face of this double session here declares its white color—extends between the candid virginity (*"fragments of candor"* . . . *"nuptial proofs of the Idea"*) of the white (*candida*) page and the white paint of the pale Pierrot who, by simulacrum, writes in the paste of his own make-up, upon the page he is. Through all the surfaces superimposed white on white, between all the layers of Mallarméan make-up, one comes across, every time, on analysis, the substance of some *"drowned grease paint"* (*The Chastised Clown* [*Le Pitre châtié*]). One can read, each within the other, the Pierrot of *Mimique* and the "*bad Hamlet*" of the *Chastised Clown* (*"Eyes, lakes with my simple intoxication of rebirth / Other than as the histrion who with a gesture evoked / As a quill the smoking lamps' ignoble soot, / I pierced a window in the canvas wall"*). Pierrot is brother to all the Hamlets haunting the Mallarméan text. If one takes account of the crime, incest, or suicide in which they are all simultaneously engaged, then it is, in the form of an I or A, the ghost of a castrated point, quill, or stick that lies therein whetting its threats. To prove this, one must go through several relays, that of all signifiers containing -IQUE, for example, and this we shall not fail to do.

The Mime is not subjected to the authority of any book: the fact that Mallarmé points this out is all the more strange since the text called *Mimique* is initially a reaction to a reading. Mallarmé had earlier had the booklet of the mimodrama in his hands, and it is this little work that he is at first commenting upon. We know this because Mallarmé had published the first version of this text, without its title, in the November 1886 issue of *La Revue indépendante*. In place of what was to become the first paragraph of *Mimique*, one could read this in particular: "A type of luxury not inferior to any gala seems to me to be, during the treacherous season all with its calls to go out, the setting aside, under the first lamp, of an evening at home for reading. The suggestive and truly rare booklet that opens in my hands is none other, in sum, than a pantomime booklet: *Pierrot Murderer of his Wife* . . ." (Published by Calmann-Lévy, new edition, 1886).[20]

It is thus in a booklet, upon a page, that Mallarmé must have read the effacement of the booklet before the gestural initiative of the Mime. That,

---

20. The editors of the Pléiade edition of Mallarmé's works have not deemed necessary to point out, in their "Notes et Variantes," that the text printed in *La Revue indépendante*, which was part of a much longer sequence, did not carry the title *Mimique*, and that the paragraph we have just quoted and broken off at the same point as the Pléiade editors was followed by a paragraph which, both in vocabulary and syntax, was quite different from the second paragraph of *Mimique*. Contrary to the rule observed for other texts, those editors have not included the variants from the second version, published in *Pages* (Brussels, 1891) in the chapter called "Le Genre ou des Modernes," still without a title. *Mimique* is a third version, published under that title in *Divagations* (1897), in the series called *Crayonné au théâtre*. When the Pléiade editors, after quoting two paragraphs from the *Revue indépendante* (up to *Pierrot Murderer of his Wife* . . .), go on to add: "These two paragraphs, in *Pages* (1891), were part (p. 135–36) of the chapter 'le Genre ou des Modernes.' They also appeared in *Divagations*, p. 186," this description is both incomplete and inexact. If we have chosen to reproduce here the two earlier versions, it is because the transformation of each paragraph (in certain of its words, its syntax, its punctuation, its play of parentheses and italics, etc.) displays the economy of the "syntaxer" at work; and also because, at the proper moment, we will draw from them certain specific lessons.

a. *La Revue indépendante* (1886) (immediately following the passage we have quoted in the body of the text) . . . "a pantomime booklet: *Pierrot Murderer of his Wife*, composed and set down by M. Paul Margueritte. A monomime, rather, I would say along with the author, before the tacit soliloquy that the phantom, white as a yet unwritten page, holds in both face and gesture at full length to himself. A whirlwind of delicate new thoughts emanates, which I would like to seize upon with security, and say. The entire esthetic there of a genre situated closer to principles than any other! nothing in this region of fantasy being able to foil the direct simplifying instinct. This: 'The scene illustrates but the idea, not any actual action, through a hymen out of which flows Dream, tainted with vice, yet sacred, between desire and fulfillment, perpetration and remembrance: here anticipating, there recalling, in the future, in the past, under the false appearance of a present. This is how the Mime operates, whose act is confined to a perpetual allusion: not otherwise does he set up a pure medium of fiction.' This marvelous bit of nothing, less than a thousand lines, whoever will read it as I have just done, will comprehend the eternal rules, just as though facing the stageboards, their humble depository. The surprise, which is also charming, caused by the artifice of a notation of sentiments by unproffered sentences, is that, in this sole case perhaps with authenticity, between the sheets and the eye silence is established, the delight of reading."

b. *Pages* (1891). "Silence, sole luxury after rhymes, an orchestra only marking with its gold, its brushes with dusk and cadence, the detail of its signification on a par with a stilled ode and which it is up to the poet, roused by a dare, to translate! the silence that I have sought ever since from afternoons of music, I have also found with contentment before the reappearance, always as original as himself, of Pierrot, that is, of the bright and sagacious mime, Paul Legrand. [This paragraph can now be found in *Crayonné au théâtre*, in *Oeuvres complètes*, p. 340.]

"Such is this *Pierrot Murder of his Wife* composed and set down by M. Paul Margueritte, a tacit soliloquy that the phantom, white as a yet unwritten page, holds in both face and gesture at full length to himself. A whirlwind of naïve or new thoughts emanates, which it would be pleasing to seize upon with security, and say. The entire esthetic of a genre situated closer to principles than any other! nothing in this region of fantasy being able to foil the direct simplifying spirit. This: 'The scene illustrates but the idea, not any actual action, through a hymen (out of which flows Dream), tainted with vice yet sacred, between desire and fulfillment, perpetration and remembrance: here anticipating, there recalling, in the future, in the past, *under the false appearance of a present*. That is how the Mime operates, whose act is confined to a perpetual allusion: not otherwise does he set up a pure medium of fiction.' This role, less than a thousand lines, whoever reads it will comprehend the rules as if placed before the stageboards, their humble depository. The surprise, too, accompanying the artifice of a notation of sentiments by unproffered sentences, is that, in this sole case perhaps with authenticity, between the sheets and the eye is established this silence, the delight of reading."

On comparing these three versions, we can draw a first conclusion: the sentence in quotation marks is indeed a simulacrum of a citation—an expli-citation, rather—an impersonal, concise, solemn statement, a kind of illustrious rule, an anonymous axiom or law of unknown origin. Aside from the fact that such a "citation" is nowhere to be found (particularly among the different booklets, prefaces, and notes), the fact that it changes slightly in the course of the three versions would suffice to prove that we are dealing with a Mallarméan fiction. Its syntax should already have suggested as much.

It is not impossible that, several years earlier, Mallarmé had *also* attended a performance by this *Pierrot*. The second edition, the "rare booklet" to which *Mimique* is responding, was indeed accompanied by the following Notice, signed by Paul Margueritte himself: "In 1881, the amusement afforded by a theatrical performance in the country, an unexpected success in the role of Pierrot, beneath the white mask and in Deburau's costume, made me suddenly become enamoured of pantomime, and write and act out, among other scenarios, this one: PIERROT MURDERER OF HIS WIFE. Having never seen a mime, Paul Legrand or Rouff, or read anything concerning this special art, I was ignorant of all traditions. I thus came up with a personal Pierrot, in conformity with my innermost esthetic self. As I sensed him and translated him, it seems, he was a modern being, neurotic, tragic, and ghostly. For lack of the proper sideshow stage, I was prevented from going on with this eccentric vocation, this veritable artistic madness that had gripped me, to which I owed certain singular personality-sheddings, strange nervous sensations, and, on the mornings after, some cerebral intoxications like those one gets from hashish. Unknown, a beginner in the world of letters, without any supporting cast or Columbine, I modestly performed a few monomimes in drawing-rooms and for the general public. Poets and artists judged my attempts curious and new: MM. Léon Cladel, Stéphane Mallarmé, J. K. Huysmans, and M. Théodore de Banville, who, in a letter sparkling with wit, tried to dissuade me, alleging that the worldly public was too . . . witty, and that the heyday of pantomime had past. *Amen*. If anything is left of my mimic efforts, it is the literary conception of a modern, suggestive Pierrot, donning at will the flowing classical costume or the tight black suit, and moving about in uneasiness and fear. This idea, set down in a little pantomime,* was one I later developed in a novel,** and I intend to use it again in two volumes that will be: a study of artistic sensations, and a collection of pantomimes. *Henceforth I should be allowed to emphasize the dates of my works*. My cup is small, but I drink it all. It would be unjust if my forthcoming books should seem to be inspired by someone else, and if I should be accused of imitation or plagiarism. Ideas belong to everyone. I am convinced that it is by mere coincidence that following PIERROT MURDERER OF HIS WIFE there should have appeared a work with a similar title and that after the character of Paul Violas in ALL FOUR there should follow a Pierrot reminiscent of him. I am just affirming my priority and reserving it for the future. This granted, the affection I feel toward the pretty art of pantomime, for Pierrots— Willette's Album, Huysmans' *Skeptical Pierrot*, and Hennique—induces me to applaud any effort that will ressuscitate, on stage or in a book, our friend Pierrot." (*Pierrot Murderer of his Wife*, 1882, Schmidt, Printer. **All Four*, a novel, 1885, ed. Giraud.)

This lengthy quotation is also of interest in that it marks the historical complexity of the textual network in which we are already engaged and in which Margueritte declares his claim to originality.

in fact, is a structural necessity, marked in the text of *Mimique*. Whether Mallarmé ever did actually go to *see* the "spectacle" *too* is not only hard to verify but irrelevant to the organization of the text.

What Mallarmé *read*, then, in this little book is a prescription that *effaces itself through its very existence*, the order given to the Mime to imitate nothing that in any way preexists his operation: neither an act (*"the scene illustrates but the idea, not any actual action"*) nor a word (*"stilled ode . . . mute soliloquy that the phantom, white as a yet unwritten page, holds in both face and gesture at full length to his soul"*).

In the beginning of this mime was neither the deed nor the word. It is prescribed (we will define this word in a moment) to the Mime that he not let anything be prescribed to him but his own writing, that he not reproduce by imitation any action (*pragma*: affair, thing, act) or any speech (*logos*: word, voice, discourse). The Mime ought only to write himself on the white page he is; he must *himself* inscribe *himself* through gestures and plays of facial expressions. At once page and quill, Pierrot is both passive and active, matter and form, the author, the means, and the raw material of his mimodrama. The histrion produces himself here. Right here—*"A veracious histrion was I of myself!"* (p. 495).

Before we investigate this proposition, let us consider what Mallarmé is *doing* in *Mimique*. We read *Mimique*. Mallarmé (he who fills the function of "author") writes upon a white page on the basis of a text he is reading in which it is written that one must write upon a white page. One could nevertheless point out that while the referent indicated by Mallarmé is not a spectacle he actually perceived, it is at least a "real" object called a booklet, which Mallarmé could see, the brochure he has before his eyes or in his hands (since he says so!: *"The suggestive and truly rare booklet that opens in my hands"*), which is firmly maintained in its self-identity.

Let us see, since we must see, this little book. What Mallarmé has in his hands is a second edition, issued four years after the first, five years after the performance itself. The author's Note has replaced the Preface by a certain Fernand Beissier. The latter had described what he had *seen*: in the barn of an old farm, in the midst of a crowd of workers and peasants, a *mimodrama*— with no entry fee—of which he gives an outline after having described the setting at length. An inebriated Pierrot, "white, long, emaciated," enters with an undertaker. "And the drama began. For it truly was a drama we attended, a brutal, bizarre drama that burned the brain like one of Hoffmann's fantastic tales, atrocious at times, making one suffer like a veritable nightmare. Pierrot, who remains alone, tells how he has killed Columbine who had been unfaithful to him. He has just buried her, and no one will ever know of his crime. He had tied her to the bed while she was asleep, and he had tickled her feet until a horrible, ghastly death burst upon her amongst those atrocious bursts of laughter. Only this long white Pierrot with his cadaverous face could have come up with the idea of this torture fit for the damned. And, miming the action, he represented before us the whole scene, simulating the victim and the murderer by turns."

Beissier describes the reaction of the audience and wonders what sort of reception Paris would give this "bizarre, tormented, bony Pierrot who seems to be slightly neurotic" ("This destroyed all my ideas about that legendary Pierrot who once made me laugh so hard . . ."). The next day, he tells us, he meets the Mime who has "become a man of the world again": it is Paul Margueritte, the brother of Victor Margueritte, the son of the general, Mallarmé's cousin. He asks Beissier to write a Preface to the booklet of *Pierrot Murderer of his Wife* which he, Paul Margueritte, intends to write and publish. That is exactly what has happened. The Preface is dated "Valvins [where Mallarmé had a vacation house.—Trans.], September 15, 1882": it is thus not improbable that Mallarmé, linked to the enterprise in all these ways, might have attended the performance and read the first edition of the booklet.

The temporal and textual structure of the "thing" (what shall we call it?) presents itself, for the time being, thus: a mimodrama "takes place," as a gestural writing preceded by no booklet; a preface is planned and then written *after* the "event" to precede a booklet written *after the fact*, reflecting the mimodrama rather than programming it. This Preface is replaced four years later by a Note written by the "author" himself, a sort of floating outwork [*hors-livre*].

Such is the object that is supposed to have served as Mallarmé's supposed "referent." What was it, then, that he had in his hands, before his eyes? At what point? in what now? along what line?

We have not yet opened the booklet "itself." The textual machination derives its complexity first of all from the fact that this little book, a verbal text aligning words and sentences, describes retrospectively a purely gestural, silent sequence, the inauguration of a writing of the body. This discrepancy or heterogeneity in the signifier is remarked upon by Margueritte in an N.B. After the physical presentation of Pierrot in which white predominates ("in a white surtout . . ." ". . . with head and hands as white as plaster . . ." ". . . a white kerchief . . ." ". . . hands of plaster, too . . ."): "N.B.—Pierrot seems to speak? —A pure literary fiction! —Pierrot is *mute*, and the drama is, from one end to the other, *mimed*." These words—"pure," "fiction," "mute"—will be picked up again by Mallarmé.

Within this literary fiction whose verbal writing supervenes after the occurrence [*coup*] of a different sort of writing, the latter—the gestural act of the mimodrama—is described as anamnesis. It is already the memory of a certain past. The crime has already taken place at the moment Pierrot mimes it. And he mimes—"in the present"—*under the false appearance of a present*," the perpetrated crime. But in miming the past in the present, he reconstitutes, in the said "present," the deliberations through which he prepared the murder, when, examining all possible means to be used, he was still dealing with a crime to come, a death to give. Pierrot has sent the undertaker away; he stares at Columbine's portrait and "points at it with a mysterious finger." "I remember . . . Let's close the curtains! I don't dare . . .(He backs up and, without looking behind him, pulls the drapes shut. His mouth trembles and then an invincible force wrenches from him the secret that has risen to his lips. The MUSIC stops, listens.)

Here [large letters, the discourse of the mute mime]:

Columbine, my charming wife, the Columbine in the portrait, was sleeping. She slept over there, in the big bed: I killed her. Why? . . . Ah, here is why! My gold, she filched; my best wine, she drank; my back, she beat, and hard, too: as for my forehead, she decorated it. A cuckold, yes, that's what she made me, and exorbitantly, but what does that matter? I killed her—because I felt like it, I am the master, what can anyone say? To kill her, yes . . . that pleases me. But how shall I go about it? (For Pierrot, like a sleepwalker, reproduces his crime, and in his hallucination, the *past* becomes *present*.) [a sleepwalker: all this is happening, if one can still say, between sleep and wakefulness, perception and dream; the words "*past*" and "*present*" are underlined by the author; we encounter them again, underlined differently, in *Mimique*. Thus, in the apparent present of his writing, the author of the booklet, who is none other than the Mime, describes in words the past-present of a mimodrama which itself, in its apparent present, silently mimed an event—the crime—in the past-present but of which the present has never occupied the stage, has never been perceived by anyone, nor even, as we shall see, ever really been committed. Never, anywhere, not even in the theatrical fiction. The booklet reminds us that the mime "is reproducing his crime," miming what he remembers, and in so doing is obliged to begin by miming, in the present, the past deliberations over a crime yet to be committed] "Of course, there's the rope—pull it tight and blam! it's done! yes, but then the tongue hanging out, the horrible face? no—the knife? or a saber, a long saber? zap! in the heart . . . yes, but then the blood flows out in torrents, streaming.—Ugh! what a devil of a . . . Poison? a little tiny vial, quaff it and then . . . yes! then the cramps, the runs, the pains, the tortures, ah! how awful (it would be discovered, anyway). Of course, there's the gun, bam! but bam! would be heard. —Nothing, I can think of nothing. (He paces gravely back and forth, deep in thought, By accident, he trips.) Ow! that hurts! (He strokes his foot.) Oof! that hurts! It's not serious, it's better already. (He keeps on stroking and tickling his foot.) Ha! ha! that's funny! Ha! Ha! No, it makes me laugh. Ah! (He abruptly lets go of his foot. He slaps himself on the head.) I've got it! (Slyly:) I've got it! I'm going to tickle my wife to death. There!"

Pierrot then mimes all the way to the "supreme spasm" the rising of ecstatic hilarity. The crime, the orgasm, is mimed doubly: the Mime plays the roles of both Pierrot and Columbine alternately. Here is simply the descriptive passage (in parentheses and in roman letters) in which the crime and the orgasm (what Bataille calls dying laughing and laughing [at] dying) take place such that in the final analysis what happens is nothing, no violence, no stigmata, no traces; the perfect crime in that it can be confused only with the heights of pleasure [*jouissance*] obtainable from a certain speculation. The author indeed disappears since Pierrot also is (plays) Columbine and since at the end of the scene he dies, too, before the spectacle of Columbine, who suddenly comes to life and, inside her portrait, bursts out laughing. Here, then, is the apparent production of the spasm or, let us already hazard the word, of the hymen: "And now, let's tickle: Columbine, it's you that will pay for this." (And he tickles wild, he tickles fierce, he tickles again, he tickles without mercy, then throws himself on the bed and becomes Columbine. She [he] writhes in horrible gaiety. One of the arms gets loose and frees the other arm, and these two crazed arms start fulminating against Pierrot. She [he] bursts out in a true, strident, mortal laugh; sits bolt upright; tries to jump out of bed; and still her [his] feet are dancing, tickled, tortured, epileptic. It is the death throes. She [he] rises up once or twice—supreme spasm!—opens her [his] mouth for one last curse, and throws back, out of the bed, her [his] drooping head and arms. Pierrot becomes Pierrot again. At the foot of the bed, he is still scratching, worn out, gasping, but victorious . . .)

After congratulating him(her)self for having, through this nonviolent crime, through this sort of masturbatory suicide, saved his (her) head from the "chopper's blow [*coup de couperet*]" of the guillotine ("I wash my hands of it, you understand"), the androgynous mime is overtaken, incoercibly, by "Columbine's tickle, like a contagious, avenging ill." He tries to escape it by what he calls a "remedy": the bottle with which another erotic scene concludes in a "spasm" and a "swoon." After the second lapse, a hallucination presents him with a Columbine who has become animate in her portrait, bursting out in laughter. Pierrot is again overcome by trepidation and tickling, and finally he dies at the feet of his "painted victim laughing still."

With all its false bottoms, its abysses, its *trompe-l'oeil*, such an arrangement of writings could not be a simple pretextual referent for Mallarmé's *Mimique*. But despite the (structural, temporal, textual) complexity of this booklet-object, one might have been tempted to consider it a system closed upon itself, folded back over the relation, which is certainly very tangled, between, let us say, the "act" of the mimodrama (the one Mallarmé says writes itself upon a white page) and the retrospectiveness [*l'après-coup*] of the booklet. In this case, Mallarmé's textual play of reference would be checked by a definite safety-catch.

But such is not the case. A writing that refers back only to itself carries us *at the same time*, indefinitely and systematically, to some other writing. At the same time: this is what we must account for. A writing that refers only to itself and a writing that refers indefinitely to some other writing might appear noncontradictory: the reflecting screen never captures anything but writing, indefinitely, stopping nowhere, and each reference still confines us within the element of reflection. Of course. But the difficulty arises in the relation between the medium of writing and the determination of each textual unit. It is necessary that while referring each time to another text, to another determinate system, each organism only refer to *itself* as a determinate structure; a structure that is open and closed *at the same time*.

Letting itself be read for itself, doing without any external pretext, *Mimique* is also haunted by the ghost or grafted onto the arborescence of another text. Concerning which, *Mimique* explains that that text describes a gestural writing dictated by nothing and pointing only toward its own initiality, etc. Margueritte's booklet is thus, for *Mimique*, both a sort of epigraph, an hors d'œuvre, and a seed, a seminal infiltration: indeed both at once, which only the operation of the *graft* can no doubt represent. One ought to explore systematically not only what appears to be a simple etymological coincidence uniting the graft and the graph (both from *graphion*: writing implement, stylus), but also the analogy between the forms of textual grafting and so-called vegetal grafting, or even, more and more commonly today, animal grafting. It would not be enough to compose an encyclopedic catalogue of grafts (approach grafting, detached scion grafting; whip grafts, splice grafts, saddle grafts, cleft grafts, bark grafts; bridge grafting, inarching, repair grafting, bracing; T-budding, shield budding, etc.); one must elaborate a systematic treatise on the textual graft. Among other things, this would help us understand the functioning of footnotes, for example, or epigraphs, and in what way, to the one who knows how to read, these are sometimes more important than the so-called principal or capital text. And when the capital title itself becomes a scion, one can no longer choose between the presence or absence of the title.[21]

We have pointed out just about all the structural elements of Margueritte's book. We know what its themes and title are. What is left? On the title page, between the author's proper name and the title on the one hand, and the name of the writer of the preface on the other hand, there is an *epigraph* and a third proper name. It is a quotation from Théophile Gautier:

> The story of Pierrot who tickled his wife,
> And thus made her laughingly give up her life.

Now we know. This whole mimodrama refers back one more step, through the incision marked by the epigraph, to another text. At least one, and whatever Margueritte may have said in his Note. An eye graft, a text extending far out of sight.

Out of sight—you are here slowly coming back to the hymen and dissemination—for there would be a certain imprudence in believing that one could, at last, stop at a textual seed or principle of life referring only to itself in the form of Gautier's *Pierrot Posthume*.[22] A notch is marked there,

---

21. For the reasons being set forth here, this concept of the textual graft would be hard to confine simply to the field of a "human psychology" of the imagination, as Bachelard defines it in the following beautifully written passage from *L'Eau et les Rêves* [*Water and Dreams*]: "What we love above all in man is what can be written about him. Does what can't be written deserve to be lived? We have thus been obliged to content ourselves with the *grafted* material imagination, and we have almost always confined ourselves to the study of the different branches of the materializing imagination found *above the graft* whenever any culture has put its mark on any nature.

"Moreover, this is not, for us, a simple metaphor. On the contrary, the *graft* appears to us to be a concept essential to the understanding of human psychology. It is, in our view, the human sign as such, the necessary sign for specifying human imagination. For us, humanity imagining is something that lies beyond nature naturing. It is the graft that can really give the material imagination the exuberance of forms. It is the graft that can transmit the variety and density of matter to the formal imagination. It forces the seedling to flower and gives matter to the flower. In a completely nonmetaphorical sense, the production of a poetic work requires that there be a union between a dreaming activity and an ideating activity. Art is grafted nature" (pp. 14–15; original emphasis). These statements are disputed, from a "psychocritical" point of view, by Charles Mauron (*Des Métaphores obsédantes au mythe personnel* [*From Obsessive Metaphors to Personal Myth*], pp. 26–27).

22. A Harlequinade in one act and in verse (done in collaboration with P. Siraudin), first performed on the Vaudeville stage on October 4, 1847. Margueritte was much later to write: "The perusal of a tragic tale by Commander Rivière along with two lines by Gautier, 'The story of Pierrot who tickled his wife, And thus made her laughingly give up her life,' determined my Satanic, ultraromantic and yet very modern conception: a refined, neurotic, cruel yet ingenuous Pierrot in whom all possible contrasts were alloyed, a veritable psychic

one that again opens onto another text and practices another reading. The analysis of all this would be infinite. Harlequin offers a mouse to Columbine under the pretext that "A woman's a cat holding us in her claws; / A mouse is the right gift to place in her paws." To which Columbine replies: "A jewel-box is nicer than thirty mousetraps." All this at the moment that Pierrot's death in Algiers is being announced by Harlequin ("Bah! nothing's surer: his obituary, / On the opening pages of each dictionary, / Is visibly written with paraphs profuse, / Just under a Pierrot attached to a noose."). Pierrot returns, and is summoned to testify to his own death: "I can rejoice no longer in seeing myself," and he wanders about like a phantom. Mistakenly, he drinks a philter of resurrection and swallows the mouse Harlequin has surreptitiously introduced into the bottle. He begins to wiggle and laugh, "mad and wild-eyed" ("If I only could slip down a tomcat inside!"), and finally decides to kill himself. And in the course of a soliloquy, as he deliberates over the various ways of putting an end to his life, *he remembers something he has read*: "Let's go commit suicide once and for all. / Hm, what about rope? No, that's no solution: / Hemp doesn't go with my soul's constitution . . . / Jump off a bridge? cold water's too chilling . . . / Smother myself in a bed with down filling? / Fi! I'm too white to be aping Othello . . . / Not feathers, nor water, nor rope for this fellow . . . / I have it: I've read in an old-fashioned story / The tale of a husband who tickled his wife, / And thus made her laughingly give up her life . . . He tickles himself. Ha! ha! I shall soon leap about like a calf / If I don't . . . Let's go on . . . How this does make me laugh! / I'm bursting! and now to move down to the feet. / I'm fainting, I'm crawling, I'm in a fire's heat! / How the universe opens before my dazed eyes! / Ho! ho! I am fainting and cannot arise." *Columbine*: "Who's this idiot pinching himself just for fun?" *Pierrot*: "A ghost who is dying." *Columbine*: "Say that again?"

After a number of other episodes (scenes of poisoning, Pierrot as a vampire figure, etc.), Pierrot turns to address the audience. This time we do not have a Mime-librettist attributing fictional status to a booklet of words

---

Proteus, a bit sadistic, quite willingly a lush, and a perfect scoundrel. Thus it is that with *Pierrot Murderer of his Wife*—a tragic nightmare *à la* Hoffmann or Edgar Allan Poe, in which Pierrot makes his wife die laughing by tickling the bottoms of her feet—I was a precursor in the revival of pantomime back in 1881; I might even say *the* precursor." (*Nos Tréteaux* [*Our Stage*], 1910). Margueritte seems not to be familiar with all the back corridors and genealogies of this scene. For example, death by foot tickling occurs in *Les roueries de Trialph, Notre contemporain avant son suicide* [*Trialph's Tricks: Our Contemporary prior to his Suicide*] by Lassailly (1833); tickling to death is already found in *The White Devil* by Webster (1612): "He tickles you to death, makes you die laughing" (V, iii), the whole time, of course, in the interval and already, so to speak, in the English language.

being substituted for a mute mimic. We have a Pierrot who, while speaking upon the stage, begs forgiveness for having done so, the entire thing being enclosed within the writing of a booklet: "Pardon Pierrot for speaking, please. Most of the time / I play my part only through grimace and mime. / I silently move like a phantom in white, / Always fooled, always beaten, and trembling with fright, / Through all the imbroglios traced out in bold / Brush-strokes by the Comedy dreamed up of old. / *Comedia dell' arte* was once this art's name, / Where actors embroidered their role as it came."

One could go on at great length in order to find out where this Pierrot had read the exemplary story of this husband who tickled his wife and thus made her laughingly give up her life. With all the threads provided by the *comedia dell' arte*, one would find oneself caught in an interminable network.[23] Bibliographical research, source studies, the archeology of all Pierrots would be at once endless and useless, at least as far as what interests us here is concerned, since the process of cross-referencing and grafting is *remarked inside* Mallarmé's text, which thereby has no more "inside" than it can properly be said to be *by* Mallarmé.

The moment at which we appeared to take leave of that text was marked by the proposition I shall here recall: setting down and composing by himself his soliloquy, tracing it upon the white page he himself is, the Mime does not allow his text to be dictated to him from any other place. He represents nothing, imitates nothing, does not have to conform to any prior referent with the aim of achieving adequation or verisimilitude. One can here foresee an objection: since the mime imitates nothing, reproduces nothing, opens up in its origin the very thing he is tracing out, presenting, or producing, he must be the very movement of truth. Not, of course, truth

---

23. Among other intersections, one would encounter a *Pierrot Dead and Alive*, a *Pierrot Valet of Death* (with a review by Nerval, who had combed all of Europe in order to study pantomime), a *Pierrot Hanged* (by Champfleury) in punishment for the theft of a book, a Pierrot disguised as a mattress on which his Colombine more or less makes love with Harlequin, after which they make a hole in the mattress cover and card the wool, which prompts Théophile Gautier to write: "A moment later some woolcarders appear and subject Pierrot to a painful quarter-hour [*quart d'heure~cardeur* (carder)]; to be carded, what a fate! it's enough to take your breath [*l'haleine~la laine* (wool)] away. Please excuse these puns, which cannot occur in pantomime, which proves the superiority of those sorts of works over all others." Elsewhere, Gautier notes that "the origin of Pierrot," "the symbol of the proletarian," is just as "interesting" as those enigmas "that have aroused the curiosity of the . . .Father Kirchers, the Champollions, etc." This is a lead to follow. I would like to thank Paule Thévenin for helping me in this library of Pierrots, who are all, including Margueritte's, at once living and dead, living more dead than alive, *between* life and death, taking into consideration those effects of specular doubling which the abundant literature of the time associates with Hoffman, Nerval, and even Poe.

in the form of adequation between the representation and the present of the thing itself, or between the imitator and the imitated, but truth as the present unveiling of the present: monstration, manifestation, production, *alētheia*. The mime produces, that is to say makes appear *in praesentia*, manifests the very meaning of what he is presently writing: of what he *performs*. He enables the thing to be perceived in person, in its true face. If one followed the thread of this objection, one would go back, beyond imitation, toward a more "originary" sense of *alētheia* and of *mimeisthai*. One would thus come up with one of the most typical and tempting metaphysical reappropriations of writing, one that can always crop up in the most divergent contexts.

One could indeed push Mallarmé back into the most "originary" metaphysics of truth if all mimicry [*mimique*] had indeed disappeared, if it had effaced itself in the scriptural production of truth.

But such is not the case. *There is* mimicry. Mallarmé sets great store by it, along with simulacrum (and along with pantomime, theater, and dance; all these motifs intersect in particular in *Richard Wagner, Rêverie d'un Poète français*, which we are holding and commenting upon here behind the scenes). We are faced then with mimicry imitating nothing; faced, so to speak, with a double that doubles no simple, a double that nothing anticipates, nothing at least that is not itself already double. There is no simple reference. It is in this that the mime's operation does allude, but alludes to nothing, alludes without breaking the mirror, without reaching beyond the looking-glass. *"That is how the Mime operates, whose act is confined to a perpetual allusion without breaking the ice or the mirror."* This speculum reflects no reality; it produces mere "reality-effects." For this double that often makes one think of Hoffmann (mentioned by Beissier in his Preface), reality, indeed, is death. It will prove to be inaccessible, otherwise than by simulacrum, just like the dreamed-of *simplicity* of the supreme spasm or of the hymen. In this speculum with no reality, in this mirror of a mirror, a difference or dyad does exist, since there are mimes and phantoms. But it is a difference without reference, or rather a reference without a referent, without any first or last unit, a ghost that is the phantom of no flesh, wandering about without a past, without any death, birth, or presence.

Mallarmé thus preserves the differential structure of mimicry or *mimēsis*, but without its Platonic or metaphysical interpretation, which implies that somewhere the being of something that *is*, is being imitated. Mallarmé even maintains (and maintains himself in) the structure of the *phantasma* as it is defined by Plato: the simulacrum as the copy of a copy. With the exception that there is no longer any model, and hence, no copy, and that this structure (which encompasses Plato's text, including his attempt to escape it) is no longer being referred back to any ontology or even to any dialectic. Any attempt to reverse mimetologism or escape it in one fell swoop by leaping out of it *with both feet* would only amount to an inevitable and immediate fall back into its system: in suppressing the double or making it dialectical, one is back in the perception of the thing itself, the production of its presence, its truth, as idea, form, or matter. In comparison with Platonic or Hegelian idealism, the displacement we are here for the sake of convenience calling "Mallarméan" is more subtle and patient, more discreet and efficient. It is a simulacrum of Platonism or Hegelianism, which is separated from what it simulates only by a barely perceptible veil, about which one can just as well say that it already runs—unnoticed— between Platonism and itself, between Hegelianism and itself. Between Mallarmé's text and itself. It is thus not simply false to say that Mallarmé is a Platonist or a Hegelian. But it is above all not true.[24]

And vice versa.

What interests us here is less these propositions of a philosophical type than the mode of their reinscription in the text of *Mimique*. What is marked there is the fact that, this imitator having in the last instance no imitated, this signifier having in the last instance no signified, this sign having in the last instance no referent, their operation is no longer comprehended within the process of truth but on the contrary comprehends *it*, the motif of the last

24. Just as the motif of neutrality, in its negative form, paves the way for the most classical and suspect attempts at reappropriation, it would be imprudent just to cancel out the pairs of metaphysical oppositions, simply to *mark off* from them any text (assuming this to be possible). The strategic analysis must be constantly readjusted. For example, the deconstruction of the pairs of metaphysical oppositions could end up defusing and neutralizing Mallarmé's text and would thus serve the interests invested in its prevailing traditional interpretation, which up to now has been massively idealist. It is in and against this context that one can and should emphasize the "materialism of the idea." We have borrowed this definition from Jean Hyppolite (". . . within this materialism of the idea he imagines the diverse possibilities for reading the text . . ." "Le coup de dés de Stéphane Mallarmé et le message," in *les Etudes philosophiques*, 1958, no. 4). This is an example of that *strategic dissymmetry* that must ceaselessly counterbalance the neutralizing moments of any deconstruction. This dissymmetry has to be minutely calculated, taking into account all the analyzable differences within the topography of the field in which it operates. It will in any case be noted that the "logic of the hymen" we are deciphering here is not a logic of negative neutrality, nor even of neutrality at all. Let us also stress that this "materialism of the idea" does not designate the content of some projected "philosophical" doctrine proposed by Mallarmé (we are indeed in the process of determining in what way there *is* no "philosophy" in his text, or rather that that text is calculated in such a way as no longer to be situated *in* philosophy), but precisely the form of what is at stake in the operation of writing and "Reading—That practice—," in the inscription of the "diverse possibilities for reading the text."

instance being inseparable from metaphysics as the search for the *arkhē*, the *eskhaton*, and the *telos*.[25]

If all this leaves its mark upon *Mimique*, it is not only in the chiseled precision of the writing, its extraordinary formal or syntactical felicity; it is also in what seems to be described as the thematic content or mimed event, and which in the final analysis, despite its effect of content, is nothing other than the space of writing: in this "event"—hymen, crime, suicide, spasm (of laughter or pleasure)—in which nothing happens, in which the simulacrum is a transgression and the transgression a simulacrum, everything describes the very structure of the text and effectuates its possibility. That, at least, is what we now must demonstrate.

The operation, which no longer belongs to the system of truth, does not manifest, produce, or unveil any presence; nor does it constitute any conformity, resemblance, or adequation between a presence and a representation. And yet this operation is not a unified entity but the manifold play of a scene that, illustrating nothing—neither word nor deed—beyond itself, illustrates nothing. Nothing but the many-faceted multiplicity of a lustre which itself is nothing beyond its own fragmented light. Nothing but the idea which is nothing. The ideality of the idea is here for Mallarmé the still metaphysical name that is still necessary in order to mark nonbeing, the nonreal, the nonpresent. This mark points, alludes without breaking the glass, to the beyond of beingness, toward the *epekeina tēs ousias*: a hymen (a closeness and a veil) between Plato's sun and Mallarmé's lustre. This "materialism of the idea" is nothing other than the staging, the theater, the visibility of nothing or of the self. It is a dramatization which *illustrates nothing*, which illustrates *the nothing*, lights up a space, re-marks a spacing as a nothing, a blank: white as a yet unwritten page, blank as a difference between two lines. "I am for—no illustration. . . ."[26]

---

25. For the reasons indicated in the preceding note, the simple erasing of the metaphysical concept of last instance would run the risk of defusing the necessary critique it permits in certain determinate contexts. To take this double inscription of concepts into account is to practice a *double science*, a bifid, *dissymmetrical* writing. Whose "general economy," defined elsewhere, does indeed constitute, in a displaced sense of the words, the last instance.

26. The context of this quotation should here be restituted and related back to what was said, at the start of this session, concerning the book, the extra-text [*hors-livre*], the image, and the illustration; then it should be related forward to what will be set in motion, in the following session, between the book and the movement of the stage. Mallarmé is responding to a survey: "I am for—no illustration; everything a book evokes should happen in the reader's mind: but, if you replace photography, why not go straight to cinematography, whose successive" unrolling will replace, in both pictures and text, many a volume, advantageously" (p. 878).

This chain of terms, Theater-Idea-Mime-Drama, can be found sketched out in one of the fragments from the unpublished plans for the *Book*:

> "*The summary of the theater*
> *as Idea and hymn*
> *whence theater* = *Idea*"

And, a bit further on, off to one side:

> "*Theater*   *Idea*
>   *Drama*
> *Hero*   *Hymn*
> *mime*   *dance*"

The stage [*scène*] thus illustrates but the stage, the scene only the scene; there is only the equivalence between *theater* and *idea*, that is (as these two names indicate), the visibility (which remains outside) of the visible that is being effectuated. The scene illustrates, in the text of a hymen—which is more than an anagram of "hymn" [*hymne*]—"*in a hymen (out of which flows Dream), tainted with vice yet sacred, between desire and fulfillment, perpetration and remembrance: here anticipating, there recalling, in the future, in the past, under the false appearance of a present.*"

"Hymen" (a word, indeed the only word, that reminds us that what is in question is a "supreme spasm") is first of all a sign of fusion, the consummation of a marriage, the identification of two beings, the confusion between two. *Between* the two, there is no longer difference but identity. Within this fusion, there is no longer any distance between desire (the awaiting of a full presence designed to fulfill it, to carry it out) and the fulfillment of presence, between distance and non-distance; there is no longer any difference between desire and satisfaction. It is not only the difference (between desire and fulfillment) that is abolished, but also the difference between difference and nondifference. Nonpresence, the gaping void of desire, and presence, the fullness of enjoyment, amount to the same. By the same token [*du même coup*], there is no longer any textual difference between the image and the thing, the empty signifier and the full signified, the imitator and the imitated, etc. But it does not follow, by virtue of this hymen of confusion, that there is now only one term, a single one of the differends. It does not follow that what remains is thus the fullness of the signified, the imitated, or the thing itself, simply present in person. It is the difference between the two terms that is no longer functional. The confusion or consummation of this hymen eliminates the spatial heterogeneity of the two poles in the "supreme spasm," the moment of dying laughing. By the same token, it eliminates the exteriority or anteriority, the independence, of the imitated, the signified, or the thing. Fulfillment is summed up within desire; desire is (ahead of) fulfillment, which, still mimed, remains desire, *"without breaking the mirror."*

What is lifted, then, is not difference but the different, the differends, the decidable exteriority of differing terms. Thanks to the confusion and continuity of the hymen, and not in spite of it, a (pure and impure) difference inscribes itself without any decidable poles, without any independent, irreversible terms. Such difference without presence appears, or rather baffles the process of appearing, by dislocating any orderly time at the center of the present. The present is no longer a mother-form around which are gathered and differentiated the future (present) and the past (present). What is marked in this hymen between the future (desire) and the present (fulfillment), between the past (remembrance) and the present (perpetration), between the capacity and the act, etc., is only a series of temporal differences without any central present, without a present of which the past and future would be but modifications. Can we then go on speaking about *time*, *tenses*, and *temporal* differences?

The center of presence is supposed to offer itself to what is called perception or, generally, intuition. In *Mimique*, however, there is no perception, no reality offering itself up, in the present, to be perceived. The plays of facial expression and the gestural tracings are not present in themselves since they always refer, perpetually allude or represent. But they don't represent anything that has ever been or can ever become present: nothing that comes before or after the mimodrama, and, within the mimodrama, an orgasm-crime that has never been committed and yet nevertheless turns into a suicide without striking or suffering a blow, etc. The signifying allusion does not go through the looking-glass: *"a perpetual allusion without breaking the ice or the mirror,"* the cold, transparent, reflective window ("without breaking the ice or the mirror" is added in the third version of the text), without piercing the veil or the canvas, without tearing the moire. The antre of Mallarmé, the theater of his glossary: it lies in this suspension, the *"center of vibratory suspense,"* the repercussions of words between the walls of the grotto, or of the glottis, sounded among others by the rhymes *"hoir"* [heir], *"soir"* [evening], *"noire"* [black], *"miroir"* [mirror], *"grimoire"* [wizard's black book], *"ivoire"* [ivory], *"armoire"* [wardrobe], etc. (see figures II and IV).

What does the hymen that illustrates the suspension of differends remain, other than Dream? The capital letter marks what is new in a concept no longer enclosed in the old opposition: Dream, being at once perception, remembrance, and anticipation (desire), each within the others, is really none of these. It declares the "fiction," the "medium, the pure medium, of fiction" (the commas in *"milieu, pur, de fiction"* also appear in the third version), a presence both perceived and not perceived, at once image and model, and hence image without model, neither image nor model, a medium (medium in the sense of middle, neither/nor, what is between extremes, and medium in the sense of element, ether, matrix, means). When we have rounded a certain corner in our reading, we will place ourselves on that side of the lustre where the "medium" is shining. The referent is lifted, but reference remains: what is left is only the writing of dreams, a fiction that is not imaginary, mimicry without imitation, without verisimilitude, without truth or falsity, a miming of appearance without concealed reality, without any world behind it, and hence without appearance: *"false appearance . . ."* There remain only traces, announcements and souvenirs, foreplays and aftereffects [*avant-coups et après-coups*] which no present will have preceded or followed and which cannot be arranged on a line around a point, traces "here anticipating, there recalling, in the future, in the past, *under the false appearance of a present."* It is Mallarmé who underlines (as of the second version, in *Pages*) and thus marks the ricochet of the moment of mimed deliberation from Margueritte's *Pierrot*: at that point—in the past—where the question is raised of what to do in the future ("But how shall I go about it?"), the author of the booklet speaks to *you* in parentheses, in the "present": ("For Pierrot, like a sleepwalker, reproduces his crime, and in his hallucination, the *past* becomes *present.*") (Underlined by the author.) The historial ambiguity of the word *appearance* (at once the appearing or apparition of the being-present *and* the masking of the being-present behind its appearance) impresses its indefinite fold on this sequence, which is neither synthetic nor redundant: *"under the false appearance of a present."* What is to be re-marked in the underlining of this circumstantial complement is the displacement without reversal of Platonism and its heritage. This displacement is always an effect of language or writing, of syntax, and never simply the dialectical overturning of a concept (signified). The very motif of dialectics, which marks the beginning and end of philosophy, however that motif might be determined and despite the resources it entertains within philosophy against philosophy, is doubtless what Mallarmé has marked with his syntax at the point of its sterility, or rather, at the point that will soon, provisionally, analogically, be called the undecidable.

Or *hymen*.

The virginity of the *"yet unwritten page"* opens up that space. There are still a few words that have not been illustrated: the opposition *vicious/sacred* (*"hymen (out of which flows Dream)*, *tainted with vice yet sacred"*; the parentheses intervene in the second version to make it clear that the adjectives modify "hymen"), the opposition *desire/perpetration*, and most importantly the syncategorem *"between"* {*entre*}.

To repeat: the hymen, the confusion between the present and the nonpresent, along with all the indifferences it entails within the whole series of opposites (perception/nonperception, memory/image, memory/desire, etc.), produces the effect of a medium (a medium as element enveloping both terms at once; a medium located between the two terms). It is an operation that *both* sows confusion *between* opposites *and* stands *between* the opposites "at once." What counts here is the *between*, the in-between-ness of the hymen. The hymen "takes place" in the "inter-," in the spacing between desire and fulfillment, between perpetration and its recollection. But this medium of the *entre* has nothing to do with a center.

The hymen enters into the antre. *Entre* can just as easily be written with an *a* (see figures II and IV). Indeed, are these two *(e) (a)ntres* not really the same? Littré: "ANTRE, s.m. 1. Cave, natural grotto, deep dark cavern. 'These antres, these braziers that offer us oracles,' *Voltaire, Oedipe* II, 5. 2. Fig. The antres of the police, of the Inquisition. 3. *Anatomy*: name given to certain bone cavities. —*Syn*: *Antre, cave, grotto. Cave*, an empty, hollow, concave space in the form of a vault, is the generic term; *antre* is a deep, dark, black cave; *grotto* is a picturesque cave created by nature or by man. *Etym*. Antrum, 'άντρον; Sanscrit, *antara*, cleft, cave. *Antara* properly signifies 'interval' and is thus related to the Latin preposition *inter* (see *entre*). Provenc. *antre*; Span. and Ital. *antro*." And the entry for ENTRER ["to enter"] ends with the same etymological reference. The *interval* of the *entre*, the in-between of the hymen: one might be tempted to visualize these as the hollow or bed of a valley (*vallis*) without which there would be no mountains, like the sacred vale between the two flanks of the Parnassus, the dwelling-place of the Muses and the site of Poetry; but *intervallum* is composed of *inter* (between) and *vallus* (pole), which gives us not the pole in between, but the space between two palisades. According to Littré.

We are thus moving from the logic of the palisade, which is always, in a sense, "full," to the logic of the hymen. The hymen, the consummation of differends, the continuity and confusion of the coitus, merges with what it seems to be derived from: the hymen as protective screen, the jewel box of virginity, the vaginal partition, the fine, invisible veil which, in front of the

hystera, stands *between* the inside and the outside of a woman, and consequently between desire and fulfillment. It is neither desire nor pleasure but
in between the two. Neither future nor present, but between the two. It is
the hymen that desire dreams of piercing, of bursting, in an act of violence
that is (at the same time or somewhere between) love and murder. If either
one *did* take place, there would be no hymen. But neither would there
simply be a hymen in (case events go) *no* place. With all the undecidability
of its meaning, the hymen only takes place when it doesn't take place, when
nothing *really* happens, when there is an all-consuming consummation
without violence, or a violence without blows, or a blow without marks, a
mark without a mark (a margin), etc., when the veil is, *without being*, torn,
for example when one is made to die or come laughing.

''Υμήν designates a fine, filmy membrane enveloping certain bodily
organs; for example, says Aristotle, the heart or the intestines. It is also the
cartilage in certain fish, the wings of certain insects (bees, wasps, and ants,
which are called hymenoptera), the foot membranes in certain birds (the
hymenopoda), a white pellicle over the eyes of certain birds, the sheath
encasing the seed or bean of plants. A tissue on which so many bodily
metaphors are written.

There exist treatises on membranes or *hymenologies*; descriptions of membranes or *hymenographies*. Rightly or wrongly, the etymology of "hymen" is
often traced to a root *u* that can be found in the Latin *suo, suere* (to sew) and in
huphos (tissue). *Hymen* might then mean a little stitch (*syuman*) (*syuntah*,
sewn, *siula*, needle; *schuh*, sew; *suo*). The same hypothesis, while sometimes
contested, is put forth for *hymn*, which would thus not be a merely
accidental anagram of *hymen* [*hymne/hymen*] (see figure V). Both words
would have a relation with *uphainō* (to weave, spin—the spider web—
machinate), with *huphos* (textile, spider web, net, the text of a work—
Longinus), and with *humnos* (a weave, later the weave of a song, by extension
a wedding song or song of mourning). Littré: . . ."according to Curtius,
'ύμνος has the same root as 'υφάω, to weave, 'υφή, 'ύφος, textile; in that
long ago era when writing was unknown, most of the words used to
designate a poetic composition were borrowed from the art of the weaver,
the builder, etc."

The hymen is thus a sort of textile. Its threads should be interwoven with
all the veils, gauzes, canvases, fabrics, moires, wings, feathers, all the
curtains and fans that hold within their folds all—almost—of the Mallarméan corpus. We could spend a night doing that. The text of *Mimique* is not
the only place where the word "hymen" occurs. It appears, with the same
syntactical resources of undecidability, handled more or less systematically,

in the *Cantate pour la Première Communion* [*Cantata for the First Communion*] composed by Mallarmé at the age of sixteen ("in this mysterious hymen / Between strength and weakness"), in *L'Après-midi d'un Faune* [*The Afternoon of a Faun*] ("Too much hymen hoped for by him who seeks the *la*"), in the *Offrandes à divers du Faune* [*Gifts of the Faun to a Few*] ("The Faun would dream of hymen and of a chaste ring"), and especially in *Richard Wagner, Rêverie d'un Poète français*, where all the elements of the constellation are named over two pages (pp. 543–45): the Mime, the hymen, the virgin, the occult, the penetration and the envelope, the theater, the hymn, the "folds of a tissue," the touch that transforms nothing, the "song, spurting out of a rift," the "fusion of these disparate forms of pleasure."

A folding back, once more: the hymen, *"a medium, a pure medium, of fiction,"* is located between present acts that don't take place. What takes place is only the *entre*, the place, the spacing, which is nothing, the ideality (as nothingness) of the idea. No act, then, is *perpetrated* ("*Hymen . . . between perpetration and remembrance*"); no act is committed as a crime. There is only the memory of a crime that has never been committed, not only because on the stage we have never seen it in the present (the Mime is recalling it), but also because no violence has been exerted (someone has been made to die of laughter, and then the "criminal"—bursting with hilarity—is absolved by his own death), and because this crime is its opposite: an act of love. Which itself has not taken place. To perpetrate, as its calculated consonance with "penetrate" suggests, is to pierce, but fictively, the hymen, the threshold never crossed. Even when he takes that step, Pierrot remains, before the doors, the "solitary captive of the threshold" (*Pour votre chère morte* [*For your dear departed*]).

To pierce the hymen or to pierce one's eyelid (which in some birds is called a hymen), to lose one's sight or one's life, no longer to see the light of day, is the fate of all Pierrots. Gautier's *Pierrot Posthume* succumbs to it, prior to Margueritte's. It is the fate of the simulacrum. He applies the procedure to himself and pretends to die, after swallowing the mouse, then by tickling himself, in the supreme spasm of infinite masturbation. This Pierrot's hymen was perhaps not quite so subtly transparent, so invisibly lacking in consistency, as Mallarmé's. But it is also because his hymen (marriage) remains precarious and uncertain that he kills himself or passes himself off as dead. Thinking that, if he is already dead in others' eyes, he would be incapable of rising to the necessary hymen, the *true* hymen, between Columbine and himself, this posthumous Pierrot simulates suicide: "I'll beat up on Harlequin, take back my wife... / But how? and with what? my soul's all my life, / I'm a being of reason, I'm all immaterial.

/ A hymen needs palpable things, not ethereal... / What a puzzle! to settle these doubts, let's not stall: / Let's go commit suicide once and for all."[27] But suicide being still another species of the genus "hymen," he will never have finished killing himself, the "once and for all" expressing precisely that which the hymen always makes a mockery of, that before which we shall always burst out laughing.

Quant au Livre [*As for the Book*] : The structures of the hymen, suicide, and time are closely linked together. "Suicide or abstention, to do nothing, why? Only time in the world, for, due to an event that I shall explain, always, there is no Present, no—a present does not exist . . . . For lack of the Crowd's declaration, for lack—of all. Ill-informed is he who would pronounce himself his own contemporary, deserting, usurping, with equal imprudence, when some past has ceased and a future is slow in coming or else both are perplexedly mixed with a view to masking the gap" (p. 372).

A masked gap, impalpable and insubstantial, interposed, slipped between, the *entre* of the hymen is reflected in the screen without penetrating it. The hymen remains in the hymen. The one—the veil of virginity where nothing has yet taken place—remains in the other—consummation, release, and penetration of the antre.

And vice versa.

The mirror is never passed through and the ice never broken. At the edge of being.

At the edge of being, the medium of the hymen never becomes a mere mediation or work of the negative; it outwits and undoes all ontologies, all philosophemes, all manner of dialectics. It outwits them and—as a cloth, a tissue, a medium again—it envelops them, turns them over, and inscribes them. This nonpenetration, this nonperpetration (which is not simply negative but stands between the two), this suspense in the antre of per-penetration, is, says Mallarmé, *"perpetual"*: *"This is how the Mime operates, whose act is confined to a perpetual allusion without breaking the ice or the mirror: he thus sets up a medium, a pure medium, of fiction."* (The play of the commas

27. The word "Hymen," sometimes allegorized by a capital H, is of course part of the vocabulary of "Pierrots" ("Harlequin and Polichinelle both aspire to a glorious hymen with Colombine," Gautier), just as it is included in the "symbolist" code. It nevertheless remains—and is significant—that Mallarmé with his syntactic play remarks the undecidable ambivalence. The "event" (the historical event, if you wish) has the form of a repetition, the mark—readable because doubled—of a quasi-tearing, a *dehiscence*. "DEHISCENCE: s.f. Botanical term. The action through which the distinct parts of a closed organ open up, without tearing, along a seam. A regular predetermined splitting that, at a certain moment in the cycle, is undergone by the closed organs so that what they contain can come out . . . E. Lat. *Dehiscere*, to open slightly, from *de* and *hiscere*, the frequentative of *hiare* (see *hiatus*)." Littré.

(*virgulae*) only appears, in all its multiplicity, in the last version, inserting a series of cuts marking pauses and cadence, spacing and shortness of breath, within the continuum of the sequence).[28] Hymen in perpetual motion: one can't get out of Mallarmé's antre as one can out of Plato's cave. Never min(e)d [*mine de rien*];[29] it requires an entirely different kind of speleology which no longer searches behind the lustrous appearance, outside the "beyond," "agent," "motor," "principal part or nothing" of the "literary mechanism" (*Music and Letters*, p. 647).

". . . as much as it takes to illustrate one of the aspects and this lode of language" (p. 406).

"*That is how the Mime operates*": every time Mallarmé uses the word "*operation*," nothing happens that could be grasped as a present event, a reality, an activity, etc. The Mime doesn't *do* anything; there is no act (neither murderous nor sexual), no acting agent and hence no patient. Nothing *is*. The word *is* does not appear in *Mimique*, which is nevertheless conjugated in the *present*, within and upon the "*false appearance of a present*," with one exception, and even then in a form that is not that of a declaration of existence and barely that of a predicative copula ("*It is up to the poet, roused by a dare, to translate!*"). Indeed, the constant ellipsis of the verb "to be" by Mallarmé has already been noted.[30] This ellipsis is complementary to the frequency of the word *jeu* [play, game, act]; the practice of "play" in Mallarmé's writing is in collusion with the casting aside of "being." The *casting aside* [*mise à l'écart*] of being defines itself and literally (im)prints itself in dissemination, *as* dissemination.

The play of the hymen is *at once* vicious and sacred, "tainted with vice yet sacred." And so, too, is it neither the one nor the other since nothing happens and the hymen remains suspended *entre*, outside and inside the antre. Nothing is more vicious than this suspense, this distance played at; nothing is more perverse than this rending penetration that leaves a virgin womb intact. But nothing is more marked by the sacred, like so many Mallarméan veils, more folded, intangible, sealed, untouched. Here we ought to grasp fully the analogy between *Mimique*'s "scenario" and the one that is spottily sketched out in the fragments of the Book. Among them, these:

28. ". . . I prefer, as being more to my taste, upon a white page, a carefully spaced pattern of commas and periods and their secondary combinations, imitating, naked, the melody—over the text, advantageously suggested if, even though sublime, it were not punctuated" (p. 407).

29. TN. In French, *mine de rien* means, in its colloquial sense, "as though it were of no importance," but literally it can mean "a mine full of nothing."

30. Cf. Jacques Scherer, *l'Expression littéraire dans l'Oeuvre de Mallarmé*, pp. 142 ff.

19 A

On the other side, both future
and past

                              (one arm, another,
                              raised, posture of

Such is what takes place   a dancer
visible
with him omitted

20 A

     to open onto[1] medium (solitary
     within the self—[2] this extends
     to the mysterious fore-stage, like the
     ground—preparation for the festival
=   intermission*

confusion of the two

with interruption of the open ground   or = **
                                        the action in
                                        the background
                                        —taking up where
                                        one leaves off

=   * intermission
      before alone   (recall the festival (regrets, etc.)
      and growing
      with the medium

and   the curtain rises—falls   the "house"
                                      and backdrop
       corresponds to ground   the beyond

and mysterious fore-stage—corresponds to
                what hides the background (canvas, etc.) makes its
                                        mystery—

---

    background = the "house"   **   with lustres

1. onto a second ground
2. solitary festival in the self—festival

21 A

               the electrical arabesque
       lights up behind—and the two
veils

       —a sort of sacred rending of the
veil, written there—or rends—

       and two beings at once bird
and scent—like the two in a
          pulpit
high (balcony) com

---

      the egg   church

22 A

      . . . .
      . . . .
      There, that is all the echo says—
double, lying, questioned
by the <u>wandering</u> <u>spirit</u> (of the wind)

24 A

      . . . .
      . . . .
      —During that time—the curtain
of the diorama deepened—shadow
more and more pronounced, as though hollowed
out by it—by the mystery—

      The blinds have rendered themselves null . . . .
      . . . .

169 A   [in the corner of a page]

      Operation*
crime   oath?
*which is neither. nor.
      . . . .

50 B

    5 years. the lustre

The Mime is *acting* from the moment he is ruled by no actual action and aims toward no form of verisimilitude. The act always plays out a difference without reference, or rather without a referent, without any absolute exteriority, and hence, without any inside. The Mime mimes reference. He is not an imitator; he mimes imitation. The hymen interposes itself between mimicry and *mimēsis* or rather between *mimēsis* and *mimēsis*. A copy of a copy, a simulacrum that simulates the Platonic simulacrum—the Platonic copy of a copy as well as the Hegelian curtain[31] have lost here the lure of the present referent and thus find themselves lost for dialectics and ontology, lost for absolute knowledge. Which is also, as Bataille would literally have it, "mimed." In this perpetual allusion being performed in the background of the *entre* that has no ground, one can never know what the allusion alludes to, unless it is to itself in the process of alluding, weaving its hymen and manufacturing its text. Wherein allusion becomes a game conforming only to its own formal rules. As its name indicates, allusion *plays*. But that this play should in the last instance be independent of truth does not mean that it is false, an error, appearance, or illusion. Mallarmé writes "allusion," not "illusion." Allusion, or "suggestion" as Mallarmé says elsewhere, is indeed that operation we are here *by analogy* calling undecidable. An undecidable proposition, as Gödel demonstrated in 1931, is a proposition which, given a system of axioms governing a multiplicity, is neither an analytical nor deductive consequence of those axioms, nor in contradiction with them, neither true nor false with respect to those axioms. *Tertium datur*, without synthesis.

31. As for the hymen between Hegel and Mallarmé, one can analyze, for example, in the *Phenomenology of Spirit*, a certain curtain-raising observed from the singular standpoint of the *we*, the philosophic consciousness, the subject of absolute knowing: "The two extremes . . ., the one, of the pure inner world, the other, that of the inner being gazing into this pure inner world, have now coincided, and just as they, *qua* extremes, have vanished, so too have the middle term, as something other than these extremes, has also vanished. This curtain [*Vorhang*] hanging before the inner world is therefore drawn away, and we have the inner being . . . gazing into the inner world—the vision of the undifferentiated selfsame being, which repels itself from itself, posits itself as an inner being containing different moments, but for which equally these moments are immediately *not* different—*self-consciousness*. It is manifest that behind the so-called curtain which is supposed to conceal the inner world, there is nothing to be seen unless *we* go behind it ourselves, as much in order that we may see, as that there may be something behind there which can be seen. But at the same time it is evident that we cannot without more ado go straightway behind appearance" [trans. Miller, p. 103]. I would like to thank A. Boutruche for recalling this text to my attention.

"Undecidability" is not caused here by some enigmatic equivocality, some inexhaustible ambivalence of a word in a "natural" language, and still less by some *"Gegensinn der Urworte"* (Abel).[32] In dealing here with *hymen*, it is not a matter of repeating what Hegel undertook to do with German words like *Aufhebung*, *Urteil*, *Meinen*, *Beispiel*, etc., marveling over that lucky accident that installs a natural language within the element of speculative dialectics. What counts here is not the lexical richness, the semantic infiniteness of a word or concept, its depth or breadth, the sedimentation that has produced inside it two contradictory layers of signification (continuity and discontinuity, inside and outside, identity and difference, etc.). What counts here is the formal or syntactical *praxis* that composes and decomposes it. We have indeed been making believe that everything could be traced to the word *hymen*. But the irreplaceable character of this signifier, which everything seemed to grant it, was laid out like a trap. This word, this syllepsis,[33] is not indispensable; philology and etymology interest us only secondarily, and the loss of the "hymen" would not be irreparable for *Mimique*. It produces its effect first and foremost through the syntax, which disposes the *"entre"* in such a way that the suspense is due only to the placement and not to the content of words. Through the "hymen" one can remark only what the place of the word *entre* already marks and would mark even if the word "hymen" were not there. If we replaced "hymen" by "marriage" or "crime," "identity" or "difference," etc., the effect would be the same, the only loss being a certain economic condensation or accumulation, which has not gone unnoticed. It is the "between," whether it names fusion or separation, that thus carries all the force of the operation. The hymen must be determined through the *entre* and not the other way around. The hymen in the text (crime, sexual act,

32. We are referring less to the text in which Freud is directly inspired by Abel (1910) than to *Das Unheimliche* (1919), of which we are here, in sum, proposing a rereading. We find ourselves constantly being brought back to that text by the paradoxes of the double and of repetition, the blurring of the boundary lines between "imagination" and "reality," between the "symbol" and the "thing it symbolizes" ("The Uncanny," trans. Alix Strachey, in *On Creativity and the Unconscious* [New York: Harper & Row, 1958], p. 152), the references to Hoffman and the literature of the fantastic, the considerations on the *double meaning* of words: "Thus *heimlich* is a word the meaning of which develops towards an ambivalence, until it finally coincides with its opposite, *unheimlich*. *Unheimlich* is in some way or other a sub-species of *heimlich*" (p. 131) (to be continued).

33. "The mixed tropes called *Syllepses* consist of taking one and the same word in two different senses, one of which is, or is supposed to be, the original, or at least the *literal*, meaning; the other, the *figurative*, or supposedly figurative, even if it is not so in reality. This can be done by *metonymy*, *synecdoche*, or *metaphor*" (P. Fontanier, *Les Figures du discours*, introduction by G. Genette, Flammarion, p. 105.) [This figure is more commonly called a *zeugma* in English.—Trans.]

incest, suicide, simulacrum) is inscribed at the very tip of this indecision. This tip advances according to the irreducible excess of the syntactic over the semantic. The word "between" has no full meaning of its own. *Inter* acting forms a syntactical plug; not a categorem, but a syncategorem: what philosophers from the Middle Ages to Husserl's *Logical Investigations* have called an incomplete signification. What holds for "hymen" also holds, *mutatis mutandis*, for all other signs which, like *pharmakon, supplément, différance*, and others, have a double, contradictory, undecidable value that always derives from their syntax, whether the latter is in a sense "internal," articulating and combining under the same yoke, *huph' hen*, two incompatible meanings, or "external," dependent on the code in which the word is made to function. But the syntactical composition and decomposition of a sign renders this alternative between internal and external inoperative. One is simply dealing with greater or lesser syntactical units at work, and with economic differences in condensation. Without reducing all these to the same, quite the contrary, it is possible to recognize a certain serial law in these points of indefinite pivoting: they mark the spots of what can never be mediated, mastered, sublated, or dialecticized through any *Erinnerung* or *Aufhebung*. Is it by chance that all these play effects, these "words" that escape philosophical mastery, should have, in widely differing historical contexts, a very singular relation to writing? These "words" admit into their games both contradiction and noncontradiction (and the contradiction and noncontradiction *between* contradiction and noncontradiction). Without any dialectical *Aufhebung*, without any time off, they belong in a sense both to consciousness and to the unconscious, which Freud tells us can tolerate or remain insensitive to contradiction. Insofar as the text depends upon them, *bends* to them [*s'y plie*], it thus plays a *double scene* upon a double stage. It operates in two absolutely different places at once, even if these are only separated by a veil, which is both traversed and not traversed, *inter*sected [*entr'ouvert*]. Because of this indecision and instability, Plato would have conferred upon the double science arising from these two theaters the name *doxa* rather than *epistēmē*. *Pierrot Murderer of His Wife* would have reminded him of the riddle of the bat struck by the eunuch.[34]

34. "And again, do the many double things appear any the less halves than doubles?— None the less.—And likewise of the great and the small things, the light and the heavy things—will they admit these predicates any more than their opposites?—No, he said, each of them will always hold of, partake of, both.—Then each *is* each of these multiples rather than it *is not* that which one affirms it to be?—They are like those jesters who palter with us in a double sense at banquets, he replied, and resemble the children's riddle about the eunuch and his hitting of the bat—with what they signify that he struck it.* For these things too equivocate, and it is impossible to conceive firmly any one of them to be or not to

Everything is played out, everything and all the rest—that is to say, the game—is played out in the *entre*, about which the author of the *Essai sur la connaissance approchée*, who also knew all about caves,[35] says that it is "a mathematical concept" (p. 32). When this undecidability is marked and re-marked in *writing*, it has a greater power of formalization, even if it is "literary" in appearance, or appears to be attributable to a natural language, than when it occurs as a proposition in logicomathematical form, which would not go as far as the former type of mark. If one supposes that the distinction, still a metaphysical one, between natural language and artificial language be rigorous (and we no doubt here reach the limit of its pertinence), one can say that there are texts in so-called natural languages whose power of formalization would be superior to that attributed to certain apparently formal notations.

One no longer even has the authority to say that "between" is a purely syntactic function. Through the re-marking of its semantic void, it in fact begins to signify.[36] Its semantic void *signifies*, but it signifies spacing and articulation; it has as its meaning the possibility of syntax; it orders the play of meaning. *Neither purely syntactic nor purely semantic*, it marks the articulated opening of that opposition.

The whole of this dehiscence, finally, is repeated and partially opened up in a certain *"lit"* ["bed," "reads"], which *Mimique* has painstakingly set up. Toward the end of the text, the syntagm *"le lit"* reproduces the stratagem of the hymen.

---

be or both or neither. . . . But we agreed in advance that if anything of that sort should be discovered, it must be denominated opinable, not knowable, the wanderer between being caught by the faculty that is betwixt and between" (the *Republic* V, 479 *b, c, d*, trans. Paul Shorey, p. 719). [*Francis M. Cornford, in his edition of the *Republic* (New York: Oxford University Press, 1945), glosses the riddle as follows (p. 188): "A man who was not a man (eunuch), seeing and not seeing (seeing imperfectly) a bird that was not a bird (bat) perched on a bough that was not a bough (a reed), pelted and did not pelt it (aimed at it and missed) with a stone that was not a stone (pumice-stone)."—Trans.]

35. The chapter of *La Terre et les rêveries du repos* [*Earth and Dreams of Rest*] which deals with *caves* does not, however, mention Mallarmé's in its rich survey of various "caves in literature." If this fact is not simply insignificant, the reason for it may perhaps appear later in the course of our discussion of Mallarmé's "imaginary."

36. From that point on, the syncategorem "between" contains as its meaning a semantic quasi-emptiness; it signifies the spacing relation, the articulation, the interval, etc. It can be nominalized, turn into a quasi-categorem, receive a definite article, or even be made plural. We have spoken of "betweens," and this plural is in some sense primary. *One* "between" does not exist. In Hebrew, *entre* can be made plural: "In truth this plural expresses not the relation between one individual thing and another, but rather the intervals between things (*loca aliis intermedia*)—in this connection see chapter 10, verse 2, of Ezechiel—or else, as I said before, this plural represents preposition or relation abstractly conceived." (Spinoza, *Abrégé de grammaire hébraique* [Vrin, 1968], p. 108.)

Before we come to that, I would like to recall the fact that in this *Mimique*, which is cannily interposed between two silences that are breached or broached thereby (*"Silence, sole luxury after rimes . . . there reigns a silence still, the condition and delight of reading."*), as a "gambol" or "debate" of "language" (figure II), it has never been a question of anything other than reading and writing. This text could be read as a sort of handbook of literature. Not only because the metaphor of writing comes up so often (*"a phantom . . . white as a yet unwritten page"*)—which is also the case in the *Philebus*—but because the necessity of that metaphor, which *nothing* escapes, makes it something other than a particular figure among others. What is produced is an absolute extension of the concepts of writing and reading, of text, of hymen, to the point where nothing of what *is* can lie beyond them. *Mimique* describes a scene of writing within a scene of writing and so on without end, through a structural necessity that is marked in the text. The mime, as "corporeal writing" (*Ballets*), mimes a kind of writing (hymen) and is himself written in a kind of writing. Everything is reflected in the medium or speculum of reading-writing, *"without breaking the mirror."* There is writing without a book, in which, each time, at every moment, the marking tip proceeds without a past upon the virgin sheet; but there is also, *simultaneously*, an infinite number of booklets enclosing and fitting inside other booklets, which are only able to issue forth by grafting, sampling, quotations, epigraphs, references, etc. Literature voids itself in its limitlessness. If this handbook of literature meant to *say* something, which we now have some reason to doubt, it would proclaim first of all that there is no—or hardly any, ever so little—literature; that in any event there is no essence of literature, no truth of literature, no literary-being or being-literary of literature. And that the fascination exerted by the "is," or the "what is" in the question "what is literature" is worth what the hymen is worth—that is, not exactly nothing—when for example it causes one to die laughing. All this, of course, should not prevent us—on the contrary— from attempting to find out what has been represented and determined under that name—"literature"—and why.

Mallarmé *reads*. He writes while reading; while reading the text written by the Mime, who himself reads in order to write. He reads for example the *Pierrot posthume* so as to write with his gestures a mimic that owes that book nothing, since he reads the mimic he thus creates in order to write after the fact the booklet that Mallarmé is reading.

But does the Mime read his role in order to write his mimic or his booklet? Is the initiative of reading his? Is he the acting subject who knows how to read what he has to write? One could indeed believe that although he is passive in reading, he at least has the active freedom to choose to begin to read, and that the same is true of Mallarmé; or even that you, dear everyreader, retain the initiative of reading all these texts, including Mallarmé's, and hence, to that extent, in that place, you are indeed attending it, deciding on it, mastering it.

Nothing could be less certain. The syntax of *Mimique* imprints a movement of (non-Platonic) simulacrum in which the function of *"le lit"* ["the bed," "reads it," "reads him"] complicates itself to the point of admitting a multitude of subjects among whom you yourself are not necessarily included. Plato's clinical paradigm is no longer operative.

The question of the text is—(for whom are) / (for whoever reads) these sheets. [*La question du texte est—pour qui le lit*; literally, can mean both: "The question of the text is for the one who reads it (or him)" and: "The question of the text is: whom is the bed for?"—Trans.]

Among diverse possibilities, let us take this: the Mime does not read his role; he is also ready *by* it. Or at least he is both read and reading, written and writing, between the two, in the suspense of the hymen, at once screen and mirror. As soon as a mirror is interposed in some way, the simple opposition between activity and passivity, between production and the product, or between all concepts in -er and all concepts in -ed (signifier/ signified, imitator/imitated, structure/structured, etc.), becomes impracticable and too formally weak to encompass the graphics of the hymen, its spider web, and the play of its eyelids.

This impossibility of identifying the path *proper* to the letter of a text, of assigning a unique place to the subject, of locating a simple origin, is here consigned, plotted by the machinations of the one who calls himself "profoundly and scrupulously a syntaxer." In the sentence that follows, the syntax—and the carefully calculated punctuation—prevent us from ever deciding whether the subject of "reads" is the role (*"less than a thousand lines, the role, the one that reads . . ."*) or some anonymous reader (*"the role, the one that reads, will instantly comprehend the rules as if placed before the stageboards . . ."*) Who is "the one?" *"The one"* [*"qui"*] may of course be the indefinite pronoun meaning "whoever," here in its function as a subject. This is the easiest reading; the role—whoever reads it will instantly understand its rules. Empirical statistics would show that the so-called "linguistic sense" would most often give this reading.

But nothing in the grammatical code would render the sentence incorrect if, without changing a thing, one were to read "the one" (subject of "reads") as a pronoun whose antecedent was *"role."* Out of this reading would spring a series of syntactic and semantic transformations in the function of the words "role," *"le* [it or him]," "placed," and in the meaning of the word "comprehend." Thus: *"Less than a thousand lines, the role* (subject, not object), *the one* (referring back to "role") *that reads* [the one that reads "*him*," not "*it*"] (referring to the Mime, the subject of the preceding sentence), *will instantly comprehend* (embrace, contain, rule, organize: read) *the rules as if placed before the stageboards* (the role is placed facing the stage, either as the author-composer, or as the spectator-reader, in the position of the "whoever" in the first hypothesis), *their humble depository.*"

This reading is possible. It is "normal" both from the syntactic and from the semantic point of view. But what a laborious artifice! Do you really believe, goes the objection, that Mallarmé consciously parceled out his sentence so that it could be read two different ways, with each object capable of changing into a subject and vice versa, without our being able to arrest this movement? Without our being able, faced with this "*alternative sail*," to decide whether the text is "*listing to one side or the other*" (*A Throw of Dice*). The two poles of the reading are not equally obvious: but the syntax at any rate has produced an effect of indefinite fluctuation between two possibilities.

Whatever might have been going on in Mallarmé's head, in his consciousness or in his unconscious, does not matter to us here; the reader should now know why. That, in any event, does not hold the least interest for a reading of the text. Everything in the text is interwoven, as we have seen, so as to do without references, so as to cut them short. Nevertheless, for those who are interested in Stéphane Mallarmé and would like to know what he was thinking and meant to do by writing in this way, we shall merely ask the following question. But we are asking it on the basis of texts, and published texts at that: how is one to explain the fact that the syntactic alternative frees itself only in the third version of the text? How is one to explain the fact that, some words being moved, others left out, a tense transformed, a comma added, then and only then does the one-way reading, the only reading possible in the first two versions, come to shift, to waver, henceforth without rest? and without identifiable reference? Why is it that, when one has written, without any possible ambiguity, this: "This marvelous bit of nothing, less than a thousand lines, whoever will read it as I have just done, will comprehend the eternal rules, just as though facing the stageboards, their humble depository" (1886),

and then this: "This role, less than a thousand lines, whoever reads it will comprehend the rules as if placed before the stageboards, their humble depository" (1891),

one should finally write this, with all possible ambiguity: "*Less than a thousand lines, the role, the one that reads, will instantly comprehend the rules as if placed before the stageboards, their humble depository*" (1897)?

Perhaps he didn't know what he was doing? Perhaps he wasn't conscious of it? Perhaps, then, he wasn't completely the author of what was being written? The burst of laughter that echoes deep inside the antre, in *Mimique*, is a reply to all these questions. They can only have been formulated through recourse to certain oppositions, by presupposing possibilities of decision whose pertinence was rigorously swept away by the very text they were supposed to question. Swept away by that hymen, the text always calculates and suspends (figure I) some supplementary *"surprise"* and *"delight."* *"Surprise, accompanying the artifice of a notation of sentiments by unproffered sentences—that, in the sole case, perhaps, with authenticity, between the sheets and the eye there reigns a silence still, the condition and delight of reading."* Supplement, principle, and bounty. The baffling economy of seduction.

enter . . . between . . . a silence

> *"Each session or play being a game, a fragmentary show, but sufficient at that unto itself..."*
> [Le *"Livre,"* 93 (A)]

II

Like *Mimique*, the double session has no middle. It is divided into two halves[37] only through the fiction of a crease. Yet each session by itself is no more whole or symmetrical for all that, being but the rejoinder or application of the other, its play or its exercise. Together they are neither more nor less than two hemitropic crystals; never, in sum, a finished volume. Never making a complete turn, for lack of presentation.

Mallarmé indeed brought the Book he was turning out back to the "necessity of folding":

37. Between the two sessions the following letter from Philippe Sollers is—necessarily—inscribed:

"le 12 (minuit).

MIMIQUE, ou plutôt mi + mi + que, c'est-à-dire deux fois les moitiés plus l'indication ou l'intimation subjonctive de la subordination mimée; mi-mais? mais-qui? mimi à que (ue)? queue de mémé?

Le *si* lance et défie le texte en excès comme ce qui succède—dans l'après mi-dit—à la répétition du rire en écho mimé (rimé) l'arrivée d'*or* étant tout d'abord musique (or-chestre) et cela fait (si + or) = *soir* au milieu des rôles et du lustre qui ment—synode meurtrier, silence tué—

(*synodique*: temps qui s'écoule entre deux nouvelles lunes consécutives)—pas tant qu'il ne soient freinés—

LIT/DES (il y en a *des* qui sont dans le *lit*) (scène primitive) (coup de dés)— queue déliant l'idée—

la scène ne rend pas illustre, sous le lustre, que lit le dés (ir)—

le vice est plus près des cieux que le rêve, sacré—

ça crée en cédant au rêve—en s'aidant au rêve—

pas de cadeau non plus (présent) apparent—le fantasme blanc—procédant,
procréant—
plissement du con, pétration du père
(ô père)
per/pro
foutre futur passé glacé opéra—
mimère—

L'I mène—

Le MIME (neutre) est un demi-moi opéré, infini borné dans son unique stalle pur de toute

227

read from the bottom

— —   — — ⌐ and have the book
                     │ present itself
    and   │ thus
.V   V.   .V   V. └
        necessity of folding   [77(B)]

    ⌐ end   ⌐ return

of the same—but almost other   [78(B)]
    serial—
folds on each side

                                    and because of that
                                        the addition of a
tucked in, at the cleft   sheet the other way around
                                        against
                                                    death
                                                    rebirth?
                                        for +

⌐ one never rediscovers
a fold in the opposite
sense   —there is another sheet
                     to (cor)respond to the possibility
└   of that other sense.

the fold that on one   ⌐ series of folds
side alone—   gilt edge—
stops the glance—   a cardboard box
and masks   in (as in the old days
                                            on the binding)
                                            [44(A)]

────────
fiction, un demi-lieu et un demi-dieu—
retour des règles—
mime/milieu = moins/millier
(qu'y le lit/qui le l'y) (lie)
très tôt en dépot : s'y taire
lignes : phrases-points, que/con, sur-prise liée—
au temps cité, luxe du silence ferré : *un si lance en qu'or*—
condiction d'hélice au regard feuilleté : dés lisses—"
[For a translation of this letter, see "Translator's Introduction"—Trans.]

The necessity of folding the page of the hymen does not involve, after the fact, a secondary procedure. You will not have been required to flex back upon itself a surface that was at first smooth and flat. The hymen, "at the cleft," does not come to adopt, here or there, some fold, indifferent as to whether you are imposing it or refusing it. In the morgue of all Pierrots, you have been able to read that the folding was being marked *in* the hymen, in the angle or cleft, in the *entre* by which, dividing itself, it related back to itself. Yet neither (is it) a fold in the veil or in the pure text but rather in the lining which the hymen, of itself, was. But by the same token *is* not: the fold in a lining by which it is, out of itself, in itself, at once its own outside and its own inside; between the outside and the inside, making the outside enter the inside and turning back the antre or the other upon its surface, the hymen is never pure or proper, has no life of its own, no proper name. Opened up by its anagram, it always seems torn, already, in the fold through which it affects itself and murders itself.

Along the undiscoverable line of this fold, the hymen never presents itself. It never *is*—in the present—; it has no proper, literal meaning; it no longer originates in meaning as such, that is, as the meaning of being. The fold renders (itself) manifold but (is) not (one).

In the title spot of this session, if you suspend the *fold*, you will find a use for some such epigraph as this:

"To detach myself from the idea of being — would that make me one or would I still be outside? I think it would be to stay outside inside, by being there, and to be there is to remain not above Evil but rather *inside*, and to be Evil itself, the kind of evil it takes God to satiate, the hymen of the Morgue, which is the fact that the fold has never been a fold..."[38]

As in *The Murders in the Rue Morgue*, which begins with a theory of games and an encomium of the "analyst" who "is fond of enigmas, of conundrums, hieroglyphics"—all of this merits rereading—it is a matter of operating along the fold, by displacing the final quotation in the story: "*de nier ce qui est, et d'expliquer ce qui n'est pas* [in French in Poe's text; it means "denying what is, and explaining what is not"—Trans.]" Edgar Allan Poe: Mallarmé called him "the absolute literary case." His is also the only proper name, it seems, to appear in the notes toward the "Book." Is this without significance? On a sheet[39] on which every word is crossed out, we find:

38. Antonin Artaud (June 1945).
39. It is the first sheet.

```
finish
conscience
     And pains        +
                      +
                    rue
      +
childhood
double
     their
crowd +
     +                              a — crime — sewer
```

And on the following page:

> I revere Poe's opinion, no vestige of any philosophy,
> ethics or metaphysics, will pierce through;
> I would add that it is necessary, enclosed and latent.

Further on, on the same page:

> The intellectural armature of the
> poem, conceals itself and—takes place—holds in the space that
>   isolates the stanzas and
> among the blankness of the white paper; a significant silence that it
> is no less lovely to compose than
> verse.

To deny what is, to explain what is not, cannot here be reduced to some dialectical operation; at most, it constitutes *mimed* dialectics. The intermission or interim of the hymen does not establish time: neither time as the existence of the concept (Hegel), nor lost time nor time regained, and still less the moment or eternity. No present in truth presents itself there, not even in the form of its self-concealment. What the hymen undoes, outwits, under the rubric of the present (whether temporal or eternal), is the assurance of mastery. The critical desire—which is also the philosophical desire—can only, as such, attempt to regain that lost mastery. That desire tends to read the hymen alternately according to this or that species of presence: the work of writing *against* time or the work of writing *effected by* time.

Working against Time. According to Jacques Scherer, the *"false appearance of a present"* amounts to the granting of a greater degree of presence or reality to a future present or a past present, or even to an eternal present:

> Another essential element of dramaturgy that Mallarmé rejects is time. He praises a pantomime in the following unexpected terms: "The scene illustrates but the idea, not any actual action . . . here anticipating, there recalling, in the future, in the past, *under the false appearance of a present.*" His elimination of action necessarily entails an elimination of time, and, denying the temporal reality of theater, which he calls a false appearance, he is led to grant a less illusory reality, paradoxically enough, to the future and the past. Elsewhere in his work it is Villiers de l'Isle-Adam who appears as the hero of atemporal theater. Mallarmé describes in the following terms the effect produced by the prestigious narrator called Villiers: "Midnights thrown off with indifference by a man standing next to himself at his own wake; time became null, those nights." Villier's talent thus enables him to cancel out not only his own existence, but time itself: theater takes us out of the temporal flow by introducing us into time regained, or eternity.[40]

Work Effected by Time. If the interim of the hymen differs (defers) from the present, or from a present that is past, future, or eternal, then its sheet has neither inside nor outside, belongs neither to reality nor to the imaginary, neither to the original nor to its representation. The syntax of its fold makes it impossible for us to arrest its play or its indecision, to fix it on any one of its terms, to stop, for example, as Richard has done, on the mental or the imaginary. Such a stopping of the works would subsume *"Mimique"* within a philosophical or critical (Platonico-Hegelian) interpretation of *mimēsis.* It would be incapable of accounting for that excess of syntax over meaning (doubled by the excess of the *"entre"* over the opposition syntactic/ semantic); that is, for the re-marking of textuality. Interestingly, it is now to the workings of *time* itself, and not to atemporality, that Richard attributes the process of unrealization designed to return writing to its proper element: the mental or the imaginary. Those are his words:

---

40. *Le "Livre" de Mallarmé*, p. 41. In citing Jacques Scherer or, in a moment, Jean-Pierre Richard, I want to stress what should in fact be obvious: that what I am doing is marking the most rigorous need for the "critical" operation and not launching some polemic, or even less seeking to discredit, however slightly, some admirable pieces of work. Every reader of Mallarmé today knows what he owes such work.

If we seek a still more perfect phantom, we encounter the *mime*: "a phantom white as a yet unwritten page," a smooth stonelike figure whose only expression is silence. Far from interposing itself between the real and the mental, his body, which is entirely negative, will serve as a free field for the play of imaginary transcription. There are no longer any signs imposed here: this face is indeed only half there; it remains neutral, malleable, hypothetical. It is not transparent—that would eliminate the possibility of reading—but it is not opaque, either, since that would arrest the flight of the fiction; it succeeds in being perfectly *here* and *elsewhere*, *now* and *then*: "hymen (out of which flows Dream), tainted with vice yet sacred, between desire and fulfillment, perpetration and remembrance: here anticipating, there recalling, in the future, in the past, under the false appearance of a present." What the theater indeed aims to abolish in each of its creations is actuality as well as materiality. The work of unrealization and vaporization is henceforth entrusted to time itself: like the woman in the *Phénomène futur* and so many other Mallarméan creations, the mime oscillates within a double call to the imagination, a call both from the future and from the past.[41]

The demonstration of this point is developed and explained further: the work of the temporal fiction, the *"dreamed-of crossing of an interval,"* the "lie," have as their aim the *"playing"* of some *"imaginary* being," the "rediscovery of the transcendence of the great yonder," in order that "we may aesthetically rejoin *our own* transcendental truth . . ."

And the mirror, too, reverses its dreamlike function: while once it bespoke the painful inaccessibility of being, now it serves to *play* a being that is inaccessible but nonetheless real, an *imaginary* being. Out of the *here* and *now*, objectified in flesh that is both opaque and contingent, theater and pantomime claim to rediscover the transcendence of the great yonder . . . . The theatrical world's existence is solely mental: under that heading one can only gain access to it by detaching oneself from the everyday world, through the dreamed-of crossing of an interval. In the form of a theatrical body, a mime's white face, or vaporous coatings of music, this interval naturally finds its model in the Mallarméan epitome of all intervals, the *windowpane*. Everything is thus turned upside down, yet everything remains the same. Transparency once signified "the azure," but barred access to it. It is now

41. Richard, pp. 406–7.

what supports, or better, gives life to, introduces among things, a new dream of Beauty. But this beauty is also nothing other, as we know, than a glorious lie, a pure creation of the mind. It is this lie that art attempts to render true, and for that it must, theatrically or artistically, put it *under glass*. The mirror henceforth constitutes the sensible field of illusion; it calls us toward it, makes us glide toward a mirage. No longer an obstacle, transparency has now become an instrument: the god it points to is within ourselves, not outside us in some celestial yonder, but imaginarily this makes little difference. If theater vitrifies its characters, if art puts the world under glass, if literature works toward the bleaching and airing of the object by means of language, it is nonetheless still in order that, through all this, we may aesthetically rejoin *our own* transcendental truth; in order that, in short, we may inject into all this the necessary dimension of the beyond. (Pp. 407–8; Richard's italics)

This "under glass" structure cannot be described, only interpreted. That, at least, is the interpretation with which we will henceforth be concerned, no doubt distractedly, from digression to digression, but without letup.

Who would think of denying the evidence of this "work of unrealization and vaporization," this idealization of "actuality" and "materiality" in Mallarmé's text? With the proviso, that is, that one read it under glass. And that one take into account the *process* of vitrification and not discount the "production" of the glass. This "production" does not consist—any more than does the hymen—simply in unveiling, revealing, presenting; nor in concealing or causing to disappear all at once; nor in creating, inventing, or inaugurating. If the structure of this glass has anything in common with that of the hymen, then its role is to dislocate *all* these oppositions. The glass must be read as a text, or, as it would have been called not long ago, as an undecidable "signifier." It will soon be proven that the effect of the signifier *verre* (glass) is almost indistinguishable from that of the signifier *vers* (verse).

Who would think of denying the evidence that for Mallarmé the world of theater is a mental world? With the proviso, of course, that one read it under glass. Mallarmé does indeed speak of "the mental medium identifying stage and house" (p. 298). And isn't the book the internalization of theater, the inner stage? In any such "ideal performance," "a theater, inherent in the mind, whoever has looked at nature with a steady eye carries it within him, a compendium of types and concordances; just as these are confronted by the volume that opens its parallel pages" (p. 328). These propositions—and the long series of their equivalents[42] —*mime* the internalization of the theater in the book and of the book in the "mental medium." The mimed operation does not, however, sum up the outside inside the inside; it does not plant the theater inside the enclosure of a mental hideaway nor reduce space itself to the imaginary. On the contrary, in *inserting* a sort of spacing into interiority, it no longer allows the inside to close upon itself or be identified with itself. The book is a "block" but it is a block composed of sheets of paper. Its "cubic perfection" is *open*.[43] This impossibility of closure, this dehiscence of the Mallarméan book as an "internal" theater, constitutes not a reduction but a *practice* of spacing. Staked on the structure of the fold and of supplementarity, this practice puts itself into play.

And hence it has to be set back on the track of its own movement: it has, literally, to be *quoted*. To write the word *insertion*—a word that here operates with all its energy according to all its possibilities ("To place within. To insert a graft just under the bark. . . . By extension, to introduce into a text or register." Littré)—so as to mark the breaking through of theater into the book, of spacing into interiority, while a certain mimic inscribes a graft in one corner, holding the antre open, "at the cleft," in the intimate recesses of a volume coiled around itself and henceforth disemboweled by "the introduction of a weapon or paper-cutter" just as it is parted from itself; to write the word *insertion* is, literally, to quote: "Another, the art of Mr. Maeterlinck who also inserted theater into the book!" (p. 329). To write the *open antre [antre ouvert]* of the stage by the book is, literally, to quote: ". . . now the book will attempt to suffice, to open into [*entr'ouvrir*] the interior scene and whisper its echos" (p. 328). To write that such a movement plays along a structure of supplementarity, surplus, and vicariousness is, literally, to quote: "With two pages and the verses they contain, I, and the accompaniment of all myself, make up for the world [*supplée au monde*]! or I perceive, discreet, its drama" (ibid.). Here, supplementarity is not, as it apparently or consciously is in Rousseau, a unilateral movement which, falling from inside to out, loses in space both the life and the warmth of the spoken

---

42. One could cite the whole of *Crayonné au théâtre*. This, for example: "A work of the genre of the one our Théodore de Banville has offered in all his vigor and wisdom is literary in essence, but does not entirely espouse all the folds involved in the play of that mental instrument par excellence, the book!" (p. 335). Or this: ". . . delightful ambiguity between the written and the acted, neither quite one nor quite the other, which pours forth, the volume being almost set aside, the impression that one is not altogether in front of the stage" (pp. 342–44).

43. Jean-Pierre Richard, pp. 565 ff.

word; it is the excess of a signifier which, in its own inside, makes up (for) space and repeats the fact of opening. The book, then, no longer repairs, but rather repeats, the process of spacing, along with what plays, loses, and wins itself in it. This, too, is literally to quote: "A book, held in our hand, if it enunciates some august idea, makes up for all theaters, not by casting them all into oblivion, but by imperiously calling them to mind, on the contrary" (p. 334). Far from replacing the stage or substituting a perfectly mastered interiority for the slipping away of space, this *suppléance* [addition/representation] implacably retains and repeats the theatrical stage within the book. Such is the relation of *Planches et feuillets* [*Stageboards and Sheets of Paper*: title of Mallarmé's essay from which most of the preceding quotations are taken.—Trans.][44]

One would clearly find no lack of references and documents to support the claim that the theatrical world is a mental world, or even an imaginary representation. With the proviso that, in *quoting* this proposition, one set it in motion, that one space it out in order to deploy what is implicit in it, displacing it and turning it around so as to let its pivot show: the mental world is already a stage; the inside of the *mens*, like the intimacy of the book that is folded back on itself, has the structure of a spacing. The spaciousness of writing, provided one takes into account the hymen of the act of miming, prohibits the ranking of the Mallarméan *fiction* in the category of the imaginary. For that category is in fact constructed out of the *ontological* interpretation of *mimēsis*. This is what we found in the course of the other session. But for that same reason, one cannot simply replace the values of the imaginary or the mental with those of actuality, reality, or even materiality, at least not if one does so by symmetrical inversion or by a simple reversal of the asymmetry.

44. It can only be a graphics of supplementarity, as we have attempted to show elsewhere, that can account for the relations between the concepts of Literature and Nature, between the "beyond" or the "nothing" and that to which it is added, the sum total of what is, or Nature. "Yes, Literature exists and, if you will, alone, excepting everything. . . . We know, captives of an absolute formula that, of course, there is nothing but what is. However, incontinent(ly) to put aside, under a pretext, the lure, would point up our inconsequence, denying the pleasure that we wish to take: for that *beyond* is its agent, and its motor might I say were I not loath to operate, in public, the impious dismantling of (the) fiction and consequently of the literary mechanism, so as to display the principal part or nothing. . . .

What is that for—

For play. . . .

For my part, I ask nothing less of writing and am going to prove this postulate.

Nature takes place; it can't be added to . . ." (*La Musique et les Lettres*, pp. 646–47). For a reading of this text as well as an interpretation of the entirety of Mallarmé's writing, see Philippe Sollers, "Littérature et totalité" (in *Logiques*) and Julia Kristeva, "Poésie et négativité" (in Σημεωτιχή).

This chain ("fiction," "hymen," "spacious," etc.), itself both spacious and mobile, *gets caught in*, but thereby disorganizes, the whole ontological machine. It dislocates all oppositions. It carries them off, impresses upon them a certain play that propagates itself through all the text's moving parts, constantly shifting them, setting them out of phase, more or less regularly, through unequal displacements, abrupt slowdowns or bursts of speed, strategic effects of insistence or ellipsis, but always inexorably. It is in this way that the "Book," the "Mind," the "Idea"—the most spectacular examples of this grand scene—begin to function like signifiers unhooked, dislodged, disengaged from their historic polarization. "The book, the total expansion of the letter, must draw from it, directly, a kind of mobility and, spacious, through correspondences, institute a play, one doesn't know, which confirms the fiction.

"Nothing fortuitous there, where chance seems to capture the idea, the machinery is the equal: not to judge, in consequence, these words—industrial or having to do with materiality: the manufacture of the book, as a whole about to issue forth, begins, as of one sentence. From time immemorial, the poet, concerned with the place for this line, in the sonnet that inscribes itself for the mind or upon pure space" (p. 380).

The letter, and what this spaciousness draws from it, through folding, flexing back, deploying, expanding, must now be considered, contemplated, and have its design retraced. We must determine the structure of Mallarmé's spacing, calculate its effects, and deduce its *critical* consequences. The pivoting of the proposition ("the mental world is already a theatrical scene") does not exempt us from—on the contrary requires of us—the posing of this question: "when," "how," "why," is that scene played *outside*, outside the mind, in the form of "theater" or "literature"? In order to set this question into its entire stratified network (following the classical distributions under "history," "economics," "psychoanalysis," "politics," etc.), it is necessary first to make clear the specific law governing this "theatrical" or "literary" effect. It is this (pre)liminary question that retains us here. But this question has also, explicitly, presented itself as the question *of the liminary*. And since this question, at least in the scene in which it is being treated here, engages and interrogates along the couplings of its concepts the very syntax of its pairs of opposing terms, the ground of its presuppositions, the entirety of the discourse in which one could articulate the question of the "entire-field" (as a question, and hence as a discourse, if one were to assume that it has any *real margins*), one can already sense that a crisis is on the march as of the very first step. One must deduce its *critical* consequences: those that would affect Mallarméan criticism, and eventually criticism in general, which is linked, as its name indicates, to the possibility of decidability, to the κρίνειν; but also the critical effects that a certain re-mark or re-tempering of spacing produces upon literary operations, upon "literature," which thereby goes into crisis.

That the blanks of this spacing and the crisis of literature are not foreign to the writing of a certain hymen (the feint of a veil in its fictive tear or fold) is set out by *Crise de vers* [*Crisis of verse*] for us to read and to traverse. That text, which exhibits a modernity that could be judged untimely, puts the dots on the *i*'s. With its little suspended dot, the *i* continually pricks and rips through—or almost—the veil, reaches a decision—or almost—about the text, as do so many Mallarméan *i*'s. Witness:

"Our phase, of recent times, is, if not closing, reaching a stop or perhaps an awareness: some attention sifts out the creative and relatively certain will.

"Even the press, whose information is usually twenty years old, is suddenly, on the correct date, busying itself with the subject.

"Literature is here undergoing an exquisite crisis, down to its very foundation.

"He who grants a place, or the primary place, to this function can recognize therein the current event: we are witnessing, as the century nears its finale, not as it was in the previous one, an upheaval; but, far from the public square, a certain disquiet stirs the veil in the temple with significant crinklings [*plis*] and, a little bit, its rending" (p. 360).

With its critical, pointed, sharpened dot, the *i* here signs the exquisite crisis "literature" is going through with significant crinkles and folds which—the hymen again—tear it "a little bit" without tearing it, fastening down the tissue. Beneath the fictive letting go of its highest point, suspended in the air (*r* [pronounced "air"—Trans.] is another seminal letter in *Crise de vers*), as if cut off from itself, the *i* draws its slash, applies its quill or its wing, its penna; it needles and scratches, assigns a place for criticism in the folds of writing, in "literary" writing or in the writing—so often called hieroglyphic—of dance, ballet, and theater.

Let us pretend to take leave of *Crise de vers* in order to read two other texts, to do no more than read them, for lack of the infinite amount of time one would need (but we will try to formalize this demand for infinite process), doing no more than recognizing the *i* as their "subject."

They are from *Crayonné au théâtre* [*Penciled at the Theater*], one page apart: (we will call them *Rejoinder I* and *Rejoinder II*).

Rejoinder I. "Criticism, in its integrity, is only, can only have value or stand almost equal to Poetry to which it contributes a noble complementary operation, if it aims, directly and superbly, also toward phenomena or the universe: but, in spite of that, despite its status as a primordial instinct placed in the secret folds of our deepest inner recesses (a divine malaise), it gives in to the attractions of a theater that shows a mere representation, for those who are not meant to see things in themselves! of the play inscribed in the folio of the sky and mimed, with the gesture of his passions, by Man" (p. 294).

What will always defy and baffle criticism is this effect of being a supplementary double. There is always one extra rejoinder, one recess or representation too many, which also means one too few. The "recess": the Mallarméan fold will always have been not only a replication of the tissue but also a repetition-toward-itself of the text that is a re-folding, a re-plying, a supplementary re-marking of the fold. "Re-presentation": theater does not show "things in themselves," nor does it represent them; it shows a representation, shows itself to be a fiction; it is less engaged in setting forth things or the image of things than it is in setting up a machine.

Rejoinder II. The reader is now invited to count the dots, to follow the fine needlepoint pattern of *i*'s and *ique*'s [-*ic* or -*ical*] which are being sprinkled rapidly across the tissue being pushed by another hand. Perhaps he will be able to discern, according to the rapid, regular movement of the machine, the stitches of Mallarmé's idea, a certain instance of *i*'s and a certain scattering of dice [*d*'s]:[45]

"Ballet gives but little: it is an imaginative genre. When some sign of scattered general beauty—some flower, wave, cloud, jewel, etc.—is isolated for the eye, if, for us, the exclusive means of being sure of it consists in juxtaposing its appearance with our own spiritual nudity so that we can feel whether it fits and whether we can adapt it in some exquisite confusion of our nudity with that analogous form in flight—if only through the rite, there, the affirmation of the Idea, doesn't it seem as if the ballerina appears, part the element in question, part humanity eager to be one with it, in the floating of a reverie?"

A "floating," among the texts: the aerial suspension of the veil, the gauze, or even of gas (this is being written in the margins of the *Adaptation of Dutch Jewish Lamps to Gas*)[46] evolves according to the hymen. Each time it

45. TN. The word *idée* [idea] is composed of the two syllables in question here: *i* and *dé* [dé = the letter "d" and the word "dice"].

46. That page, in which it is possible to detect a watermark of all, or almost all, the other texts, is from *La Dernière Mode* (p. 736). The semantic condensation, like the index of a glossary, which goes along with the semblance of a description, collects itself of its own accord, incomparable in that it keeps adding to itself one application after another; that is, it produces its own fold, the fold of a writing or whatever one henceforth wants to call it.

appears, the word *floating* suggests what Mallarmé calls suggestion: barely revealing at all, on the point of disappearing, the indecision of that which remains suspended, neither this nor that, between here and there, and *hence* between this text and another, along with their ether, a "gas . . . both invisible and present" (p. 736). Between this and that hovers a penna, "the ballerina, part the element in question, part humanity eager to be one with it . . ." Between the two, there is both confusion *and* distinction ("exquisite confusion"), hymen, the dance of the penna, the flight of the Idea, *confusion exquise d'elle (d'aile)* [exquisite confusion of it (of the wing)] "with that analogous form in flight—if only through the rite, there, the affirmation of the Idea, doesn't it seem as if the ballerina appears, part the element in question, part humanity eager to be one with it, in the floating of a reverie." This floating, within the text, recalls "many an undecided floating of an idea deserting accidents . . ." (p. 289). The hesitations of the "veil" [*voile*], the "flight" [*vol*], the "leap" [*voltige*], as they condense down toward the point of an idea or of a dancer's toe (one should here reread the opening lines of *Crayonné au théâtre*), are always, *in addition*, descriptions/inscriptions of the structure and movement of the literary textile, a "hesitation" turning into writing. In folding it back upon itself, the text thus *parts* (with) reference, spreads it like a V, a gap that pivots on its point, a dancer, flower, or Idea. "One of them divulges his intuition, theoretically and, it may well be, vacuously, as of this date: he knows that such suggestions, touching on the literary art, ought to proclaim themselves firmly. The hesitation, however, to uncover everything abruptly of what does not yet exist, weaves, for modesty's sake, out of the general state of surprise, a veil."

Again, it is a question of luminaries: even though the lustre is not named, it is possible to follow, within the infinite word-for-word play, "a horizontal stream of light" concerning which it is impossible to decide whether it should be considered written or spoken, proceeding as it does from a multitude of pens or mouths, that is, produced by *becs* [becs = "beaks," "pen nibs," and "gas burners."—Trans.] (". . . six copper *becs*, each projecting a horizontal stream of light . . . that object, six tongues of flame held together by metal, suspends a merry Pentecost—no, a *star*, for in truth any impression of Judaic ritual has disappeared." Among the "different applications of this luminary," which illustrate *once again* the question of writing, we find the "work table" or the "study . . . where the master would linger during the premature September evenings").

Now [*Or*]—this gas[light], so to speak, does not cross the threshold; it remains, veiled, on the doorstep: "Gas does not penetrate further, in our interiors, than the stairway or sometimes the landings: it can pass through the door of the apartment to light up the anterooms only in a vague, softened form, veiled by the transparent paper of a Japanese or Chinese lantern."

Richard, too, examines, from another viewpoint (p. 502), the theme of electricity, "gas and the sun" in *La Dernière Mode* (p. 825). On the phallic symbolism of pulley lamps, cf. Freud, *A General Introduction to Psychoanalysis*, trans. Joan Rivière (New York: Liveright Publishing Co, 1920), p. 138.

"Let us ascribe to daydreams, before the start of the reading, in an audience, the attention solicited by some fluttering white butterfly, at once everywhere, nowhere—it vanishes; yet not without leaving a bit of sharp, ingenuous nothing, to which I just reduced the subject, which has passed and re-passed, insistently, before the general astonishment" (p. 382).

Ever marking the threshold, this hesitation, suggestion, flotation, with its bit of sharpened nothing, this operation is about to break through—the hymen. Sewing the text together, here is what, with the *i*'s and the *ique* of *Mimique*, the subject is reduced to:

"... in the floating of a reverie? The operation or poetry, par excellence and theater. Immediately the ballet turns out allegorical: it will enlace as well as animate, so as to mark each rhythm, all correlations or Music, latent at first, between its postures and many a type, to such an extent that the figurative representation of earthly accessories by the Dance contains a test relative to their degree of esthetic quality; a consecration occurs therein, giving proof of our Treasures. To deduce the philosophical point at which the dancer's impersonality is located, between her feminine appearance and some mimed object, for what hymen: she sticks it with a confident point and sets it down; then unrolls our conviction in a cipher of pirouettes prolonged toward another motif . . ."

Let us freeze for a moment, just at this point, these cinematographic acrobatics. This entire paragraph is woven like a textile, a copious veil, a vast and supple fabric being spread out before us, but also being regularly stitched down. In the play of this tacking, there is nothing but text; the histological operation treats a tissue with the point of a sewing instrument that *at once* pierces and joins, strings together. The text—for what hymen— is at once cut through and gathered up. The "cipher of pirouettes prolonged toward another motif" is, like the whole of the text, ciphered to the second power. This is remarked by its cipher in that, while designating the dancer's pirouette as a cipher or hieroglyphic, it also enciphers the sign "pirouette," which it causes to pirouette or turn upon itself like a top, this time designating the movement of the sign itself. The cipher of pirouettes is also the pirouette as a cipher, as the movement of the signifier that refers, through the fiction of this or that visible dancing pirouette, to another pirouetting signifier, another "pirouette." In this way, the pirouette, like the dancer's pointed toe, is always just about to pierce with a sign, with a sharp bit of nothing, the page of the book or the virginal intimacy of the vellum. And hence, the dance of the signifier cannot be said to confine itself simply to the interior of a book or an imagination. Cf. *Le Genre ou des modernes* [*Genre, or Concerning Certain Moderns*]: ". . . its ill-concealed gaslights immediately lighting up, in various general postures of adultery or theft, the imprudent actors in this banal sacrilege.

"I understand.

"Dance alone, from the fact of its evolutions, along with mime appears to me to necessitate real space, or the stage.

"Strictly speaking, a piece of paper would suffice to evoke any play: with the aid of his own multiple personality anyone could play it inside himself, which is not the case where pirouettes are concerned" (p. 315). As a pirouette, the dance of the hieroglyph cannot be played internally in its entirety. Not only because of the need for "real space, or the stage"; not only because of the point that pierces the page or the plate of the book; but most especially because of a certain lateral movement: in turning incessantly on its point, the hieroglyph, the sign, the cipher moves away from its "here and now," as if it were endlessly falling, forever here en route between here and there, from one here to the other, inscribing in the *stigmē* of its "here" the *other* point toward which it continually drifts, the other pirouette that, in each vaulting spin, in the whirls of flying tissue, is instantly remarked. Each pirouette is then, in its twirling, only the mark of another pirouette, totally other and yet the same. The "cipher of pirouettes prolonged toward another motif" thus suggests the line—which unites but also divides— between two "words" or "signifiers," for example between the two occurrences of the signifier "pirouette" which, from one text to the other and first of all in the blank space of the inter-text, entrain, entail, and encipher each other, moving about like silhouettes, cut out like black shadows against a white background, profiles without faces, sketches forever presented askew, turning around the shaft of a wheel, the invisible axis of writing, a potter's wheel endlessly spinning away.

This mute writing, like that of a circling bird,[47] rises up, removes its point at the very instant it jabs. On the page facing *Mimique*,[48] Mallarmé names "Dance . . . that subject, virginal as muslins . . ." He speaks of "living folds." The graphics of the hymen will perhaps nowhere have been so strongly stressed as here: "A certain framework, belonging to no woman

---

47. For all this [*pirouette, silhouette, muette* (mute), etc.—Trans.] will have been calculated to suggest the wing sweep or pen sweep of the signifier *ette*, which is to be found in the unmarked intertext or else in the other text, marked; for example—all geared to rhyme with *souhaite* [wish] — find *chouette* [owl], *alouette* [skylark], *fouette* [whip], *girouette* [weathercock], and even the little wheels of the *brouette* [wheelbarrow], sprinkled through the occasional verse (pp. 118, 119, 120, 122, 137). So many pennas to keep track of. Rhyming with the "wish [*souhait*] to see too much and not enough."

48. (P. 311). "We have no information on the origin of this fragment," note the editors of the *Oeuvres Complètes*.

in particular, whence its instability, through the veil of generality, exerts an attraction toward this or that fragment of form revealed and therein drinks the flash that renders it divine; or else exhales, in return, through an undulation of tissues, floating, palpitating, diffuse, this ecstasy. Yes, the suspense of the Dance, a contradictory fear or wish to see too much and not enough, requires a transparent prolongation . . . for some spiritual acrobatics ordering that one follow the slightest scriptural intention, exists, but remains invisible, in the pure motion and displaced silence stirred by the dance. The next-to-nudity, apart from a brief radiating of skirts, whether to muffle the fall or, inversely, to heighten the lifting of the pointed toes, reveals, first and last, two legs—bearing some other than personal signification, like a direct instrument of an idea."

While literature, theater, drama, ballet, dance, fable, and mimicry are all forms of writing that are subject to the law of the hymen, they nevertheless do not all form one and the same text. There is more than one kind of writing: the different forms and genres are irreducible. Mallarmé has sketched out their system. What these types of writing have in common has been propounded here as the rule of the *cast-aside-reference*, the *being aside*, or the hymen. The range of differentiation within this common rule could not have been better demonstrated than on the occasion of the *Two Pigeons*, apropos of which Mallarmé distinguishes between Drama, Ballet, and Mime. But only after recapitulating the generality of writing: the hymen, reference cast aside by difference (the double show and the difference between the sexes), the play of the penna (bird, wing, feather, quill, beak, etc.), and the process of metaphorical production incessantly being relaunched by the gap, or the setting-aside, of being. And this generality of writing is nothing other than the production, by writing, of generality: the weaving, along the gap of the referent, of this "veil of generality" "belonging to no woman in particular." Witness, in the case of the *Two Pigeons*, the syntax of the *point* [= "point" or "not"] and the *pas* [= "not" or "step"]: "Such, a reciprocity, from which results what is *un*-individual, in the prima donna and in the whole company, about the dancing being, never anything but emblem not someone . . .

"The judgment or axiom to affirm when it comes to ballet!

"That is, that the dancer *is not a woman dancing*, for these reasons juxtaposed that she *is not a woman* but a metaphor summing up one of the elementary aspects of our form (sword, cup, flower, etc.) and that *she is not dancing*, suggesting, through a marvel of short cuts or surges, with her bodily writing what it would take paragraphs of prose dialogue or description to express on paper: a poem freed from any scribe's equipment. . . . The dance is wings; it concerns birds and takeoffs into the ever-after, along with returns as vibrant as an arrow. . . . One of the lovers shows them to the other, then shows himself, an initial language, comparison. Little by little the couple's demeanor turns, under the dovecote's influence, to a series of little pecks or leaps, swoons, until an invasion of aerial lasciviousness slips over them, with breathless resemblances. Once children, here they are birds, or the opposite, from birds they have become children, according to how one wishes to view the exchange in which forever after, he and she, would have to express the double game: perhaps the whole adventure of sexual difference! . . . with the intercalation of a celebration toward which everything will turn under a sudden storm, and then the anguishing lovers, one ready to flee and the other to forgive, will unite: it will be . . . You can imagine the hymn of the final triumphal dance in which the space put between the fiancés by the necessity of their journey diminishes down to the source of their joyful exhilaration!" Each pair in the circuit will always have referred to another pair, signifying *in addition* the very operation of signifying, the "initial language, comparison," the "double game" of the signifier, and "sexual difference" each indefinitely proposing itself as an example with respect to the others. Hence the dancer "sums up the subject through her divination mingled with pure, disturbing animality, designating at every turn uncompleted allusions, just as she invites, before any step, with two fingers, a quivering fold of her skirts and simulates an impatience of plumes toward the idea. . . . Then, through a kind of commerce whose secret her smile seems to pour forth, without delay she imparts to you, through the last veil that remains forever, the nudity of your own concepts, and silently proceeds to write your vision in the manner of a Sign, which she is."

While this difference opens up the common play of all types of writing, one neither can nor should erase the rigorous distinctions between the genres. One instance of "cheating" has already been denounced: the importation of Fable into Ballet: "With the exception of a distinctly perceived relation between the habitual demeanor of flight and many a choreographical effect, and then the importation, not without cheating, of Fable into Ballet, there remains a certain love story. . . ."[49]

All the "genres" of this generalized writing, including Fable, which actually tells a story, are distinguished by trace effects whose structure is in each case original. The different "silences," for example, never merge. "An art holds the stage, a historical one in the case of Drama; with Ballet, on the

49. Pp. 305–7. Cf. also Richard, pp. 409–36.

other hand, it is emblematic. To be allied but not confused; it is not from the outset and by treating them as the same that one ought to join two attitudes jealous of their respective silences, mime and dance, suddenly hostile if forced into too close proximity. For an example illustrating this: while it might have been tempting, a moment ago, in order to render one and the same essence—that of a bird—through two performers, to imagine placing a mime beside a dancer; this is to confront too much difference! . . . The distinct trait of each theatrical genre that is brought into contact or opposed finds itself commanding the work, which employs the discrepancy in its very architecture: what remains is to find the communications among them. The librettist ordinarily does not know that the dancer, who expresses herself by means of steps, understands no other form of eloquence, not even gesture" (p. 306). "Always, theater alters, toward a special or literary point of view, the arts it adopts: music cannot contribute to it without losing some of its depth and shadow, nor song, its solitary lightning, and, strictly speaking, it is possible not to grant to Ballet the name of Dance; which latter is, in a sense, hieroglyphic" (p. 312).

The different genres, which do not fuse into a total art (an indication of Mallarmé's discreet, ironic, but insurmountable qualms about Wagner), nevertheless exchange properties according to the infinite circulation of the scriptural metaphor; they are congeneric in that they do not actually show anything at all, and are *conjoined* around an absent focus: the lustre again, from *Rejoinder II*: ". . . for what hymen: she sticks it with a confident point and sets it down; then unrolls our conviction in a cipher of pirouettes prolonged toward another motif, given the fact that everything, in the evolutions through which she illustrates the meaning of our ecstasies and triumphs sounded by the orchestra, is, as art itself demands, in the theater, *fictive or momentary*.

"Sole principle! and just as the lustre glistens, that is to say, itself, the prompt exhibition, under all its facets, of whatever, and our adamantine sight, a dramatic work shows the succession of exteriorities of the act without any moment's retaining any reality and that in the final analysis what happens is nothing.

"Old-fashioned Melodrama, occupying the stage, conjointly with Dance, and also under the management of the poet, fulfills this law. Moved to pity, the perpetual suspense of a tear that can never be entirely formed nor fall (still the lustre) scintillates in a thousand glances, now, like gold, an ambiguous smile. . . ."

Now, once the crisis of literature has thus been remarked, would any criticism whatsoever—as such—be capable of facing up to it? Would such criticism be able to lay claim to any *object*? Doesn't the project of the χρίνειν itself proceed precisely out of the very thing that is being threatened and put in question at the focal point of this remodeling, or, to use a more Mallarméan word, this re-tempering of literature? Wouldn't "literary criticism" as such be part of what we have called the *ontological* interpretation of mimesis or of metaphysical mimetologism?

It is in this de-limitation of criticism that we will henceforth be interested.

If we take into account a certain time lag and some significant historical developments, it can be said that the elements in Mallarmé's text that re-mark these "critical" boundaries have now been recognized. But this recognition cannot be reached by one viewer alone or in one fell swoop. It must be something other than mere recognition, and it must entail a certain stratified repetition. On the one hand, "contemporary criticism" has now recognized, studied, confronted, and *thematized* a certain number of *signifieds* that had long gone unnoticed, or at least had never been treated as such, systematically, for more than half a century of Mallarméan criticism. And on the other hand, the whole formal crafting of Mallarmé's writing has recently been analyzed in detail. But never, it seems, has the analysis of the way the text is assembled seemed to block access to the thematic level as such, or, more broadly, to meaning or the signified as such. Never has an overall meaning system or even a structural semantics seemed to be threatened or thwarted by the very progression or onward *march* of the Mallarméan text, and this according to the workings of a regular law. That law does not apply only to the text of "Mallarmé," even though he "illustrates" it according to a "historical" necessity whose entire field needs to be mapped out, and even though such an illustration entails a general reinterpretation of everything.

What we will thus be concerned with here is the very possibility of thematic criticism, seen as an example of modern criticism, at work wherever one tries to determine a meaning through a text, to pronounce a decision upon it, to decide that this or that *is* a meaning and that it is meaningful, to say that this meaning is posed, posable, or transposable as such: a theme.

It is obvious—and this will later receive further confirmation—that the fact that we have chosen to focus on the "blank" and the "fold" is not an accident. This is both because of the specific effects of these two elements in Mallarmé's text and precisely because they have systematically been recognized as *themes* by modern criticism. Now, if we can begin to see that the "blank" and the "fold" cannot in fact be mastered as themes or as meanings,

if it is within the folds and the blankness of a certain hymen that the very
textuality of the text is re-marked, then we will precisely have determined
the limits of thematic criticism itself.

Is it necessary to point out that *l'Univers imaginaire de Mallarmé*
[*Mallarmé's Imaginary Universe*] (1961) remains the most powerful of all
works of thematic criticism? It systematically covers the whole of the
textual field of Mallarmé; or at least, it *would* do so if the structure of a
certain crisscrossed groove (the blankness of a fold or the folding of a blank)
did not turn the "whole" into the *too much* or the *too little* of the text. And
vice versa. Thus, let us say, the whole of Mallarmé's textual field would be
covered.

The questions we will ask of this book, for the same reason, will not be
directed toward it as a "whole," the "whole" being the imaginary version of
a text. They will be addressed to a certain determinate part of its procedure,
particularly to the theoretical and methodological formulation of its project: its thematicism. In this, we will be dealing with the book on a level
that is still too thematic. But one would not be able to redirect our own
critique against us in the end without confirming its legitimacy and its
principle.

At the point at which the theoretical project of the book is stated in the
Preface, it is explained by means of two examples. Although these are given
as two examples among many, and although what is exemplary or excep-
tional about them is never rigorously examined by Richard, it is not
without cause that they have found their way to such a key position. The
examples in question are precisely the "themes" of the "blank" and the
"fold." We must here quote a long and beautifully written page of the
Preface. Inquiring into "the very notion of a *theme*, on which [our] whole
enterprise is based,"[50] Richard has just noted the "strategic value" or the
"topological quality" of the theme. "Any thematics will thus derive both
from cybernetics and from systematics. Within this active system, the
themes will tend to organize themselves as in any living structure: they will
combine into flexible groupings governed by the law of isomorphism and
by the search for the best possible equilibrium. This notion of equilibrium,
which first arises out of the physical sciences but whose crucial importance
in sociology and psychology has been demonstrated by Claude Lévi-Strauss

50. I shall not go into the seemingly very particular problem posed by the transference of
the word *theme*, in the sense in which Mallarmé indeed reproduces the definition in *Les Mots
anglais*, to its conventional technical and grammatical sense (p. 962). For all sorts of reasons,
is it not hard, "in applying it to fields other than philology" (Richard, p. 24), to consider
oneself authorized to do so by Mallarmé?

and Jean Piaget, seems to us to be of considerable utility in the understanding of the realms of the imaginary. One can indeed observe how themes arrange themselves into antithetical pairs, or, in a more complex manner, into multiple compensating systems. In his dream of the idea, for example, Mallarmé appeared to us to oscillate between the desire for an opening (the idea bursting apart, *vaporized* into suggestion or silence) and a need for closure (the idea *summoned*, summed up in a contour or a definition). The closed and the open, the clear and the fleeting, the mediate and the immediate, these are a few of the mental pairings whose presence we believe we have discerned on a number of very diverse levels of the Mallarméan experience. The important thing is then to observe how these oppositions are resolved, how their tension is eased into new synthetic notions or into concrete forms that realize a satisfactory equilibrium. The opposition between the closed and the open thus engenders certain beneficent figures in which both contradictory needs can be satisfied, successively or simultaneously: for example the *fan*, the *book*, the *dancer* . . . The essence succeeds at once in summoning and in vaporizing itself in a synthetic phenomenon: *music*. At other times the equilibrium is established in a static manner, through a play of forces very precisely pitted against each other, whose total balance amounts to the euphoria of a 'suspension.' It is thus that Mallarmé himself indeed envisioned the internal reality of a poem and the ideal architecture of the objects the poem must reorder within. itself: grottos, diamonds, spiderwebs, rose windows, kiosks, shells, all stand as so many images which translate the search for a total correlation of nature with itself, a perfect equalization of all things. The mind or spirit then becomes the keystone of this architecture, functioning as the absolute center through which everything communicates, balances out, and is neutralized (Mallarmé adds 'is annulled' . . . .). Thus Mallarmé's thematics itself provides us with the technical tools needed for its own elucidation. What we have tried to do is to see how the profoundest tendencies of reverie succeed in going beyond their inherent conflict toward some state of equilibrium. To that end it was in fact enough to reread the most beautiful of the poems, where that balance is achieved effortlessly and spontaneously, poetic felicity— what is called 'felicity of expression'—being doubtless nothing other than the reflection of lived felicity, that is, a state in which a being's most contradictory needs are all satisfied at once, and even satisfy *each other*, in a harmony composed of connections, oscillations, or fusions" (pp. 26–27).

Let us interrupt the quotation for a moment. Not in order to ask—as Richard does not, throughout the length of the book—what "the most beautiful of the poems, where that balance is achieved effortlessly and spontaneously" might be, but in order to point out a coherent group of concepts: "living structures," "law of isomorphism," "best possible equilibrium," "mental pairings," "beneficent figures," "synthetic phenomenon," "euphoria of a suspension," "total correlation of nature with itself," "happy states of equilibrium," "felicity of expression," "reflection of lived felicity," etc. These concepts belong to a critical "psychologism." Gerard Genette has analyzed the *transitive* character of this approach, along with its "sensualist" and "eudaemonist" postulates.[51] Using this concept of "reflection" (of "lived felicity"), so loaded with history and metaphysics, such a representative psychologism makes the text into a form of expression, reduces it to its signified theme,[52] and retains all the traits of mimetologism. What it retains in particular is that *dialecticity* that has remained profoundly inseparable from metaphysics, from Plato to Hegel:[53]

51. *Bonheur de Mallarmé?* [*Mallarméan Felicity?*] in *Figures* (Seuil, 1966), pp. 91 ff.

52. We will attempt to show elsewhere that this type of thematicism has as its very vocation to be eudemonistic or hedonistic (and vice versa), and that it is not in principle incompatible with Freud's psychoanalysis of the work of art, at least in the guise in which it operates in the essays prior to *The Uncanny* (1919) and *Beyond the Pleasure Principle* (1920), that is, particularly in the *Traumdeutung* (1900), *Der Witz...* (1905), *Gradiva* (1906), *Der Dichter und das Phantasieren* (1907), *Introduction to Psychoanalysis* (1916). Freud acknowledges that he is going beyond the formal limits of the text toward the theme (*Stoff*), or the author, and that that entails a number of inconsistencies. He analyzes the work as a *means* in the service of the pleasure principle *alone*: situating it between a preliminary pleasure (*Vorlust*) or bonus of seduction (*Verlockungsprämie*) produced by the formal achievement and a final pleasure linked to the releasing of tensions (*Der Dichter . . .* in fine). This does not mean that after 1919–20 such propositions will be entirely superseded, but they nevertheless will seem to circulate within a modified frame of reference. The problematics of this displacement still remains to be constituted.

Among the valuable biographical and other elements collected by Jones relating to this problem (*The Life and Work of Sigmund Freud*), I will cite only a letter from 1914. This time Freud seems to be putting all pleasure on the side of form. And he betrays a surprising irritation toward those he categorizes rather strangely as "given up to the pleasure principle": "Freud remarked once in a letter to me describing an evening he had spent with an artist: 'Meaning is but little to these men; all they care for is line, shape, agreement of contours. They are given up to the *Lustprinzip*.' " (III, 412).

On this problem cf. also Sollers, "La Science de Lautréamont," in *Logiques* (Paris: Seuil, 1968) and Baudry, "Freud et la création littéraire" in *Théorie d'ensemble* (Paris: Seuil, 1968).

53. If one wishes to identify the specificity of the writing operation or of the operation of the textual signifier (the graphics of supplementarity or of the hymen), one must focus one's critique on the concept of *Aufhebung* or sublation [*relève*], which, as the ultimate mainspring of all dialecticity, stands as the most enticing, the most sublating, the most "relevant" way of (re)covering (up) that graphics, precisely because it is most similar to it. This is why it has seemed necessary to designate the *Aufhebung* as the decisive target (cf. *Of Grammatology*, p. 25). And since thematicism presents itself not only as a dialectic but also, and rightly so, as a "phenomenology of the theme" (p. 27), let us here recall by analogy the fact that it was the possibility of "undecidable" propositions that presented phenomenological discourse with such redoubtable difficulties (Cf. my Introduction to *L'origine de la géométrie, de Husserl*, (Presses Universitaires de France, 1962), pp. 39 ff).

we have already shown in what way the dialectical structure is incapable of accounting for the graphics of the hymen, being itself comprehended and inscribed within the latter, almost indistinguishable from it, separated from it only by itself, a simple veil that constitutes the very thing that tries to reduce it to nothing: desire.

This dialectical intention animates the whole of Richard's thematicism, reaching its fullest expansion in the chapter entitled "The Idea" and in its subsection "Toward a dialectics of Totality." This dialectics of totality intervenes in the Preface just after the passage cited above, precisely in connection with the examples of the "blank" and the "fold": "If one wishes to approach the psychological reality of the theme from another angle, one can do so through that other product of the imagining function: the symbol. In a recent study of the work of M. Eliade, Paul Ricoeur gives an excellent analysis of the different modes of comprehension at our disposal for dealing with the symbolic world: his remarks could be applied with little modification to a phenomenology of the theme. The theme, too, 'makes us think'. To understand a theme is also to 'deploy [its] multiple valences': it is, for example, to see how Mallarmé's dream of the *blank* can incarnate now the ecstasy of virginity, now the pain of an obstacle or of frigidity, now the happiness of an opening, of a liberation, or of a mediation, and then to connect these diverse nuances of meaning into one single complex. One can also, as Ricoeur suggests, understand a theme through another theme, progressing from one to the other following 'a law of intentional analogy' until one has reached all the themes linked by relations of affinity. This would involve, for example, moving from the azure to the windowpane, to the blank paper, to the glacier, to the snowy peak, to the swan, to the wing, to the ceiling, not forgetting the lateral branchings that occur at each point in this progression (from the glacier to the melted water, to the blue eyes, and to the amorous bath; from the white paper to the black marks that cover and divide it; from the ceiling to the tomb, the priest, the sylph, and the mandolin). And finally, one can show how the same theme 'unifies several experiential and representational levels: the internal and the external, the vital and the speculative.' The Mallarméan figure of the *fold*, for example, enables us to join the erotic to the sensible, then to the reflective, to the metaphysical, and to the literary: the fold is at once sex, foliage, mirror, book, and tomb—all are realities it gathers up into a certain very special dream of intimacy" (pp. 27–28).

This passage (in which each connotation calls for analysis) is flanked by two brief remarks. One cannot, it seems, subscribe to it without acknowledging two objections in principle to the phenomenological, hermeneutic, dialectical project of thematicism. The first involves the differential or

diacritical character of language: "Then another difficulty arises: to construct a lexicon of frequencies is to suppose that from one occurrence to
another the meaning of words remains fixed. But in reality, meaning varies;
it is modified both within itself and according to the horizon of meanings
that surround, sustain, and create it. Languages, as we now know, are
diacritical realities; each element within them is in itself less important than
the *gap* that distinguishes it from other elements. . . . Neither a mathematical study nor even an exhaustive list of themes can therefore ever account
for their intention or their richness; what will above all be left out is the
original relief of their system" (p. 25). Out of this fundamental diacriticity
whose design should also be further complicated, we will later draw another
consequence: a certain inexhaustibility which cannot be classed in the
categories of richness, intentionality, or a horizon, and whose form would
not be simply foreign to the order of mathematics. Nevertheless, it can be
seen that even in the eyes of Richard himself, diacriticity already prevents a
theme from being a theme, that is, a nuclear unit of meaning, posed there
before the eye, present outside of its signifier and referring only to itself, in
the last analysis, even though its identity as a signified is carved out of the
horizon of an infinite perspective. Either diacriticity revolves around a
nucleus and in that case any recourse to it remains superficial enough not to
put thematicism as such into question; or else diacriticity traverses the text
through and through and there is no such thing as a thematic nucleus, only
theme *effects* that give themselves out to be the very thing or meaning of the
text. If there is a textual system, a theme does not exist (. . . "no—a present
does not exist . . ."). Or if it *does* exist, it will always have been unreadable.
This kind of nonexistence of the theme in the text, this way in which
meaning is nonpresent or nonidentical with the text, has in fact been
recognized by Richard, however—this is the second of the two remarks
mentioned above—in a note dealing with the problems of ordering and
classifying themes. These problems are by no means secondary: "We cannot
help admitting, however, that this order is far from satisfactory. For in fact
it is actually the multiplicity of lateral relations that creates the *essence* of
meaning here. A theme is nothing other than the sum, or rather the putting
in perspective, of its diverse modulations" (p. 28. Similar remark on p.
555).

This concession still allows for the hope, the "dream," of reaching a sum
and of determining a perspective, even if these are infinite. Such a sum or
perspective would enable us to define, contain, and classify the different
occurrences of a theme.

To this we would oppose the following hypotheses: the sum is impossible to totalize but yet it is not exceeded by the infinite richness of a content of meaning or intention; the perspective extends out of sight but without entailing the depth of a horizon of meaning *before* or *within* which we can never have finished advancing. By taking into account that "laterality" Richard mentions in passing, but by going on to determine its law, we shall define the limit otherwise: through the angle and the intersection of a re-mark that folds the text back upon itself without any possibility of its fitting back over or into itself, without any reduction of its spacing.

The fold, then, and the blank: these will forbid us to seek a theme or an overall meaning in an imaginary, intentional, or lived domain beyond all textual instances. Richard sees the "blank" and the "fold" as themes whose plurivalence is particularly rich or exuberant. What one tends not to see, because of the abundance of his sample, is that these textual effects are rich with a kind of poverty, I would even call it a very singular and very regular monotony. One does not see this because one thinks one is seeing themes in the very spot where the nontheme, that which cannot become a theme, the very thing that has no meaning, is ceaselessly re-marking itself—that is, disappearing.

All this in the movement of a fan. The polysemy of "blanks" and "folds" both fans out and snaps shut, ceaselessly. But to read Mallarme's *éventail* [fan] involves not only an inventory of its occurrences (there are hundreds, a very large but finite number if one sticks to the word itself, or an infinite number of diverse possibilities if one includes the many-faceted figure of wings, pages, veils, sails, folds, plumes, scepters, etc., constituting and reconstituting itself in an endless breath of opening and/or closing); it involves not only the description of a phenomenological structure whose complexity is also a challenge; it is also to remark that the fan re-marks itself: no doubt it designates the empirical object one thinks one knows under that name, but then, through a tropic twist (analogy, metaphor, metonymy), it turns toward all the semic units that have been identified (wing, fold, plume, page, rustling, flight, dancer, veil, etc., each one finding itself folding and unfolding, opening/closing with the movement of a fan, etc.); it opens and closes each one, but it also inscribes *above and beyond* that movement the very movement and structure of the fan-as-text, the deployment and retraction of all its valences; the spacing, fold, and hymen *between* all these meaning-effects, with writing setting them up in relations of difference and resemblance. This surplus mark, this margin of meaning, is not one valence among others in the series, even though it is *inserted* in there, too. It has to be inserted there to the extent that it does not exist outside the text and has no transcendental privilege; this is why it is always *represented* by a metaphor and a metonymy (page, plume, pleat). But while belonging in the series of valences, it always occupies the position of a supplementary valence, or rather, it marks the structurally necessary position of a supplementary inscription that could always be added to or subtracted from the series. We will try to show that this position of the supplementary mark is in all rigor neither a metaphor nor a metonymy even though it is always represented by one trope too many or too few.

Let us set the fan down here as an epigraph at the edge of the demonstration.

The "blank" appears first of all, to a phenomenological or thematic reading, as the inexhaustible totality of the semantic valences that have any tropic affinity with it (but what is "it"?). But, through a reduplication that is always represented, the "blank" *inserts* (says, designates, marks, states—however one wishes to put it, and there is a need here for a different "word") the blank as a blank *between* the valences, a hymen that unites and differentiates them in the series, the spacing of "the blanks" which "assume importance." Hence, the blank or the whiteness (is) the totality, however infinite, of the polysemic series, *plus* the carefully spaced-out splitting of the whole, the fanlike form of the text. This *plus* is not just one extra valence, a meaning that might enrich the polysemic series. And since it has no meaning, it is not *The* blank proper, the transcendental origin of the series. This is why, while it cannot constitute a meaning that is signified or represented, one would say in classical discourse that it always has a delegate or representative in the series: since the blank is the polysemic totality of everything white or blank *plus* the writing site (hymen, spacing, etc.) where such a totality is produced, this *plus* will, for example, find one of these representatives representing nothing in the blankness or margins of the page. But for the reasons just enumerated, it is out of the question that we should erect such a representative—for example the whiteness of the page of writing—into the fundamental signified or signifier in the series. Every signifier in the series is folded along the angle of this remark. The signifiers "writing," "hymen," "fold," "tissue," "text," etc., do not escape this common law, and only a conceptual strategy of some sort can temporarily privilege them as *determinate* signifiers or even as *signifiers* at all, which strictly speaking they *no longer are.*

This non-sense or non-theme of the spacing that relates the different meanings to each other (the meaning of "blank" or "white" along with the others) and in the process prevents them from ever meeting up with each other cannot be accounted for by any *description*. It follows, then, firstly, that there is no such thing as description, particularly in Mallarmé's work: we have already shown through one or two examples that while Mallarmé was pretending to describe "something," he was *in addition* describing the operation of writing ("there is at Versailles a kind of wainscotting in scrollwork tracery . . ."). It follows, secondly, that any description of "themes," particularly in Mallarmé's work, will always run aground at the edges of this *greater* or *lesser* extent of theme which makes it possible that "there is" a text, that is, a readability without a signified (which will be decreed to be an unreadability by the reflexes of fright): an undesirable that throws desire back upon itself.

If polysemy is infinite, if it cannot be mastered as such, this is thus not because a finite reading or a finite writing remains incapable of exhausting a superabundance of meaning. Not, that is, unless one displaces the philo-sophical concept of finitude and reconstitutes it according to the law and structure of the text: according as the blank, like the hymen, re-marks itself forever as disappearance, erasure, non-sense. Finitude then becomes in-finitude, according to a non-Hegelian identity: through an interruption that suspends the equation between the mark and the meaning, the "blank" marks everything white (this above all): virginity, frigidity, snow, sails, swans' wings, foam, paper, etc., *plus* the blankness that allows for the mark in the first place, guaranteeing its space of reception and production. This "last" blank (one could equally well say this "first" blank) comes neither before nor after the series. One can just as easily subtract it from the series (in which case it is determined as a lack to be silently passed over) or add it as an extra to the number, even if the number is infinite, of the valences of "white," either as an accidental bit of white, an inconsistent discard whose "consistency" will show up better later, or else as another theme which the open series must liberally embrace, or else, finally, as the transcendental space of inscription itself. As they play within this differential-supplementary structure, all the marks must blend to it, taking on the fold of this blank. The blank is folded, is (marked by) a fold. It never exposes itself to straight stitching. For the fold is no more of a theme (a signified) than the blank, and if one takes into account the linkages and rifts they propagate in the text, then *nothing* can simply have the value of a theme any more.

And there is more. The supplementary "blank" does not intervene only in the polysemous series of "white things," but also *between* the semes of *any* series and *between all* the semantic series in general. It therefore prevents any semantic seriality from being constituted, from being simply opened or closed. Not that it acts as an obstacle: it is again the blank that actually liberates the effect that a series exists; in marking itself out, it *makes us take* agglomerates for substances. If thematicism cannot account for this, it is because it overestimates the *word* while restricting the *lateral*.

In his taxonomy of "whites," Richard indeed distinguished the *principal* valences, which he designated by abstract concepts or names of general essences ("the ecstasy of virginity, the pain of an obstacle or of frigidity, the happiness of an opening, of a liberation, of a meditation"), and the *lateral* valences exemplified by material things, enabling one to "move from the azure to the windowpane, to the blank paper, to the glacier, to the snowy peak, to the swan, to the wing, to the ceiling, not forgetting the lateral branchings . . . from the glacier to the melted water, to the blue eyes and to the amorous bath; from the white paper to the black marks that cover and divide it; from the ceiling to the tomb, the priest, the sylph, and the mandolin"). This leads one to believe that some sort of hierarchy lines the lateral themes up with the principal themes and that the former are but the sensible figures (metaphors or metonymies) of the latter, which one could *properly conceive* in their literal meaning. But without even resorting to the general law of textual supplementarity through which all proper meanings are dislocated, one has only to turn to one of Richard's own lateral remarks ("In fact it is actually the multiplicity of lateral relations that creates the *essence* of meaning," [p. 28n]) in order to undercut such a hierarchy. And since there is never, textually, anything but a silhouette, one can hold up against any frontal conception of the theme the way in which Mallarmé writes *on the bias*, his *double play* ceaselessly re-marking its *bifax*. Once more: ". . . it will be (the) language whose gambol this is.

"Words, of themselves, are exalted on many a facet known as the rarest or having value for the mind, the center of vibratory suspense; whoever perceives them independently from the ordinary sequence, projected, on the walls of a cave, as long as their mobility or principle lasts, being that which of discourse is not said: all of them quick, before becoming extinct or extinguished, to enter into a reciprocity of fires that is distant or presented on the bias as some contingency.

"The debate—which the average necessary obviousness deflects into a detail, remains one for grammarians." Elsewhere translated as "there is a double-faced silence" (p. 210).

The grammar of the *bias* and of *contingency* is not only concerned with treating lateral associations of themes or semes whose constituted, smoothed, and polished unit would have as its signifier the form of a word. And in fact, the "relation of affinity" which interests the thematic critic only brings together semes whose signifying face always has the dimensions of a word or group of words related by their meaning (or signified concept). Thematicism necessarily leaves out of account the formal, phonic, or graphic "affinities" that do not have the shape of a word, the calm unity of the verbal sign. Thematicism as such necessarily ignores the play that takes the word apart, cutting it up and putting the pieces to work "on the bias as some contingency." It is certain that Mallarmé was fascinated by the possibilities inherent in the *word*, and Richard is right in emphasizing this (p. 528), but these possibilities are not primarily nor exclusively those of a body proper, a carnal unit, "the living creature" (p. 529) that miraculously unites sense and the senses into one *vox*; it is a play of articulations splitting up that body or reinscribing it within sequences it can no longer control. That is why we would not say of the word that it has "a *life* of its own" (ibid.); and Mallarmé was just as interested in the dissection of the word as in the integrity of its life proper. It is a dissection called for by the consonant as much as by the vowel, the pure vocable; called for no less by the differential skeleton than by the fullness of breath. On the table or on the page, Mallarmé treats the word as something dead *just as much as* something living. And how is one to separate what he says of the science of language in *Les Mots anglais* [*English Words*] from what he *does* elsewhere:

"Words, in the dictionary, are deposited, the same or of diverse date, like stratifications: in a moment I will speak of layers. . . .Akin to all of nature and hence comparable to the organism that stands as the depository of life, the Word presents, in its vowels and diphthongs, something like flesh; and, in its consonants, something like a skeleton delicate to dissect. Etc., etc., etc. If life feeds on its own past, or on a continual death, Science will uncover this fact in language: which latter, distinguishing man from the rest of things, will also imitate him in being factitious in essence no less than natural; reflective, than fated; voluntary, than blind" (p. 901).

This is why it is difficult to subscribe to the commentary Richard offers on the sentence from *Les Mots anglais* ("the Word presents . . . to dissect") at the very moment he recognizes that thematicism stops short before Mallarmé's formal analyses, here his work with phonetics: "If one wishes to know completely the profound orientation of a poet, one must perhaps attempt a phonetic phenomenology of his key words. In the absence of such a study, let us at least recognize in the word the mystery of the flesh joined with the felicity of structure: a union that suffices to make the word a complete, closed system, a microcosm" (p. 529). It is difficult to subscribe to this: (1) because such a phonetic phenomenology would always, as such, have to lead back to plenitudes or intuitive presences rather than to phonic differences; (2) because the word cannot be a complete system or a body proper; (3) because, as we have tried to show, there cannot be any such thing as key words; (4) because Mallarmé's text works with graphic differences (in the narrowest ordinary sense of the term) as much as with phonic differences.

While it is far from being the only example, the play of *rhyme* is doubtless one of the most remarkable instances of this production of a new sign, a meaning and a form, through the "two-by-two" (cf. Richard, passim) and the magnetization of two signifiers; it is a production and a magnetization whose necessity imposes itself against contingency, arbitrariness, and semantic, or rather semiological, haphazardness. This is the operation of verse, whose concept Mallarmé, as we shall see, extends and generalizes; it is *not limited to rhyme* ("Verse, which, out of several vocables, remakes a total new word foreign to the language and as if incantatory, achieves that isolation of speech: negating, in a sovereign stroke, the haphazardness remaining in each term despite the artifice of its alternate retempering in sense and sound . . ." [p. 858]). Mallarmé's bias is also worked out with a file [*à la lime*; rhymes with *à la rime*, "at the rhyme"].[54] The "total new word foreign to the language": through this (signifying) difference, it is truly the effect of a transformation or displacement of the code, of the existing taxonomy ("new, foreign to the language"); and it is also, in its newness, its otherness, constituted out of parts borrowed from the language (the "old" language), to which, however, it cannot be reduced ("total"). But no astonishment at this poetic production of new meaning should make us forget—and to read Mallarmé is to be sufficiently reminded of it—that while it works *upon* the language, the total new word foreign to the language also *returns* to the language, recomposes with it according to new networks of differences, becomes divided up again, etc., in short, does not become a master-word with the finally guaranteed integrity of a meaning or truth.[55] The "effect" (in the Mallarméan sense of the word: "to paint not the

54. "*Lime*: from Lat. *lima*, related to *limus*, oblique, because of the obliquity or curvature of the teeth of a file" (Littré, from whom we are asking for anything but an etymology here).

55. This at least is the hypothesis on the basis of which we would question certain formulations in the remarkable analyses Richard entitles *Formes et moyens de la littérature* [*The Forms and Means of Literature*] (chap. 10). Formulations like these, for example, concerning the "new word": "this word is new because it is total, and it seems foreign to our language because it has been restored to that primordial language of which ours is but a fallen echo. . . . New, that which is of the order of the recreated original, that is, no doubt, of the eternal" (p. 537). "The pessimism of the word thus gives way in Mallarmé to a marvelous optimism of verse or sentence, which indeed is but a kind of confidence in the inventive or redemptive powers of the mind" (p. 544). "What pours forth here in the form of flowing fabric or a half-open spiritual strongbox is indeed the certain revelation of meaning" (p. 546).

thing but the effect it produces")[56] of totality or novelty does not make the word immune to difference or to the supplement; the word is not exempt from the law of the bias and does not present itself to us squarely, with its own singular face.

In the constellation of "blanks," the place of the semic content remains practically empty: it is that of the "blank" meaning insofar as it refers to the non-sense of spacing, the place where nothing takes place but the place. But that "place" is everywhere; it is not a site fixed and predetermined; not only, as we have already noted, because the signifying spacings continually reproduce themselves ("Indefectibly the white blank returns") but because the semic, metaphoric, or even thematic affinity between "white" [blanc] and "blank" [blanc] (spacing, interval, the entre, etc.) means that each

---

Since the value of virginity (newness, wholeness, etc.) is always overlaid with its opposite, it must ceaselessly be subjected—and would indeed submit of its own accord—to the operation of the hymen. The "presence" of words like "wholeness," "nativeness," "ingenuousness," etc., in Mallarmé's text cannot be *read* as a simple or simply positive valorization. All evaluations (optimism/pessimism) immediately pass into their opposite according to a logic that Richard describes elsewhere in its greatest complexity—at least up until the moment when, by a regularly repeated decision, what is undecidable or unprecedented in this logic, in this "almost impracticable" (p. 552) poetics, is reconstituted as a dialectical contradiction that must be gone beyond (p. 566), that Mallarmé would have wished to overcome through "a perfect synthetic form" (The Book) (p. 567); through the affirmation, produced by the space of its own absence, of a center of truth; through an aspiration toward unity, truth, "the happiness of a truth that is both active and closed" (p. 573), etc.

56. From a letter to Cazalis (1864, *Correspondance*, p. 137): ("I have finally begun my *Hérodiade*—in terror, for I am inventing a language that must necessarily arise from a highly new poetics, which I could define in the following two words: *To paint, not the thing, but the effect it produces*. The line of verse should not then be composed of words but of intentions, and all speech should efface itself before sensation." At that date, the first interpretation of the "highly new poetics" is formulated in a language that is naïvely sensualist and subjectivist. But the exclusion is clear: poetic language will not be a description or imitation or representation of the thing itself, of some substantial referent or of some primal cause, and it should not be *composed* of words taken as substantial or atomic units that are precisely undecomposable or uncompoundable. This letter (which should of course be interpreted with the utmost caution, without falling into retrospective teleology, etc.) seems at any rate to proscribe, under the terms of this new poetics, that a thing or cause in the last instance be what is signified by a text. ("There is no such thing as the true meaning of a text," said Valéry; of Mallarmé, he wrote: "But what one finds pronounced there on the contrary is the most daring and sustained attempt ever made to overcome what I shall call naive intuition in literature.") But it could be asked whether "sensation" or "intention" are not here simply occupying the place vacated by the referent, and are now to be *expressed* rather than *described*. This is no doubt the case, except if, in being placed in radical opposition to *the thing* with all its predicates, which is what Mallarmé is doing, they are in effect being displaced otherwise by a discourse, a practice, a writing.

Like almost all the texts I cite (and this is why I do not mention it each time), this letter is given a different commentary by Richard (p. 541).

"white" in the series, each "full" white thing in the series (snow, swan, paper, virginity, etc.), is the trope of the "empty" white space. And vice versa. The dissemination of the whites (*not* the dissemination of whiteness) produces a tropological structure that circulates infinitely around itself through the incessant supplement of an extra turn: there is *more* metaphor, *more* metonymy. Since everything becomes metaphorical, there is no longer any literal meaning and, hence, no longer any metaphor either. Since everything becomes metonymical, the part being each time greater than the whole and the whole smaller than the part, how could one arrest a metonymy or a synechdoche? How could one fix the *margins* of any rhetoric?

If there is no such thing as a total or proper meaning, it is because the blank *folds over*. The fold is not an accident that happens to the blank. From the moment the blank (is) white or bleaches (itself) out, as soon as there is something (there) to see (or not to see) having to do with a *mark* (which is the same word as *margin* or *march*), whether the white is marked (snow, swan, virginity, paper, etc.) or unmarked, merely demarcated (the *entre*, the void, the blank, the space, etc.), it re-marks itself, marks itself twice. It folds itself around this strange limit. The fold does not come up upon it from outside; it is the blank's outside as well as its inside, the complication according to which the supplementary mark of the blank (the asemic spacing) applies itself to the set of white things (the full semic entities), plus to itself, the fold of the veil, tissue, or text upon itself. By reason of this application that nothing has preceded, there will never be any Blank with a capital B or any theology of the Text.[57] And yet the structural site of this theological trap is nevertheless prescribed: the mark-supplement [*le supplément de marque*] produced by the text's workings, in falling outside of the text like an independent object with no origin other than itself, a trace that turns back into a presence (or a sign), is inseparable from desire (the desire for reappropriation or representation). Or rather, it gives birth to it and nourishes it in the very act of separating from it.

The fold folds (itself): its meaning spaces itself out with a double mark, in the hollow of which a blank is folded. The fold is simultaneously

---

57. If the *blanc* extends both the marks and the margins of the text, then there is no reason to give any special status to the whiteness of what we think we know literally under the name *page* or *paper*. The occurrences of this type of white are less numerous (examples are found in *Mimique* and *Deuil* and on pp. 38, 523, 872, 900, etc.) than others, the white of all the fabrics, the flying wings or foam, the sobs, fountains, flowers, women, or nudes in the night, the agonies, etc. The white involved in spacing slips in between all the others and can be remarked in the word *spacious*, whether it intervenes directly ("what leaps and if more spacious . . ." p. 312; "here the spacious illusion intervenes," p. 414; cf. also pp. 371, 404, 649, 859, 860, 868, etc.), or figuratively.

virginity, what violates virginity, and the fold which, being neither one nor
the other and both at once, undecidable, *remains* as a text, irreducible to
either of its two senses. "The act of folding . . . with respect to the page
printed large," the "intervention of folding or *rhythm*, that which initially
causes a closed page to contain a secret; silence remains in it," "the folding
back of the paper and the undersides this installs, the shadow dispersed in
the black lettering" (p. 379), "the virginal folding back of the book" (p.
381),[58] such is the closed, feminine form of the book, protective of the secret
of its hymen, the "frail inviolability" preceding "the introduction of a
weapon, or letter opener, to mark the taking of possession," before "the
consummation of any encroachment." We have never been so close to
Mimique, and the femininity of the virgin book is surely suggested by the
place and form of the verb "prête" [as a verb, it means "lends," as an
adjective, it means "ready" or "willing" in the feminine.—Trans.], clearly
ready to offer itself as an adjective with the copula understood ("The
virginal folding-back of the book, again, willing/lends for a sacrifice from
which the red edges of the books of old once bled"). The masculine is turned
back upon the feminine: the whole adventure of sexual difference. The
secret angle of the fold is also that of a "minuscule tomb."

But in the same blow, so to speak, the fold ruptures the virginity it
marks as virginity. Folding itself over its secret (and nothing is more
virginal and at the same time more purloined and penetrated, already in and
of itself, than a secret), it loses the smooth simplicity of its surface. It differs
from itself, even *before* the letter opener can separate the lips of the book.[59] It
is divided from and by itself, like the hymen. But after the fact, it still
remains what it was, a virgin, beforehand, faced with the brandished knife
("the fact is, in the actual case, that, for my part, however, on the subject of
pamphlets to be read according to common usage, I brandish a knife, like a
cook slaughtering fowls"). After the consummation, more folded up than
ever, the virginity transforms the act that has been perpetrated into a
simulation, a "barbarous simulacrum." What is intact is remarked by the
mark that remains intact, an immarcescible text, at the very edge of the
margin: "The folds will perpetuate a mark, intact, bidding one to open or
close the page, according to the master" (p. 381).

58. Emphasis mine. "Yes, the Book or that monograph it becomes of a type (the
superimposition of pages as in a jewel case, defending an infinite, intimate, tucked-in
delicacy of (the) being in itself against brutal space) is sufficient with many a truly new
procedure analogous in rarefaction to the subtlest features of life" (p. 318).

59. On the (anagrammatic, hymenographic) play between *livre* [book] and *lèvres* [lips],
read over the development opened up in *Crayonné au théâtre* on the House, the Stage, and the
"absent mime" (pp. 334–35).

Perpetual, the rape has always already taken place and will *nevertheless* never have been perpetrated. For it will always have been caught in the foldings of some veil, where any and all truth comes undone.

Indeed: if all the "whites" accrue to themselves the blanks that stand for the spacing of writing—the "blanks" that assume importance—it is always by way of a signifying relay through the white canvas or sail, a cloth that is folded and stitched, the surface on which all marks apply themselves, the sheet of paper where the pen or the wing comes to propagate itself ("Our triumphal frolic, so old, out of the crypt-book / Hieroglyphics that so exalt the multitudes /Propagating with the wing a familiar shiver!" [p. 71]).[60] The blanks are always applied, directly or indirectly, to something woven: whether it be "the white solicitude of our canvas" (*Salut*), "the banal whiteness of the curtains" (*Les Fenêtres*), the white in the *Albums* (where "white reflection" rhymes with "simulation") or in the *fan* poems (". . . wool / . . . white flock"), the white of the bed sheet or the pall, the shroud (extending through a number of texts *between* the "sole fold" in the *Homage* to Wagner and the vellum in the *Overture* to *Hérodiade* ("She sang out, sometimes incoherently, a lamentable / Sign! the bed with the vellum pages, / Such, useless and so cloistral, is no linen! / Which no longer keeps the cryptic folds of dreams, / Nor the sepulcral canopy's deserted moire")) in which the book is wound ("The lovely paper of my ghost / Together sepulcher and shroud / Thrills with immortality, a tome / To be unfurled for one alone" (p. 179)) or in which the Poet is draped ("The flash of a sword, or, white dreamer, he wears a cope, . . . Dante, in bitter laurel, in a shroud is draped, / A shroud . . ." (p. 21)), icy like the paper, or frigid (which rhymes, in one dedication, with "Gide": "Awaiting what he himself will add / You sheets of paper now so frigid, / Exalt me as a great musician / For the attentive soul of Gide" (p. 151)). These veils, sails, canvases, sheets, and pages are at once the content and the form, the ground and the figure, passing alternately from one to the other. Sometimes the example is a figure for the white space on which they are inscribed, that which stands out, and sometimes it is the infinite background behind. White on white. The blank is colored by a supplementary white, an extra blank that becomes, as in *Numbers*, a blank open on all four sides, a blank that is written, blackens itself of its own accord, a false true blank sense [*sens blanc*], without a blank [*sans blanc*], no longer countable or totalizable, counting on and discounting itself at once, a blank that indefinitely displaces the margin and undoes

60. *"Sois, Louys, l'aile qui propages / A quelque altitude ces Pages"* ["Louys, be the wing that propagates / To some altitude these Pages"] (p. 151).

what Richard calls "the unitary aspiration of meaning" (p. 542) or the "sure revelation of meaning" (p. 546). The white veil that slips between the blanks, the spacing that guarantees both the gap and the contact, enables us no doubt to see the blanks; it determines them. It could therefore never be lifted without blinding us to death, either by closing or by bursting. But inversely, if it were never lifted, if the hymen remained sealed, the eye would still have no greater capacity to open. The hymen, therefore, is not the truth of an unveiling. There is no *alētheia*, only a wink of the hymen. A rhythmic fall. A regular, *(w)inclined* cadence.

The dream of the "sure revelation of meaning" proposed to us by *L'Univers imaginaire de Mallarmé* thus appears to be a hymen without a fold, a pure unveiling without a snag, a "felicity of expression" and a marriage without difference. But in this wrinkle-free felicity, would there still be such a thing as an "expression," not to speak of a text? Would there be anything beyond a simple parousia of meaning? Not that, in the absence of such parousia, literature would be an infelicity of expression, a romantic inadequacy between expression and meaning. What is in question here is neither a felicity nor an infelicity of expression—because there is no longer any expression, at least in the ordinary sense of the word. No doubt the hymen, too, would be one of those "beneficent figures" engendered by "the opposition between the closed and the open," "in which both contradictory needs can be satisfied, successively or simultaneously: for example the *fan*, the *book*, the *dancer* . . ."(pp. 26–27). But such dialectical happiness will never account for a text. If there is text, if the hymen constitutes itself as a textual trace, if it always leaves something behind, it is because its undecidability cuts it off from (prevents it from depending on) every—and hence *any*—signified, whether antithetic or synthetic.[61] Its textuality would not be irreducible if, through the necessities of its functioning, it did not do without (deprivation and/or independence: the hymen is the structure of *and/or*, between *and* and *or*) its refill of signified, in the movement through which it leaps from one to another. Thus, strictly speaking, it is not a true sign or "signifier." And since everything that (becomes) traces owes this to the propagation-structure of the hymen, a text is never truly made up of "signs" or "signifiers." (This, of course, has not prevented us from using the word "signifier" for the sake of convenience, in order to designate, within

61. It would be useful to quote in their entirety—and perhaps discuss some of the speculative moments—the analyses put forth by R. G. Cohn concerning what he calls Mallarmé's "antisynthesis" and "dual-polarity" (*L'Oeuvre de Mallarmé*, pp. 41–42 and Appendix 1).

the former code, that facet of the trace that cuts itself off from meaning or from the signified.)

And now we must attempt to write the word *dissemination*.

And to explain, with Mallarmé's text, why one is always at some pains to follow.

If there is thus no thematic unity or overall meaning to reappropriate beyond the textual instances, no total message located in some imaginary order, intentionality, or lived experience, then the text is no longer the expression or representation (felicitous or otherwise) of any *truth* that would come to diffract or assemble itself in the polysemy of literature. It is this hermeneutic concept of *polysemy* that must be replaced by *dissemination*.

According to the structure of supplementarity, what is added is thus always a blank or a fold: the fact of addition gives way to a kind of multiple division or subtraction that enriches itself with zeros as it races breathlessly toward the infinite. "More" and "less" are only separated/united by the infinitesimal inconsistency, the next-to-nothing of the hymen. This play of the integral unit excrescent with zeros, "sums, by the hundreds and beyond," is demonstrated by Mallarmé under the title of *Or* [this word is both a noun signifying "Gold" and a conjunction marking a turning point in an argument.—Trans.] (expert as he was in alloying—in the literal alchemy of such an ironic, precious, and overinflated signifier—the sensible, phonetic, graphic, economic, logical, and syntactical virtues of this stone in which the "two ways, in all, in which our need is bifurcated: esthetics on the one hand and also political economy" intersect (p. 399; cf. also p. 656)):

"OR

. . . The currency, that engine of terrible precision, clean to the conscience, smooth to consciousness, loses even a meaning.

. . . a notion of what sums, by the hundreds and beyond, can be. . . . The inability of numbers, whatever their grandiloquence, to translate, here arises from a case; one searches, with the indication that, when a number is raised and goes out of reach toward the improbable, it inscribes more and more zeros: signifying that its total is spiritually equivalent to nothing, almost."[62]

62. OR, which is condensed or coined without counting in the illumination of a page. The signifier OR (O + R) is distributed there, blazing, in disks of all sizes: "outdoORs" [*dehORs*] "fantasmagORical," "stORe" [*trésOR*], "hORizon," "mORe" [*majORe*], "exteriOR" [*hORs*], not counting the O's, the zeROs, the null opposite of OR, the number of round, regular numerals lined up "toward the improbable." Referring by simulacrum to a fact—everything seems to turn around the Panama scandal ("Those are the facts," affirms the first version, which has not yet erased its referent, "the collapse of Panama." I will study elsewhere the textual operations involved here)—this page, less than thirty-two lines, seems

at least to retain gold as its principal signified, its general theme. *Or*, through a clever exchange, it is rather the signifier that this page treats, the signifier in the full range of its registers, whose orchestration Mallarmé illustrates here and elsewhere. For even the theme, were it present as such, is but another addition to the order of the signifier: not the metallic substance, the thing itself involved in "phraseless gold," but the metal as a monetary sign, the "currency," "signifying that its total is spiritually equivalent to nothing, almost," and which "loses even a meaning" (p. 398).

The whole is mounted in a picture frame, the semblance of a description, a fictive landscape of "fantasmagorical sunsets" whose play of lights would already, indefinitely, arrest the eye on the shadow of its ores. Such "avalanches of gold" (p. 33) methodically defy any phenomenology, any semantics, any psychoanalysis of the material imagination. They systematically outwit and undo the oppositions between the syntactic and the semantic, between form and content, ground and figure, figural and literal, metaphor and metonymy. The demonstration must be announced under the title of khrysis and threads (sons) of gold.

Or, *Igitur*'s ascendancy comes, logically, *before* the consequence [*Igitur* in Latin means "therefore"; thus this adverb-name has grammatical affinities with *or*.—Trans.], but it also, through its etymological ascendants, marks the *hour* (*hora*, which would give a reading not only of all the "hours" and "*ors*" in *Igitur* but also of all Mallarmé's *encor*(es), whether or not they rhyme with *or*: *hanc horam*): ". . . an eclipse: *or*, the hour has come, for here is Pierrot . . ." (p. 751). *Or*, that substantive noun, that adverb of time [*or* also, archaically, means "today," "presently."—Trans.], that logical conjunction, a veritable throw of linguistic dice—Mallarmé's syntax organizes not only its polysemy, its polygraphy, and its orchestral polyphony, but also, most particularly, its out-of-line ex-centricity and its brilliant suspension. I have chosen three examples among many. From the first version: "*or*, because he would not understand, it will be deferred forever." From *Crayonné au théâtre*: "Moved to pity, the perpetual suspense of a tear that can never be entirely formed nor fall (still the lustre) scintillates in a thousand glances, *or*, an ambiguous smile unpurses the lip . . . throughout the labyrinth of anxiety led by art—really not in order to let myself be overcome as if my fate were not enough, a spectator attending a gala; but in order to plunge, in some way, back into the populace . . ." (p. 296). From the *Quant au Livre* (the book being always, as we shall see in a moment, associated with gold): "*Or*—

"The act of folding is, with respect to the page printed large, an indication . . ." (p. 379).

The limits of thematicism, as one could once again verify text in hand (I will not do so here), have never been so striking as in the case of "*or*," and not only because dissemination stands confirmed through the affinity between the seed sown and that very precious substance, because dispersal is goldenly consumed in the Book ("ashes-total-gold-" 32 [A]), but first and foremost because that signifier "loses even a meaning," becomes extenuated, devalued, mined out. Names no longer.

In another vein—to be looked into—*or* colors the bedtime hour of all sunsets, beside all of Mallarmé's "beds"; he also plays on all its tunes: "the golden hues of sundown," from *Petit Air*, ". . . a gold / Is dying according perhaps to the dec*or* / Of unic*or*ns . . . / . . . once m*or*e . . ." from the *Sonnet in* —*yx* (in which the folds of its rhyme alternate with those of the ptyx), the end of the "afternoons of music," "an orchestra only marking with its gold, its brushes with thought and dusk . . ." from *Mimique*. At the end of the sun's course, after-noon, gold repeats and (re)doubles, after midnight, the horror and the aurora. It always serves as their rhyme (through rhythm or through number). "This gold moon-rise . . ." (p. 109) always serves as the closing for—a march. A book: "O golden clasps of olden missals! O hieroglyphs inviolate in papyrus scrolls!" (p. 257). A mine or a tomb: ". . . by the pearly star of their nebulous science held in one hand, and by the golden spark of their volume's heraldic clasp in the other; of the volume of their nights" (*Igitur*, p. 437).

Or—in its impurity—will never simply have been either the dense fullness of sensible matter (or even of music or rays of light, "shafts of vibratory gold," (p. 334)), nor the transparent alloy of a logical conjunction. Molten *or*. Golden time, neither sensible nor intelligible, not even a sign, then, or a signifier or signified; at least as much *"Il Signor," "qui s'ignore"* ["who does not know himself"] (which, in the *Triolets*, rhymes with *"signe, or"* ["sign, gold"]) as it is a sign —*or*, this *or* is consistently mounted according to the double syntax of the goldsmith and the watchmaker, in the golden antre of a glottis (*glossa* can once have had the meaning *gold ingot*, and Littré notes that "the once-held etymology that derives *lingot* [ingot] from the Latin *lingua*, because of its form, still remains possible"). Hearing, seeing, reading: "A hundred posters soaking up the uncomprehended gold of days, a betrayal of the letter . . ." (p. 288).

Has it ever been noted ("buried / Endlessly in blinding scholarly abysses / Unknown gold . . ." p. 470) that the first paragraph of *Igitur* (*the Midnight*) links the words "hour," "*or*," and "gold work," and rereads "the infinite accident of conjunctions"? "Certainly there subsists a Midnight presence. The hour has not disappeared through a mirror, nor has it buried itself in drapes, evoking furniture through its vacant sonority. I remember that its gold [*son or*] was about to feign in absence some null jewel of reverie, something rich and useless that had survived, unless it was that upon the watery and starry complexity of a work of gold the infinite accident of conjunctions could be read.

"This revealer of the Midnight has never before indicated such a conjuncture, for this is the one unique hour . . . I was the hour that has to make me pure."

"Son or" follows right after "vacant sonority." *"Or"* is more than once preceded by the possessive adjective *son* [his, her, its]: which in effect gives us *sonore* ["sonorous"], and which, through an unconscious lateral pressure, transforms the possessive adjective into a noun, *le SON or* ["the sound, 'or' "] and the noun into an adjective, *le son OR* ["the sound *or*"].

The "sound *or*" re-marks the signifier *or* (the phonic signifier: of the conjunction or of the noun, which latter is also the signifier of the substance or of the metallic signifier, etc.), but it also re-marks music. Which is to be expected since music, for Mallarmé, is almost always golden, while *or* is reduced by this play to the vacant sonority—with its chance decor—of a signifier. Thus; "On the credenzas, in the empty parlor: no ptyx, / Abolished bauble of sonorous inanity, / (For the Master has gone to fetch tears from the Styx / With that object alone that is the pride of Nothingness [*dont le Néant s'honore*])/ But near the casement vacant to the north, a gold / Is dying according perhaps to the decor / Of unicorns . . . ," or *Mimique* again: ". . . an orchestra only marking with its gold [*son or*], its brushes with thought and dusk, the detail of its signification on a par with a stilled ode . . ."

One can also bring in the diverse *or*'s from the text on Villiers de l'Isle-Adam: the "gold shield" and the "thread of gold" are spread out under the "heraldic sunset," and strange conjunctions overlay the "jewelry": "*or* such a childlike and powerful amalgam . . ." (p. 483), "*or* here it is, so overwritten it has become a palimpsest, or, I have to say, excessive wear has obliterated the tenor, so that it does not present anything decipherable" (p. 486, cf, also pp. 497–500). In the same vein, in the *Chevelure*, which announces the "jewel of the eye" and the "exploit / Of sowing rubies": "But without *or* sighing that this lively cloud . . ." (p. 53). How could the categories of classical rhetoric possibly account for such displacements? [Not to speak of the categories of translation.—Trans.]

Corresponding to the Oedipal hymen, to the "infinite accident of conjunctions" and of the "conjuncture" in *Igitur*'s *or*, there is "that supreme conjunction with probability" in the SI ["if," "whether," "yes"] or the *Comme SI* ["as IF"] in the *Coup de dés*. Hence—if, in one fell swoop, the plays of *Or* and *Donc* are constellated with the powerful positioning of the Mallarméan SI, an infinite sentence unfolds, suspending itself among SI, OR, DONC, in which the order can as well be reversed from *Igitur* to the *Coup de dés*. (Can one then conclude, as does J. Scherer (in the course of a chapter of his thesis devoted to *The Conjunction* in which none of these three "words" are named) that "conjunctions seldom attract his [Mallarmé's] attention", (p. 127) or "play a role of little importance" (pp. 287)?)

Or—that singular plural, such is the ring of hour and species set in the balance of Mallarmé.

Why does this almost-nothing lose the glint of a phenomenon? Why is there no phenomenology of the hymen? Because the antre in which it folds back, as little in order to conceal itself as in order to denude itself, is also an abyss. In the recoiling of the blank upon the blank, the blank colors itself, becomes—for itself, of itself, affecting itself ad infinitum—its own color-less, ever more invisible, ground. Not that it is out of reach, like the phenomenological horizon of perception, but that, in the act of inscribing itself on itself indefinitely, mark upon mark, it multiplies and complicates its text, a text within a text, a margin in a mark, the one indefinitely repeated within the other: an abyss.

Now [Or], isn't it precisely such writing *en abyme*[63] that thematic criticism—and no doubt criticism as such—can never, to the letter, account for? The abyss will never have the glint of a phenomenon because it becomes black. Or white. The one and/or the other in the squaring of writing. It whitens (itself) in the incline of *A Throw of Dice*.

EVEN WHEN TOSSED UNDER
ETERNAL CIRCUMSTANCES
FROM THE DEPTHS OF A SHIPWRECK
WHETHER
       the Abyss
whitened
     spreads out
       furious
           under an incline
              hovers desperately
                on the wing
                  its own
                    in

advance fallen in its pains to straighten its flight
           and covering the upbursting swell
             leveling off the surging leaps

---

63. TN. The expression *en abyme*, popularized by Gide, was originally used in heraldry to designate the status of the figure of a small shield used to decorate a shield. Now used whenever some part of a whole can be seen as a representation of that whole, often ad infinitum, as in the Quaker Oats box on which a man holds up a Quaker Oats box on which a man . . . etc.

very inwardly sums up
the shadow buried in the deeps by this alternative sail
to the point of adapting
to the span
its gaping depth as the hull
of a structure
listing to one or the other side...

Thus reconstituted in each of its stitches, the hymen still echoes from every side. Reflecting, for example, *A la nue accablante tu* (*To the crushing nude cloud silenced*). If one repeats a fragment here and there, hearing what resonates from one side to the other, counting the A's, as white as foam, here perhaps is what the hymen will always have disseminated ("tossed under..."): SPERM, the burning lava, milk, spume, froth, or dribble of the seminal liquor. I shall now underline a number of letters, reserving the A's and the *Tu*'s, along with the sonnet's form, for some future reading:

To the crushing nude cloud silenced
Basalt base of bass and *lava*
Even through the slavish echoes
By a *trumpeting sans virtue*

What *sepulchral shipwreck* (you do
Know it, *spumy* depths, but *drivel*)
One supreme *between* the flotsam
Can *abolish* the *bare masthead*

Or this that in (de)*fault furious*
Of some sort of *high perdition*
All the *vain abyss unfolded*

In the hair *so white* that straggles
Avariciously will *drown* the
Childlike haunches of a *siren.*[64]

64. TN. The original French text with Derrida's emphasis is:

A LA NUE accab*lante* tu
Basse de basalte et de *laves*
A même les *échos* esclaves
Par une *trompe sans vertu*

Quel sépulcral *naufrage* (tu
Le sais, *écume*, mais y *baves*)
Suprême *une entre* les épaves
Abolit le *mât dévêtu*

While it is not exhausted by it, no more than is the affirmation of any text, this sonnet articulates both the scenography and the syllabary of the double session. Which is condensed there, and indefinitely displaced, much more than is required by the efforts of any "commentary." Dissemination skims and froths the flight and theft of the seminal: a vain, blank loss in a wet dream in which the masthead, *pour qui le lit* [*for the one that reads / for which the bed exists*], blots itself into abysses of lost veils, sails, and children. *A « bo / lit*.[65] The *"so white."*

In a demonstration that leaves no room for doubt, Robert Greer Cohn has reconstituted the links in the chain that unites the white with the seminal, both through direct attribution and through the semic constellation of milk, sap, stars [*étoiles*] (which so often rhyme with *sail / veil* [voile]) or through the milky way that inundates Mallarmé's "corpus."[66] And let us reread once more: "to seek support, according to the page, upon the blank space, which inaugurates it . . . for an ingenuousness . . . and, when, in a break—the slightest, disseminated—chance is aligned, conquered word by word, indefectibly the white blank returns. . . . Virginity . . . divided into its fragments of candor, the one and the other, nuptial proofs of the Idea" (p. 387). And reread the letter to Cazalis (1864): " . . . terror, for I am inventing a language that must necessarily arise from an extremely new poetics" but then further on: "I would never touch my quill again if I were floored. . . . Alas! the baby is going to interrupt me. I've already been interrupted once by the presence of our friend—toward whom, even, the imp of perversity pushed me to act very bitter, I don't know why—. And then the weather is so sad and grey, a time when

> *the drowned poet dreams of obscene lines.*

"I've even written some, but I won't send them to you, because the nightly emissions of a poet ought to be milky ways, and mine are just shameful stains."

Ou cela que *furibond faute*
De quelque *perdition haute*
Tout l'*abîme vain* éployé

Dans le *si blanc* cheveu qui traîne
Avarement aura *noyé*
Le *flanc enfant* d'une sirène

65. TN. *A/bo/lit*. The word *abolit* means "abolishes." A homonym would be *à beau lit*, ("with/to a beautiful bed"). A related expression would be *(il) a beau lire*, ("he reads in vain"). Again, a certain obliteration marks the bed and the page, sleeping and reading, copulation and interpretation.

66. See Cohn, *L'Oeuvre de Mallarmé*, esp. pp. 137–39.

And to Régnier, in September 1893, he writes: "I am also reworking my deepest stores and whitewashing, by drinking milk, my inmost cell."

Appearances to the contrary, the endless work of condensation and displacement does not end up leading us to dissemination as its ultimate meaning or primary truth. The emission here is not that of a message: Mallarmé's *dispersal*. Following a pattern we have already experienced in the "*entre*," the quasi-"meaning" of dissemination is the impossible return to the rejoined, readjusted unity of meaning, the impeded march of any such *reflection*. But is dissemination then the *loss* of that kind of truth, the *negative* prohibition of all access to such a signified? Far from presupposing that a virgin substance thus precedes or oversees it, dispersing or withholding itself in a negative second moment, dissemination *affirms* the always already divided generation of meaning.[67] Dissemination—spills it in advance.

67. No more than can castration, dissemination—which entails, entrains, "inscribes," and relaunches castration—can never become an originary, central, or ultimate signified, the place proper to truth. On the contrary, dissemination represents the affirmation of this nonorigin, the remarkable empty locus of a hundred blanks no meaning can be ascribed to, in which mark supplements and substitution games are multiplied *ad infinitum*. In *The Uncanny*, Freud—here more than ever attentive to undecidable ambivalence, to the play of the double, to the endless exchange between the fantastic and the real, the "symbolized" and the "symbolizer," to the process of interminable substitution—can, without contradicting this play, have recourse both to castration anxiety, behind which no deeper secret (*kein tieferes Geheimnis*), no other meaning (*keine andere Bedeutung*) would lie hidden, and to the substitutive relation (*Ersatzbeziehung*) itself, for example between the eye and the male member. Castration is that nonsecret of seminal division that breaks into substitution.

It should not be forgotten that in *Das Unheimliche*, after having borrowed all his material from literature, Freud strangely sets aside the case of literary fictions that include supplementary resources of *Unheimlichkeit*: "Nearly all the instances which contradict our hypothesis are taken from the realm of fiction and literary productions. This may suggest a possible differentiation between the uncanny that is actually experienced (*das man erlebt*), and the uncanny as we merely picture it (*das man sich bloss vorstellt*) or read about it (*von dem man liest*)" [Freud, *On Creativity and the Unconscious*, ed. Benjamin Nelson (New York: Harper & Row, 1958) p. 155] "The Uncanny as it is depicted in *literature*, in stories and imaginative productions (*Das Unheimliche der Fiktion—der Phantasie, der Dichtung*—) merits in truth a separate discussion" (p. 157). ". . . fiction presents more opportunities for creating uncanny sensations than are possible in real life (*die Fiktion neue Möglichkeiten des unheimlichen Gefühls erschafft, die in Erleben wegfallen würden*). . . . It is clear that we have not exhausted the possibilities of poetic license and the privileges enjoyed by story-writers in evoking or in excluding an uncanny feeling" (p. 160). (To be continued)

"Appearing there then as half	"hemisphere
two halves of a troop"	—and the monster eye
[17(A)]	that looks at them—
	but something still they
	lack" [18(A)].

We will therefore not return to dissemination as if it were the center of the web. We return to it, rather, as to the fold of the hymen, to the somber white of the cave or of the womb, to the black-on-white upon the womb, [68] the locus of scattered emissions, of chances taken with no return, of separations. We will not follow up the "arachnoid thread."

Like Mallarmé (pp. 308–82 and elsewhere), Freud encountered the riddle of the butterfly. Let us pin it down with a couple of indications, in order to be able to reread it later, perhaps. It is in *Wolf Man*: "His fear of the butterfly was in every respect analogous to his fear of the wolf; in both cases it was a fear of castration. . . . He was also informed that when he himself was three months old he had been so seriously ill . . . that his winding-sheet had been got ready for him. . . . The world, he said, was hidden from him by a veil; and our psychoanalytic training forbids our assuming that these words can have been without significance or have been chosen at haphazard. The veil was torn, strange to say, in one situation only; and that was at the moment when, as a result of an enema, he passed a motion through his anus. He then felt well again, and for a very short while he saw the world clearly. The interpretation of this 'veil' progressed with as much difficulty as we met with in clearing up his fear of the butterfly. Nor did he keep to the veil. It evaporated into a sense of twilight, into '*ténèbres*,' and into other impalpable things. It was not until just before taking leave of the treatment that he remembered having been told that he was born with a caul. . . . Thus the caul was the veil which hid him from the world and hid the world from him. The complaint that he made was in reality a fulfilled wish-phantasy: it exhibited him as back once more in the womb. . . . But what can have been the meaning of the fact that this veil, which was now symbolic but had once been real, was torn at the moment at which he evacuated his bowels after an enema? . . . If this birth-veil was torn, then he saw the world and was re-born. . . . The necessary condition of his re-birth was that he should have an enema administered to him by a man. . . . Here, therefore, the phantasy of rebirth was simply a mutilated and censored version of the homosexual wish-phantasy. . . . The tearing of the veil was analogous to the opening of his eyes and to the opening of the window. . . . The wish to be born of his father . . . , the wish to present him with a child—and all this at the price of his own masculinity— . . . in them homosexuality has found its furthest and most intimate expression." And this note: "A possible subsidiary explanation, namely that the veil represented the hymen which is torn at the moment of intercourse with a man, does not harmonize completely with the necessary condition of his recovery. Moreover it has no bearing upon the life of the patient, for whom virginity carried no significance." (A rather strange remark, when we are talking of someone who wanted to "return to the womb," at least.) [Freud, *Three Case Studies*, ed. Philip Rieff (New York: Collier Books, 1963), pp. 288–94.]

From the butterfly's wing to the hymen, via the head hooded with a caul. In the meantime, one can refer to the "veil of illusion" and the "hood" ["*coiffe*"] from the *Coup de dés*—and elsewhere—to the "hymen" from *Pour un tombeau d'Anatole* [*For Anatole's Tomb*] (ed. J. P. Richard, Paris: Seuil, 1961): to the son: "... to us / two, let us make / an alliance / a hymen, superb / — and the life / that remains in me / I will use it for— / no mother / then? ..." (leaves 39–40) "child, seed / idealization" (16) "the double side / man woman / — sometimes for / profound union / one, for the other, whence / and you the sister / " (56–57).

68. Follow for example the play of the "finger" (the die, *datum* or *digitum*) in the *Prose des fous* (Mysticis Umbraculis) which "trembled" next to the "navel," "and her flesh seemed like snow on which, / While a golden ray lit the forest, / The mossy nest of a gay goldfinch had fallen" (p. 22).

As soon as one has recognized, from all the disseminated webs, the fold of the hymen—with all that this supplement is henceforth woven of—one has read not only the "nubile folds" in the *Tombeau de Verlaine* but also the endless multiplication of folds, unfoldings, foldouts, foldures, folders, and manifolds, along with the plies, the ploys, and the multi-plications. Every determinate fold unfolds the figure of another (from the leaf to the sheet, from the sheet to the shroud, from the bed to the book, from the linen to the vellum, from the wing to the fan, from the veil to the dancer, to the plumes, to the leaflet, etc.) and of the re-mark of this fold-upon-itself of writing. It would be easy to verify the preceding demonstration for the polysemy of the fold: under the constraints of the differential-supplementary structure, which constantly adds or withdraws a fold from the series, no possible theme of the fold would be able to constitute the system of its meaning or present the unity of its multiplicity. If there were no fold, or if the fold had a limit somewhere—a limit other than itself as a mark, margin, or march (threshold, limit, or border)—there would be no text. But if the text does not, to the letter, exist, then *there is* perhaps a text. A text one must make tracks with.

If there were no text, there would perhaps be some unimaginable "felicity of expression," but there would no doubt be no literature. If literature—the literature Mallarmé still produces under that name, allowing for the reservations set forth above concerning "literarity" (the essence or truth of literature)—is engaged in this fold of a fold, then it is not a mere subsection of foldedness: it can give its name to anything that resists, within a given history, the pure and simple abolishing of the fold. Anything that resists being used as an example:

> The Mallarméan figure of the *fold*, for example, enables us to join the erotic to the sensible, then to the reflexive, to the metaphysical, and to the literary: the fold is at once sex, foliage, mirror, book, and tomb—all are realities it gathers up into a certain very special dream of intimacy. (Richard, p. 28)

But the fold is not a form of reflexivity. If by reflexivity one means the motion of consciousness or self-presence that plays such a determining role in Hegel's speculative logic and dialectic, in the movement of sublation (*Aufhebung*) and negativity (the essence is reflection, says the greater *Logic*), then reflexivity is but an effect of the fold as text. In a chapter called *Reflexivity*, Richard analyzes the fold along the dialectical, totalizing, eudemonistic lines we have already questioned. He turns the fold, so to speak, only in the direction of the "very special dream of intimacy," toward the reserved, protected, "modest" insides of self-consciousness ("Conscious of itself, intimacy becomes reflexivity"):

> To reflect intellectually is already to fold in upon oneself. . . . The folding-back also protects a secret dimension of the object; it reserves an inside for being. . . . The fold is perfect then because intimacy can dwell there in both the security and the equality of the exact adequation of two *sames*, and in the shimmering, the active consciousness, born of the encounter between two *others*. Each self possesses itself in an other it nonetheless knows to be only another self. At the farthest reach of Herodiade's narcissism, and doubtless even more perfect than that because it would introduce into the reflexive circuit the exciting presence of pseudo-otherness, there exists perhaps in Mallarmé the temptation, entirely on the mental level, of what would elsewhere be called homosexuality. . . . Within the folded object—book, bed, wing—the intimate space annuls itself with so much intimacy: the self and its image are no longer separated, as in a mirror, by any distance. (Pp. 177–78)

Even supposing that the mirror does unite the self with its image, this analysis, while not in truth unjustifiable, deliberately and unilaterally closes the fold, interprets it as a coincidence with self, makes opening into the precondition of self-*adequation*, and reduces every way in which the fold also marks dehiscence, dissemination, spacing, temporization, etc. This confirms the classical reading of Mallarmé and confines his text within an atmosphere of intimism, symbolism, and neo-Hegelianism.

Dissemination in the folds of the hymen: that is the "operation." Its steps allow for (no) *method*: no path leads around in a circle toward a first step, nor proceeds from the simple to the complex, nor leads from a beginning to an end ("a book neither begins nor ends: at most it pretends to" [the "Book" 181 (A)]). "All method is a fiction" (1869, p. 851).

We here note a point/lack of method [*point de méthode*]: this does not rule out a certain marching order.

Which does not get under way without our investing, at the risk of losing it, a pretty penna.[69] If—as a folded sail, candid canvas, or leaflet—the hymen always opens up some volume of writing, then it always implies

---

69. We ought doubtless to have untangled the threads of this penna [*penne*] sooner: it is also, as we shall see, a term used in weaving. We turn again to Littré, from whom we have never, of course, been asking for the *truth*:

"1. PENNE, s.f. 1. The name given to the long wing- and tail-feathers of birds. The wing pennae are called remiges and the tail pennae, rectrices, on account of their particular

and implicates the pen [*plume*]. With the range of all its affinities (wing, bird, beak, spear, fan; the form sharpened into an *i* of all the points: swan, dancer, butterfly, etc.), the quill brings into play that which, within the operation of the hymen, scratches or grafts the writing surface—plies it, applies it, stitches it, pleats it, and duplicates it. "Your act is always applied to paper" (p. 369). It would be difficult to count Mallarmé's changes of pen, from writing quills to ostrich plumes, from the "feathered cap" of *Le Guignon* [*The Jinx*], the histrion's quill which in the *Pitre Châtié* [*Chastised Clown*] "pierced a window in the canvas wall" ("As a quill . . . I pierced"), the feather in Hamlet's toque (p. 302), all the feathers, wings, plumages and ramifications in *Hérodiade*, the "feathery candor" in *l'Après-midi d'un Faune* [*Afternoon of a Faun*], the "instrumental plumage" in *Sainte*, all the way to the "solitary erratic quill" in *A Throw of Dice*, standing alone, except for "except," on one page facing the following, in which we have lined up the words, flattening the typographical syntax ("solitary erratic quill /except / if a midnight toque meets or brushes it / and immobilizes / in the velvet rumpled by a somber chuckle / this rigid whiteness / laughable / in opposition to the sky / too much / not to mark / exiguously / whichever one / bitter prince of the reef / covers his head with it as if donning the heroic / irresistible but contained / by his little virile reason / thunderstruck/"), along with all the swords, wings, daggers, stems, etc.[70] Turn to *Hérodiade*

functions; the former execute the flight, the latter direct it. . . . 2. A term of falconry. The large feather of birds of prey. 3. *Penne marine*, a species of zoophyte also called "sea feather." 4. (Heraldry) . . . Sometimes said of the feathers of an arrow. E. . . . from the Latin *penna*, feather, wing. . . . In French there is another *penne* signifying cloth, from the Latin *pannus*.

"2. PENNE, s.f. 1. Weaver's term. The beginning, the head of the chain. Penne threads: threads that remain attached to the loom after the cloth has been removed. . . . 2. A thick wool cordon fixed as a tassel at the end of a baton. E. Lower Breton, *pen*, end, head.

"3. PENNE, s.f. 1. Name of a type of beam. 2. Nautical term. One of the two rods composing the lateen yard or the main yard. E. Probably same as *penne* 2; that is, from the Celtic *pen*, head, end."

To this we will add not the definition of *penis* but that of "PÉNIL, s.m. *Anatomy*. The part in front of the pubic bone, the lowest part of the abdomen. . . . 'The bone called in Latin *os pubis* is called in French the *os du pénil* or *os barré*,' (Paré, IV, 34). In Provençal, *penchenilh*. The Provençal word undoubtedly comes from a form derived from the Latin *pecten*, which, in addition to signifying "comb," also has the sense of *pubes*. But through the form *panil* it tended to become confused with the common word *panne* or *penne*, meaning cloth, rag. This can also be seen in *penilien*, which signified both the *pénil* and a type of clothing. In Brittany, *pénille* signifies the frayed edges of a piece of worn clothing: 'please cut off these *pénilles*.' "

70. For a list of all these *plumes* and an analysis of this plumage or pen-box, cf. R. G. Cohn, pp. 247 ff. As far as its further implications are concerned, let us merely note that the raising of the quill always marks the imminence or the occurrence of its fall. We have the "terrible struggle against that mean old plumage now fortunately laid low: God" from the famous letter to Cazalis, the "faithful plumage" in the *Sonneur* [*Bell Ringer*] ("... worn out

and reread how much writing is gathered up, in its vicinity, by *"Une d'elles"* ["one of these"] p. 42. Elle, aile, L: masculine/feminine.

In the *Notes and Documents* that follow the chapter entitled *Toward a Dialectics of Totality*, Richard fans out the array of feathers (including the fan) in a series of pages of great beauty, moving from their angelic (seraphic) value to their "Luciferian, or at least Promethean, signification" (p. 445). Near the end of this extensive note (which is almost four pages long), following a parenthetical remark concerning the "phallic allusion" that Robert Greer Cohn "sees in the feather," Richard expresses some mistrust of a certain extension of polythematicism. Here is his justification: "For the word *plume* [feather] has also been understood to be the *plume* [pen] of the *writer*, and it is particularly upon this analogy that R. G. Cohn has founded his whole exegesis. This relation, which is certainly possible, appears to us, however, to remain unproven: the analogy seems excessively conceptual, both in its origin and especially in the details of its consequences. It seems to me difficult, and contrary to the genius of Mallarmé, to read *A Throw of Dice* as a literal allegory (even if, as Cohn would have it, that allegory is charged with spontaneous echoes and more or less conscious ambiguities). On this double meaning of *plume*, however, see the following text from

---

from having pulled in vain / O Satan, I shall move the stone and hang"), the "heraldic plumage" and "black plumage" in *Herodiade*; beside the "naked gold" and "Aurora," there are "my two featherless wings / — At the risk of falling for all eternity?" in *Les Fenêtres* [*Windows*]; "Black, with a pale bleeding wing, deplumed, / Through the glass burnt with incense and gold, / Through the icy panes, alas! mournful still / The dawn threw itself on the angelic lamp. / Palms! . . ." (*Don du Poème* [*Gift of a Poem*]), ". . . the plumage is caught" (*Le vierge, le vivace . . .* [*The virgin, vivacious . . .*]), the hat "without feathers and almost without ribbons" of "my poor wandering beloved" (*La pipe*), ". . . the expected interval, having, indeed, the double opposition of the panels as its lateral partitions, and, facing out, in front and in back, the null-doubt opening reflected by the extension of the sound of the panels, where the plumage escapes, and doubled again by the explored equivocity . . ." (*Igitur*). There is an opposition between black and white: *jet* (and its homonyms *geai* [jay], *jet* [water spout], *j'ai* [I have]) is a black substance or glass that can be painted white. The evening gown is a vision of plumes and jet ("Evening gowns . . . trimmed either with gauze or with embroidered tulle, and then with borders of white jet and feathers, with jet fringes, indeed with every possible trimming for a ballroom gown: can be worn at the theater, at a Grand Dinner, at an Intimate Evening, *but open in a square or quite squarely, never decolleté*" (p. 781, emphasis Mallarmé's); but the bridal gown is featherless, there is only a "veil of generality," like the dancer's hymen (*Rejoinder* II): ". . . the ancient custom of feminine attire par excellence, white and vaporous, as it is worn at a Wedding. . . . It is not loud, a Bridal Gown: it is remarked, as it appears, mysterious, following and not following the fashion . . . with brand new details enveloped by generality as by a veil. . . . A veil of fine tulle [*tulle illusion*] and orange blossoms skillfully woven into the hair. The whole is worldly and virginal. . . . Your ringlets will drop their curls in the space between two wings. A brilliant conception, isn't it?" (pp. 763–64).

1866: ' . . . I am very tired of work, and the nightly *plumes* I pull out of myself every morning to write my poems with do not grow back again by afternoon' (Corr. p. 219)."

Why should a "literal allegory" be "contrary to the genius of Mallarmé"? What *is* Mallarmé's genius? Does the idea of a "literal allegory" imply a monosemy that would reduce all quills to the writer's pen? But Cohn is conducting a completely different operation: he is establishing a network that *also* passes through the "phallic allusion." (Interestingly, despite the proximity of his references, Richard dissociates the "phallic allusion" by putting it in parentheses, and dissociates further from that "allusion" the critical paragraph we have just quoted.) Then, too, what is an "excessively conceptual analogy"? Why should what is "possible" be improbable? What is the nature of a proof of thematic affinity? Even without quoting the whole textual mass whose network Cohn displays (and which would provide us with quasi-certainty if recourse to such norms had any pertinence here), why wouldn't the text cited as a "however"—which confirms at least once[71] the possibility in question—give us reason enough to suppose that the writer's quill is always, on however virtual a level, implied and implicated in the cloth, wing, or tissue of every other kind of feather? This letter of 1866 (to Aubanel), juxtaposed with the one to Cazalis, will not fail to produce certain grotto effects. "Nightly emissions" and "nightly *plumes*": the solitary quill errs through a semblance of milky ways.[72] An operation (1 + 0 + 0) in which it expands its identity to exhaustion.

These grottal effects are usually also glottal effects, traces left by an echo, imprints of one phonic signifier upon another, productions of meaning by reverberations within a double wall. *Two* with no *one*. Always one extra, or one too few. The decisive, undecidable ambiguity of the syntax of "any more" [*plus de*] (both supplement and lack).

Are we letting go of the pen?

In the final paragraph of the same note, which is just as isolated as the one we have just cited, from which it is separated by a whole development,

71. Other examples can be found in the *Autobiographie* (p. 661) and in the *Bibliographie* to the 1898 edition of the poems ("studies with an eye toward something better, as one might try out the nibs of one's pen [*plume*]"), etc.

72. TN. A number of wordplays are lost here. The original sentence—*La plume solitaire et (est) perdue dans un semblant de voie lactée*—literally means: "The solitary (lost) quill (is lost) in the semblance of a milky way." Behind the sentence stands its homonym, *plume solitaire éperdue* ["solitary erratic quill"] from the *Coup de dés*. In addition, the idea of *loss* is lost when *pertes nocturnes* [literally, "nocturnal losses"] is translated, as here, "nightly emissions." In this text in which what is added is zeros, it is perhaps no accident that what is lost in translation is, precisely, losses.

Richard adds a "phonetic" detail. Everything would lead one to believe that he considers it a purely accessory curiosity: "And finally, phonetically, the word 'plume' seems to have lent itself to a very rich play of imaginary associations in Mallarmé's mind. A few pages of notes included by Bonniot in his edition of *Igitur* (Paris: N.R.F., 1925) reveal that this one word was linked to a reverie on the personal pronouns (and thus associated with the dream of subjectivity) and to the related image of the upward surge ("*plus je—plume—plume je—plume jet*" ["more I—quill—quill I—quill jet of water"]. *Plume* is also a cousin of *palm*" (p. 446). These notes published by Bonniot are also quoted by Cohn (p. 253).

We include here a reproduction of that page.[73] Even assuming, which we do not, that only a secondary, reserved attention need be paid to the

---

73. This page makes apparent, among other things, the beveled construction of *Igitur*, in which the anagrammatical calculus of forms ending in –URE (*pliure* [fold], *dechirure* [tear], *reliure* [binding]) is even more condensed than elsewhere. This is the grating sound of the file of erasure. *Erasure* belongs to lite*rature* and even rhymes with it (pp. 73, 109, 119,

"spontaneous echoes" and "more or less conscious ambiguities"—do we find many of those in this play of the plume?

I also recall here the *"plume . . . j'ai troué"* ["quill—I pierced"; "j'ai" sounds like "jet."—Trans.] in the *Chastised Clown*, and the cluster composed of *j*'s, jet, echo, more, plume, and wing, turning like a gull, carried along on a play of the *winds*:

> Her American lake where the Niagara winds,
> The winds have been frothing the sea-grass, which pines:
> "Shall we any more mirror her as in times past?"
> For just as the seagull, o'er waves it has passed,
> Enjoins joyous echoes or drops a wing feather,
> She left her sweet mem'ry behind her forever!
> Of all, what remains here? What can one show?
> A name! . . . (*Her grave is closed*, 1959, p. 8).[74]

298), as well as with *Igitur* (which plays on *ci-gît* [here lies] combined with doors—*fors* [outside], *hors Tur* [outside the door], the "sepulchral door," the enclosure of tombs and of sleep, of *sommes* ["(we) are," "sums," "naps"], "it was the scansion of my measure, a reminiscence of which came back to me prolonged by the noise in the corridor of time at the door of my sepulcher, and by my hallucination . . ." (p. 439), and including the words "luminous suture," "hour," "former," "grandeur," "pure"—"I was the hour that has to make me pure," "furniture," *heurt* ["bump"] (at least six times), "endure," "pallor," "aperture," "future," "aura," "superior," "pasture," etc.). An anagrammatical hallucination, delirium, folly [*folie*], an anagram of phial [*fiole*] ("the empty phial, folly, all that is left of the castle?"). A crisis of the phial, but, it is worth remembering, also a phial of verse [*vers*] ("The Dream has agonized in this phial of glass [*verre*] . . ." p. 439). The seminal play of *coupes* ["cuts/cups"] (pp. 27 and 178): phial, vial, violate (p. 59), veil, *vol* [flight], *col* [neck] ("Would sow upon my veil-less neck [*col sans voiles*] / More kisses than there are stars [*étoiles*] / Than there are stars in the sky!"). *Voile-étoiles-voie lactée-voile*: masculine / feminine. [*Voile* can either be masculine, meaning "veil," or feminine, meaning "sail." The milky way (*voie lactée*) can also be seen as both masculine (scattering of starry sperm) and feminine (milk).—Trans.] *Dorure* [gilding]. [The word *"dorure,"* which combines both *or* and *ure*, thus punctuates these word plays as a superbly condensed anagram for what is going on in footnotes 62 and 73.—Trans.]

74. "Wing feather [*plume de l'aile*] . . . her memory [*souvenir d'elle*]" ["aile" (wing) rhymes with "elle" (she, her).—Trans.]. The unfolding of this aviary and of this fan is perhaps infinite. Just to give an Idea of this *défi d'ailes* ["challenge of the wings"; *ailes* also sounds like *l*'s.—Trans.]: there is always a supplementary *l*. One *l* too few (produces a fall) or one *l* too many forms the fold, "a spacious writing . . . folds back the too-much-wing" (p. 859), guarantees the flight of the "winged writing" (p. 173), of the "Wing that dictates his verses" (p. 155). The wing, which can be "bleeding" (blank sense) and "featherless" (p. 40), can also at times be held as a quill ("Hold my wing in your hand," p. 58), "in the event that the written word be threatened, and [it] summons the literary Supremacy to erect in the form of a wing, with forty courages grouped into one hero, your brandishing of frail swords" (p. 420). And eventually, later on, to conjugate *i* with *l*. Henceforth he [*il*] will have, himself/lit up [*lui*], gathered up his powers. *l:i*—. [*lit* = "reads," "bed."—Trans.]

These plays (on "plume," on "winds," etc.) are anathema to any lexicological summation, any taxonomy of themes, any deciphering of meanings. But precisely, the crisis of literature, the "exquisite crisis, down to the foundations," is marked in a corner of this cast-off excess. The figure of the *corner* [*le coin*], with which we began, would testify to this in all the recastings and retemperings that have marked its course (an angle, an open recess, a fold, a hymen, a metal, a monetary signifier, a seal, a superimposition of marks, etc.). The *coin-entre*. If this crisis is indeed one of verse, it is first and foremost because the formal structure of the text, which is called *verse* in Mallarmé's logical generalization of it, is precisely what historically organizes, with the omission of the author (*plus je*), just such a form of excess. It has often been said that Mallarmé, without apparently having made many actual innovations in this domain, constructed his entire literary praxis out of the necessities of verse and rhyme: that is, once these two concepts have been transformed and generalized, upon repercussions set off among signifiers, which are in no way dictated or decided in advance by any thematic intentionality. Rhyme—which is the general law of textual effects—is the folding-together of an identity and a difference. The raw material for this operation is no longer merely the sound of the end of a word: all "substances" (phonic and graphic) and all "forms" can be linked together at any distance and under any rule in order to produce new versions of "that which in discourse does not speak." For difference is the necessary interval, the suspense between two outcomes, the "lapse of time" between two shots, two rolls, two chances. Without its being possible in advance to *decide* the limits of this sort of propagation, a different effect is produced each time, an effect that is therefore each time "new" [*neuf*], a game [*jeu*] of chance forever new, a play of fire [*feu*] forever young [*jeune*]—fire and games being always, as Heraclitus and Nietzsche have said, a play of luck with necessity, of contingency with law. A hymen between chance and rule. That which presents itself as contingent and haphazard in the *present* of language (this is a question raised by *English Words*: "Beforehand, we must define this point: the Present of Language" [p. 1049]) finds itself struck out anew, retempered with the seal of necessity in the uniqueness of a textual configuration. For example, consider the duels among the *moire* [watered silk] and the *mémoire* [memory], the *grimoire* [cryptic spell book] and the *armoire* [wardrobe]: while they might function in one singular way and have only one textual outcome in the *Homage* to Wagner, they are nevertheless open to a whole chain of virtualities including *miroir* [mirror], *hoir* [heir], *soir* [evening], *noir* [black], *voir* [to see], etc.

These spacings and repercussions are put forth by Mallarmé both as contingency ("a reciprocity of fires that is distant or presented on the bias as some contingency") and as "chance conquered,"[75] as the interlacing, by verse, of the necessary with the arbitrary. And we find ourselves back in the *Crise de vers* ("Now, a subject, fated . . ."): "The pure work implies the elocutionary disappearance of the poet. . . . The makeup of a book of verse occurs innate or everywhere; it eliminates chance; it is still needed in order to omit the author; now, a subject, fated, implies, among the assembled pieces, a certain accord concerning the spot in the volume that corresponds. There is a susceptibility rationally proportional to the fact that each cry possesses an echo—the motifs belonging to the same movement will

75. We refer the reader here to the last two pages of *Quant au Livre* (pp. 386–87). These pages are inexhaustible; one should return to them again and again. The scattered quotations we have cited ought now to be gathered together. But we have not yet even pulled out this one, which conducts them, to be seen, or heard, or read: "The abrupt, high plays of the wing, will be mirrored, too; the one that conducts them, perceives an extraordinary appropriation of structure, in its limpidity, in the primal cataclysms of logic. A stuttered utterance, as the sentence appears to be, here ploughed down beneath the use of subordinate clauses, is multiplied, composed, and lifted into some superior equilibrium, where planned inversions balance each other out." Just above, we find the statement of the law of pivoting or undecidability, the "alternative that is the law." "What pivot, I understand, in these contrasts, for intelligibility? A guarantee is needed—
"Syntax—"
To guarantee intelligibility is not to assure univocity. It is, on the contrary, to calculate—through simple syntactic linkages—the precise play of an indefinite theft, flight, fluctuation, or acrobatics of meaning. *Entre, hymen,* and *le lit* are far from being the only examples of this play. Jacques Scherer (pp. 114–16) has pointed out many words that can alternately take on different grammatical functions within the same sentence, sometimes verb and adjective (*continue* ["continues" or "continuous"]), sometimes verb and noun ("offer"). I would add that Mallarmé himself has stated the law governing this procedure. That statement occurs in connection with the interjection, which Mallarmé so often employs to well-calculated effect. The monosyllabic *or* is an example of this rich alloy. While postponing the study of what *Les Mots anglais* still owes to historical linguistics, let us lift out this quotation (in which Mallarmé defines a law of three states): "Primordial laws . . . Here they are. The Aryan, Semitic, or Turanian involve the genetic distribution of Language, but another one, which models its phases more directly upon the development of forms themselves, would be: Monosyllabism, like Chinese, which is certainly a primitive stage, then Agglutination, or that junction analogous to what juxtaposes two Compound Words among themselves or adds Affixes to the Body of a Word almost without alteration, and finally Flexion, or the elimination of certain intermediary or final letters in contractions or case declensions. Whether it be this isolation pure and simple of the unalterable Word, or this copulation of several Words whose meanings are still discernible; everything down to the very disappearance of meaning, which leaves only abstract, empty vestiges to be accepted by thought, is but an alloy of life with death, a double means, both facticious and natural; *or,* to each of these *three states*, rich with all their consequences, there corresponds some aspect of English. It is Monosyllabic in its original vocabulary, which takes on that status in the passage from Anglo-Saxon to the King's English; one could even call it interjectional, the same identical word often serving as both verb and noun" (pp. 1052-1053).

balance each other out, reaching, at a distance, their equilibrium, neither the incoherent sublime of Romantic verses on the page, nor that artificial unit once measured into the book as a block. Everything becomes suspense, fragmentary disposition with alternation and face-to-face, concurring in the total rhythm, which would be the poem silenced, in the blanks; . . ." (pp. 366–67).

It is neither the natural arbitrariness nor the natural necessity of the sign, but both at once, that obtains in *writing*. It must be written. And sometimes the very gambols of Language itself bring this to the attention of the poet "or even the canny prose writer" (p. 921). Just before wondering whether "strict observance of the principles of contemporary linguistics will yield before what we call *the literary point of view* . . ." Mallarmé had led up to the question of alliteration via onomatopoeia: "A bond so perfect between the meaning and the form of a word that it seems to produce a single unified impression, that of its success, on both mind and ear, is frequent, but occurs especially in what is called ONOMATOPOEIA. Would one believe it: these admirable words, all of a piece, find themselves placed, relative to others in the language (we shall make exception for words like TO WRITE, which imitates the scratching of a pen as far back as the Gothic WRITH), in a condition of inferiority" (p. 920).

Hence, the practice of versification is coextensive with literature, which "goes beyond genre" (p. 386) and exceeds, in its effects and in its principle, the bounds of the vulgar opposition between prose and poetry: ". . . the form called verse is simply in itself literature; there is verse as soon as diction is accentuated, rhythm from the moment there is style" (p. 361). ". . . in Verse, the dispenser and organizer of the play of pages, the master of the book. Visibly, if its integrality appears, among the margins and the blanks; or else it is dissimulated, call it Prose, nevertheless it remains, if there is any secret pursuit of music in the reserve of Discourse" (p. 375).

The crisis of verse (of "rhythm," as Mallarmé also puts it) thus involves all of literature. The crisis of a *rythmos*[76] broken by Being (something we

---

76. In thus carrying the conjoined question of rhythm, rhyme, and mime to the *limits* of both the philosophical and the critical, one ought to include the lateral approaches provided by the following associations: (1) the definition of the literary, or more exactly, of verse, by rhythm (". . . the literary game par excellence; for the very rhythm of the book, which then would be impersonal and alive right down to its pagination, juxtaposes itself with the equations of this dream, or Ode," p. 663). "Verse is everywhere in language where there is rhythm, everywhere, except on posters and on the fourth page of newspapers. Within the genre called prose, there are lines of verse, sometimes admirable lines, of all rhythms. But in truth, there is no such thing as prose: there is the alphabet and then there are verses that may be more or less finely wrought . . ." (p. 867); (2) the relation between the rhythmic

began by spinning off in a note toward Democritus) is "fundamental." It solicits the very bases of literature, depriving it, in its exercise, of any foundation outside itself. Literature is at once reassured and threatened by the fact of depending only on itself, standing in the air, all alone, aside from Being: "and, if you will, alone, excepting everything."

Thus: rhythm, decline, inclined cadence, decadence, *fall* and return: "For, ever since that white creature ceased to be, strangely and singularly, I have loved everything summed up in the word: fall. Thus, in the year, my favorite season is the very last languid days of summer that come immediately before autumn, and, in the day, the time I choose for walking is the moment when the sun rests just before sinking, when there are rays of yellow copper on the grey walls and of red copper on the windowpanes. In the same way, the kind of literature in which my spirit looks for pleasure will be the dying poetry of Rome's final hours, as long, however, as it in no way breathes with the rejuvenating approach of the Barbarians and does not stammer out the childish Latin prose of the early Christians" (*Plainte d'Automne* [*Autumn Lament*] p. 270).

Literature, all along, in its exquisite crisis, shivers and flaps its wings, and goes trembling through the great divestment of a winter. I found myself wondering at first what might have prompted a title as strange as *Crise de vers*. Sensing that it harbored other virtual associations, I varied or toyed with certain elements. Unfailingly, the *i* and the *r* remained: *crise de nerfs* or *hystère* [hysterics], "*bise d'hiver*" or "*brise d'hiver*" [winter winds] (cf. the play on "winds" and the winter atmosphere in *Sa fosse est fermée* [*Her Grave is Closed*]), added to "*bris de verre*" [sliver of glass], which retains a glint of so many other Mallarméan "*brisures*" [breaks], reflecting a certain "*bris de mystère*" [whiff of mystery] ("Yes, without the folding back of the paper and the undersides this installs, the shadow dispersed in the black lettering would present no reason to emanate like a whiff of mystery, on the surface, in the parting prodded by the finger" [pp. 379–80]).

These associations are consonant with the first paragraph of *Crise de vers*. Like *Mimique*, like *Or*, that essay begins with the simulacrum of a descrip-

---

cadence—or case— and all the falls, including the silent fall of the pen ("memorable rhythmic case," p. 328). "There falls / the pen / the rhythmic suspense of the sinister / to become buried / in the original spume / not long ago from which delirium with a start leaped to a peak / withered / by the identical neutrality of the gulf / NOTHING / of the memorable crisis . . ." (pp. 473–74); (3) the play between rhythmic suspense and mimic suspense, between rhythm and laughter ("*or*, the hour has come, for here is Pierrot . . . the Verse which, always clownish, exquisite, sonorous, splits into a moon from ear to ear or withdraws back into a rosebud, what with each smile or laugh contained in its syllables alone, moves the mouths of Mimes delighted to speak; and to speak with rhythm" [p. 751]).

tion, a scene without a referent. In all three cases, moreover, the music reserved for that opening spot consists in preparations for a finale: the evening in *Mimique* ("Silence, sole luxury after rhymes, an orchestra only marking with its gold, its brushes with thought and dusk . . . "), the "sunsets" in *Or*, and the winter afternoon in *Crise de vers*, spent in a glassed-in library with its closed bookshelves from which one has read all the books, shelf after shelf of old-fashioned literature, a "swishing of brochures" in a wintry atmosphere of icy paper and of open tombs, during a storm perceived through the pane of a window, a tempest seen from inside a glass:

"Just now, letting myself go, with the lassitude produced by one dispiriting afternoon of bad weather after another, I let drop, without curiosity seemingly having read everything twenty years ago, the fringe of multicolored pearls that smooths the rain, again, upon the swishing of brochures in the library. Many a work, beneath the beaded glass curtain, will line up its own scintillation: I love to follow, as in a ripened sky, against the glass, the play of lights of a storm" (p. 360). In an illusion of lights and swishings, you will almost have seen, in a burst of lightning, what a scintillation has flashed by—by him who seems to have read it all. Unless it (he) has rained (reigned).

Like *Mimique* (1886–1891–1897) and like *Or*, *Crise de vers* composes its transformations in three beats (1886–1892–1896). Among the three afternoons, the fabric is very tightly woven. In *Pages* (1891), what is to become the first paragraph of *Mimique* follows two other paragraphs beginning thus:

"Winter is for prose.

"With the splendor of autumn, verse ceases. . . .

"Silence, sole luxury after rhymes. . . ." (P. 340)

In this atmosphere bespeaking the end of history, the exhausted library plays out, swishing, all its scales; during the flood, it is swept away and yet protected by the thin transparent casing of a pane of glass [*verre*], by the fortunes of a verse [*vers*] or hymen; it is threatened with being eaten away from the inside.[77] The pane of glass, which serves as both an insulator and a

---

77. The opposition between metaphor and metonymy, which is an entirely semantic opposition, is deconstructed in practice by the superficial, profound, that is, abyssal operation of *versification* (*ver* [worm] —*vers* [toward]—*vers* [verse]—*versus*—*verre* [glass]), a constant process of fragmentation and reconstitution (*hiver* [winter]—perverse—reverse—verso—traverse—vertigo—reverie). All possible condensations and displacements are tried out by "Mr. Mallarmé. Who quite perversely / Left us for a breath of woodland charm / My letter, do not follow him aversely / To Valvins, near Avon, in the Seine-et-Marne." The network of these effects of versification would necessarily include the translation of Poe's "Conquerer Worm" [*le Ver vainqueur*] ("An angel throng, bewinged, bedight in veils . . . Sit

contact between the library and the turmoil, reflects all Mallarmé's other windows and mirrors, and affords a view, inside, of "many a work, beneath the beaded glass curtain." Beads [*verroterie*]: little bits of minutely worked *verre* (or *vers*) strung together like fragile poems, a "fringe" of "multicolored pearls," like a work that "will line up its own scintillation." Abolished baubles. A ptyx.

A sampling of feathers (and) of glass in *la Dernière Mode* [*The Latest Fashion*] will retemper the swishing alloy made out of winter and glass: "Breastplates, braces, corselets, etc., the whole charming, defensive getup that has long pervaded feminine attire will not discontinue the use of jet, with its steely scintillations, nor abandon steel itself, either. While not neglecting the rich array of feathers: natural rooster, peacock, and pheasant feathers along with ostrich plumes sometimes dyed blue or pink, we have continued to believe (here our predictions differ from those of others) that for the length of the winter the use of sequins, beads, and metal will go on" (p. 832).

All this intimate space, however, seals itself off only so as to remark a certain historical storm—the crisis—the final inanity of that of which there will never again be quite so much. It is the end and repetition of a year, a cycle, a ring. And the return of a rhythm: "Chimera, to have thought of that attests, through the reflection of its scales, to what extent the present cycle or last quarter century is undergoing some absolute strike of lightning—whose disheveled showers running down my windows wash across the streaming turmoil, until it illuminates this—that, more or less, all books contain the fusion of a few numbered rephrasings: and there might even be but one—in the world its law—bible as it is simulated by each nation" (p. 367).

I thus began to sprinkle the crisis of verse with splinters diverse: with slivers of glass, with bits of pearl, with "whiffs of mystery," with icy "winds" and dispiriting weather, with libraries and rain in winter [*hiver*]—*hi/ver*, *win/ter*, the sounds reflect, repeat, and condense the opposition in which they are found (I/R [*Crise de Vers*]), the function of the descriptive back-

---

in a theater / . . . Mimes, in the form of God on high . . . The mimes become its food, / And the angels sob at vermin [(!)—Trans.] fangs / In human gore imbued "[*Great Tales and Poems of Edgar Allan Poe* (New York: Pocket Books, 1956), pp. 397–98]), the rhyme between *vers* and *pervers* (p. 20), *envers* ("*vierge vers* / . . . *a l'envers* [p. 27]), *travers* (pp. 29 and 152), and *hivers* (pp. 128 and 750). One can also follow that "luxury essential to versification, which enables it, in certain places, to space itself out and disseminate itself" (p. 327) in "*Surgi de la croupe et du bond* / *D'une verrerie éphémère* / . . . / . . . *ni ma mère* . . ." and in "*Une dentelle s'abolit*/ . . . / *Qu'absence eternelle de lit* / . . . / *Telle que vers quelque fenêtre* / *Selon nul ventre que le sien* / *Filial on aurait pu naître*" (pp. 74 and 333).

ground periodically becoming an element in the abyss, a décor made to be carried away by repetition, made to engage there the whole of the library, the literature of yesteryear [*hier*], missing the V of the hymen.

In order to set up the library behind *Crise de vers*, the "author" has offered us its "bibliography." The *Bibliographie* appended to *Divagations* notes: "*Crise de vers*, a study from the *National Observer*, reincluding some passages omitted from *Variations*: the fragment 'An undeniable desire in my time . . .' appeared separately in *Pages*." The Pléiade editors add: "The first three paragraphs of *Crise de vers* reproduce: 1. the opening lines of one of the Variations on a Subject, which appeared in the September 1, 1895, issue of *La Revue blanche* under the title: VIII, *Averses ou Critique* [*Downpours or Criticism*]. . . ."

The word *Averses* thus operates like a hidden line linking the crisis of literature to the crisis of criticism, to rain, to winter, to the storm, to the *reversal* of the golden age. A seasonal cycle with seasonable weather. Winter facts [*faits d'hiver*: sounds like *faits divers*, "news items," the title of another of Mallarmé's series of articles.—Trans.]. Mallarmé was unlikely to miss the channel running between *averse* and the English word *verse*, not only because that second language is always superimposed in some way on his syntax and vocabulary[78] but also because *Crise de vers* was originally published in the *National Observer*. Like the *Grands Faits Divers* [*Great News Items*] (in which *Or* is found).

The crisis of the alternative, of the binary opposition, of the *versus* (V), is thus inscribed in an atmosphere of death and rebirth, an atmosphere both funereal and joyous. It is a moment of wakefulness [*veille*], a wake for the dead, an awakening of birth, a watch [*veille*] and an eve [*veille*], a hymen between yesterday and tomorrow, a waking wet[79] dream on the eve of now.

78. This is not just a biographical fact. Witness the author's view of the subject in a context in which he discusses the theoretical question: "First and foremost, where are we French situated, when we undertake to study English? . . . There is a difficulty both here and there for anyone not gifted with universal knowledge, or not English; *or*, what should one do? Study English simply from out of French, since one has to stand somewhere in order to cast one's eyes beyond; but nevertheless check first whether this vantage point is a good one. . . . Reader, you have before you this, a piece of writing . . ." (*Les Mots anglais*, p. 902). "You have seen announced in our Preliminaries the third case of linguistic formation, which is neither artificial nor absolutely natural: the case of a quasi-formed language poured into an almost-formed language, a perfect mix occurring between the two. . . . Grafting alone offers an image that can represent the new phenomenon; indeed, French has been grafted onto English: and the two plants have, all hesitation past, produced on the same stalk a magnificent and fraternal generation" (p. 915), born of an "indissoluble hymen" (p. 914).

79. *Veille mouillée*: again, we encounter *Les Mots anglais*, and are forced to begin rereading. "There is not one consonant in French, nor even any vocal gesture of greater complexity, that is not represented, by one or several letters, in English: except the *L mouillée*

[palatalized]. Should we just change the pronunciation of a large number of our vocables by saying the two LL's as one, emitted in its ordinary way? that is too easy a subterfuge: for while our case consists in the modulation of a very weak, invisible I *after* the single or double L, the fact is that the said I always appears in writing *before*. Read *eventa-i-l, ve-i-lle, fam-i-lle*, and *dépou-i-lle*. Three solutions offer themselves to the recalcitrant foreign organism: to eliminate the I, as in APPAREL, CORBEL, COUNSEL, and MARVEL, for E; and MALL (a *mail*), MEDAL, PORTAL, RASCAL (from *racaille*), REPRISAL with A: or to join the I, making a diphtongue, to the preceding vowel, as in DETAIL, ENTRAILS, etc. (prounounced ai-l). And if one language gives in and bends to imitate the other, it will be, precisely, by moving the same *i* from before to after, that is by offering an image of our pronunciation, as we have analyzed it above: MEDALLION, PALLIASSE (a *paillasse*), PAVILION, VALIANT, and VERMILION. There is a total indifference to the number of L's, both there and in our case, the question focusing where I have placed it: on the I. It can nevertheless be said, to the detriment of the terminal *mute E* and to the benefit of this fundamental I, that while the latter is necessarily kept and the former sometimes dropped, the simple IL does not remain without some reminiscence of the *palatalized sound [son mouillé]*" (pp. 981–82). And, as close as can be to the L, *son mouillé*, is the M, an upside-down double V ("you have before you this, a piece of writing"), of which all the examples, without exception, bend to the law of the *hymen* and of *mimique*. We shall cite not the examples but only the statement of the law: "A letter which, while it can precede vowels alone or indeed the full range of diphtongues, begins as great a number of English words as any other, M translates the power to make or do, hence a joy at once male and maternal; next, according to a signification springing from the distant past, it indicates measure and duty, number, meeting, fusion, and the middle term; and finally, through a change that is less abrupt than it appears, it can imply inferiority, weakness, or anger. All these meanings are very precise and do not group a multiple commentary around the *m*" (p. 960).

We had earlier, interrupting the flight of the dancer (*Rejoinder* II), suspended the case of the *i*. It must have appeared daring and risky—indeed, wasn't it?—to read the little point cut off—decapitated, unglued—from the body of the *i*, from the jabbing, dancing pointed toe, right beside the castrated pike or pointer, above. Since it is now possible to glimpse what goes (on) between the pen and its head, nib (*bec*), or end (*pen*), it is time to clarify this point. The rule is that nothing be touched on the spot [*séance tenante*]. Since what is in question is *one*—body proper.

Might Mallarmé not have been blind to what cuts the *i* off from what is proper to it? Perhaps; although the question of "eliminating the I," of the "benefit of this fundamental I," "the question focusing where I have placed it," would seem to indicate some attention on his part. In any event, he did not neglect the reverse of this figure: the sub-scribed point of exclamation! His syntax so often plays with it, interrupting the flow of a sentence with this strange pause, this disconcerting hiatus. He preferred it, in its verticality, to suspension points. And he saw in it the scanned agitation of a quill, head down:

About the exclamation point.
"Dujardin, that point is drawn
So as to imitate a plume." (p. 168)

And finally, the capital I — isn't it the English *je*, the ego (echo and looking-glass of the self)? *Les Mots anglais*: "I, *je*, Lat. ego; ice, *glace*; . . ." (p. 925). And the extra-text from *Igitur*: *écho — ego — plus-je*, etc.

The I (capitalized) disseminates in advance the unity of meaning. It — multiplies it, deploys it, fans it out in the rainbow of the signifier, *iridesces* it. Instead of wondering whether the I of Idea is hypostatized in the orbit of Plato or Hegel, one ought to take into account its literal (I + Dé) *irisation* ("the capacity of certain minerals to become iridesent," Littré).

A filing question [*Question de la lime*]: *Idée* rhymes, cross-grained (or-referenced), with *orchidée*, which rhymes with *décidée* (pp. 92 and 171). *Gloire du long désir, Idées* ["Glory of the

The *Homage* to Wagner is teetering there, too. Here, the mortal remains are those of Victor Hugo. But in both texts we find the same structure, the same words, the same veil and fold and "a little bit, its rending." The same underside worn through, traversed, reversed, versified, diversified.

In a hymen depending on the verse, blank once more, composed of chance and necessity, a configuration of veils, folds, and quills, writing prepares to receive the seminal spurt of a throw of dice. If—it were, literature would hang—would it, on the suspense in which each of the six sides still has a chance although the outcome is predetermined and recognized after the fact as such. It is a game of chance that follows the genetic program. The die is limited to surfaces. Abandoning all depth, each of the surfaces is also, once the die is cast [*après coup*], the whole of it. The crisis of literature takes place when nothing takes place but the place, in the instance where no one is there to know.

No one—knowing—before the throw—which undoes it (him) in its outcome—which of the six—(die falling).

---

long desire, Ideas"] rhymes with *La famille des iridées* ["The iris family"] (p. 56). The iris, the flower absent from all bouquets, is also the goddess of the rainbow and a membrane in the eye [(!) —Trans.] ("The conjunctiva extends over the white of the eye up to the circle called the iris," Paré), etc.

Or how is a reading decided?

Displaced almost at random — but that is the law, for along with delirium one *wants* writing — dislocated, dismembered, the "word" is transformed and reassociated indefinitely. Le *dé lit l'idée, le dais, ciel de lit, plafond et tombeau, dé à coudre tous les tissus, voiles, gazes, draps et linceuls de tous les lits de Mallarmé, "lit aux pages de vélin," "absence éternelle de lit" ("lit vide," "enseveli," "aboli," "litige," etc.). Il l lit. Il l l'I. Il se renverse dans (le) lit. Il se sépare dans l'I "* . . . *d'où sursauta son délire jusqu'à une cime l flétrie l par la neutralité identique du gouffre l* RIEN *de la mémorable crise* . . ."

TRANCE PARTITION (2)

phal: but it foreshadows, in financial terms, the future credit, preceding capital or reducing it to the humility of small change! With what disorder are such things pursued around us, and how little understood! It is almost embarrassing to proffer these truths, which imply neat, prodigious dream transfers, thus, cursively and at a loss."

Mallarmé

"The words of Harlequin, introducing himself, are as follows:

"I HAVE COME TO HAVE THEM EXTRACT FROM ME THE LAPIS PHILOSOPHALLUS."

Increasing the silence after each segment of the sentence . . .
A short pause after: I have come—a long one after: from me—a still longer one, indicated by a suspension of gestures on: -phallus."

Artaud

Dissemination

First version published in *Critique* (261–62), 1969. The text was there accompanied by a preliminary editorial note, which we here reproduce: "The 'present' essay is but a tissue of 'quotations.' Some are in quotation marks. Generally faithful, those taken from *Nombres* [*Numbers*] by Philippe Sollers are written, unless otherwise indicated, both in quotation marks and in italics (Editor's note)."

I

*not so much
that it does not enumerate
upon some vacant superior surface
the successive bumping
sidereally
of a total account in process of formation*

Some such other enumeration, altogether squarely written, would nevertheless remain undecipherable.

This is a question we are posing, knowing it—were it not already repeated from further away and from later on—to be yet unreadable, protruding like a toothing-stone, waiting for something to mesh with. And like a cornerstone, as it can, by chance or by recurrence, be gathered from the registering of certain trade-marks.

1. The Trigger [*Le déclenchement*]

DÉCLENCHEMENT, n. 1. The automatic release of a mechanism. 2.
Any device in a position to engage or to stop the moving parts of a
machine. 3. The act of triggering the motion of a machine by means
of such a device.

DÉCLENCHER, v. tr. 1. To lift the latch of a door in order to open
it. . . . 2. To trigger; to effect a *déclenchement*. R. Sometimes written
déclancher, which is an error since the verb derives from the noun
clenche [latch]. In lower Normandy, popularly used to mean: to
speak. "*Il est resté une heure sans déclencher*" ("He stayed for an hour
without unclenching his teeth").

Littré

These *Numbers* enumerate themselves, write themselves, read themselves.
By themselves. Hence they get themselves remarked right away, and every
new brand [*marque*] of reading has to subscribe to their program.

The text is remarkable in that the reader (here in exemplary fashion) can
never choose his own place in it, nor can the spectator. There is at any rate
no tenable place for him opposite the text, outside the text, no spot where
he might get away with *not* writing what, in the reading, would seem to
him to be *given, past*; no spot, in other words, where he would stand before
an already *written* text. Because his job is to put things on stage, he is on
stage himself, he puts himself on stage. The tale is thereby addressed to the
reader's body, which is put by things on stage, itself. The moment
"therefore" is written, the spectator is less capable than ever of choosing his
place. This impossibility—and this potency, too, of the reader writing
himself—has from time immemorial been at work in the text in general.
What here opens, limits, and situates all readings (including yours and
mine) is hereby, *this time at last*, displayed: as such. It is shown through a
certain composition of overturned surfaces. And through an exact material
mise en scène.

Or rather—since this sort of exhibition and the "as such" of phenomena are no longer in the last instance in control here, but are rather being maneuvered as inscribed functions and subordinate mechanisms—what is in question here, this time at last, finds itself not displayed but given play, not staged but engaged, not demonstrated but mounted. Mounted with a confectioner's skill in some implacable machinery, with "consummate prudence and implacable logic."

Mounted: not in a mechanism that has this time at last become visible but in a textual apparatus that gives way, gives place, and gives rise, on only one of its four series of surfaces, to the moment of visibility, of the surface as what is facing out, of presence as what is face-to-face, thus calculating the opening, counting out the phenomenon, the in-person-ness, the being-in-flesh-and-blood, in a theater that takes the un-representable into account this time and

> "The Read.
>   or
> each term
> concealing and revealing

pages] <u>Theater</u>......

that, with the help of the <u>Book</u>

The whole thing modernized....

. . . .

according to Drama . . . ," which is something that can be exhausted neither in the presentation nor in the representation of anything whatsoever, even though it *also* opens up the possibility and formulates the theory of such presentations and representations. And it does so in one single movement that, however highly differentiated, is unified and unique.

This time at last. "This time at last" does not mean that what had always obscurely until now been sought has finally, in a single blow—a stroke of the pen or a throw of dice—been accomplished. Nothing could be more foreign to any eschatology, particularly any eschatology of or by way of literature, than the finite-infinite seriation of these numbers. What is being effected is on the contrary a generalized putting-in-quotation-marks of literature, of the so-called literary text: a simulacrum through which literature puts itself simultaneously at stake and on stage.

"This time," as the reader has already been able to gather, expressly stands for the multiplicity—the entirely intrinsic multiplicity—of an event that is no longer an event since its singularity, from the word go, is doubled, multiplied, divided, and discounted, immediately concealing itself in an unintelligible "double bottom" of nonpresence, at the very moment it seems to produce itself, that is to say, to present itself.

Because it begins by repeating itself, such an event at first takes the form of a story. Its first time takes place several times. Of which, one, among others, is the last. Numerous and plural in every strand of its (k)nots (that is, (k)not any subject, (k)not any object, (k)not any thing), this first time already is not from around here, no longer has a here and now; it breaks up the complicity of belonging that ties us to our habitat, our culture, our simple roots. "In *our* country," says Alice, "there's only one day at a time." Hence, it would seem that what is foreign would have to reside in repetition.

"*1. ... Air / « Because of something said in another language, accentuated, repeated, sung—and straightway forgotten—, I knew that a new story had been triggered off. How many times had that happened?*"

The story that seems to be thus triggered off—for the first, but innumerable, time—then begins to function according to modalities in which death is affiliated with the (metaphor of the) textual machine in which ultimately

"*4.92.(. . . all is effaced before this volume, this functioning without a past, without a body... All is lost and nothing is lost; you find yourself back without anything, yet steadier, quickened, cleansed, irrigated, changed, and deader...)*"

Born of repetition ("*something said...repeated...*") even in its first occurrence, the text mechanically, mortally reproduces, ever "*steadier*" and "*deader*," the process of its own triggering. No one is allowed on these premises if he is afraid of machines and if he still believes that literature, and perhaps even thought, ought to exorcise the machine, the two having nothing to do with each other. This technological "metaphor"—technicity as a metaphor that transports life into death—is not added as an accident, an excess, a simple surplus, to the living force of writing. Or at any rate it is necessary to account for the possibility of what comes to inscribe itself here as an extra, a supernumerary that, instead of falling outside of life or perhaps in its very act of falling, provokes these *Numbers*, deploys that "living force" by dividing it, making room for it, enabling it to speak. Plugging it in and triggering it off:

"*3. ... ... and this game was using me as one figure among others . . . the operation of which I was the object . . .*"

"4. (... *the text is interrupted, folds back upon itself, lets the voices come back like an endless recording*—...)"

"2.10. ... *just as I knew that something had gotten underway that I could no longer stop...*"

"4.12. (*for as soon as the first propositions are introduced into the mechanism, as soon as the minimum program is decided upon and plugged into you, nothing is going to remain motionless, nothing is going to be spared, avoided, concealed... Everything repeats itself and returns, repeats itself and still returns, and you are entrained in this chain of earth and air and fire and blood and stone; man and woman alike, you are all caught in these deranged permutations...*)—"

"4.16. (...*This is evidently what the mechanism is trying to say, what the machine wants to show in its changes, without any need to decipher the story or the interpretation it cancels out in its way of being at every moment and all at once... It is a functioning difficult to grasp in its way of sliding, breaking off, and bringing together, in its lack of a center or goal, in its ramified tissue of laws*)—"

"2.18. ...*All that was necessary was to be plugged into it through her...*"

"4.20. (...*the peak of the effect triggered off when, after having located the three animate surfaces, you turn toward the fourth, is thus characterized by multiplied violence ...*)—"

"3.43. ... ... *Nothing could resist the story thus triggered off...*"

"2.46. ... ... *What was opening up by means of me thus remained nameless, threatened, and yet more and more assured, pushing, growing, and triggering fear within fear and at the same time a global distancing, a new beginning... Upon questioning and, on the level of time, rediscovering certain living terms like so many germs, there was thus a beating envelope and I was on its border, one dead person among many that designated their deaths by all the disjoined bodies on the living surface on which death inscribes itself... That indication could be presented simply: 'for the future, a detour through the imperfect'—but it was most particularly a matter of a needle, a dull ray going directly through each organ, at the point at which each is necessarily glued to its own explosion, which is directly plugged into the outside...*"

"2.62. ... *Those among us who had disappeared could nevertheless be detected in the overall productivity; they held onto their active, diffuse position, and that indeed was the political reality of the operation that had been triggered off, the side where nothing could be isolated, where nothing could cross the crumpled flange ...*"

"4.64. (... *The orient thus slipping underneath the page, being there in the beginning... you yourself caught up in a rotation that is, as it were, historical; sent back upon the appearance of reports and relations summed up on the page but which immediately trigger off its bashing-in, the arrival of new forces bearing the reason for inequalities in development...*)—"

"4.76. (... *All of that being thought out in an ever more active retreat, a black,
thoughtless, dreamless retreat flowing out of the depths of the tissue where each face
appears directly plugged into the utilization of the volumes, in the crucible that, in
sum, becomes generalized:* . . . .)"

Et coetera, for everything in this text is generalized in sum. The *triggering*
(which unclenches the teeth of discourse, loosens the teeth of the machine,
allows the face to speak, feigns a frontal exposure, a face-to-face view,
whereas it simultaneously entrains the face toward enumeration by *plugging*
it [*en le branchant*] into the numbers tree and the square roots) takes place
much more often, at stages that are much more numerous. You will be
expected—let us mark it here in the hollow of a mute, invisible angle
(about which more later)—to measure, to sum up, in a statistical accumulation of "quotations," the well-calculated, rhythmically regulated effects of
a recurrence. Like the constraints of that angle, this accumulation will be
the only means, not of presenting, but of feigning to present the text that,
more than any other, writes and reads *itself*, presents its own reading,
presents its own self-presentation, and constantly deducts this incessant
operation. We will hence be inscribing—simultaneously—in the angles
and corners of these *Numbers*, within them and outside them, upon the
stone that awaits *you*, certain questions that touch upon "this" text "here,"
the status of its relation to *Numbers*, what it pretends to add to "that" text in
order to mime its presentation and re-presentation, in order to seem to be
offering some sort of review or account of it. For if *Numbers* offers an account
of *itself*, then "this" text—and all that touches it—is already or still "that"
text. Just as *Numbers* calculates and feigns self-presentation and inscribes
presence in a certain play, so too does what could still with a certain irony be
called "this" text mime the presentation, commentary, interpretation,
review, account, or inventory of *Numbers*. As a generalized simulacrum,
this writing circulates "here" in the intertext of two fictions, between a
so-called primary text and its so-called commentary—a chimera, as it
would have been called by the disappearing author of that *Mimique* in which
the "idea" is certainly not what one thinks, nor is its illustration: "The
scene illustrates but the idea, not any actual action, in a hymen (out of
which flows Dream), tainted with vice yet sacred, between desire and
fulfillment, perpetration and remembrance: here anticipating, there recalling, in the future, in the past, *under the false appearance of a present*. That is
how the Mime operates, whose act is confined to a perpetual allusion
without breaking the ice or the mirror: he thus sets up a medium, a pure
medium, of fiction."

The mirror in which these *Numbers* are read, in its capacity for seeing you, will of course be broken, but it will reflect that breaking in a fiction that remains intact and uninterrupted.

If "this" moment in the fiction comes back to itself, asks itself about its own power, and attempts a passage toward the other, it can therefore only do so by fitting itself into the angles between the surfaces of *Numbers*, along the line of an opening/closing (since angles open and close at once), in the inter(sur)face of the spaces that are already filled and prescribed by *Numbers*, in (the) place of the articulation between one surface and another, one tense and another. Not that the angle of articulation itself is an absent or invisible theme, far from it. It is in fact, in *Numbers*, quite insistent and blue, of a blue that is illegible outside a deliberately distributed chromatic system. It is a *"night"* that *"was nothing other than this insistent, blue passage of all the tenses into each other, the twist, for example, through which the present and the imperfect communicate among themselves without remarking each other..."* (1.5).

Hazarding themselves out into that night, pressing into the corners that squarely relate the three surfaces of the imperfect to the single surface of the present, our superadded inscriptions will only, in the end, have succeeded in re-marking the passage itself in its own insistence, repeating the square by the closing of the angle, fictively loosening the rigor of the text through the opening of another surface of writing to come, in a certain play of the cardinal points or the hinges (*cardo* = hinge) that has been triggered off. What sort of angle is this angle writing? concave? projecting? an angle of reflection? Because we cannot yet know what that will all have meant, let us put "this" writing forth as a kind of *angle remark*, considering all lines broken.

We thereby remark, as far as the statistical reading just outlined is concerned, that such a reading has already been thoroughly authorized by the text itself: these *Numbers*, with intended frequency, proclaim themselves the contemporaries and inhabitants of *"cities—where the mute machines are henceforth capable of reading, deciphering, counting, writing, and remembering—..."* "We are living in this city (this book)" (*Drama*).

As a way of introducing this book of self-rejoining, self-escaping repetition, as a way of designating the strange logic that will be articulated in it, "this time at last" thus does not point to some unique ultimate accomplishment but also to a displacement and a rift, to the open system consisting of the repetition of rifts.

Whence the continued impossibility of choosing one's place and the even greater difficulty of getting one's bearings in it. Yet the impossibility thus mounted is never simply stated, no more than it was ever simply *shown*. It is not declared merely as a *theorem*, even though, on occasion, in the form of reinscribed logicomathematical statements (Hilbert, Frege, Wittgenstein, Bourbaki, etc.), the latent proposition is sometimes roused through the enormous, condemned margins of our domestic library (Islamic, Mexican, and Indian mythologies, the Zohar, the Tao Tö King; Empedocles, Nicholas of Cusa, Bruno, Marx, Nietzsche, Lenin, Artaud, Mao Tse-tung, Bataille, etc.; and within another margin, more internal or less visible, effaced: Lucretius, Dante, Pascal, Leibniz, Hegel, Baudelaire, Rimbaud, and others). The impossibility is *practiced*.

What is to be said about this praxis? If to produce is to draw out of darkness, to bring to light, to unveil or to manifest, then this "practice" does not content itself with the act of making or producing. It cannot be governed by the motif of truth whose very horizon it *frames*, for it is just as rigorously accountable for *non*production, for operations of nullification and deduction, and for the workings of a certain textual zero.

2. The Apparatus or Frame

> "It is these weights and measures, these frames, these meridians,
> and these artificial horizons which, in their very construction,
> possess a kind of rigor that is absolute and general, mathematical."

Within the system of this strange countable practice, the one who is ultimately accountable, the single, unique accountant, will be no less than the reader, or even the author, whom you will not be in a position to name. *Numbers*—in which the weakness that would consist in the naming of works and authors (as you have just done for a moment as a concession) is prohibited—*Numbers* begins by putting the signer's name in an umbra, *"in the column of numbers, of names in the umbra"* (4.52). The old theatrical organization has become unjustifiable, is no longer answerable to anyone; the old phantoms called the author, the reader, the director, the stage manager, the machinist, the actor, the characters, the spectator, etc., have no single, unique, fixed place (stage, wings, house, etc.) assigned to themselves by themselves, except in the representation they make of it to themselves, of which an account must be given. That is where the story (history) will have taken place, if it takes place, where something will have been seen, recounted, summed up as the meaning or presentable substance of the book.

But these *Numbers* dismantle such a representation; they take it apart as one deconstructs a mechanism or as one disconcerts the self-assured pretensions of a claim. At the same time, in this very gesture, they assign a determinate place to what they take apart, granting it a relative position within the general movement of the apparatus. Classically speaking, this place would be that of illusion and error, about which Spinoza and Kant have demonstrated, along paths that are as different as one could wish, that it is not enough to become aware of them in order for them to cease to function. Such moments of awareness belong in the category of theatrical effects. One might even, prudently, take the analogy further, whether in the direction of the illusion necessary for perception, inherent in the very structure of sensible presentation, or in the direction of a transcendental illusion at play within the very law that constitutes the object, that presents the thing as an object, as that which stands opposite me, facing me.

In the *frame* of the text, one side of the square, one surface of the cube will represent this nonempirical error, this transcendental illusion. More simply put, it will *represent*: it will be the opening to the classical representative scene. In representing representation, it will reflect and explain it in a very singular mirror. It will speak representation, proffering its discourse through a kind of "square mouth," "oblivion closed by the frame."

You will ceaselessly be required to take this structural illusion into account. You should remark here only that it does not arise as an aberrant error, an uncontrollable disorientation, or a capricious contingency of desire. On the contrary, it has to belong to a necessity inscribed *in situ*, within the overall organization and calculable functioning of the topography, so that the theater can finally succeed in being cruelly generalized, so that no nonplace whatsoever is left out of it, so that no pure origin (of creation, of the world, of the word, of experience, of all that is present in general) can stand guard over the stage as if derived from the intactness of some absolute opening. If that which, once it is framed, appears to be an element or an occurrence of opening is no longer anything but an aperture-effect that is topologically assignable, then nothing will indeed have taken place but the place.

Out. Any attempt to return toward the untouched, proper intimacy of some presence or some self-presence is played out in illusion. Because illusion, as its name already implies, is always an effect of play; and also because illusion entails a theater in which a certain definite relation between the unrepresentable and representation is engaged. And lastly because the whole of the text, as in *Drama*, is through and through put into play, powerfully reinstituting the square horizontality of the page, of the "checkerboard serving as a figure for time," of that "invisible chessboard," within the theatrical volume of a certain cube. Within this hanging-in-the-balance with its numerous intersecting planes, he who says *I* in the present tense, in the so-called positive event constituted by his discourse, would be capable of only an illusion of mastery. At the very moment he thinks he is directing the operations, his place—the opening toward the present assumed by whoever believes himself capable of saying *I*, I think, I am, I see, I feel, I say (you, for example, here and now)—is constantly and in spite of him being decided by a throw of dice whose law will subsequently be developed inexorably by chance. *Déclenchement*: a release, an opening, the unlatching of a door, which has a lock, a padlock, and keys that from now on you ought not to forget; and *cadre* [frame]: an inscription in a square; hence, an opening comprehended and reflected in a quadrangle, a squared opening, a certain singular mirror, which awaits you. Once again it is the city, with its doors and mirrors, the labyrinth:

> "1.17. ... *And just as one might in darkness approach the busy night life of a city surrounded by nothing, just as one might find oneself willed by a throw of dice into one of the bad squares of the forgotten game, just as some combination of numbers chosen at random might open this or that armored door, just so did I enter back into my own form without having foreseen what awaited me... The frame in which I found myself was of course impossible to fill if one evoked only the millions of stories that were in the process of unfolding... the millions of sentences spoken, transmitted, or fleetingly at work in the process... This was a new form of torture raised to the second degree, which traversed all the living inhabitants of that time, opened up the possibility of their eyes and their words...*"

And, in order that you not lose all trace of the key nor of a certain clasp toward which you are being led, behind a "black mirror":

> "3.15. ... *Also saying: 'the palace is furnished with fifty doors. These are open upon all four sides, forty-nine in number. The last door is not on any side and it is not known whether it opens upward or downward... All these doors have a single lock and there is only one little opening into which the key can be introduced, and that spot is indicated only by the trace of the key...' "*
>
> "3.35. ... *and once again I found the key, and each time it was with the same surprise at discovering how to walk and knowing how to walk...*"

The illusion—that is to say, the truth, of that which seems to present itself as the thing itself, facing me, in the entirely "natural," ceaselessly self-regenerating opening of my face or of the scene on stage—will therefore have been only an effect of what is often called the *"apparatus"* (*"a constantly active, distorting apparatus."* 3.43).

"...That device was me, it is that device which just wrote this sentence." Not that the apparatus can be considered my self or my property, but it stands in my place and *I* is only the differentiated structure of this organization, which is absolutely natural and purely artificial, differentiated enough to count within its structure the moment or the place of the autarchic illusion or the sovereign subject.

This apparatus explains itself. Its self-explanatoriness does not imply, however, that one can explain it, that it can be comprehended by an outside observer: rather, it itself explains itself and already comprehends any observer whatever. It becomes more explicit as it multiplies, *"folding and unfolding the roots of its slightest signs"* (ibid.). The *Numbers* thus explain themselves—whence the contortions with which you are pretending to grate, scratch, or graft some supplement in the corner—up to a certain limit which does not bound all the text's powers from the outside but rather, on the contrary, through a certain folding-back or internal angle of the surfaces, conditions their envelopment and development in the finite/infinite structure of the apparatus.

The latter does not merely explain itself; it also reads its explanation, which is not some discourse emanating from somewhere else that would, outside the text, come to comment, interpret, decipher (you are beginning to understand why this text is undecipherable), teach, or inform about the technical secrets of its assemblage. These explanatory discourses spring up regularly, engendered in the course of sequences that are themselves part of the quadrature of the text, belonging precisely to one of the four faces, the one that seems to be open for the perception of the spectacle, for the "now" of consciousness faced with its object, for the present tense of discourse—belonging, in a word, to the face as what one faces, a surface of envisaged presence. This face—the *frons scaenae* of classical theater—also contemplates itself as the originary, immediate, unconditioned opening of *appearing*, but it explains itself as an *apparent* opening, a conditioned product, a surface effect. The explanation of "illusion" is being offered to you in the present, in the tense of the "illusion" thus reflected; and it is always a partial explanation that must forever be started anew, prolonged, tied together; its importance arises more from the pressures it exerts on the general text than from any "truth" it is supposed to reveal, its conveying of information or deformation. Although it passes itself off as the hearth or focal point where the overall story gathers itself together, it has its own particular history just

like each of the other surfaces. The specific logic of its unfolding should be
followed. Every term, every germ depends at every moment on its place and
is entrained, like all the parts of a machine, into an ordered series of
displacements, slips, transformations, and recurrences that cut out or add a
member in every proposition that has gone before.

3. The Scission [*La Coupure*]

"... forever this margin, this scission, this slim and latent immensity...
   He writes:
   'Never the problem directly... The functioning of the general
organization prevents us from posing it...' " (*Drama*).

"The virginal folding-back of the book, again, willing/lends for a
sacrifice from which the red edges of the books of old once bled; the
introduction of a weapon, or letter-opener, to mark the taking of
possession. How much more personal and forward would consciousness be without this barbarous simulacrum: when it will
become participation, in the book taken from here, from there,
varied according to different airs, divined like an engine—almost
remade by oneself. The folds will perpetuate a mark..."
   "There is a knife that I do not forget."

Clip out an example, since you cannot and should not undertake the infinite
commentary that at every moment seems necessarily to engage and immediately to annul itself, letting itself be read in turn by the apparatus
itself.

So make some incision, some violent arbitrary cut, after you recall that
Numbers actually prescribes such scissions, and recommends "beginning"
with one. It is of course a beginning that is forever fictional, and the
scission, far from being an inaugural act, is dictated by the absence—unless
there exists some illusion to discount—of any de-cisive beginning, any pure
event that would not divide and repeat itself and already refer back to some
other "beginning," some other "event," the singularity of the event being
more mythical than ever in the order of discourse. Scission is necessary
because of the fact (or as a consequence of the fact, as you will) that the
beginning is plied and multiplied about itself, elusive and divisive; it
begins with its own division, its own numerousness. "*1.9. ... there was thus,
in the beginning, what I am obliged to call 'the leap,' the scission one can get across
only by leaping...*"
   Within what you will provisionally call the general polysemy of *Numbers*,
this "scission" marks the text's interruption ("*when the text is interrupted,*

folds back on itself"...) and also marks the arbitrary insertion of the letter-opener by which the reading process is opened up indifferently here or there, the cutting edge of writing which begins with the reading of some sentence clipped out from there or here, the chancy but necessary repetition of the already-thereness of some (other) text, the sharp blade of decision in general, of decided decision, of decision undergone as well as decision deciding (*"3.11. ... The great decision was swooping down on me now, and fear was gnawing into every sign..."*), the passage from nothing to "here," from here to "there," *"a detonation and break in which the body is shot like a shell from out of the absence of range,"* the violent decision explosively projecting the shell-body, which is as sharp-edged as a *knife* (*"she was groaning, twisted, as though night were flowing out of her throat, as though she were no longer anything but this emission of night opened up with a knife in the full mass of the afternoon, keeping that darkness in her mouth..."*).

Such a decision is a castration, at least acted out or feigned, or a circumcision. This is as it always is, and the knife that with obsessive frequency slashes the tree of *Numbers* hones itself as a phallic threat: the phallus is both threatening and threatened by the very instrument it is. The "operation" of reading/writing goes by way of *"the blade of a red knife."*

The castration that is at stake must be read as indistinguishable from the detonation or projection of the shell. In their alliterations and permutations, the associations *"term/germ"* (2.46) or *"deader/steadier"* (4.92), which you have already encountered, never mark an opposition but rather a co-implication that is utterly internal and irreducible. The threat of the letter-opener from which the red edge bled opens or erects, hence broaching or breaching (the) decision in its present with one stroke; that is how the teeth become unclenched, the sewn-up mouth opened:

"1.29. meanwhile I found my body mutilated and one would have said that the flesh had been plowed, and the sex was sewn together and upright like an ear of grain hardened and closed, and I looked at this first model from before the fall enclosed inside a narrow cell into which the sun penetrated... This first copy, wounded but more sexed... It was me, I was sure, I had been waiting for my sleep... There, I was coming out of the earth, I was coming back disfigured but speaking, isolated but strong enough to go on to the end, in the egg... More precisely, there were two of us, now: the one whose intact skin could be shown to everyone, the one whose outer envelope did not immediately provoke horror, and the other riddled with gashes and holes, the flesh cut to the quick, crimson and purple, skinned like a steer..."

The severed head: these *Numbers* are written in red, the red of the coming revolution. *"We are dancing on a volcano"* (1.29): this was spoken during a ball given by the Duke of Orleans for the King of Naples, on the eve of one revolution. In *Numbers*, this anonymous quotation must be placed in relation to the regular cadence or fall of a severed head, the "operation." *"1.5. ... And there was the echo or rather the incision or rather the fallout connected with this unit: 'fait' {last syllable of "imparfait" ("imperfect"); also means "done," "makes," and "fact."—Trans}: the blood doesn't gush out instantaneously... I saw the head, severed but still alive, the mouth open upon the only word that cannot be pronounced or captured... Upon touching this sequence, I understood that a single murder was constantly in progress, that we were coming from it only to return to it via this detour..." ... "2.14. ... Similar, now, to that engraver who, a hundred years ahead of time, represented the king's execution on the chopping block even though the mechanism had not been produced... I, in my turn, was entirely able to relive the scene... The drumroll that finally covers this voice before the blade has dispatched the organ of this voice into the basket, not without the head's having been brandished as proof of a sacrilegious, dirtied reduction... A unique act, which is equaled only by the massacres of priests finally permitted or again by the parading of that skinned head on the end of a pole all through the cries—"*

You are beginning to follow the relation between a certain brandished erection and a certain head or speech that is cut off, the brand or the pole rising up in the manifestation of the scission, unable to *present* themselves otherwise than in the play, or even the laughter—the display of sharply pointed teeth—of the cut. To be presented, that is, to stand upright. Uprightness always announces that a single murder is in progress.

"2.66. ... She, rising upright—the laugh, the rictus—the lips, tensing up and exposing what it is that cuts (the teeth)... The head seen severed and she carrying it off, and I unbalancing her and holding her tight while moving, and I again urging her on to the finish, and leaping—"

Castration—always at stake—and the self-presence of the present. The pure present would be the untouched fullness, the virgin continuity of the nonscission, the volume that, not having exposed the roll of its writing to the reader's letter-opener, would therefore not yet be written on the eve of the start of the game. But the pen, when you have followed it to the end, will have turned into a knife. The present can only present itself as such by relating back to itself; it can only aver itself by severing itself, only reach itself if it breaches itself, (com)plying with itself in the angle, along a break [*brisure*] (*brisure*: "crack" and "joint," created by a hinge, in the work of a locksmith. *Littré*): in the release of the latch or the trigger. Presence is never present. The possibility—or the potency—of the present is but its own limit, its inner fold, its impossibility—or its impotence. Such will have been the relation between presence and castration in play and at stake. What holds for the present here also holds for "history," "form," the form of history, etc., along with all the significations that, in the language of metaphysics, are indissociable from the signification: "present."

The presence of the present only forms a surface, only enters squarely on stage, only institutes itself as something face-to-face—something present—, only triggers off discourse—speech *in praesentia*—, only unclenches its teeth, in the play of this cut, this scission.

"*4.44. (... history then takes this form: the muscle rising upright, showing its red swollen head, and her hand closed around it, her lips approaching its blood and her teeth gently seizing what is called present)—*"

"What is called present"—that which erects itself freely before me, upright, close at hand, that which is appearing—can be given as such, as a pure upsurge owing to nothing, only in a mythical discourse in which difference would be erased. If account be taken of what divides it, cuts it up, and folds it back in its very triggering, then the present is no longer simply the present. It can no longer be named "present" except through indirect discourse, in the quotation marks of citation, storytelling, fiction. It can only go out into language by a sort of ricochet. Transformed here into a regular device, this ricochet confers a quality of indirection, a detour or angle upon every so-called simple, natural, obvious evidence of presence in itself. Already *Drama* had confined within the angle of these quotation marks "my life," "alive," "my life before birth"; "the brief silence of the 'I live, you live, we live' "; and elsewhere " 'living' is manifested in the following manner..."; or again: " 'His life' coming toward him from the facades, the deserted sidewalks—passing near him, brushing against him, going off into the distance... In a few seconds, under the rain, the city becomes another city, vaster, floating... As though nothing had yet begun..." *Numbers:* "*1.29. ... Not only 'me' and 'my whole life'... Not only that, but also the set of which I was a member, in which I will be without knowing what I am in reality, exactly as at this moment when 'I am' does not signify anything precise... The set, the long accumulation without a look, the weight of what is, constructs, moves, manufactures, transmits, transports, transforms, and destroys...*" "*2.94. ... what is still called life... .*"

These privileged examples form an organic series. Presence and life, the presence of the present and the life of the living, are the same thing here. The exit out of the "primitive" mythical unity (which is always reconstituted retrospectively in the aftermath of the break [*dans l'après-coupure*]), the scission, the decision—which is both deciding and decided—,the shot/throw/blow [*le coup*] parts the seed as it projects it. It inscribes difference in the heart of life ("it is that very difference ['that implacable difference'] which is the condition for their operation. No thing is complete in itself, and it can only be completed by what it lacks. But what each particular thing lacks is infinite; we cannot know in advance what complement it calls for. We can thus only recognize by the authority of fact and by our spirit's secret taste when the effective harmony, the essential, generative mother-difference, had been found... A difference: the cause is radically that. It is not a positive difference, nor is it one included within the subject. It is what the subject is essentially lacking."); numerical multiplicity does not sneak up like a death threat upon a germ cell previously one with itself. On the contrary, it serves as a pathbreaker for "the" seed, which therefore produces (itself) and advances only in the plural. It is a singular plural, which no single origin will ever have preceded. Germination, dissemination. There is no first insemination. The semen is already swarming. The "primal" insemination is dissemination. A trace, a graft whose traces have been lost. Whether in the case of what is called "language" (discourse, text, etc.) or in the case of some "real" seed-sowing, each term is indeed a germ, and each germ a term. The term, the atomic element, engenders by division, grafting, proliferation. It is a seed and not an absolute term. But each germ *is* its own term, finds its term not outside itself but within itself as its own internal limit, making an angle with its own death. It would be possible to reconstruct the network through which *Numbers* is infiltrated by references to all kinds of atomistic theories, which are also theories of sperm. Let yourself be guided, in *Numbers*, through the vocabulary of germination or dissemination, by the word "group"—the set of elements dispersed. Swarm. *Numbers* are caught in a mathematicogenetic theory of groups.

If this in itself were intended to mean something, it would be that there is nothing prior to the group, no simple originary unit prior to this division through which life comes to see itself and the seed is multiplied from the start; nothing comes before the addition in which the seed begins by taking itself away, before what *Drama* announced as "a proliferation which would never have begun," before what *Logics* set down as a swarm of bees, a division at work: "Language becomes that state of beginning *speaking up from all sides* whose soundless effects are immediately going to reverberate on that linguistic hinge or pivot: comparison. Just so, the bees in the temple of Denderah: ..."

It is proliferation, furthermore, because the disappearance, or rather the substitution of the unit that adds and effaces itself—counts itself out—of its own accord in the moment of triggering ("*1.41. ... we were participating in the calculation that effaced us and replaced us—*" ..."*4.84. (... 'the rod he is holding in his hand represents the central square, the unit that does not count but that equals and makes the whole set—the distributor, the pivot' / 'the unit is not added on but simply produces a mutation and becomes indistinguishable from the whole thing, the total within which the mutations operate' / ... And thus, the atom 'I' ...—*") engenders in one blow both number and the innumerable. "*Germs, seeds sown in innumerable number...*" ... "*Seminaque innumero numero summaque profunda.*"

A fictive beginning, a false entrance, a false exit, a kind of writing of innumerable number—these will still have to be reread by you.

You are authorized to do so by the law of the cut; it is henceforth prescribed that you clip out an example, and dismember the text:

"*4. (but since there is this scission, and this recoil, which are constantly present and at work; since the lines disperse themselves and sink down before they appear turned back on the dead surface where you see them, the imperfect provides the motion and the unreachable double bottom—and that all dies and comes back to life in a thought that in reality belongs from the beginning to no one, a transparent column where what takes place remains suspended at a greater or lesser height, and when you wake up you say to yourself: 'hey, I was there,' but nothing comes to explain that sentence, and that is what regards you... That column does not leave you any distance; it keeps watch while you are asleep; it is slipped in between you and you... Less and less suspected, less and less remembered where you are walking without seeing me... It is only for us, however, that night is turning and forming itself above the cities—where the mute machines are henceforth capable of reading, deciphering, counting, writing, and remembering—, and one sees a conversation break off, its gestures stand still, here, among the fabrics, the objects assembled, 'something has not been said.' They are talking, now, but something of their silence subsists; they are represented here by a mist, a reflection, 'no, no, it's just the opposite,' 'I do indeed think that that can be affirmed': I am veritably writing what is going on, and of course it is impossible to be there totally, it is done sideways, on the bias, without stopping—but after all we are together, no reason to wait or to stop—*

it is hard to accept this interval, this blank intact; it is nevertheless very hard to

confirm without this forgetting which comes back and forces one's hand—when the
text is interrupted, folds back upon itself, lets the voices come back like an endless
recording—

    each time necessary not to listen, 'what are you talking about,' 'be more precise'—
    since they come from an infinite series of rotten, cleansed, burned, canceled,
accumulated elements, whereas up ahead others are already searching for their words
and will cover what is said today again,—and I am like them, among them, among
you, in the operation, in the number, $1 + 2 + 3 + 4 = 10$—   —*)"*

Here, then, is the 4.

4. The Double Bottom of the Plupresent

                  |Book |
"The four volumes are one| | the same
presented twice inasmuch as its two halves,
the first of one and last of the other juxtaposed to
last and first of one and the other: and little by
little its unity is revealed, with the help of this work
of comparison

                       |showing that it makes a whole
in two different senses,| inasmuch as a fifth
part, formed of the set of these four fragments,
apparent or two repeated:
this will thus take place 5 times
or 20 fragments grouped together
in 2(3) by 10, found identical
    [........]
    [........]

    Thus one has 4 volumes, 5 times
i.e. once (quadriga) the 4   or to begin
first volumes   by the middle
concurrently, of the four
books that are each in
five volumes: and so forth,
    inasmuch
as a quadruple Play juxtaposed
in five acts, until the exhaustion of the whole. Whereas then it
turns out that there are four
    books (from four contestants)
Each in [2]5 volumes..."

You had just recognized, crowning the formula $1 + 2 + 3 + 4 = 10$ (*si* in its phonetic transcription), the Chinese ideogram for 4. The text's card had been played, was beginning to sketch out its outlines.

You did not in fact cut just anything or just anywhere. The sequence you cut is the "first" in a series of 25 sequences bearing the number 4. It is the fourth in a set containing 100: the "operation" as it is called by the disappearing author of the text cited above as an epigraph, the operation of reading-writing, with no subject or object but the book.

The text's chart will have been played. It will have stated the present as a cut, a scission, an interruption *of* the text put into play *in* the text. But it is in the present that it will have stated the presentness of the scission. For nothing says the present better, it seems, than *there is*. But what *there is* here is a scission ("there is this scission"), and what is *"constantly present and at work"* is a *"recoil."*

Which is also to be understood as the recoil of a firearm and the possibility of its triggering.

Like all the sequences that begin with the number 4, the one you have just read is placed in parentheses, its tense is the present, and it is addressed to "you." Constituting one of the faces of the 25 squares (which are doubly numbered: in periodic fashion, from 1 to 4, and in linear fashion, from 1 to 100), it is the opening carved out in the form of a scene that is at this very moment visible and vocal, speaking to the spectator-reader: "you." You: reading, seeing, speaking. *Numbers*, reading you, seeing you, speaking to you, in the process of reading, seeing, speaking; "in the process" here meaning "at the moment in which presently" you read, see, speak, etc. You live in the present, in "what is called present," in consciousness; you witness what seems to be in front of you, what is upright before you, advancing toward you, what stands out against the very horizon of the world, becomes a figure against that ground, takes shape as it faces you, exposed and examinable before your eyes, your brow, your mouth, your hands. You are receiving or upholding in the form of what is called present, i.e. according to consciousness or perception, a certain discourse.

This opening of presence is surface number four. Claiming to be originary, wild, and irreducible like the incessant, ever-virginal arising of the world, it has its own "history" or rather it is plunged by that "history" into a limitless time that is neither a "present" nor a "history." According to the history of this present, the fourth surface is affiliated with the stage of the old representative theater. This surface is therefore a *"dead surface"*: it is dead like the structure of that old-fashioned theater, and, too, it is dead because the consciousness that stands as spectator and consumer of the represented present or meaning—"you"—believes itself to move in the

freedom of pure appearing, while it is only an effect, the drifting, reverber-
ating, transported, cast-off effect forever turned back or thrown away, the
crust or the shell shed by a force or a "life" that does not present itself, has
never presented itself. What is invisible in this scene of visibility is its
relation to the ciphered and seminal production that organizes it.

  "*4. ... since the lines disperse themselves and sink down before they appear turned
back on the dead surface where you see them...*"

This scission, this opening, this pure appearance of appearing through
which the present seems to free itself from the textual machine ("history,"
numbers, topology, dissemination, etc.) in fact denounces itself at every
moment. The operation puts "illusion" into play as an effect or product.
"Presence," or "production," is but a product. The product of an arithmetic
operation. The apparent immediacy of what seems to be given to present
perception in its original nakedness, in its nature, is already shed as an
effect; it falls: under the sway of a machinated structure that never gives
itself away in/to the present, which has nothing to do with it.

Nor should the imperfect, the tense of the other three series of sequences
(1, 2, 3), be read as an *other* present, a modified present, a past present, the
past of what once at least was present, upon some other surface one might
once have seen arising before one, and which one might still be able to see if
one were to make the rounds of the theater or of one's memory, of the
theater of memory (one should read within the layers of *Numbers* the
sedimentation of all sorts of arts of memory, of all the "theaters of memory"
and all the plans that designed them, from the *Ad Herennium* to the *Ars
memoriae* by Robert Fludd, including the projects of Giulio Camillo,
Giordano Bruno, etc.). The imperfect is therefore not another present, a
has-been-present; it is another thing entirely than the present; it has no
essence. That is why it *"provides the motion and the unreachable double bottom."*

The present presents itself as the simplicity of a bottom or ground. A past
tense that would mark only another present would assure itself of the
grounding of a simple foundation, hidden behind the surface of present
appearances. What the double bottom of the imperfect summons up, here
at least, is a time without grounding, foundation, or limit, a tense that
would no longer be a *tempus*; it is a presentless time, the total account
depriving the square of its ground, leaving it suspended in the air. As soon
as there is a double bottom, there is no bottom or ground at all in process of
formation, and this law will not cease to confirm itself from now on.

The imperfect will have provided the motion. The illusion of the
present, the illusion which, playing upon the dead surface, makes us
believe in the secure foundation of an originary donation or providence, is

also denounced, as you can see, and set in motion by the touch of a whip "with thongs of steel." But that denunciation takes place in a sequence that is itself written in the present.

What about this new present? Why and how is this fourth sequence *at the same time* a "presentation" and a critical discourse, a summons addressed to "you" concerning the presentation? Why does this convocatory interpretation, which constantly refers back to the imperfect, remain in the present? And what is its relation to the imperfect which provides the motion?

Perhaps it has to do with some unknown mirror. You are getting hot as you approach that icy looking glass and the key to a certain clasp.

This new present is more perceptible in the opening of the *Drama*. Its story was *apparently* written in the present. Of course. In that way, too, it can be found reinserted, transplanted, re-cited, with all the effects of textual transformation this implies, within the more encompassing set and the more complex temporality of *Numbers*. You will have many a chance to verify this. But the *Drama*'s present was never in fact simple. In the structure of the *I Ching*, on the checkerboard, between the present outside the quotation marks and the present of what "he writes," a disjuncture creeps in, a duplicity in which something abysmal happens to the founding present, to what is called present. Following this "duality triggered off by writing," there is thus already, on the same page, a simple present, the effect produced by what provides the motion, and the present that enounces or denounces its relation to the other tenses in a "scientific" discourse, "scientific" in its presentation, which tells, in the present, the truth (about truth as a naive present). Just as in sequence four of *Numbers*.

This total, differentiated, equivocal present, which must not be reduced to the simple present it violently throws into question; this structured, bottomless present, which is related to the double bottom that comprehends but *is* not the present, is called, in *Drama*, the "plupresent" ["*plus-que-présent*"].

Although it is neither squarely the imperfect in *Numbers*, nor the double or dialogic present of the fourth interpellation, the plupresent will have laid the groundwork for both of these: it will, through a kind of future perfect [*futur antérieur*], have lodged itself in the one and in the other, or rather in the very exchange through which they were supposed to "remark" each other. Such a future perfect, always making one text circulate inside another, excludes any and all eschatology merely by dint of being the future perfect of an innumerable imperfect, an indefinite past that will never have been present.

Even before the confirmation brought by other parentheses, this sequence of parentheses, in *Drama*, will have prescribed that thought for you:

"... But on this side of 'speech,' he discovers an absence of limits: this can be endlessly described, this can be endlessly described in the process of being described, etc. (The sign 'etc.,' moreover, is ludicrously inadequate here; one ought to invent something that would signify the incessant or the innumerable, something that could serve as an abbreviation of vertigo within the general dictionary). His method nevertheless allows for access at all times to the entire set of declensions, agreements, figures, persons— taking them so to speak the other way around. A story of thought contained in words and vice versa. An ablative absolute. That does not happen in time but on paper, where one can make use of tenses. A page present for the plupresent. 'The past is not behind us but beneath our feet.' The page is white but it has been written on from time immemorial; it is white through forgetfulness of what has been written, through erasure of the text on which everything that is written is written. And yet nothing is truly written, all this can change at every moment, and it is still and interminably the first time (one ought to write 'the first time'). (He sees himself again seeing the ocean for the first time: grey at the end of a street, the effect was null. It seemed to him only later that the sea on the shore immediately represented sound and consequently an explanation of the horizon which does and does not exist.) Here is how he goes about it: he calls up a simple possibility of image, a prior bit of speech isolated in that unlocatable country which is at the same time what he sees, thinks, has seen or dreamed, could have thought or seen, etc., a limitless and yet available country, which makes a screen."

You have just, through this quotation, through this motif from *Drama*, come within sight of a "horizon which does and does not exist," and then of a certain "screen." You are almost there.

So one ought to have invented "something that would signify the incessant or the innumerable." Inventing it, of course, in the interval. Inventing the sign for this "being-in-the-process-of," for a movement that is at once uninterrupted and broken, a continuity of rifts that would nevertheless not flatten out along the surface of a homogeneous, obvious present. Our language always takes up this movement in the form of a becoming-present: to become present, a present in the process of becoming, the becoming of the present, a reprise of the movement of writing in the tense of "living" speech: a self-proclaimed traceless present. It was therefore necessary to turn to what is outside *our* language in order to signify that incessant extrapresent. And what is outside speech, too. Two "Chinese" characters mark that "*something constantly reanimated and unappeased—* 動 —"(1.37), that incessant movement of the "*being in the process of and precisely* — 正 —" (2.62).

The plupresent in sequence four thus envelops both the present ("lived," by you, in the "illusion" of one who lives, reads, speaks in the present, your eyes riveted to the classical scenario) and its violent reinscription in the theatrical, arithmetical machine: *Numbers*, read, see, and speak, you, in the process of reading *you*, seeing *you*, speaking (to) *you*, "in the process" here meaning at the moment that, non-presently, you are being read, seen, spoken, etc. This reinscription *takes place*; *there is* its violence. This "there is" of the "taking place" is in the present only through the "illusions" of statement or utterance. The content and act of this speech are immediately open upon the extrapresent. What takes place, what there is, is writing, i.e. a machination in which the present is no longer anything but a whirligig. Thus it is that *Drama* will have put the present in place in writing, in the taking-place of the place, in the ex-centered composition of the plupresent: "His story is no longer his story, but simply this statement: something takes place. He tries to become the center of this new silence, and indeed everything comes up and becomes hesitant and unbalanced in his vicinity... Spoken words and gestures (beside him, outside) rediscover their geometric roots: he enters into a generalized graph."

The machination of tenses, in *Numbers*, merges with the distribution of persons. For example (what else can you do here but pick an example out of the innumerable or draw a lot?), the "we" will no more have been just a person among others than the imperfect a simple past present. The "we" is the nonpresent, nonpersonal, imperfect, limitless element in which the personal present, the properness of the persons *you*, *I*, *he*, we are cutting out, cut themselves out. The "we" is but the place of the permutation of persons. Hence it takes place as the "dawning indication of an unsituated—unsituable—presence, but which remains and reconstitutes itself irresistibly. There is doubtless nobody there, but the roles are permuted..." That is why the other persons present themselves, frontally so to speak, and can be faced, counted, discounted; the "we" is never presented full face: the imperfect or plupresent: "*1. ... Yet meanwhile, there was a 'we.' This 'we' got lost, came back, trembled, and kept coming back...*" Everything has thus "begun" by that "we" and yet it is never representable at the front of the scene. It is enlisted like an oblique force in a war without a front, like this numberless group...

"*1.80. ... 'The finite and the infinite are inseparable'/ ... Coming from the rotation and breaking our journey for a moment in the sign 'us' inscribed within us in profile... Thus taking the form of a whole people animated and grouped around its articulations, its voice of sex and exchange, becoming the moving force of translations and divisions... All that, stirring by us and through us now, seeming to arise out of an acceleration of sleep, to issue from the current and to deposit by us and through us its past and future germs... Germs, grouped and disseminated..."*

"By us" and "through us." In the "us," the function of the personal agent is opened, traversed by the anonymous force, the proliferating, working imperfect of the swarm.

The edges of the chart are appearing more clearly to you. "And in that way he finds the turning plate of his present again, where he has at his disposal all tenses, persons, verbs (he reviews his cards and his charts), in a sort of navigation or aerial view..." (*Drama*).

Make another cut through *Numbers* and skip to the second of the sequences numbered four. That is where a representation of the machine is feigned in its first approximation:

"4.8. (and since it is impossible to communicate to those of long ago or far away that the operation is unfolding both on the ground on which they move and beneath the depths they could not fail to see if they but raised their eyes, the construction is presented thus: three visible sides, three walls if you like, on which the sequences are in reality inscribed—transitions, articulations, intervals, words—, and one absence of side or wall defined by the three others but enabling one to observe them from their point of view.

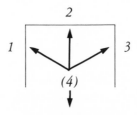

This fourth surface is in a sense carved out of the air; it enables speeches to make themselves heard, bodies to let themselves be seen; consequently, it is easily forgotten, and that is doubtless where illusion and error lie. Indeed, what is thus too easily taken to be the opening of a stage is nonetheless a panel that distorts, an invisible, impalpable, opaque veil that plays toward the other three sides the role of a mirror or reflector, and toward the outside (i.e. toward the possible but consequently always repelled, multiple spectator) the role of a negative developer on which the inscriptions simultaneously produced on the other planes appear inverted, righted, fixed. As if the hypothetical actors came and traced or pronounced their text backwards, in front of you, without your being aware of it—nor they, either—by virtue of the apparatus in question. Whence the impression of witnessing a projection, whereas it is ultimately a matter of the very product of the surface—of the darkroom transformed into a surface. Whence the tendency to imagine that something is happening in three-dimensional space, whereas, initially and in closing, there are only two dimensions: neither stage

nor house but on the contrary, enveloping both stage and house, a single sheet capable
of giving at once the sensation of depth, representation, and reflection: the page, for the
moment, stands as an indication of that sheet, its most obvious envelope, the place
where, for that which appears and for him to whom it appears, the very passage of
time upon bodies is played. But this must be added: this envelope is the epitome of
flatness and depth, of platitude and profundity; it corresponds to your life through
and through, in its slightest details; it is the reason for space in its multitude of
grains falling in the night; it covers the sum total of your acts as of right now; it is
very precisely, here, what makes a sign to you, poorly perhaps, without lying and
without telling the truth, but with the distinct desire to destroy you and live in the
heart of this stroke)—"

The chart sketched out in this "second" of the fourth sequences (4.8) will
henceforth continually be filled in, made more complex, shifted regularly
about, through a process of transformation you will be able to follow, which
stops to explain itself periodically, from quarter to quarter, sometimes
fixing its mutations and reversals in some new schema (4.52; 4.48...).

5. wriTing, encAsIng, screeNing

"What! perfect writing rejects even the slightest adventure, so as to
delight in its chaste evocation, on the tain of memories as drawn by
some extraordinary figure, both the eternal ghost and the breath!
when nothing immediate or outward is happening, in a present that
plays (at being) effaced so as to cover some more hybrid undersides.
If our external agitation is shocking, on the screen of printed pages,
all the more so on the stageboards, a materiality upright in gratuitous obstruction. Yes, the Book or that monograph it becomes of
a type (the superimposition of pages as in a jewel-case, defending an
infinite, intimate, tucked-in delicacy of (the) being in itself against
brutal space) is sufficient with many a truly new procedure analogous in rarefaction to the subtlest features of life."

"Parenthesis. In the margin. Blank. Title. Contact... It would only
take one of those short theatrical productions that seem to perform
the operation of extracting themselves from themselves for me to be
led here, to the edge... this veil passes over everyone's vision—a
white film covering the eye of birds that are still warm and
stiff—with a kind of discretion, a hesitation, scarcely tainted with
disgust..." (*Drama*)

What gives the structural necessity to "illusion," "error," and "forgetting," is thus the strange "opening" of this quadrangle, its missing side.
The opening *already* goes unnoticed *as* opening (aperity, aperture), as a
diaphanous element guaranteeing the transparency of the passageway to

whatever presents itself. While we remain attentive, fascinated, glued to
what presents itself, we are unable to see *presence* as such, since presence does
not present itself, no more than does the visibility of the visible, the
audibility of the audible, the medium or "air," which disappears in the act
of allowing to appear.

But it is not enough to call presence to mind, to make the air *itself* appear,
supposing that to be possible, in order to erase forgetfulness, illusion, or
error. For not only is the air not a simple medium—nor is the "air" (this
will be remembered since one can only say it, not see it) a univocal
signification—but the opening carved out of it is in fact a closed opening,
neither quite open nor quite closed. It is a false exit. A mirror.

And it is not just any mirror. It should be added that this mirror will
have been turned toward the back of the stage, "toward the other three
sides," offering us only the sight of its tain, in sum.

Which would (not) be *anything* if the tain were not also transparent, or
rather transformative of what it lets show through. The tain in this mirror
thus reflects—imperfectly—what comes to it—imperfectly—from the
other three walls and lets through—presently—the ghost of what it
reflects, the shadow deformed and reformed according to the figure of what
is called present: the upright fixity of what stands before me; *"the inscriptions
...appear inverted, righted, fixed."*

Once this ether, the presence of the present, has been called to mind, it is
necessary to mark the fact that the plupresent is not merely *presence*, but also
a kind of deformation irreducible to any form—and hence to any present—a
transformation based on no original form, no raw material, no first matter
in the last instance. To mark this is to remark that the alleged simplicity of
the opening, of the aperity—the letting-be, the truth that lifts the veil-
screen—is already regulated according to a mirror, and in particular a
tainless mirror, or at any rate a mirror whose tain lets "images" and
"persons" through, endowing them with a certain index of transformation
and permutation.

Numbers are of such a cast: their ink is drawn from this tain, a sort of metal
covered with liquid mercury (the $10 = 1 + 2 + 3 + 4$, which is the
number of the *letter* in the Kabbalah and of the *Sphinx* in Tarot, is also the
number of *Mercury* in astrology and these *Numbers* filled with *"quasi stellar
sources"* could be read, will soon begin to be read, as an astrographical
constellation). The mercury, the tain of this ink, forms a screen. It shelters
and conceals. Holds in reserve and exposes to view. The screen: at once the
visible projection surface for images, and that which prevents one from
seeing the other side. The structure of this screen-mirror, this tain, this
"stray verso lined with metal" (4.100), entails that it give itself out—this is

the *case* in *Numbers*—as something that must be broken, absolutely gone
through en route to the true source, toward which it lures you, for

"3.95. ... / 'A mirror is not a source' / ..."

The mirror takes place—try to think out the taking-place of a mirror—as
something designed to be broken. "Since I am feigning not to know that
my look can put even the planets turning in space to death, he who claims
that I do not possess the faculty of memories will not be wrong. What
remains to be done is to smash this mirror to smithereens" (quoted in
Logics).

It is hard to know whether such a mirror is the space of the classical stage
or the generalized space, irreducible and plupresent, in which the old
theater is inscribed, dismantled, and denounced. This uncertainty should
not be dispelled. The mirror and the extramirror, the implication and the
issuance, are together prescribed by the structure of this uncertain speculum. Such is the *obligation* that *Numbers* will have made such a case out of.

*"2.70. ... Hence, obliged to tear the veil again and to attack again the plane of
sleeps, tearing the screen anew, breaking the mirror, the error..."*

*"3.79. ... She was thus obliged to seek support from what made her into one value
among others, one nerve in the constant network forcing its way to knowledge; she was
forced at a certain point to sell her rhythm, her gestures—seeking the mirror,
necessarily summoning the opposite of what was becoming dead in all the mirrors..."*

You will have begun, but not finished, pinning down the above allusion
to "value" only in the mirror in which we in turn quote a quotation from
Numbers. Before 3.79, in 3.67, you had read, for example: *"By means,
therefore, of the value-relation expressed in our equation, the bodily form of
commodity B becomes the value-form of commodity A, or the body of commodity B acts
as a mirror to the value of commodity A..."*

Not a single atom of *Numbers* escapes this play of recurrences, as one can
well suspect, and as one can indeed unceasingly verify. No statement can be
sheltered, like a fetish, a commodity invested with value, even potentially
"scientific" value, from these mirror effects through which the text quotes,
quotes itself, sets itself in motion of its own accord, through a generalized
graph that undoes all certainty derived from the oppositions between value
and nonvalue, respectable and nonrespectable, true and false, high and low,
inside and outside, whole and part. All these oppositions are thrown out of
whack by the simple "taking-place" of the mirror. Each term takes over the
other and excludes itself from itself; each germ becomes steadier and deader

than itself. The element envelops and deducts itself from what it envelops. The world comprehends the mirror which captures it and vice versa. In the whole of what it captures, and because it can capture the whole, each part of the mirror is larger than the whole; but then it is smaller than itself. The fourth surface is the paradigm of this relation, which does not prevent it from being caught in it itself; as the mirroring effect of the whole, as present, it re-forms, in the indefiniteness of the plupresent, all possible deformations. "*3.35. ... For here, the text was flattened out, and the whole could at every moment be lesser than one of its parts...*"

And since nothing has preceded the mirror, since everything begins in the folds of citation (you will later learn how to read this word), the inside of the text will always have been outside it, in what seems to be serving as the "means" toward the "work." This "reciprocal contamination of the work and the means" poisons the inside, the body proper of what was once called the "work," just as it poisons the texts which are cited to appear and which one would have liked to keep safe from this violent expatriation, this uprooting abstraction that wrenches them out of the security of their original context. Interestingly enough, in *Numbers*, poison is affirmed. The mercury in its tain is a poison. It is mentioned by name, a name whose frequent occurence you will have been able to follow: "*dry poison,*" "*subtler poison,*" "*methodical poison,*" "*a more secret, more poisoned blow,*" "*the poison I had recognized in my veins,*" "*letting the opposite of the metal come back, something poisoned and slowed down,*" "*the orient...transformed by its occident, but in turn not leaving the latter intact, infiltrating it and poisoning it in its sentences,*" etc.

The relation between opposing terms, between contrary germs, is thus one of venomous tain. Metals of course can well be, and be termed, "venomous."

To try to resist the removal of a textual member from its context is to want to remain protected against this writing poison. It is to want at all costs to maintain the boundary line between the inside and the outside of a context. It is to recognize the legitimacy of the relative specificity of each text, but it is also to believe that any system of writing exists *in itself*, as the relation of an inside to itself, particularly when it is "true." This amounts above all to an imposition of fundamentally classical limits upon general-ized textuality. It is a kind of discontinuity prompted by resistance and protectionism.

Everything "begins," then, with citation, in the creases [*faux plis*] of a certain veil, a certain mirrorlike screen. Even the model itself is not exempt from this rule. For example, in describing the composition of mirrors, screens, and walls in *Numbers*, in delineating the general structure of the machine, one is already anchored in the citation or pre-scription of another "book," which thereby finds itself reinscribed in these *Numbers*, preventing them by the same token from closing around their own order. The mirror of a mirror. Witness this description, already, in *Drama*, and store up in your memory each one of its details, for instance those columns of white smoke rising above the factories. Later, you will already have read:

"There is a tranquillity there composed of words that are false and lacking in importance, a frozen rotation in which, while I am asleep, I live through my own disappearance (and I am sorry, I insist: about the total destruction of my hand and the precisely symmetrical destruction of your eyes and mine). On the page... A white screen spewing out of a factory located far from the city, in the midst of the forest that burns almost every summer, a factory with its putrid smoke (one drives past it hurriedly, keeping the car windows shut) spreading a grey area around it, a factory in which wood is precisely turned into paper... Sometimes the fire is at the gates of the city, day is no longer day, everything is swept by a dry storm, and ashes fall slowly, at random, so that there drops for example upon one's plate a charred bit of fern carried there by the wind... Black afternoons, red evenings... All this can be found in the word 'fern' if one really stops to think about it... And that is where the problem lies: how is one to follow the solicitations, the appeals, the diagonal lines of such rapid visions ('fern' is also the presence of the hidden sun, the carpet of luminous patterns in which all autumns come to be imprinted), unless it be through a system of reflection and framing which makes the rest exist and which, in its repetitions and closures, sets it free? This system, perhaps: 'a succession of crisscrossed but always parallel lines that come back to meet themselves at right angles.' Which defines and opens each fresco, isolating it, allowing it to take place and be seen, but which also limits it, wipes it out, or rather recalls its origin and end... (I am writing this legibly, it seems to me?) A wall and a mirror. (And if you write next to the looking glass, your right hand is writing no less truly than your left, in front of you, and the shock can be as self-evident as you please; it still in your eyes lags behind your incomprehensible and ever-changing self.)"

You would be mistaken to think that the matrix of *Numbers* is merely outlined in *Drama*, barely sketched out by that "screen," those "diagonal lines," that "system of reflection and framing which makes the rest exist and which, in its repetitions and closures, sets it free," that "right angle," that "wall," that "mirror," that "lag." You would be mistaken to think that that matrix is merely outlined in *Drama*, and only once at that, one "first time." Everything in *Drama* proclaims itself only "*as if* for the first time": "then the curtain rises, he recovers his sight, escapes, watches himself struggle with the spectacle that is neither inside nor outside. And then he enters on stage as if for the first time. Hence, it is a matter of theater: everything begins again." In the passage quoted above concerning the "page present for the plupresent" and the "first time," this procedure was already, there too, written. To repeat: "Here is how he goes about it: he calls up a simple possibility of image, a prior bit of speech isolated in that unlocatable country which is at the same time what he sees, thinks, has seen or dreamed, could have thought or seen, etc., a limitless and yet available country, which makes a screen."

The screen, without which there would be no writing, is also a device described *in* writing. The writing process is reflected in what is written.

And here is another screen, a "provisional screen," another matrix of the "operation," caught in another of *Drama*'s textual refractions, another citation you will have read all the way down to the citation of another mirror within it: "He lives in this country, this city... His face raised, he feels more and more replaced, dilated, by the night, tries to become its mirror and direct reflection... And ever so slowly, his eyes regain their autonomy and, as though filling with tears, they cause the whole extent of space to well up and drift about, spreading over and through it in a traceless, borderless flow. His sight, however, is not altered; it remains sharp, precise (making out the scattering of stars more and more clearly, seeming to multiply them, to raise them to a cold incandescence, a kind of calculus with principles and laws unknown to him), but it now secretes its own milieu in which distances become equalized and lost—in which the absence of direction (of sense) is at once unveiled and seized... He is in the midst of the night he is. He is holding it out, reduced, before his eyes—but he himself has disappeared in it (he verifies in sum the fact that there is no 'subject'—no more than on this page). Thus, from time to time, motionless before the band of yellow sky that unfurls the horizon, he takes careful stock of his position, his limitations. The furthest point he is able to see or imagine coincides with the one that is most 'withdrawn' (in virtual space, which also represents the future)—and, between the two, there is this provisional screen on which the operation depends... A suspended, free-floating sphere is constituted in silence, half visible if one looks through him... The word he can pronounce here will also be the thing that is furthest away, and the thing that is nearest at hand will be an existing but absent word... 'Each substance, moreover, is like an entire world, a mirror of the whole universe, which is expressed by each substance in its own way, somewhat as the selfsame city is variously represented according to the different positions occupied by the person observing it'..."

JUST AS the city here mentioned refers back to what you will later refuse to call a "thematics" of the city ("We are living in this city (this book)..."), which permeates and virtually encompasses the entire architecture of *Drama* and *Numbers*, their common yet different design; JUST AS this latest mirror captures in its "citation" the most powerful and most arithmological thought about the mirror or echo as the universal characteristic; JUST AS that "scattering of stars" raised to a "cold incandescence, a kind of calculus whose principles and laws would be unknown to him" implicates an entire textual constellation (from *Drama* again: "while the mass of stars invades the nocturnal void..." ..."always the same fixed star endlessly in the midst of falling to the keenest limit of the fixed eyes..."), a whole magnetic field from which you are here choosing to detach this diamond, which is more than fragmented by the arbitrary violence of abstraction, being compared to another diamond extracted from a box of writing and dream, of silence and death or, if you prefer, from a clasp or jewel-case you will encounter later on:

after "the sky is not sowing fewer stars across her shadow" (*Her grave is closed*)

there will have been

"IF [SI]

IT WAS
Stellar outgrowth

IT WOULD BE
    worse

        not

            more nor less

                    indifferently but just as much

EXCEPT   **NOTHING**

    at the altitude

        PERHAPS

            as far as one location

THE NUMBER

WERE IT TO EXIST

otherwise than as a scattered hallucination of agony

WERE IT TO COMMENCE AND CEASE

welling up yet denied and closed when in view

at last

through some widespread profusion of rarity

WERE IT TO BE CIPHERED

evidence of the sum if only there is one

WERE IT TO ILLUMINATE

CHANCE

WILL HAVE TAKEN PLACE

BUT THE PLACE

fuses with beyond

outside the interest

indicated as far as it is concerned

in general

according to such-and-such obliquity by such-and-such declivity

of fires

toward

it must be

the Septentrion just as North

A CONSTELLATION

cold with oblivion and disuse

not so much

that it does not enumerate

upon some vacant superior surface

the successive bumping

sidereally

of a total account in process of formation

« *qu'elle n'énumère* [that it does not enumerate]:

The constellation is not so cold that it does not give any sign of life in the *number* of stars that compose it; this sense of the continued fertility of the mother-site (an androgynous mixture of stars and sky: *con* [female sexual parts] and *st* [testes?]) is borne out by the elements *mère* [mother], *elle* [she], the caudal *qu'elle* [cf. *queue*, tail, male organ], the link *né* [born], and the element *nu* [nude] recalls the nudity of procreation (both on the physical and on the mental level), and this is in line with another usage of *mère*: 'pure fem. adj.' (*Larousse*). The unit *mère* is being used consciously, as is shown by the rhyme between '*énumère*' and '*mère*' ('*On trouve ici, bonheurs que j'énumère / La grande mer avec petite mère*' ['One finds here, joys that I enumerate / The huge sea along with little mother'] *On some pebbles from Honfleur*), and the expression '*la Muse nue et mère*' ['the nude mother Muse' "]; '*nue et mère*' is a permutation of the syllables in '*énumère*.'—Trans.] (from the preface to *Les Raisins bleus et gris* [*Blue and Grey Grapes*]) provides an excellent indication of one of the levels of signification... Childbirth, the final Throw of Dice, comes from an androgynous procreator: nature, summed up in the constellation; its products are later stages of itself in the process of becoming symbolized by the garland of individual stars in the Dipper; these stars are products that are ambiguously male: sperm; and female: eggs; or both at once: children, and all three ideas are summed up in the word 'seed': the letter *m* in *énumère* is thus a good example of 'M translates the power to make, hence a joy that is both male and maternal...number...' (*English Words*)... The idea of stars as seeds is a traditional one in poetry, cf. 'your conversation sows jewels into my inner winter' (letter to Cazalis, December 4, 1868). The star-seeds will be linked with male and female milk in association with the milky way; see *successif*, below...

le heurt successif [the successive bumping]

This is the 'supreme game' itself, the act, or its products, its children, the stars of the constellation *in process of formation*, with an eye to the *total account*.

This erotic *bump* intended toward consummation is amply confirmed by: 'the mechanical salutation inflicted by the way the tool bumps, incessantly, toward the Sum' (*Confrontation*), particularly if we recall 'that shovel and that pick, sexual tools—whose metal, epitomizing the pure force of the worker, fecundates the terrain' (*Conflicts*). The 'disseminating' power of the 's' is entirely appropriate here; *successive* is used in the literal sense of dissemination [having *successors*]: to sow [*semer*] seeds: note the word 'incessantly' in the passage just quoted and the word 'incessant' in 'the incessant, successive coming-and-going' (*As for the Book*)...»

SO TOO, then, does each sequence of the text, through this mirror-effect that germinates and deforms, comprehend some *other* text each time, which by the same token comprehends *it*, so that, in one of these parts that are smaller than themselves and greater than the whole they reflect, the theoretical statement of this law is guaranteed a housing. That statement would moreover not itself be exempt from the law of recurrence and metaphorical displacement in which, in elementary fashion, being both end and middle, term and milieu, it expropriates itself:

Drama: ... "but it now secretes its own milieu..." ... "...He is in the midst of the night he is..."

Numbers: "3.19. ...It was a more and more differentiated, acidic material that kept biting into its own fire—"

"1.77. ... I could nevertheless transform what was happening since I was no longer stuck upon a single surface, able on the contrary to see the organisms constantly functioning on several levels, as if leafed through and superimposed upon themselves, recharged like batteries immersed in their own acid, which has been elaborated or neutralized, traversing and being traversed, modifying and being modified..."

Do not try your hand at temporal "intuitions" or impracticable variations; you will perhaps have better declined this double-bottomed, plupresent imperfect by drawing the figure of a quadrangle complicated by the structure of a very strange mirror. A mirror which, despite the aforementioned impossibility, does indeed come to stand as a source, like an echo that would somehow precede the origin it seems to answer—the "real," the "originary," the "true," the "present," being constituted only on the rebound from the duplication in which alone they can arise. This is why the *"echo"* is an *"incision"* (1.5). The "effect" becomes the cause. A word that would not be repeated, a unique sign, for example, would not be *one*. A sign becomes what it is only through the possibility of its reissue.

"1.77. ... each word found the echo that was its cause."

What has become of the present here? the past present? the future present? "You"? "Me"? "Us" will have been in the imperfect of that echo.

6. The Attending Discourse [Le discours d'assistance]

"... The sound box, the vacant space in front of the stage: the absence of anyone, where those attending are held back, and which the character does not cross" ... "Let a critic plant himself in front of the gaping stage!"

Imagine Plato's cave not simply overthrown by some philosophical movement but transformed in its entirety into a circumscribed area contained within another—an absolutely other—structure, an incommensurably, unpredictably more complicated machine. Imagine that mirrors would not be *in* the world, simply, included in the totality of all *onta* and their images, but that things "present," on the contrary, would be in *them*. Imagine that mirrors (shadows, reflections, phantasms, etc.) would no longer be *comprehended* within the structure of the ontology and myth of the cave—which also situates the screen and the mirror—but would rather envelop it in its entirety, producing here or there a particular, extremely determinate effect. The whole hierarchy described in the *Republic*, in its cave and in its line, would once again find itself at stake and in question in the theater of *Numbers*.

Without occupying it entirely, the "Platonic" moment inhabits the fourth surface. But the fourth surface also comprehends, as you know, the discourse that dismantles the "Platonic" order of presence (present speech leading us to the visibil*ity* of the phenomenon, to the visibility of the *eidos*, of what *is*, in its truth, behind the veil or screen, etc.).

That which, on this stage, plupresently, proffers itself in the present, so as to deconstruct the "illusion" or "error" of the present, will be named the "attending discourse." It unites the motif of *presence* (the presence, the pressing solicitude of the interlocutory voice that calls you "you," thus invoking the presence of the reader-spectator who *attends* the spectacle or discourse while it is happening) with the motif of the *auxiliary* (a discourse

324

of aid, of indefatigable attentiveness, of vigilant prevention, a kind of Platonic *boetheia* that supports with its speech—its present speech—the faltering and frightened infirmity of an *ekgonos*, a dispossessed son, a stray product, a seed exposed to all the violence of writing: you).

The attending discourse—which is proliferating here—is addressed to the spectator (who attends the spectacle and is carefully attended in his attendance) and assists him in his reading of the moving structure of the play as a whole in all of its four faces, in its generalized writing and its total account in process of formation.

But who is it that is addressing you? Since it is not an "author," a "narrator," or a "deus ex machina," it is an "I" that is both part of the spectacle and part of the audience; an "I" that, a bit like "you," attends (undergoes) its own incessant, violent reinscription within the arithmetical machinery; an "I" that, functioning as a pure passageway for operations of substitution, is not some singular and irreplaceable existence, some subject or "life," but only, moving between life and death, reality and fiction, etc., a mere function or phantom. A term and a germ, a term that disseminates itself, a germ that carries its own term within it. Strengthening its breath with its death. The seed is sealed; the sperm, firm.

"3.11. ... becoming like you: not knowing who I am. But retaining what permits me to say 'I', this sudden start, this flaw in the syllables at the moment they are all at once there... I woke up talking, like a bolt of lightning slipping into a blackened whirlwind of words, I had thus been talking forever before finding myself among you... In the bloody knot of space, myself and all those who could say myself, all of us found ourselves caught in this implacable numeration, both the living and the dead, straining, lifted above the rivers, the cold vertiginousness of water and windows, all of us who are thus turning about inside the cage, with this learned new change, are ceaselessly placed in echo-positions, with these letters that approach, only by falling back, the cry felt from on high..."

Turning about inside the frame, the cage, or the park, "I" catches—two sequences later, coming from the wall across the way—the distorted repercussions of its language. "I" is caught in the violent impact of those repercussions as of the very first redoubled blow:

"1.13. ... The tale had begun abruptly when I decided to change languages within the same language . . . , when repetitions began to invade all their traits... That, however, did not involve any doubling . . . . . . When the operation—during which I had passed through mounds of disfigured flesh, skinless and speaking, as well

as through the retchings and churnings of nerves and blood turned into ciphers detached and lost in the exchange—had reached its term, I became that reversal... I opened my eyes, I saw coming toward me what would in sum force me to say 'I'..."

Being but "reversal," repercussive percussion, a passing passageway for permutation, subject to the violence of the blow and the "operation," this "*I*," which is forced to be said in sum, and which serves as your attendant, attends your attendance, and leans on its attending presence,

"*4.28. (...You open your eyes, you enumerate what passes before them... For you there is always something to see, something that fills the day in which you find yourself and the night in which you think you are sleeping and forgetting yourself... I am passing through here as that which marks and strikes the tale in progress, making it derive from itself, giving it the vertigo in which you were born...),"*

this "*I*" is the name of the full force of writing which, in one blow [*d'un coup*], triggers off the tale and keeps it in progress; but it is above all the simulacrum—and that simulacrum must be understood as a force—of an identity that is ceaselessly dislocated, displaced, thrown outside itself, precisely by this kind of writing by force,

"*3.47. ...'myself,' however, more and more lost in the text, posed, arrested in a corner of the text and no longer really doing anything but passing through, still detecting myself everywhere and in everything but to the point where everything was growing dark with the motion of its force..."*

This is the darkroom of that writing force where we developed pictures that "I" and "you" will never have had anything but the negatives of. The simulacrum of attendance would therefore require that the discourse of the "I" (which serves as your attendant and attends your attendance) be different, in writing, from what it says it is: proclaiming itself true instead of stating the truth of the story in progress, it is a simulation, and it deludes "you" by feigning to transform the imperfect point by point into the present, an operation it knows is impossible (4.48). In this duality triggered off by writing, it pretends to account—and to give a reason—for what you are seeing, feigning to tell you the presence of your present, whereas this pretense is itself part of a writing process. That is to say, a process of de-presentation and expropriation. And you are sucked into a new form of dizziness: in what does the present consist? Does it *consist* at all, since it divides itself thus in its attendance [*assistance*]? What would standing upright on stage amount to for something that is not consistent with itself?

While it is feigning to speak to you, to assist you, the "I" that passes through requires, as a surface vacant of itself, that something supplement *it*, and this in that very simulacrum of attendance. By ruse, it foments the cruel dispossession through which you will be dragged into the writing of the red tale. Preparing new reports for the red moment *("3.83. ... I was there, though breathing in the depths... Preparing new reports for the red moment . . . , desiring the massive ascent of the East, the orient finally forced to show its color...")*, the "I" foments against you; it foments, i.e. prepares a substance felt to be injurious—a poison—which makes the story redder and redder, carrying you off in the movement of its dispossessive writing until it reaches the simulacrum point at which it can both stain the tissue and feign to tell you about it in truth, in the form of attendance or, in a face-off, in the form of a barefacedly threatening provocation or summons. Go on reading, but watch out for this, which should already have started to make your head spin: that each separate fragment is only readable within the well-calculated play of an extremely numerous recurrence and an innumerable polysemy. Here, for example and at least, it is of the kind that affects the words "column," "frame" [*"cadre"* also = an executive], "blow" [*"coup"*], "poisoned," "products," "squares," "red," etc., and transforms them, throughout the length of *Numbers*, in the most baffling and necessary, surprising but obsessive ways. Hence you might see the "present" passage "quoted" as though it referred only to itself:

"4.40. (...Here, however, the tale continues, and it is like an empty column, a series of empty cadres designed to help the enemy in depth, to deliver you a more secret, more poisoned blow intended to deprive you of the use of your products and of the mastery of your discourse whose function is to mask everything, to arrange everything into neat, regular formulas... As though you were passing, with your eyes closed, from one square to another, from some decorated land to a land that has been bombed, with respect to which you are already beginning to spin... The red tale...)—"

Such a simulacrum of attendance only operates within parentheses. The twenty-five occurrences of sequence four are in parentheses, which signifies, in its duplicity, at once:

1. that a (present) discourse is claiming to go outside the text, to interrupt the (written) tale, through the rectitude of frank speech and the explanations of an accomplice, as if the discourse presently being held owed

nothing to anyone in its immediate, frontal disclosure, proffering itself of its own accord in all consciousness and without prior history;

2. that it nevertheless returns to writing, that the irreducibly graphic function of parentheses belongs within the general fabric of the tale just as the extratextual claims are really a form of dressing-room gossip, now being unmasked by the attending voices, or rather restored to their masks and theatrical effectiveness:

"4. (... *it is hard to accept this interval, this blank intact; it is nevertheless very hard to confirm without this forgetting which comes back and forces one's hand— when the text is interrupted, folds back upon itself, lets the voices come back like an endless recording*—...)

If there is no extratext, it is because the graphic—graphicity in general—has always already begun, is always implanted in "prior" writing. You have indeed read *implanted* here, and with the sowing of this allusion to grafting, transplantation, and emphyteosis, you can premeditate the idea of seeing it bud somewhere later on.

There is nothing before the text; there is no pretext that is not already a text. So that, at the moment the surface of attendance is broached and the opening opens and the presentation is presented, a theatrical scene was.

In the imperfect. Was already in place, even though presently invisible, at work without letting itself show, without being spoken by any present statement, prior to the "first" act. "It was/stellar outgrowth/the number/."
Numbers thus has no proper, unified, present origin; no one, outside the mask or simulacrum of some very clever pseudonym, is entitled to the property rights or author's royalties... Authority and property still remain, though, as pretentions of the attending discourse and as dead surface effects. (Even though, if two specific emblems are taken into account, while the proper name of the author is disappearing in a constant equivocal motion of death and safekeeping or salvation, the name is only in fact in hiding; it conceals itself behind the screen, behind *"the multiplication of screens as emblems of this new reign"* (1.25), or finds refuge, without ceasing to shine, a gem without air at the bottom of the book, the clasp, or the jewel-case, thanks to *"that writing that comprises a tangle of serpents, plumes, and the emblem of the eagle, which refers to the tensed force of the sun—a precious stone—a stone that must be reached if one wishes to go on behind the sun"* (2.34), behind death. A proper name, then, as it was once penciled at the theater, "always ready to regain control. An intact jewel [*joyau*] beneath the

disaster." All you will have had to do, once this stone has been thrown out, is to go a bit further, behind the citing of the solar [*solaire*] star (sun = death = mirror) in order to glimpse a poisoned ring. Then an antidote and then the key. Which are all the same.)

What will already have begun its play in the imperfect (or in a certain aorist, a certain unlimitedness in which the very horizon is lost, and which can also be confused with a future that will never become present ("2.6. ... *As though I were able for a moment to grasp myself from the viewpoint of an empty future, without any bounds (Ø), as though the play, the crowd, the sky which were now comprehended in the present—there I am—were coming from a past I had yet to go through...*")); what will have been written—the past of an anterior future or the future of an anterior past—in the "unreachable double bottom," which is itself neither anterior nor ulterior; what constantly returns to that imperfect *does not belong*. But not because it has been wrested from some primal presence or state of belonging. What is in question here is not a thing—a "reality" or "meaning"—that would come to achieve inscription as an extra option, after its original "production" or first marketing. This non-belonging—textuality as such—intervenes, i.e. interrupts, as of the very "first" trace, which is already marked by duplication, echoes, mirrors, presenting itself something like "the trace of its reflection" (*Drama*), always at least geminated into two parts, each one greater than the whole.

> « ———— it is only by virtue of two texts
> being repeated that one can enjoy
> any one part whole
>
>   or by virtue of
>   the turning around
>   of the same text
>
>   — of a second way
>   of rereading
>   that allows for having
>   the whole
>   successively......
>
> . . . .
>   Until that moment
>   print on quality paper
> or edit separately—
>   seek—
>
>   . . . . »

II

7. The Time before First

"... However, *somebody* killed *something*: that's clear, at any rate—"
"But oh!" thought Alice, suddenly jumping up, "if I don't make
haste, I shall have to go back through the Looking-glass, before I've
seen what the rest of the house is like! Let's have a look at the garden
[*le parc*] first!"

You are retracing your steps. The last vestiges lead you deeper into the park;
you are advancing backward, toward it natively. "The triangle with its
point downward, the lower part of Solomon's seal, is a traditional symbol of
the feminine principle, exploited extensively in *Finnegans Wake*. It goes
without saying that the value of the letter V is more justly derived from a
vague, vast group of associations. The classic Mallarméan example is found
in 'Hérodiade'..."

All oppositions based on the distinction between the original and the
derived, the simple and the repeated, the first and the second, etc., lose
their pertinence from the moment everything "begins" by following a
vestige. *I.e.* a certain repetition or text. Better than ever you will have
understood this in reading *Numbers*.

Everything there goes on *beyond* the opposition between *one* and *two* (etc.);
everything plays itself out despite or against the distinction between
perception and dream, perception and memory, consciousness and the
unconscious, the real and the imaginary, story and discourse, etc. Beyond
these oppositions or *between* these terms, but not in total confusion. In a
different distribution. *Two* is no more an accident of *one* than *one* is a
secondary surplus of *zero* (or vice versa), unless we reconsider our whole
notion of the values of accident, secondariness, and surplus: the sole
condition for being able at last to consider the text, in the movement of its
constellation, which always proceeds by number.

Far from being simply erased, the oppositions deactivated by this arithmetical theater are, in the same blow, reactivated, thrown back into play,

but this time as effects, not rules, of the game. Since the trace can only imprint itself by referring to the other, to another trace ("the trace of its reflection"), by letting itself be upstaged and forgotten, its force of production stands in necessary relation to the energy of its erasure. The power of expropriation never produces itself as such but only arises through an alteration of the effects of property. Upon the historical stage of the fourth surface, disappropriation is misapprehended, and necessarily so ("*4.52 ... There is a law for this misapprehension*"); it is violently confiscated within the domestic organization and representative economy of property. Coming to terms with desire (the desire for the proper), and taking into account the contradictions among its forces (for properness limits disruption, guards against death, but also regards death closely; absolute property, one's undifferentiated proximity to oneself, is another name for death; the space of property thereby also coincides with the "dead surface"), the text, quite squarely, makes the stage spin. Expropriation operates by violent revolution. Writing lays bare that which "*dies and comes back to life in a thought that in reality belongs from the beginning to no one*" (4 and 4.100); it modulates expropriation, repeats it, regularly displaces it, and tirelessly enumerates it, "*... and I was thus one mark among other marks...... But no one was any more myself; what was going to happen, in fact, happened for no one; there was nothing but this series of ciphers counting and recording and voiding the whole of the outside—*" (3.7).

Other suns, another revolution, a different arithmetic: "Something counts inside me, adds 1, rounds out the critical number which the chariots of the sun are waiting for in order to fill up the harness. I know that I have been constructed in order to measure..."

Expropriation is not ciphered merely by the mark of numbers, whose nonphonetic operation, which suspends the voice, dislocates self-proximity, a living presence that would hear itself represented by speech. The "stilled melodic encipherment"—as *Music and Letters* puts it—is the violent death of the subject, the reading subject or the writing subject, in the mute substitution of *Numbers*, in the dream of its fastened clasp, in its silent strongbox. Your own. ("*1.5. ... Upon touching this sequence, I understood that a single murder was constantly in progress, that we were coming from it only to return to it via this detour...*") But this encipherment is *melodic*; a kind of chant or song beats out the measures of all the marks in *Numbers*. In all senses of the word, it is a cadence that you must follow.

The "stilled ode," in *Mimique*, seals only the decease of a certain voice, a particular function—the representative function—of speech, the reader's voice or the authorial voice that would be there only for the purpose of re-presenting the subject in his inner thoughts, so as to designate, state, express the truth—or presence—of a signified, to reflect it in a faithful mirror, to let it show through untouched, or to become one with it. Without any screen, without any veil, or with excellent tain. But the death of that representative voice, that voice which is already dead, does not amount to some absolute silence that would at last make way for some mythical purity of writing, some finally isolated graphy. Rather, it gives rise to an authorless voice, a phonic tracing that no ideal signified or "thought" can entirely cover in its sensible stamp without leaving something out. A numerous pounding here subjects all representative outcroppings to the effects of its rhythm; and that pounding is itself adapted to the cruel, ordered deployment and theatrical arithmography of a text that is no more "written" than "spoken" in the sense of *the alphabet henceforth outmoded for us*" (2.22). The disappearance of the "authorial voice" ("The Text speaking there of itself and without the voice of an author," as Verlaine was told) triggers off a power of inscription that is no longer verbal but phonic. Polyphonic. The values of vocal spacing are then regulated by the order of that tainless voice, not by the authority of the word or the conceptual signified, which the text, moreover, does not fail to utilize, too, in its own way.

A "poem silenced," following those *Variations on a subject* ("Everything becomes suspense, fragmentary disposition with alternation and face-to-face, concurring in the total rhythm, which would be the poem silenced, in the blanks"), *Numbers* is also a poem in a fully raised voice. Try it. Note its broad yet controlled, tense, restrained, yet pressing clamor. It is the clamor of a song that puts the vowel on stage, along with the articulation whose prior echo it precipitates onto the wall surfaces, reflecting, from one panel to the other, in hundredfold repercussion, each bounce. This occurs in a different metal each time; it is the sculpting of another liquid, the traversing of some unheard-of material. An authorless voice, a full-throated writing, a song sung out at the top of the lungs:

"3. ... *and the voice was saying so, now, and it really was my voice being raised from the colored vision or rather from the burning background of the colors; it was my voice I heard modulating a pressing, fluid conspiracy in which the vowels lined up, changed places, and seemed to apply themselves to the text through my breath. Their sequence acted directly on each detail, repulsed the hostile elements, formed a rhythmic chain, a specter that collected and distributed the roles, the facts, and this game was using me as one figure among others; I was for it simply a grain picked up and hurled... The vocal relief of the letters inserted into the detached inscription—which, without them, would have remained stable, opaque, undecipherable——; the activity of these atoms which thus enabled me to intervene by reversing the operation of which I was the object; the emission and projection whose discreet power I had returned in mid-flight; all that was opening up the distance, the outside—and I can again see the sounds penetrating the purple sky down to the bottom of the eyes. The formula could be stated thus: I-O-U-I-A-I provided one straightway impresses upon it a kind of constant undulation, something that sounds drunk... . . . —And that is how my voice left me... . . ."*

This loss of voice is sung elsewhere in the transformed recurrence of the same sequence, following a *"partition of water"* and a *"sun that comes to set it on fire," "and there was this moment before the collapse, this moment that takes off in the song: a pressing conspiracy in which the vowels lined up, changed places; a formula that could have been stated I-O-U-I-A provided one straightway impresses upon it a kind of constant undulation, something that sounds drunk, precipitous..." (3.55).* You will have remarked the cadence, and, in the second occurrence, the dropping of the I at the end, *"the last note held for a long time"* in the first occurrence; where you would see the announcement of a certain dismemberment if you went back to look, just before the mark according to which the organ of *"my voice left me."*

"... red I, etc. ... of course, one can't attribute color to a consonant. But isn't it obvious that each of them, and each letter in general, has a different dynamism, that each one does not *work* in the same way, that it can be compared to a mechanical device which, having a single form, can nevertheless be used in all sorts of different ways? ... Just recently I was reading in a book... that the letter D, the Delta (Δ), is, according to Plato, the first and most perfect of all the letters in the alphabet, the one out of which all the others are born, since it is composed of equal sides and angles. And we are also told that in the Law the Savior did not come in order to remove that dot, that apex, which is located on the top of the I."

Expropriation thus does not proceed merely by a ciphered suspension of voice, by a kind of spacing that punctuates it or rather draws its shafts from it, or at it; it is also an operation *within* voice. Mainly, if thought belongs from the beginning to no one, if "impersonification" is what is initial, then this is quite simply because the text never in fact begins. Not that its rifts are erased or its "positive" ruptures blurred and blended into the continuum of something always-already-there. But precisely because the rifts in it never stand as origins: they always transform a preexisting text. No archeology of *Numbers* is possible from the moment they are read. You find yourself being indefinitely referred to bottomless, endless connections and to the indefinitely articulated regress of the beginning, which is forbidden along with all archeology, eschatology, or hermeneutic teleology. All in the same blow. *"The new text without end or beginning"* (3.99) can be neither maintained nor contained in the clasp of a book. The text is out of sight when it compels the horizon itself to enter the frame of its own scene, so as to "learn to embrace with increased grandeur the horizon of the present time."

Thus, for example: *Numbers* does seem to begin at the beginning: with the one of the first sequence. Yet on the eve of this opening:

1. the initial capital letter is suspended by the three dots that precede it; the origin is suspended by this multiple punctuation and you are immediately plunged into the consumption of another text that had already, out of its double bottom, set this text in motion. It is a citation, an inchoative in-citation, which gets the organization of everything cited [*de chaque cité*, also = "of every city"] moving again;

2. this cited text, this prior past that is still to come, isn't it precisely itself not only consumed but indeed the consummate statement of consumption or consummation as such? Its theoretical statement, as they say? and quite expert at that? For example: the "beginning" of *Numbers* is but a propagation, rolled up in the same flame, of the last burning page of *Drama*. You can read: "1. ... *the paper was burning, and it was a matter of all the sketched and painted things being projected there in a regularly distorted manner, while a sentence was speaking: 'here is the outer surface.' Before the eyes or rather as if retreating from them: this page or surface of browned wood curling up consumed."*

The "last" page of *Drama*:

"thinking that he will still have to write:

'one ought to be able to consider that the book is washed up here— (burns) (erases itself) (in a thought that has no last thought—"more numerous than the grass"—"the agile one, the one most rapid of all, the one that leans upon the heart")—.' "

Writing, fire, erasure, the "without end," the number, the innumerable, the grass, are all citations and cited statements about the necessity of these citational effects. These effects do not describe the line of a simple relation between two texts or two fiery consumptions; they carry you off in the displacement of a constellation or labyrinth. They no longer fit "inside the frame of this piece of paper." Not only are the references infinite, but they conduct you through texts and referral-structures that are heterogeneous to each other. Sometimes the citations are "quotations" of "quotations" (you are still reading this word in quotation marks before subjecting it, when the time comes, to a thorough examination); the references can be lateral or direct, horizontal or vertical; they are almost always doubled, and most often presented on the bias. One example from out of the number: the fire in this paper does not spread merely from *Drama* to *Numbers*; it has as one focus [*foyer*, also = "hearth"], a focus more virtual than real, another such "burning paper" yearning for dawn [*en mal d'aurore*, cf. "Maldoror"], which is in turn consumed—"cited"—("symbolic figures traced upon burning paper, like so many mysterious signs living with latent breath") in *Logics*, which, in a mode that is no longer simply theoretical but perhaps repeats the attending surface of the tetralogy (*Le Parc, Drame, Nombres, Logiques*), sets forth the "transfinite" motion of writing: the "generalized putting-in-quotation-marks of language" which, "with respect to the text, within it...becomes entirely citational."

No event, then, is being recounted; everything happens in the intertext; only one principle is observed: that "in the final analysis, what happens is nothing." There is always another book beginning to burn at the moment "he closes the book—blows out the candle with that breath of his which contained chance: and, crossing his arms, he lies down on the ashes of his ancestors."

The duality between original text and quotation is thus swept away. In the process of squaring. And as of the second square, you have been warned: *"1.5. ... something had begun, but this beginning in turn revealed a deeper layer of beginning; there was no longer any before or after; it was impossible to turn around ...—"*

Any statements about the pre-beginning, about the fiction of the origin, about the indeterminacy of the seminal imperfect into which the pluperfect of some event without a date, of some immemorial birth, is inserted ("something had begun...") cannot themselves escape the rule they set forth. They recite themselves, leading you back for example to the native enclosure of the *Park*: "...read the beginning of a sentence: 'The exercise-book is open on the table,' make quite sure that it contains nothing that I wanted to give it (nothing that might be compared with the original project), that one word is not enough to save the rest, that this whole complacent, numbing succession of words must be destroyed; tear it up, tear it up, throw it away, make a clean sweep, recreate the space that will gradually extend and expand in every direction."

This "beginning of a sentence" creates a relation of attraction between a certain piece of paper and a certain "surface of browned wood" on which *Numbers* will be tabled. But they have already followed a path marked above in *The Park*: "The exercise-book is open on the table of brown wood feebly lit by the lamp. The cover is already a bit torn and the pages, covered one after another by small, fine handwriting in blue-black ink, follow each other slowly, progress over white squared [*quadrillé*] paper, making it impossible to go back, to begin again this meticulous and useless work that demands to be completed to the yet distant final page, where one day it will stop of its own accord."

Like this graph paper in *The Park*, the checkerboard in *Drama* houses, from the very outset of the game, the impossibility of beginning, which is also the impossibility of "*turning around*" (*Numbers*), of "going back" (*The Park*): "All contaminated, significant. No beginning can provide the necessary guarantees of neutrality." This contamination of origins will also have been indicated by the "poison" in *Numbers*.

From where you stand, please note, in an angle of the graph paper (*The Park*), in the checkerboard squares (*Drama*), in the squares or cubes (*Numbers*), this opening paradoxically wrought like a thing that closes, the one playing itself off against the other. The necessary exit lays siege; it surrounds the text indefinitely, and also imperfectly, by referring—by exiting—toward another text. A false exit extends out of sight. The mirror is shown the door. Or squared. The enclosure—the grille—in *The Park*, *Drama*, and *Numbers*, is shaped like an opening, a little opening where the key can be inserted, an innumerable opening since it is but a grid (a relation between the lines and angles in the network). It is therefore both necessary and impossible. Urgent and impracticable, literally obsessive, as this will already have been situated and reserved in the *Park*: "Flat on my belly, my face buried in the pillow, I must attempt the experiment again. All the elements, if I wish, have been known for all time; I know, I can know; I could get out, find the imperceptible crack, the way out that nobody before me has been able to attempt."

Further on, still in the *Park*, you will have trodden on the numerous grass from *Drama* and *Numbers* as you plunge deeper into the place beyond the mirror which divides up the entire geometry of the text to come: "Quite near, behind me, beyond the mirror where, when I lower my eyes, I can see myself sitting on this chair, the grass is thick in spite of the pebbles, the dead leaves, and the twigs; in spite of the winter and cold, the grass is unalterably green, barely a tad less green."

This text full of keys harbors no secret. Nothing in sum need be deciphered except the sum the text itself is. There is nothing inside the clasp. Nothing behind the mirror. The obsessive quest for the way out is due, all other motivation being excluded, particularly that of some "author," solely to the structure of the text. And to that bunch of keys it provides, which you don't know what to do with. The obsession will always have been a textual one. "He said it was necessary to tie me to a fence." Textuality is obsidional. It is an undecidable process of opening/closing that re-forms itself without letup. Under orders and in order (*arithmos*).

It will be said—but things are not so certain if one takes a good look—that this minute, useless, obstinate, tireless composition of uneven squares that don't mean anything, that don't show anything but their regular irregularity, their frames and their colors, doesn't make up a very jolly world. This may be, but it is not a matter of psychology here, or of an author's world, his "world view" (or yours), or of some "experiment" to be performed, or of some spectacle to be described or recounted. Not a sight to do with it.

Such will have been the fence in this undecipherable text. A text latticed in the mirror. There are still other grille designs made to foil all deciphering and keep you constantly sidetracked by throwing switch after switch. The geometry of this text's grid has the means, within itself, of extending and complicating itself beyond measure, of its own accord, taking its place, each time, within a set that comprehends it, situates it, and regularly goes beyond its bounds after first being reflected in it. The history of the text's geometries is a history of irrefutable reinscriptions and generalizations.

An example, once again from among so many others: *The Park* "began" thus, with a blue that was later to clear up: "The sky above the long, gleaming avenues is dark blue." In the curling in which the volume of *Numbers* is consumed, you will have read: "*3.15. ... Also saying: 'the palace is furnished with fifty doors. These are open upon all four sides, forty-nine in number. The last door is not on any side and it is not known whether it opens upward or downward... All these doors have a single lock and there is only one little opening into which the key can be introduced, and that spot is indicated only by the trace of the key... It contains, opens, and closes the six directions of space'... Thus understanding that we would have to go through a goodly number of series before directly reaching the return of the architecture into the medium from which it had arisen... With its terraces, its domes, its gardens, its inhabitants, its ceremonies... 'The sky above the long, gleaming avenues is dark blue': that, in sum, was the sentence from which I took off—.*"

In the same way, the "first" sentence of *Drama* is reconstituted in one of the fourth sequences in *Numbers*, where you will have been able to read it, in the present, without knowing where it comes from: "*4.32. (... 'Firstly (first draft, lines, engravings, the game begins) it is perhaps the stablest element that is concentrated behind his head and forehead...' ...).*" The text thus trussed up (twisted, bent inward) always leads you back to the whole bundle, stringing you along in its ring of keys.

3. The first sequence of *Numbers* is not merely older than itself, like the wake of a prior text (which already, itself, etc.). If it is straightway plural, divided or multiplied, this is also because of its power of germination or seminal differentiation, which will proceed to engender or will have given birth to a whole chain of other sentences that are both similar and dissimilar, sentences that reflect and transform each other in a regularly irregular way, throughout the length of the text to come, separated each time by the mark or margin of some small difference. In 4.12, for example, the entire first sequence is modified by a preceding "as if." The *"Grand space already extending beyond measure"* has become, in another key, a *"Grand harmony already extending beyond measure."* The *"Grand object dropped and undone"* has been changed to a *"Grand volume dropped and undone."* These "numbered rephrasings" could be multiplied indefinitely.

What you have thus ascertained about the "first" or "last" sentences can also be demonstrated of the pre-first words of the text, the epigraphs or dedications, those fictive extratexts which also come to be violently reinscribed within the system of *Numbers*. The epigraph, a sentence from "Lucretius" (quoted in his originally foreign language: *Seminaque innumero numero summaque profunda*), ceases to be a quotation, pinned or glued to the superficial front of the book, from the moment it is worked over and itself sets to work inside the very body of the text (*"4.80. (... / 'Desire appeared first, wandering about over everything. It already existed before the germ of any thought' / ... Germs, seeds sown in innumerable number, and the sum of which reaches the depths in which the word 'you' and the thought 'you' are carving out a passageway through chance toward you)*—... *"1.81. ...past and future germs... Germs, grouped and disseminated, formulae that are more and more derivative..."*

The epigraph does not stand outside the text [*hors d'oeuvre*]. Neither does the dedication, even though it presents itself as a proper name ["for ЮЛИЯ"] (marked in its originally foreign writing, brought in from the East, like the Chinese characters sown throughout the text) whose vowels compose an ideogrammatic formula which *Numbers* will in several senses decompose and recompose, impressing a kind of constant undulation upon it, by expropriation and anagrammatical reappropriation, translating it, transforming it into a common noun, playing with the vowels that compose it (and *"4.32 (...'Consonants are heard only through the air that makes the voice, or vowel' /)*—"), marking the color of each one, insisting on the I, which is red like the *"red moment of history."* But these writing-effects, which will henceforth be called paragrammatical effects, are much more numerous than these examples might lead one to believe.

4. The "first" sequence, therefore, is not a discourse, a present speech (in the beginning *was* the number, not the word, nor, in what presently amounts to the same, the act); or rather the apparently "present" statement is not the statement of any present, not even of any past present, of any past defined as having taken place, as having been present. Far from any essence, you are straightway plunged by the imperfect into the already opened thickness of another text. And what is said or written (the "signified") is already the performing of a cut within a graphic substance that retains and distorts traces of all sorts: forms, sketches, colors, half-silent ideograms and spoken words, etc.:

"*1. ... the paper was burning, and it was a matter of all the sketched and painted things being projected there in a regularly distorted manner, while a sentence was speaking: 'here is the outer surface.' Before the eyes or rather as if retreating from them: this page or surface of browned wood curling up consumed.*"

Just as in *The Park*, the total milieu in which the book is written (the bedroom, the "former room" that keeps reappearing, the table, the exercise-book, the ink, the pen, etc.) is constantly being reinscribed and thrown back into play in *Drama* and *Numbers*. Each time, writing appears as disappearance, recoil, erasure, retreat, curling-up, consumption. This is how *The Park* closes (you will note the reflection of the trace of the key): "dark; while another day, with the exercise-book on a table in the sun or, this evening, taken out of the drawer of which she alone has the key, the exercise-book will be read for a moment, then closed; the exercise-book with the orange cover, patiently filled, heavily written over with regular handwriting and leading to this page, this sentence, this period, by the old pen frequently and mechanically dipped into the blue-black ink."

There remains this column of ink, after, before the final period. Dipped mechanically, ready to light into another text.

Drama, which ends where *Numbers* begins, nevertheless begins at the same point ("and we can say that he begins in fact at the point where he ends"), with the already-there-ness of a text that also carves out the space of a game: "Firstly (first draft, lines, engravings—the game begins)..."

8. The Column

"As for the textual motion (which carries off the whole of the *Songs*), it is of the sort that becomes 'accelerated with a uniform rotation in a plane parallel to the axis of the column.' " (*Logics*)

"A dream comes and reminds him that he is to construct obelisks, which is to say solar rays of stone, on which he is to engrave letters that are said to be Egyptian."

"Do you know that according to Aristotle a person who dies crushed by a column does not die a tragic death? And yet here is that nontragic death hanging over you."

"It was necessary to find a formation that would make use of the masses, and this was discovered in the *column*."

"The column of faeces, the penis, and the baby are all three solid bodies; they all three, by forcible entry or expulsion, stimulate a membranous passage..."

Thus, in the indefiniteness of a past that has never been present, at the moment a scission triggers off the game and lights into the text, "*a sentence was speaking.*" Further on: "*3.11... I woke up talking, like a bolt of lightning slipping into a blackened whirlwind of words*"... Just before this: "*1.9. ...Doubtless I had awakened; but this awakening was but a delayed effect, a germination...*"

It is always a matter of waking up, but never of some *first* awakening. My own presence to myself has been preceded by a language. Older than consciousness, older than the spectator, prior to any attendance, a sentence awaits "you": looks at you, observes you, watches over you, and regards you from every side. There is always a sentence that has already been sealed somewhere waiting for you where you think you are opening up some virgin territory, "*4. (...—and that all dies and comes back to life in a thought that in reality belongs from the beginning to no one, a transparent column where what takes place remains suspended at a greater or lesser height, and when you wake up you say to yourself: 'hey, I was there,' but nothing comes to explain that sentence, and that is what regards you...)—"*

The text occupies the place before "me"; it regards me, invests me, announces me to myself, keeps watch over the complicity I entertain with my most secret present, surveys my heart's core—which is precisely a city, and a labyrinthine one—as if from the top of a watchtower planted inside me, like that "transparent column" which, having no inside of its own, is driven, being a pure outside, into that which tries to close upon itself. The column puts space into time and divides what is compact. Its transparence is also reflective. Imagine that you have swallowed a cylindrical mirror. Upright, bigger than you are. *"4. (...that column does not leave you any distance; it keeps watch while you are asleep; it is slipped in between you and you... Less and less suspected, less and less remembered where you are walking without seeing me...)."*

This glass column traverses, dominates, regulates, and reflects, in its numerous polysemy, the entire set of squares.

It is a Tower of Babel in which multiple languages and forms of writing bump into each other or mingle with each other, constantly being transformed and engendered through their most unreconcilable otherness to each other, an otherness which is strongly affirmed, too, for plurality here is bottomless and is not lived as negativity, with any nostalgia for lost unity. It engages on the contrary both writing and song. *"1. ... Air / / Because of something said in another language, accentuated, repeated, sung—and straightway forgotten—, I knew that a new story had been triggered off"* (also in 2.90).

The Tower of Babel, the text's spinal column, is also a phallic column woven according to the thread of the work. "In place of phalli, says Herodotus, they came up with other objects about a cubit long, which had a thread attached; these were carried by women who, by pulling on the threads, were able to make the objects stand upright, a reproduction of the male genital organ, almost as big as the rest of the body."

"4.56. (...You are able, following this rhythm, to stand up slowly, to gather up your patch of space, to feel the column of bones become more flexible inside you while your hands recover their fingers...)—" "2.6. ...a syllable that does not exist in any other known language... I was then almost at the top of a cylinder whose extension I could not control, its base rooted in the heaviest of metals. We were thus going up, by the thousands, toward the white opening..." "1.49. ...not succeeding in grasping

the reason for this trip through the mirror, for this double uprooting, and why it was done precisely with her, her eyes, her tapered end, the sword hidden in the column that enveloped her..."

Isn't this *"transparent cylinder going through the worlds and their eras"* (2.38) also the ungraspable column of air in the Zohar (3.43. ... *"he engraved great ungraspable columns of air"* / ...)? These mirror-columns, these columns of mercury, these *"physical and atmospheric columns"* (1.85) indeed reach into the Kabbalah in that they also involve a *"column of numbers"* (4.52), *"1.45. ...in the dissemination with no images and no earth, the leap out of the marked, accumulated pain—which is luminous, though, and dry and contoured; successions of proofs ('the minimum number of rows—lines or columns—that contain all the zeros in a matrix is equal to the maximum number of zeros located in any individual line or column')...,"* and the columns of numbers are, there too, trees (1.45 and *"3.15. ... Aside from the four naked walls and the tree that went through the room, there was thus nothing there besides the hidden outside's insensible respiration, turning red ..."*). All of which, joined to the authority of the number 10 (1 + 2 + 3 + 4), might, if such a privilege were not too richly polysemous to be mastered in one fell swoop, represent the tree of the ten *sephiroth* which correspond to the ten archetypal names or categories. *Safar* means "to count," and *sephiroth* is sometimes translated "numerations." The tree of the *sephiroth*, an engraving of the whole, reaches down into the En Sof, "the root of all roots"; and this structure is entirely recognizable in *Numbers*. That would be only one of the numerous textual grafts through which the Kabbalah is reproduced there; numerous: plural, disseminated, and also suffused with rhythm and cadence, measured, calculated, marked on *"the entire reach"* (2.74), falling in time, like heads on the chopping block, like voices in endless recordings, in *"the motionless fall of the numbers"* (1.33).

A marching column, a column of numbers, a mirror-column, a column of air, a column of mercury, a column of *gold*: gold in fusion, a name brand alloy, "My magnificent palace is built with walls of silver, columns of gold . . ." The column is nothing, has no meaning in itself. A hollow phallus, cut off from itself, decapitated (i), it guarantees the innumerable passage of dissemination and the playful displacement of the margins. It is never itself, only a writing that endlessly substitutes it for itself, doubling it as of its very first surrection: "Two columns, which it was not difficult, much less impossible, to take for baobabs, could be seen in the valley, bigger than two pins. In fact, there were two huge towers. Now although, at first sight, two baobabs do not look like two pins, or even like two towers, nevertheless, by adroit use of the strings of prudence, one may affirm, without fear of error (for if this affirmation were accompanied by the least scrap of fear, it would be no affirmation; although a single name expresses these two phenomena of the soul whose characteristics are sufficiently well-defined as not to be easily confused), one may affirm that a boabab is not so very different from a column that comparison between these two architectural forms should be forbidden... or geometrical forms... or both... or neither... or rather high and massive forms. ... Two hugh towers could be seen in the valley; I said so at the beginning. Multiplying them by two, the result was four... but I could not see very clearly the necessity of this arithmetical operation."

An entire reading of the volume could circulate in the intertext or in the paragrammatical network that enlightens and fans the fire of consumption, from *Drama* to *Numbers* (the "burning resumé" of the city or the book, "*the paper was burning,*" etc.) and the fires of the Torah, the black fire and the white fire: the white fire, a text written in letters that are still invisible, becomes readable in the black fire of the oral Torah, which comes along afterward to draw in the consonants and point the vowels, "3.43. / ... *The path of the black fire where I burned myself on the white fire...*" Even while so many fires are tossed out, projected by the text, never is reference made to any "real" consumption in which, after all texts have been exhausted and outworn, one can finally hope to reach the focal hearth. The fire, indeed, is nothing apart from this "transference" from one text to another. Not even a "stilled object." Consumption (the relation between death and a certain sun that has been in question more than "once") is, like dissemination, textual through and through ("the book suppresses
time ashes")
Which does not mean that it is reduced (to ashes) but that your thinking about the text has been set on fire. The fact that, cut off from any ultimate, "real" referent—which would keep the fire at a reassuring distance—this sort of consumption seems to consume only traces, ashes, and to shed light on nothing that would be present, in no way prevents it from burning. But it is still necessary to find out what "burning" means. What is fire *itself?* In *Drama*: "Nothing distinguishes a flame from fire; fire is nothing more than a flame, and what is in question is the meaning of words, not the things *in* the words. It is useless to picture a fire, then a flame: what they are has nothing to do with what one sees." Like the crime, this consumption or consummation never "really" takes place. It hovers *between* desire and fulfillment, perpetration and remembrance. This is what the *hymen*, "tainted with vice yet sacred," doubly names in *Mimique*; the penetration, the act perpetrated by what *enters* [*entre*], consumes, and sows confusion

between [*entre*] the partners; but also, inversely yet in the same blow, the unconsummated marriage, the vaginal partition, the virginal screen of the hymen standing *between* the inside and the outside, the desire and its fulfillment, the perpenetration and its remembrance. A suspension of the "perpetual allusion": such is this PIERROT MURDERER OF HIS WIFE (Margueritte's mime in this hymen that goes out of sight).

The Kabbalah is not only summoned up here under the rubric of arithmosophy or the science of literal permutations ("*2.42. ... 'He tripled the sky, doubled the earth, and supported himself with numbers' ...*" "*3.95. ... The science of letter combinations is the science of superior interior logic / ...*"); it also cooperates with an Orphic explanation of the earth. As in *Drama* ("At the start, everything is present, but nothing exists. Then vision creates its successive screens..." . . . "... If I copy over this passage: 'now, I am returning to the time when the world was fresh and new, when the earth was still soft' ..."), the first sequence of *Numbers* mimes a sort of cosmogonic mythology. It is a repetition of the absolute present of the undifferentiated origin, but not at the zero-point of a pre-face numbered 4, some 0.4, already in the (1.): "*the paper was burning*" already at the origin of the world.

Interestingly, through the importance it gives to the dot, the air, etc., this Orphic explanation also describes an analogue of the *pleroma*, which is a sort of original space, a pneumatic layer (*tehiru*) in which the *zimzum*, the crisis within God, the "drama of God" through which God goes out of himself and determines himself, takes place. This contraction into a dot, this withdrawal and then this exit out of self located within the original ether, is of course linked to the mythology of "Louria," but it can also arise by way of "Hegel," "Boehme," etc. ("*2.54. ... 'He produced a simple dot that was transformed into thought, and within that thought, he executed innumerable sketches and engraved innumerable engravings. And then he engraved the spark, and the spark was the origin of the work, which existed and did not exist, and which was very deeply buried, unknowable by name...' ...*").

Even while it keeps the texts it culls alive, this play of insemination—or grafting—destroys their hegemonic center, subverts their authority and their uniqueness. Indeed, reduced to its textuality, to its numerous plur-ivocality, absolutely disseminated, the Kabbalah, for example, evinces a kind of atheism, which, read in a certain way—or just simply *read*—it has doubtless always carried within it. "... number, the only thing you so-called atheists have believed in..."

Numbers are thus a kind of cabal or cabala in which the blanks will never be anything but provisionally filled in, one surface or square always remain-ing empty, open to the play of permutations, blanks barely glimpsed as blanks, (almost) pure spacing, going on forever and not in the expectation of any Messianic fulfillment. It is a spacing that is merely attended. For there exists a whole interpretation of spacing, of textual generation and polysemy, of course, revolving around the Torah. Polysemy is the possibility of a "new Torah" capable of arising out of the other ("Torah will issue out of me"). "Rabbi Levi Isaac de Berditschew: 'Here is the way it is: the blanks, the white spaces in the Torah's role also arise from the letters, but we cannot read them as we do the blackness of the letters. When the Messianic era comes, God will unveil the white in the Torah in which the letters are now invisible to us, and this is what the term "new Torah" implies.' "

Here, on the contrary, it is always possible for a text to become new, since the blanks open up its structure to an indefinitely disseminated transformation. The whiteness of the virgin paper, the blankness of the transparent column, reveals more than the neutrality of some medium; it uncovers the space of play or the play of space in which transformations are set off and sequences strung out. It is air. *"L'air blanc"* (4.36).

Air: the ether in which, from the "beginning," the "One..." is caught or *raised: "1. ... Air / ... Air / / ... Air / / / ...."*

Air is also, to all appearances (that is, the airs of the air; air squared: 1, 2, 4 lines), mythically, the undifferentiated atmosphere in which the first present seems to congeal or take shape, a sort of origin of the world and of sensible certainty, mimed with "the false appearance of a present":

"1. ... At this point, precisely, there is no longer room for the slightest word. What one feels right away is a mouth: full, dark—grass, clay—one is inside. No need to move, to turn around. Everything is filled, satisfied, without any discrepancy, interval, or gap. Further on? It is here. Otherwise? Here."

The air from which the square of the world (4.24), the breath of the voice (4.32), and the appearance (the air) of the present are taken ("4.8 (... *This fourth surface is in a sense carved out of the air; it enables speeches to make themselves heard, bodies to let themselves be seen; consequently, it is easily forgotten, and that is doubtless where illusion and error lie...)")* provides the rhythm behind the melody.

"Air blanc": drawn from the column, isn't this air also the work environment, the *milieu* of the workplace, both in the sense of an element or medium in which work takes place and in the sense of a central furnace installed in the middle [*milieu*] of the factory (you recall the "putrid smoke" and the "white screen spewing out of a factory" from *Drama*)? *Numbers:* *"3.75... and thinking about the cruel concrete work ultimately produced in the void,*

and for that very reason all the more concrete and universal, with nothing beyond it, without limitation, without appeal... 'The factories and docks you see in these pages can be leveled, the columns of white smoke cease to rise in the sky, but this port cannot be subjugated' | 'the people alone are the author of universal history' | ..."

But "before" being the milieu of work and of production as a *breakthrough* (1.24; 3.43), air is "air": a "quotation." From *Drama*, for example: "... as though he were thinking or dreaming of a book... A book in which every element (words, sentences, pages) would be animated with a veiled rotation, in such a way as to make one believe one is attending the revolution of a multiple sphere... What comes out of this book is air." You would have been able thus to reconstruct the citational network of "spheres," "rotations," etc. . . .

Hence, this air is not merely a "quotation": it is the empty medium of the text as generalized quotation, the citation of citation, the citedness of what is summoned.

This overdetermined "air" (but there is never anything *but* overdetermination, once one is outside the "illusion" of originary presence on the fourth surface) regenerates little by little within itself, leaping over "Hegel" 's *"Physics"*—in other words all of philosophy—, the texts of the Presocratic cosmogonies. The one by "Anaximander." The one by "Anaximenes" in particular, which defines the original *apeiron* (the boundless, the aorist, the imperfect in sum) as *air*, which, in its rarefaction, would give rise to fire. And, for "Anaximander," isn't the earth which floats upon the air a "column base," a "cylindrical column" of calculable proportions (the diameter of the base being equal to a third of the height), which is swollen at its upper tip and inhabited by us? *Numbers*: "2.6. ... I was then almost at the top of a cylinder whose extension I could not control, its base rooted in the heaviest of metals..."* What follows in this sequence seems to simulate the description of one of the *Scenes from Paradise* by "Bosch," which you will have been able to see at the *Palazzo Ducale* in Venice; it makes a certain "white circle," in the upper right hand corner of the painting, open onto the Way of the *"Tao Tö King"* ("*The crucible, the factory, in which we were each being elaborated with respect to the others, was thus at once the reminder and the development of a formula previously inscribed in the white circle that was the way. The way, or perhaps, on the contrary, the entrance to a new path, the same but going in the opposite direction, the same but seen in the mirror, or rather transforming the one that had just taken place into a mirror, in which we were still spinning slowly beyond what had once been called a mirror or reflection...*"), all of the *Numbers* thus getting their fictive start in the thickness of this plural text, mixing the body of writing with the space of myth, dream, painting, and the strange tain of what can no longer even be called a mirror.

The literal air (*r* [pronounced "air" in French]) cannot be dissociated from number (of which it is the elemental column) and from sperm (term/germ), for which it makes room and to which it gives rise. "Anaxagorus" and "Empedocles," in particular, associate these things systematically. "The air and the ether filled everything, both being infinite; for in all things, those two excel in number and volume . . . in all compounds, there are numerous and varied parts, the seeds (*spermata*) of all things, presenting forms, colors, and flavors of every sort." The "separation" that introduces difference into the "all together" makes each thing "appear." Beforehand, *"in the mixture prior to the mirror"* (3.31), "a large quantity of earth was contained, along with seeds in infinite quantity which bore no resemblance to each other." And finally, is it necessary to remind you that the members of the Pythagorean sect, who also believed that air constitutes the medium of the world, swore by the tetractys $(1 + 2 + 3 + 4)$ and represented numbers by means of dots arranged on small objects similar to dominoes? You will have known this, in the illusion of that future perfect in which presently, on the point of running aground, you are ceaselessly drifting about.

9. The Crossroads of the *"Est"*

"...toward the East [*Est*]? The bridges are cut? No map? ... It would take only a mistake in pronunciation and hup! a mountain? You're oversimplifying; this can't be serious. But the East? I'm asking you how to go toward the East? What are those vague gestures for? incomplete? the East? E, A, S, T? Toward the right side of the picture, in sum. There isn't much point in being painted together in the same painting if people refuse to give each other information." (*Drama*)

"*Carrefour* [crossroads], from *quadrifurcus*, having four forks... In a Latin-French glossary from the Twelfth Century, *theatrum* is translated by *carrefourc*." (*Littré*)

What are you in fact doing with these various examples of polysemous programs and textual grafts? You often hear yourself saying: this *is* [*est*] that; and then that; and also that. The air *is* the *apeiron* of Presocratic physiology, the *tehiru* of the Kabbalah, the possibility of presence, of visibility, of appearance, of voice, etc. "Air" *means* this, *is-trying-to-say* that, etc. It could also have been said that: the *square* [*carré*] is

1. The graph paper or the grille in the *Park*, the checkerboard in *Drama*, the dial [*cadran*] and the tetralogical configuration that takes shape in *Numbers*, along with *Logics* and the (IV × 4) four times four propositions in its *Program*: "that is, a multiple tetralogy deploying itself parallel to a cycle of years begun again, and suppose that its text be incorruptible like the law: that's it, almost!";

2. The "four roots of all things" described by "Empedocles," or the square root (4.32);

3. "Square writing," the form of Chinese writing in general and of a certain ideogram that "means [*veut-dire*]" "to write" ("*3.23. However, it was necessary to choose between East and West, and this was like trying to opt for a past with a false face of futurity or for a future still made of figures from the past... On one side, a cemented, cross-hatched immensity, shot through with waves and images, where black and white don't have the same value, where sex and sex are separated and withdrawn... On the other, the muddy, overturned earth, transformed into undifferentiated corporal multitudes, the earth that speaks and is armed and seems to be waking up from a calculated sleep... In the West, the massacre of the red earth forgotten under tons of iron and steel . . . In the West, the crowd; in the East, the people. In the West, the image; in the East, the stage. . . . . . . the invisible force of complete mutations that leave nothing out, the square writing that shakes the firmest ground...*");

4. And finally, the square of the earth or the world. And no one will be allowed into this theater if he does not know how to take the measurements of the earth squarely. ("*4.24. (... The square we are passing through here is the earth, but these four filled-in surfaces refer to a center which isn't there and which doesn't count, so that the complete figure*

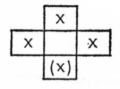

contains an empty square for the one moment impossible to live, fate... And yet I progress through this maze of words . . . we turn as we transform ourselves in this airless labyrinth carved out of air..." Then: "*1.77. ... 'They make them appear by using fire (high, sky) on the square base part (earth) of the tortoise shell' | ..."*), so that the square of writing informs both the places where writing is filled in and the blanks of that empty square or sheet which receives something like its seed

> "The 25th sheet missing
> and me presenting myself 25th
> and taking the 24: between
> which I establish a relation
> and bind into a volume
>
> ⎯⎯⎯⎯
>
> on which is
> developed that absent sheet
>
> The sessions go 4 by 4
> and in that way make an ensemble
>
> ...."

"*tetra*, which marks the double polarity, shows up in the *x* in *excepté, feux* [fires], and in the cross described by *such-and-such obliquity by such-and-such declivity*, but even more strikingly in the image of the Bear q.v. *têt* in fact epitomizes the combination cross-circle, which is the essence of the title-sentence and of the double polarity: '*têt* [*tête (head)* ... *téter* (to nurse) ... *têtard* (tadpole) ... *testicule* (testicle) ...]: the ninth letter of the Hebrew alphabet, corresponding to our *t* pronounced with greater emphasis (its earliest form, in the Phoenician alphabet, is that of a circle around a cross. This is the prototype of the Greek *theta*. It is supposed that the word *têth* once meant "serpent")' (*Nouveau Larousse*). The idea is that of the 'omnipresent Line spaced out from every point to every other point' (648), along with the serpent of the Fall, the sperm (of the milky way) that coils around itself like the snake in the Kabbalah in an eternal return, just as the ideogram, comet, tail, or slope of becoming bends back toward its head (its origin)—that is, the beginning of the Poem. The final Throw of Dice is the potential germ (sperm) of the whole Poem, and repeats the initial Throw of Dice."

The word "square" ["*carré*"] is thus a square word, a word with square corners, a crossroads-word ["*un mot carrefour*"]. Because of its empty square, its open surface, its discounted face, it does not enclose but rather leaves the way open for the intersection of meanings. The square proliferates.

But it is not a matter here of restoring some sort of mystique or poetry of numbers. We can no longer wonder "what poet will come to sing this panpythagorism, this synthetic arithmetic that begins by giving every being its four quanta, its four-digit number...," hunting down the *tetragram* as others do the *tetrapharmakon*. Here there is no longer any depth of meaning.

For when you say "this *is* that," " 'this' means 'that' " (don't take any more examples: the square, paradoxically, was only one—one element, therefore—and every term in the text could have done just as well, since the sum and substance of *Numbers* lies in this power of substitution and formalizing abstraction), the very form of your proposition, the "is" [*"est"*] affiliated with *trying-to-say*, essentializes the text, substantializes it, immobilizes it. Its motion is thus reduced to a series of stances and its writing to a thematic exercise. But one must choose between the text and the theme. It is not enough to install plurivocity within thematics in order to recover the interminable motion of writing. Writing does not simply weave several threads into a single term in such a way that one might end up unraveling all the "contents" just by pulling a few strings.

This is why it is not in all rigor a question of polythematicism or of polysemy here. Polysemy always puts out its multiplicities and variations within the *horizon*, at least, of some integral reading which contains no absolute rift, no senseless deviation—the horizon of the final parousia of a meaning at last deciphered, revealed, made present in the rich collection of its determinations. Whatever interest one might find in them, whatever dignity one might grant them, plurivocity, the interpretation it calls for, and the history that is precipitated out around it remain *lived* as the enriching, temporary detours of some passion, some signifying martyrdom that testifies to a truth past or a truth to come, to a meaning whose presence is announced by enigma. All the moments of polysemy are, as the word implies, moments of meaning.

Now, *Numbers*, as numbers, have no meaning; they can squarely be said to have no meaning, not even plural meaning. "The currency [*numéraire*], that engine of terrible precision, clean to the conscience, smooth to consciousness, loses even a meaning...." At least, in their movement (writing squared, writing about writing, which covers all four surfaces and is not pluri*vocal* for the simple reason that it does not reside essentially in the *vox*, in the word), *Numbers* have no present or signified content. And, a fortiori, no absolute referent. This is why they don't show anything, don't tell anything, don't represent anything, aren't trying to say anything (3.31). Or more precisely, the moment of present meaning, of "content," is only a surface effect, the distorted reflection of the writing on the fourth panel, into which you keep falling, fascinated by appearance, meaning, consciousness, presence in general, attendance (upon no one in danger). That "horizon"-value, that pure infinite opening for the presentation of the present and the experience of meaning, suddenly becomes framed. Suddenly it is a part. And just as suddenly apart. Thrown back into play. And into question. Its de-formations are no longer even negatively regulated by any *form,* which is another name for presence. The transformations of meaning no longer hinge on any enrichment of "history" and "language" but only on a certain squaring of the text, on the obligatory passage through an open surface, on the detour through an empty square, around the column of fire.

The concept of polysemy thus belongs within the confines of explanation, within the explication or enumeration, in the present, of meaning. It belongs to the attending discourse. Its style is that of the representative surface. It forgets that its horizon is framed. The difference between discursive polysemy and textual dissemination is precisely *différence* itself, "an implacable difference." This difference is of course indispensable to the production of meaning (and that is why between polysemy and dissemination the difference is very slight). But to the extent that meaning presents itself, gathers itself together, says itself, and is able to stand there, it erases difference and casts it aside. Structure (the differential) is a necessary condition for the semantic, but the semantic is not itself, in itself, structural. The seminal, on the contrary, disseminates itself without ever having *been* itself and without coming back to itself. Its very engagement in division, its involvement in its own multiplication, which is always carried out at a loss and unto death, is what constitutes it as such in its living proliferation. It exists in number. The semantic order is of course entangled there, too, and thereby also has a relation to death. The fourth surface is indeed a deathly surface, a dead surface of death. The semantic, as a moment of desire, signifies the reappropriation of the seed within presence, the attempt to keep the seed abreast of itself in its re-presentation. The seed thus contains itself, so as to preserve itself, see itself, observe itself. Hence, the semantic is also the seminal's dream of death. The clasp [*fermoir*] (and all its rhymes). In the dial's finite apparatus, the polysemous phase of dissemination reproduces itself indefinitely. The game is no more finite than it is infinite. "*3.83. ... / 'The number belonging to the concept "finite number" is an infinite number' / ...*"

Such is the square dance of *Numbers*: you can no longer say "the column *is* [*est*] this, and this, and that." The column *is not*; it is nothing but the passage of dissemination. As transparent as the burning air in which the text carves out its path. A process or trial opened up by (in) the seminal text. And the "phallic" significance of the column is itself only a semic effect—

"what is called present"—a reflection on the fourth surface, the described center and represented mastery of dissemination. But, filled with air, it can always be replaced, precisely by some other column, in the empty square, in the column of substitutable numbers or objects.

It is the frightening quality of such a necessity that comes to be limited and made more reassuring by the construction of a quarte and of meaning. Which is always the *meaning of Being*. The "is," which is "Being" as an indication of presence, procures this state of calm, this consciousness of ideal mastery, this power of consciousness in the act of showing, indicating, perceiving, or predicating, in the operation of the fourth surface. Whose discourse tells you: the column *is* this or that, *is there*; whether it is obvious or hidden behind the multiplicity of apparitions, the column *is*. But the column *has* no Being, nor any being-there, whether here or elsewhere. It belongs to no one. You have no hold over it, you will never absolutely control its extension. You will not take it from somewhere else and put it here. You will not cite it to appear. And from this column's not being (a being), from its not falling under the power of the *is*, all of Western metaphysics, which lives in the certainty of that *is*, has revolved around the column. Not without seeing it but on the contrary in the belief that it sees it. And can be sure, in truth, of the contours of its collapse, as of a center or proper place.

This is a subversion of the *"est"* that assures the West of all its fantasies of mastery (including the mastery of its fantasies). In *Numbers*, the powers of the *"est"* are not simply canceled out. They are enumerated. Account is given of them by situating them, framing them. Just like the horizon. Like the meaning of Being. The present indicative of the verb "to be," the tense of the great parenthesis and of the fourth surface, is thus caught up in an operation that divides it by four. Its predominance is properly discarded [*écartée*]—that is, (s)played—(drawn and) quartered [*écartelée*] by being framed [*encadrée*] on all (four) sides. From now on you will have to read the *"est"* in this *écarté* or this *écart* [gap] (*"écart*: a term of heraldry. One quarter of a shield divided into four parts. The principal arms of the house are placed in the 1st and 4th *écart*, that is, the two in the upper half of the shield; in the lower two are the arms obtained by marriage or from the maternal line"), in which the West as a whole is separated from itself.

Even though it is only a triangle open on its fourth side, the splayed square loosens up the obsidionality of the triangle and the circle which in their ternary rhythm (Oedipus, Trinity, Dialectics) have always governed metaphysics. It loosens them up; that is, it de-limits them, reinscribes them, re-cites them (*"4.84 (... that comes from the fact that the line now no longer closes up into a point or a circle ('science is the circle of circles') and also no longer rejoins its own repetition...)*—").

"4 being the figure for completion in the abstract or for the cross within the circle . . . the circle, which contains the 4, and rules over it through the Triad, which is the first module, the first effigy, or the first image of separation from unity."

"here, the *squaring of the circle* is the uniting of the masculine sex and the feminine sex into a whole, just as it is possible to unite into a single figure the framed circle or the circled square." ... "...he who follows the philosophers through winds and tides ought necessarily to set off in quest of the philosopher's stone, the squaring of the circle..."

In the "senseless gaps [*écarts*]" of *Drama*, in the "*quasi stellar sources*" of *Numbers*, "*subject to wide deviations* [*écarts*]," the metaphysical triangle, the "path that is philosophical and more certain," can no longer achieve closure. What remains invisible—because one thinks one sees into it—is a fourth side, a quarter, not a third ("like an angle extending out of sight formed by chilly cranes meditating at great length . . . it is perhaps a triangle, but it is not possible to see the third side constructed in space by these curious migrating birds").

It is thus not possible to rest upon the copula. Coupling is a mirror. The mirror is traversed of its own accord, which is to say that it is never traversed at all. This being-traversed is not something that happens by accident to the mirror—to the West—; it is inscribed within its structure. This is as much as to say that, forever producing itself, it never comes to be. Like the horizon.

And yet the "*est*," which has always tried to say what is beyond narcissism, is captured in the mirror. Read in the gap, it never comes to be. Insofar as it is turned toward the "*est*," Being henceforth confines itself to its own crossing-out as a criss-crossing. It can only be written beneath the grid of the four forks.

So, rather than quoting from the immense arithmosophistic literature, and instead of adding to the tetragon—or sacred quaternary—of Pythagoras, to the four cardinal points of the Kabbalah, to the Great Quaternary of Eckartshausen (four is the number of Force, and out of it springs the 10, the universal number: "The multiplication of the number, the extraction of its root, its multiplication by itself, and the consideration of the proportion of all root numbers with their root numbers, is the greatest secret of the doctrine of numbers. This is what is to be found in all secret writings behind the expression: knowledge of the great quaternary"), in place of quotations from Saint-Martin or Fabre d'Olivet, from *Louis Lambert* or *Seraphita*, etc., let us graft here one of the thoughts of the day, which will perhaps incite you to measure another gap, between gaps.

For example, on the basis of this text about another text concerning the crossing of a line ("Über die Linie," which can be translated either *trans lineam* or *de linea*): "Accordingly, a thoughtful glance ahead into this realm of 'Being' can only write it as B̶e̶i̶n̶g̶. The drawing of these crossed lines at first only repels, especially the almost ineradicable habit of conceiving 'Being' as something standing by itself and only coming at times face to face with man... The symbol of crossed lines can, to be sure, according to what has been said, not be a merely negative symbol of crossing out. Rather it points into the four areas of the quadrangle (*des Gevierts*) and of their gathering at the point of intersection... The meaning-fullness of language by no means consists in a mere accumulation of meanings cropping up haphazardly. It is based on a play which, the more richly it unfolds, the more strictly it is bound by a hidden rule. Through this, meaning-fullness plays a part in what has been selected and weighed in the scale whose oscillations we seldom experience."

Still in order to keep the gap open and to give it its chance, let us throw one more thing into play: "Earth and sky, divinities and mortals dwell *together all at once*. These four, at one because of what they themselves are, belong together. Preceding everything that is present, they are enfolded into a single fourfold (*das Geviert*)... Each of the four mirrors in its own way the presence of the others. Each therewith reflects itself in its own way into its own, within the simpleness of the four. This mirroring does not portray a likeness. The mirroring, lightening each of the four, appropriates their own presencing into simple belonging to one another... The mirroring that binds into freedom is the play that betroths each of the four to each through the enfolding clasp of their mutual appropriation... This expropriative appropriating is the mirror-play of the fourfold... This appropriating mirror-play of the simple onefold of earth and sky, divinities and mortals, we call the world... That means: the world's worlding cannot be explained by anything else nor can it be fathomed through anything else... The unity of the fourfold is the fouring (*die Vierung*). But the fouring does not come about in such a way that it encompasses the four and only afterward is added to them as that compass. Nor does the fouring exhaust itself in this, that the four, once they are there, stand side by side singly. The fouring, the unity of the four, presences as the appropriating mirror-play of the betrothed, each to the other in simple oneness. The fouring presences as the worlding of world. The mirror-play (*Spiegel-Spiel*) of world is the round dance of appropriating (*der Reigen des Ereignens*). Therefore, the round dance does not encompass the four like a hoop. The round dance is the ring that joins while it plays as mirroring. Appropriating, it lightens the four into the radiance of their simple oneness. Radiantly, the ring joins the four, everywhere open to the riddle of their presence..."

"*4.28. (and here is the side turned toward you: what you understand by 'nature'* ......)—"

10. Grafts, a Return to Overcasting [*Retour au surjet*]

"The essential thing is to set the song in motion as a *graft* and not as a meaning, a work, or a spectacle." (*Logics*)

"Let us therefore turn our eyes like the religious Chaldean toward the absolute sky where the stars, in an inextricable cipher, have set out the record of our birth and are keeping a graft of all our pacts and oaths. But in the absence of a polestar to provide the point, without any planet to give the height, without a sextant, without a horizon, look . . ."

That is how the thing is written. To write means to graft. It's the same word. The saying of the thing is restored to its being-grafted. The graft is not something that happens to the properness of the thing. There is no more any thing than there is any original text.

Hence, all those textual samples provided by *Numbers* do not, as you might have been tempted to believe, serve as "quotations," "collages," or even "illustrations." They are not being applied upon the surface or in the interstices of a text that would already exist without them. And they themselves can only be read within the operation of their reinscription, within the graft. It is the sustained, discrete violence of an incision that is not apparent in the thickness of the text, a calculated insemination of the proliferating allogene through which the two texts are transformed, deform each other, contaminate each other's content, tend at times to reject each other, or pass elliptically one into the other and become regenerated in the repetition, along the edges of an *overcast seam* [*un surjet*]. Each grafted text continues to radiate back toward the site of its removal, transforming that, too, as it affects the new territory. Each is defined (thought) by the operation and is at the same time defin*ing* (think*ing*) as far as the rules and effects of the operation are concerned. For example, in the case of content and form, "*1.33. . . . ('Content and form have changed because, conditions having changed, no one will be able to furnish anything but his own labor')...—*") or in the case of the elliptical: "*2.98. ... 'The differentiation of commodities into commodities and money does not sweep away these inconsistencies, but develops a modus vivendi, a form in which they can exist side by side. This is generally the way in which real contradictions are reconciled. For instance, it is a contradiction to depict one body as constantly falling towards another, and as, at the same time, constantly flying away from it. The ellipse is a form of motion which, while allowing this contradiction to go on, at the same time reconciles it' / —.*" You shall no longer stray very far from the elliptical.

These transplantations are legion. "...the cause is never the same, but the operation as of a sum that grows..." ..."I cull here and there out of several books such sentences as please me, not to keep them in my memory (for I have none to retain them), but to transplant them into this work, where, to say the truth, they are no more mine than they were in the places from whence I took them." Inserted into several spots, modified each time by its exportation, the scion eventually comes to be grafted onto itself. The tree is ultimately rootless. And at the same time, in this tree of numbers and square roots, everything is a root, too, since the grafted shoots themselves compose the whole of the body proper, of the tree that is called present: the subject's career or quarry.

All this is possible only in the gap that separates the text from itself and thus allows for scission or for the disarticulation of silent spacings (bars, hyphens, dashes, numerals, periods, quotation marks, blanks, etc.). The heterogeneity of different writings is writing itself, the graft. It is numerous from the first or it *is not*. Thus it is that the phonetic writing in *Numbers* finds itself grafted to nonphonetic types of writing. Particularly to a tissue of Chinese ideograms, as they are called, from which it derives nourishment like a parasite. Up until now the use of Chinese graphic forms—one thinks of "Pound" in particular—had as its aim, according to the worst hypothesis, the ornamentation of the text or the decoration of the page through a supplementary effect of fascination, which would haunt it by freeing the poetic from the constraints of a certain system of linguistic representation; according to the best hypothesis, it was intended to allow the forces of the designs themselves to play directly before the eyes of those who are not familiar with the rules of their functioning.

Here, the operation is altogether different. Exoticism has nothing to do with it. The text is penetrated otherwise; it draws a different kind of strength from that graphy that invades it, framing it in a regular, obsessive manner, which becomes more and more massive and inescapable, coming from the other side of the mirror—from the *est*—, acting within the so-called phonetic sequence itself, working it through, translating itself into the latter even before appearing, before letting itself be recognized after the fact, at the point at which it is dropped like a textual tail, like a remainder, like a sentence upon the text. Its active translation has been clandestinely inseminated; it has for a long time been (under)mining the organism and the history of your domestic text, just as it now punctuates its end, like the registered trademark of a kind of labor that is finished, yet still in progress—

And the powerful force of this labor is due less to any isolated character than to "sentences," to what is already a text, to a quotation. Never will any citation have so aptly meant both "setting in motion" (the frequentative form of "to move"—*ciere*) and, also since it is a matter of shaking up a whole culture and history in its fundamental text, solicitation, i.e., the shakeup of a whole.

The thickness of the text thus opens upon the beyond of a whole, the nothing or the absolute outside, through which its depth is at once null and infinite—infinite in that each of its layers harbors another layer. The act of reading is thus analogous to those X rays that uncover, concealed beneath the epidermis of one painting, a second painting: painted by the same painter or by another, it makes little difference, who would himself, for lack of materials or in search of some new effect, have used the substance of an old canvas or preserved the fragment of a first sketch. And beneath *that*, etc. ... All this requires that you take into account the fact that, in scratching upon this textual matter, which here seems to be made of spoken or written words, you often recognize the description of a painting removed from its frame, framed differently, broken into, remounted in another quadrilateral which is in turn, on one of its sides, fractured.

The entire verbal tissue is caught in this, and you along with it. You are painting, you are writing while reading, you are inside the painting. "Like the weaver, then, the writer works backwards." "4.36. (. . .*you are at present that figure in the painting who is looking toward the background—so that there is no longer any back, nor any face, and you are swallowed up by the 'canvas,' but if you try to take a note of that, your dizziness returns, a black whirling that lights up the essence of any horizon or water . . .)—"*

Thanks to the incessant movement of this substitution of contents, it appears that the painting's border is not that through which something will have been shown, represented, described, displayed. A frame *was*, and assembles and dismantles itself, that's all. Without even showing itself, as it is, in the con-sequence of those substitutions, it forms itself and trans-forms itself. And this operation, which reminds you, in the plupresent, that there was a frame for this double bottom, and that it opened, i.e.

closed, upon a mirror—*that* is what you will implacably be kept on the alert for.

On (the) edge. Alert to the border itself. Attentive to the edge of the turning dial [*cadran*] and held at the edge of dizziness, for, looking "toward the back [*fond*] of the painting"—where you are—you will have found out that its infinite depths were also bottomless [*sans fond*]. Perfectly superficial. This volume, this cube was without depth. That is why you can indifferently have confused it with a flat square, a (sun: death) dial drawn on the ground, hiding the ground where its "*needle*" (2.46), its "*rod*" (4.84), its stalk is planted ("Sundial, an instrument that indicates the solar hour directly by means of the shadow cast by a stalk parallel to the earth's axis, which is called a style." (*Littré*)). You will have made the rounds of this dial, indefinitely, dizzily, always being thrown outside by the powers of reference. You are not settled outside, since the absolute outside is not outside and cannot be inhabited as such; but you are forever being expelled, always involved in a process of expulsion, projected outside the column of light through its force of rotation, yet also pulled in by it. Through the opening of the fourth surface or through the empty square in the center of the four squares, you will have been entrained, carried off, overcast in a kind of unfinished, interminable labor. The square or, as you wish, the cube, will never be closed up. One would have had to go on forever trying to *équarrier* ("to cut off the rough edges of a parchment") or to *équarrir* ("to square off [timber or stone]"), "*4.100. (. . . you, carried, all the way to the stone which is not the stone, a transversal multitude that is read, fulfilled, effaced, burned, and refuses to close itself up in its cube and in its depth) — (1 + 2 + 3 + 4)² =*
100 — 立方 —

Here you stand, close to the first—undecipherable—stone, which is not one, or which—of all those stones, whether petrified by the Medusa, precious or not, that have marked your path—*was*, numerous. *Calculus*. Pebbles used in counting. Gravel.

XI. The Supernumerary

"And as I journeyed I came to the place where, as you say, this king met with his death. Jocasta, I will tell you the whole truth. When I was near the branching of the crossroads…"

Oedipus

"And it told him that it was fate that he should die a victim at the hands of his own son, a son to be born of Laius and me. But, see now, he, the king, was killed by foreign highway robbers at a place where three roads meet…"

Jocasta

"Well, when he came to the steep place in the road, the embankment there, secured with steps of brass, he stopped in one of the many branching paths. This was not far from the stone bowl that marks [the] covenant. . . .

"… But after a little while as we withdrew, we turned aound—and nowhere saw that man…"

Messenger (Oedipus at Colonus)

These *Numbers* define themselves, several times, through various *detours*. They thereby comprehend all discourses you can have proffered about them. The excesses of such discourses had already come to term and then been discounted in advance. Whence these *Numbers* remark themselves of their own accord. The 10 comprehends the XI. Their imperfect overruns your future perfect.

So that, after this lengthy tour around the compass, here you are back to the cornerstone—and to that toothing stone that awaits you—carried along all the way to the stone that is not the stone, the stone that will have been posed in the form of a liminary question; why should some such other enumeration, altogether squarely written, have remained in reserve, undecipherably?

Why doesn't this outside text, a drama this time without mystery

("Myst gives Dr
Dr gives Myst

Each text of the Oe is given twice
                are only the same thing around

Myst and Dr, Dr and myst. and   presenting
the one outside what
the other hides inside . . . "

"supposing that drama is something other than a mere semblance or
trap for our unreflectiveness, that it represses, conceals, and always
contains the sacred laughter that will be its undoing... that the riddle
behind this curtain exists only thanks to a revolving hypothesis here
and there given a gradual solution by our lucidity: moreover, that the
leaping of gas or electricity graduates it, the instrumental accompaniment, a dispenser of Mystery.")

without a secret, without a riddle, and above all without a key, allow itself
to be *deciphered* in its exact, premeditated architecture?
   It is indeed a question of stone and architecture, of theater *(carrefourc)*, of
temples, columns, and the *limen*, as you have just remarked, of the *pronaos*:
"The *pronaos* was a separate part of the vestibule; it often formed a rather
large square area circumscribed on the right and left sides by the walls of the
cella." *Quatremère de Quincy.*
   It is a question posed on the crossing of paths, a question of bifurcation or
of bifurcation squared, a question of the crossroads, where each way marked
with a stone becomes double, triple, quadruple. The hesitation there is
Parmenidean or, if you prefer, Oedipal. Which is already readable through
the wrought iron railings of the *Park*:
   "There's plenty of time. Again, I stretch my legs out, resting my slippers
against the wrought-iron railings. . . . Over there, a little boy bangs the
table with the back of his spoon; heads turn towards him, voices are raised
in reprimand. The tall, dark woman—it could be her, sitting opposite me,
carefully selecting food for her plate, sitting on my left in the large room,
looking out of the bay window at the dark water, the dark countryside and
the rapid, intermittent brightness of the traffic lights, one-two-three-
four—nothing—one-two—nothing—one-two-three-four; raising a glass
to her lips, pointing her fork in my direction. . . ." And further on: "Thus,
hidden in the old maple tree, hidden in his cabin or castle (two planks of

wood nailed to a forked branch) could the child observe what happened in the garden; the opening, into the house, of a window or a door; he could weigh up the strength of his forces, position his troops, his equipment, his banners; from the bamboos (beyond the seas) he could silently command..."

Move away from the railings of this *Park*, from the insomnia of this child, from the "bed with its vellum pages." Sequence 1 had already spread out a *"net"*: *"2.46. ... thus learning to recognize me, and it was like a net, a grille whose bars (walls, lines, words) were placed against my face, which from then on had no end, no repose . . . No one, then, had told his story. . . . "*

It is a lithograph of this question about the undecipherable, born of the very *ellipsis* of birth, missing like a letter from a word or a word from a sentence (*"4.88 (. . .'something has not been said' . . . —"*), and springing from a murderous blindness set against an unreserved obviousness (*"1.5 . . . I understood that a single murder was constantly in progress, that we were coming from it only to return to it via this detour..."*). This was the elliptical prescription in *Drama*: "On the other, there is   . (A dot inside a blank space, that's it.) I can imagine a trap set to function at the precise moment I think I am most free. For I know and am capable of knowing other languages; I could employ some other syntax—but at bottom nothing would be changed . . .)." Numbers: *"1.13. .... The tale had begun abruptly when I decided to change languages within the same language..."*

Of what you have just read diagonally through this tetralogy, here is a very deep impression, an impression still embedded in stone. You will have read, in the ancient traces, of a certain knife and a certain air, between NATUS and NAOS, the ellipsis of birth (a certain A that leads to all manner of origins) and the replacement of the U by a certain closed O. The undecipherable yields itself up there as what is easiest to understand:

"3.19. ...then there was a crossroads, a bifurcation, and it was necessary to choose between two ways, and the ordeal was clearly indicated by the inscriptions scratched on the walls with a knife... However, the sentences engraved there were at once easy to comprehend and impossible to read; it was possible to know in advance what they suggested but forbidden to verify them. In one of them, for example, one could make out:

N T O S

which did not correspond to any known or whole word... One would have said that the letters had long ago been superimposed upon those three great facades that stood there, without explanation, in the burnt out evening

*one would have said that
they formed the ruined pictures of a bygone history and that the air itself had incised
the stone so as to deposit there the thoughts of the stone which the stone was unable to
see..."*

(You will have compared this Y [called a "Greek *I*" in French] with the
Chinese I in sequence 3, and then to a certain V) "The ring that encircles it,
in the part adjoining our position, is marked with a longitudinal groove
that indeed, seen from our region, gives it the vague appearance of a capital
Y... ... we can say of our Sun that it is positively situated on that point of
the Y where the three lines composing it meet, and, figuring that this letter
possesses a certain solidity, a certain thickness, quite minimal compared
with its length, we can say that our position is in the middle of this
thickness. By considering ourselves to be situated thus, we will no longer
have any trouble accounting for the phenomena in question, which are
solely phenomena of perspective."

Numbers remain undecipherable by the very fact of their being facade
inscriptions—but inscriptions on facadeS (S disseminating you [*vouS*], "S, I
say, is the analytical letter, dissolving and disseminating, par excellence...
I take this opportunity to assert the existence—outside of both spoken
words and wizards' books—of a certain secret direction confusedly indicated by orthography...") between which your reading will have bounced
back and forth, ultimately eluding its own grasp. As a surbedded column,
these *Numbers* tirelessly extract themselves from the crypt where you would
have thought them ensconced. They remain undecipherable precisely because it is only in your own representation that they ever took on the aplomb
of a cryptogram hiding inside itself the secret of some meaning or reference.
X: not an unknown but a chiasmus. A text that is unreadable because it is
only readable. Untranslatable for the same reason. What was inscribing
itself there at knifepoint could not have been said, translated, taken up
again in an interpretive discourse, for nothing in it belonged to the order of
discursive meaning or trying-to-say. Un-de-cipherable, therefore, because

1. what links the text to numbers, to its cipher (a kind of writing that
does not say, that no longer speaks), cannot be decomposed, un-done,
unstitched, de-ciphered;

2. something, somewhere within the text, something that is not really
anything and does not even take place, cannot be counted, recounted,
numbered, ciphered, deciphered.

These two propositions return upon each other, double for each other, and contradict each other. They make up a square circle: *Numbers* would be considered undecipherable because something in them surpasses mere number or cipher; and yet they would also be undecipherable because everything in them is *not* ciphered, but rather "cipherly." They are undecipherable because they are numerable, and undecipherable because they are innumerable. Scription contra-diction. To be reread. The circle of the squaring.

First of all—this seems to be the easiest way to think about it—the innumerable, seen as a numerous "crowd," is not at all foreign to the essence of number. It is quite possible to conceive, without contradiction, of innumerable numbers. *Numbers* always maintain their links with unlimited dissemination—of germs, of the crowd, of the people, *etc.* (the very *et coetera* itself, which, along with the modification mentioned earlier, constitutes the first ideogram (qúnzhòng) that comes after that of the square): "*2.22. . . . Millions of hearts that go on beating, millions of thoughts being constantly disguised—and, here, the entrance of space, of the masses—*

群众 —." The innumerable here is the greater number as a force that cannot be numbered, classed, represented, ruled, a force that always surpasses the speculation or the order of the ruling class, and even exceeds its own representation. "*2.42. . . . And I could see once more the mist-filled square, with the workers gathered together holding their banners and weapons, and through the white fog the red blotches of the strips of cloth unfurled, thus answering the call ... Innumerable in the early dawn, innumerable and for the moment marginal, surrounded, blind, in the force that passes through them without being held in check, the only chance for multiplied, violent thinking... I let go ....*" Subjected to this force—the force of the innumerable number—, the numerable number (of the closed square or of the nondiscounted fourth surface) loses its theatrical grip. It plays a reactive role, opposing its order and its frames to all disseminal wanderings. It exhausts itself in attempting to control them, breaks down as it squares off and counteracts them.

But all of this is happening *among numbers*. The innumerable, which seems to blow up (or out of) all frames, is something you will nevertheless have taken into *account*. The innumerable does not simply come to exceed or bound the numerical order along its borders, from the outside. It works through it from the inside. The supernumerary belongs in a way to the column of numbers—to its overhang. Number is always just beyond or just short of itself, in the "deviation" or "spread" ["*écart*"] that the machine is designed to read. The plus and the minus, excess and lack, proliferate and condition each other in the supplementary articulation of each with the other. "In all things excess is a defect." "*3.75. ... / 'Who is capable of presenting a surplus to what is lacking?' / ...*" In the same way, the trace can only trace itself out in the erasure of its own "presence," so that tracing is not simply the mere other or outside of erasing. Scription contra-diction. Number, the trace, the frame—each is at once itself and its own excess facing [*débord*]. *The Park* already graphed a "silence that encloses without leaving a trace," a silence that is nevertheless also, necessarily, subject to "interminable steps." *Drama*, too, regularly records the erasure and blur-ring of traces, the "traceless, borderless flow." This relation to the absence of traces, to the innumerable—which is also the unnamable—is marked in *Numbers* as a relation to what is called my death. It is constitutive of my "unity," my "unit-ness," that is, my inscription and my substitution within the series of numbers.

This is the condition both of possibility and of impossibility for any transcendental subjectivity. A decipherable-undecipherable unit or unity: "*2.10. ... I had at once to mark the fact that I was a unit among others, but a unit impossible to encipher, perpetually aroused by its own end... My death was indeed starting to swell up in the background, and would extend pretty far—*"

E-numeration, like de-nomination, makes and unmakes, joins and dis-members, in one and the same blow, both number and name, delimiting them with borders that ceaselessly accost the borderless, the supernumer-ary, the surname. That is the way the (jewel-) case opens and shuts. Names and numbers are lacking in the production of writing, and by that very fact they cooperate in it, provoking overproduction—and surplus-value—without which no (trade) mark ever gets registered. "*1.41. ... there was no longer any explanation capable of saying what was happening to me . . . I was lodged in unfolding and deployment, and what is being explained here, in my place, has to be restated otherwise, destroyed... I remained turned toward the trench that does not go through the eyes, that could not for a moment change into a trace or a number, toward the knot, the overlap, the ravine, the uselessness of the words 'knot,' 'overlap,' 'ravine' ...*"

Just as the fourth surface, which is *part* of the square, reflects, distorts, and opens the righted *whole*, exposes to view without being seen; just as each angle of the square belongs to the totality of the surface but yet multiplies it by folding it back upon itself—breaking it rather than bending it—remarks it, closes it, and fractures it by the same token by always leaving room for a supplementary attending surface, a proliferating laterality that does up for the eye that which hasn't a sight to do with it; so, too, the supernumerary is part of the numeral and belongs to the very milieu it exceeds. It makes the excessive proliferate in its invisible column. The column of words, the column of numbers, is thus supernumerary. It is the supernumerary element (both term and medium) of numbers—standing erect, poised, (in) the middle of the sundial [*(au) milieu du cadran solaire*], extending out of sight. *"4.36. (... But that thought is not found: it comes in the mass whose fury is, however, restrained like a torrent changed and formed into a column of words, and it is precisely in the sign that is one too many—)— 屌 —"* (dong: *penis*).

This invisible column, which you are venturing to identify with some *"milieu with which numbers haven't a sight more to do—"* (3.59), is at once, undecidably, undecidable (its effects being propagated in a chain), unique, and innumerable. Unmasterable in its height, uncontrollable in its extension. It is unique and innumerable like what is called (the) present. The unique—that which is not repeated—has no unity since it is not repeated. Only that which can be repeated in its identity can have unity. The unique therefore has no unity, is not a unit. The unique is thus the *apeiron*, the unlimited, the crowd, the imperfect. And yet the chain of numbers is made up of uniqueS. Try to think the unique in the plural, as such, along with the "unique Number that cannot be another." You will witness the birth of *"millions of tales"* and you will understand that one and the same term can germinate twice—a geminate column—disseminating itself in overproduction. "O crossroads . . . O marriage, marriage! [*O hymen, hymen*] ["tainted with vice yet sacred," fixed but hollow, like a glowing screen, like an eye (1.45)] you bred me and again when you had bred, bred children of your child and showed to men brides, wives and mothers and the foulest deeds that can be in this world of ours." "...Unmeasured Time, fathering numberless nights, unnumbered days [*"/ 'time is as foreign to number itself as horses and men are different from the numbers that count them, and different from each other' /"*]: and on one day they'll break apart with spears this harmony— all for a trivial word. And then my sleeping and long-hidden corpse, cold in the earth, cadavre par le bras écarté du secret qu'il détient plutôt que de jouer en maniaque chenu, will drink hot blood of theirs, if Zeus endures; if his son's word is true... However, there's no felicity in speaking of hidden things. Let me come back to this: be careful that you keep your word to me; for if you do you'll never say of Oedipus that he was given refuge uselessly— or if you say it, then the gods have lied." (*At Colonus*) For "the world is Zeus's play or, in physical terms, the play of fire with itself. The One is at the same time the Multiple in this sense alone." Fire is always playing with fire.

With these *Numbers* disporting themselves around this extraneous invisible column, and within it, he who hasn't a sight to do with the operation will justifiably complain of there being nothing to see. And nothing to take. Indeed. He will already have complained here or there, clinging to his mother tongue, observant yet blind—because he is blind—to blindness, in that crumpled column, which prevents him from reading, from week to week... "the serial, heading up most of the columns... colonnades full of merchandise..." But who is dead? he will baldly have asked. "Our sympathies would lie with the newspaper, which is exempt from such treatment: its influence is nevertheless unfortunate in that it imposes upon the organism, the complex organism, which is required by literature, upon the divine old book, a certain monotony—always that unbearable column simply being redistributed, filling out the dimensions of the page, hundreds and hundreds of times."

   "4.48. (... Here you are starting to comprehend what this novel is pursuing in the wisdom of its detour; you now know that it is the rejection of all birth, the calculation that causes you to fall with open eyes into other relations)—"

You will have just begun. And it was necessary to begin again. "What is explaining itself here, in my place, must be restated otherwise, destroyed (1.14)." "Readings having no other end than that of showing these scientific relations." You will have fallen with your eyes wide open into other relations: such has been the cadence of the supernumerary singing its head off.
   The limits of the square or the cube, the indefinitely specular unfolding and refolding of the spectacle, will not have been limits at all. What stopped there was already working the space of its own reinscription as an opening and was already being invested and besieged by another polyhedron. There was another geometry to come. Altogether other. The same.

   In order to begin to comprehend, "it was thus necessary to go back over all the points of the circuit, to pass through its net at once hidden and visible, and to try simultaneously to reignite one's memory like that of a dying man reaching the turning moment..." (3.87).
   $(1 + 2 + 3 + 4)^2$ times. At least.

* * *

Moving off of itself, forming itself wholly therein, almost without remainder, writing denies and recognizes its debt in a single dash. The utmost disintegration of the signature, far from the center, indeed from the secrets that are shared there, divided up so as to scatter even their ashes.
   Though the letter gains strength solely from this indirection, and granted that it can always not arrive at the other side, I will not use this as a pretext to absent myself from the punctuality of a dedication: R. Gasché, J. J. Goux, J. C. Lebensztejn, J. H. Miller, others, *il y a là cendre*, will recognize, perhaps, what their reading has contributed here.

December 1971